Thriving, Surviving, or Going Under: Coping with Everyday Lives

Edited by

Erica Frydenberg

University of Melbourne, Australia

≡IAP

INFORMATION AGE
PUBLISHING

80 Mason Street • Greenwich, Connecticut 06830 • www.infoagepub.com

Library of Congress Cataloging-in-Publication Data

Thriving, surviving, or going under : coping with everyday lives /
edited by Erica Frydenberg.
    p. cm. — (Research on stress and coping in education series)
  Includes bibliographical references.
  ISBN 1-59311-196-7 (hardcover) — ISBN 1-59311-195-9 (pbk.)
  1. Adjustment (Psychology) in adolescence. 2. Child rearing. 3.
Educational psychology. I. Frydenberg, Erica, 1943- II. Series.
  BF724.3.A32T47 2004
  370.15—dc22

                                              2004011525

Cover Art:

Rhythms of Life, 1996, Andrew Rogers, Melbourne Australia
Bronze, height 2.2 meters
Installed at Stonebriar Park, Dallas, Texas, 2002; International Conference Centre,
Jerusalem, 2001; Victorian Arts Centre, Melbourne, Victoria, Australia, 2002; and
World Square, George Street, Sydney, N.S.W., Australia, 2003.

Printed in the United States of America

CONTENTS

Part III.
Teaching Coping Skills

Part IV.
Teacher and Parent Coping

ACKNOWLEDGMENTS

When one works in the field of coping it is heartening to see the interest in the field and the opportunity to contribute to a series on the topic that is directed at educators is welcome. Such a volume enables cutting edge research from the international community to be brought together. My acknowledgments and appreciation go to the series editors Mimi Wolverton and Gordon Gates for initiating the series and providing the opportunity for scholars to bring their work to a wide audience. There are the contributors who need to be acknowledged for the way that embraced the opportunity and produced the high-quality outcomes with enthusiasm and most willingly. My personal thanks go to Jodie Lodge who has acted as the on-site editor through various stages of the compilation process. Her competent assistance has helped to see this project to completion. My appreciation goes to the University of Melbourne which provides the stimulating environment where research endeavors are possible, where excellent students enrich the academic enterprise, and from where the support for my academic endeavors emanates. Finally to my family, my husband and lifelong partner Harry who provides the support and recreational pursuits that enable a balance to be reached between work and leisure and who makes the difference between thriving and surviving, and to my children Joshua and Lexi who thrive in their careers and always provide the encouragement for my out-of-family endeavors.

Erica Frydenberg
March 2004

FOREWORD

The other day while driving to work I switched on the radio to catch up on news of the world, however what I ended up listening to was the re-broadcast of an interview with Edward Said discussing his published memoir *Out of Place*. I remember still much of the content of the interview and desire to read the book. A couple of days later I purchased the paperback and began. There are many thoughts that I would like to share about this memoir of his early childhood to young adulthood, but I'll limit myself to two. First, I am struck by how much of his portrayed perspective I identified with given my experience growing up. I expected clear cultural boundaries between us demarked by national origin (he Palestinian and I Canadian), ethnicity (he Arab and I Irish/German), class (he upper and I middle), religion (he Protestant-Christian and I Fundamentalist-Christian), education (he private and I public), generation (he 1930s-1950s and I 1960s-1980s), and even lengthier list of assorted influences such as political events, familial relationships, and physical attributes to name a few. Yet, as I read his struggles, worries, and humiliations as well as comforts, hopes, and triumphs I could not help reflect on my past and recognize much as familiar—which brings me to my second thought. My reflections formed as Edward Said[1] wrote of his everyday life and of his feelings of awkwardness and grace, aloneness and belonging, naivety and expertise, shame and bravado, love and hate. His is a memoir that chronicles surviving and thriving. It offers a tale of coping, sometimes well and sometimes not so well, by a child and later youth.

The following book, *Thriving, Surviving, or Going Under*, edited by Erica Frydenberg, speaks in a different way to this important issue of coping by young people, their parents, and teachers. Over the past several years as I have listened at the Annual Conference of the American Educational Research Association (AERA) to Erica present findings of tested theory based on various research projects and read her publications in numerous leading academic journals I have come to appreciate her passion and commitment to helping youth live well. This edited volume—the second in the *Research on Stress and Coping* series—offers further evidence of her dedication to such cause.

Thriving, Surviving, or Going Under, is Erica's fourth book on the subject and her influence on this field of study is evident throughout its chapters. However, given that the book presents a compilation of writings by various scholars in Australia, United Kingdom, Israel, and America, it is a source that builds on a diversity of knowledge to provide for readers an accessible resource of theory, research, and application. Erica and her fellow authors write from a perspective that embraces the possibilities of human action, yet the very nature of their interest exposes failings in human society be they at institutional, familial, or individual levels. The bad and good news is that while youth appear to be facing greater challenges than ever before, efforts to understand their resiliency and address their resources are also increasing. Indeed, *Thriving, Surviving, or Going Under*, details multiple projects and programs directed at such labor. And those who work with and assist youth toward healthy living will benefit from the practical insights and understandings on the particular problems and selected strategies of coping used by youth offered throughout each of its chapters.

I would be remiss if before concluding I failed to draw attention to the political nature of this edited volume. Although the various authors tend not to make explicit or focus on the politics of their subject matter, *Thriving, Surviving, or Going Under* is concerned with equity, justice, and care involved in educational, social, and medical policies and practices. For example, the chapters elicit important questions about differences in access or use of various resources, the organization of conflict, and feelings of safety and anxiety given variables such as gender, age, ability, and role. In identifying such politics I hope to encourage both the authors of these chapters and the reader to strengthen discourse on social justice in the stress and coping literature. There is valuable work to be done in helping children survive and thrive given challenges and discrimination due to differences of nationality, ethnicity, class, religion, gender, ability, sexual orientation, age, and so forth. Thus, I commend Erica and her colleagues for this volume as I believe it offers much that if pursued as research, instituted as policy, or engaged in as practice can result in the amelioration of inequities in stress and coping, as well as improvement to the everyday life of children, their parents, and teachers.

Gordon S. Gates
Washington State University

NOTE

1. Edward Said (1935-2003) held the position of professor in the Department of English and Comparative Literature at Columbia University. Many of his writings on literary and cultural criticism have received wide acclaim.

INTRODUCTION

Erica Frydenberg
University of Melbourne

Two important developments in psychology have provided the impetus for this volume. The first is psychology's focus on positive approaches to human endeavor which was signaled at the beginning of the twenty-first century by Martin Seligman and Mihaly Csikszentmihalyi (2000). These eminent psychologists, along with many others, called on us to explore human capacity rather than focusing on failings or inadequacies. In 2000 the *American Psychologist* devoted much of the sixth issue of Volume 55 to papers that made the argument from many perspectives. Additionally the *Handbook of Positive Psychology* (Snyder & Lopez, 2002) continues the theme. We are well on the way to looking at what helps us to thrive and survive rather than go under. The second is the research field of stress and coping. Arguably it has been the most highly researched area in psychology in recent decades. What that means is that a volume such as this can draw on a vast body of literature and bring that, along with new insights and understandings, to the educational domain.

Many of the chapters within this volume highlight the fact that schools are increasingly being called on to contribute to the development of resilience in young people in order to be proactive and prevent the consequences of poor, social-emotional health and well-being. The focus of prevention is on building resiliency in students through programs that

Thriving, Surviving, or Going Under: Coping with Everyday Lives, xiii–xvi
Copyright © 2004 by Information Age Publishing

foster adaptive coping skills. The critical role of teachers in the social-emotional development of students in their care is also acknowledged. However, a recent literature review found that few programs addressing coping and emotional well-being were available for implementation in school settings. Furthermore, the longer-term success of any health-promotion program requires not only the translation of sound theory into practical applications, but that these programs need to be evaluated. Within this volume a number of different coping programs are presented and some are evaluated (see chapters in the third section).

Despite coping being one of the most widely researched areas in the field of psychology today, much of our understanding of young people's coping derives from research with adults. In more recent years research with children and adolescents has provided new advances in the field. This volume seeks to contribute to our understanding of coping with young people and their coping, as well as adult coping being represented. The implications of theorizing for educational practice are also considered.

The book is divided into four sections: Understanding Coping; Resources and Coping with Prevalent Problems; Teaching Coping Skills; and Teacher and Parent Coping. The sections are there to aid the reader in selection. In reality many of the chapters transcend these section divides. Each section is introduced by a brief summary of the contents of the section and each chapter is introduced by an abstract that serves to contextualize the contribution. It is intended that the chapters stand-alone for the reader. Many of the chapters provide a substantial overview of the coping process (In particular see chapters 1, 2, 4 and 9). In an edited volume the reader and researcher have the benefit of multiple authors and multiple data sets so that each chapter can make a distinct contribution. Sometimes this leads to inevitable overlap, but it never compromises the integrity of a chapter. Where possible, links are made and the chapters are cross-referenced.

Many of the chapters come from the same laboratory where we are endeavoring to extend our theoretical understandings of the coping process, particularly as it relates to the lives of young people. Additionally, many chapters in this volume utilize a common language of coping as exemplified by the Adolescent Coping Scale (Frydenberg & Lewis, 1993) and the Coping Scale for Adults (Frydenberg & Lewis, 1997).

Each of the chapters provides a unique insight into the coping process. Examples of theory which have direct implications for educational practice includes Chapter 1 which identifies coping skills that work to assist in thriving, those that contribute to surviving, and those that prevent going under. Similarly an understanding of how accurate and helping young people's assessment of their own coping is enables educators to better understand elements of the coping process (see Chapter 2). The theoretical links between resources and coping are presented in Chapter 4. Two chapters report how it is helpful to distinguish between different types of aggression (see Chapter 6) or different types of anxiety (see Chapter 5) so that appropriate ways of helping young people can be developed. How parent illness impacts on young people's coping behavior is considered in a British study by Cogan, Riddell, and Mayes (see Chapter 3). Some chapters describe teaching coping to young people through a universal set of skills, while one chapter focuses particularly on teaching coping skills to young people who experience particular forms of anxiety (see chapters 7, 8, and 9). Johnson and Johnson's chapter on the three keys to thriving (see Chapter 11) guides us to an understanding of the importance of cooperative relationships, conflict management skills, and the importance of civic values.

The chapter by Cinamon and Rich (see Chapter 10) anticipates the difficulties young people will experience in family work-role conflict. It prepares adolescents for the likelihood of having to juggle multiple roles in their adult lives and it is a good example of proactive coping, where goal management is considered as part of young people's preparation for life. It is another example of how the educational system can become a "primary social institution," an agency to provide guidance.

The impact of adults on young people's management of their lives is recognized in a chapter by Rollin, Dao, and Holland, who describe a program for parents of children at risk. These writers emphasize problem management that comes from the problem-solving models of adaptation (see Chapter 12). The chapter focuses on parents with children at risk, giving particular examples of children at risk of learning difficulties and substance abuse.

Finally, in all work-related settings, and no less in schools, teachers can avoid burnout by learning to deal effectively with their own stress. The ways adults learn to cope with stress is going to impact their charges both directly and indirectly (See Chapter 13).

Collectively the chapters make up a rich tapestry of coping research that draws on established theory, brings new insights into the arena, and at all times makes it evident that these understandings are helpful in the educational context. They provide knowledge—materials that can be directly adapted. At other times they just provide the building blocks for furture research or new educational activities.

REFERENCES

Frydenberg, E., & Lewis, R. (1993). *Adolescent Coping Scale.* Melbourne: Australian Council for Educational Research.

Frydenberg, E., & Lewis, R. (1997). *Coping Scale for Adults.* Melbourne: Australian Council for Educational Research.

Seligman, M. E. P., & Csikszentmihalyi, M. (2000). Positive psychology. *The American Psychologist, 55,* 5-14

Snyder, C. R., & Lopez, S. J. (2002). *Handbook of positive psychology.* New York: Oxford University Press.

PART I

UNDERSTANDING COPING

The three chapters in this section add to the vast literature on coping and provide an introduction to the concepts. There are strategies that help us to thrive, those that just assist us to survive and those that help us to avoid sinking. It is not only the use of a coping strategy that is important but the perceived efficacy of what one does makes a difference. Additionally it is also important to recognize that students generally evaluate their coping appropriately but nevertheless a minority resort to the use of nonproductive coping strategies. The third chapter in this section addresses the fact that there are familial patterns on coping but when it comes to children who are at risk because their parents experience mental health problems it is important to be able to intervene so that the young people's coping potential can be developed.

CHAPTER 1

THRIVING, SURVIVING, OR GOING UNDER

WHICH COPING STRATEGIES RELATE TO WHICH OUTCOMES?

Ramon Lewis
La Trobe University, Australia

Erica Frydenberg
University of Melbourne, Australia

ABSTRACT

Early research in the field of coping in the adolescent area has generally focused on the coping process without taking outcomes into account. Later research has more frequently addressed outcomes, but the interest has generally been on dysfunction. As psychology is moving to emphasize health and well-being rather than focusing solely on prevention of maladaptation, there is an interest in resilience, in addition to dysfunction (see Chapter 7 by Israelashvili and Chapter 12 by Rollin et al., this volume). This chapter examines the relationship between measures of well-being and dysfunction in a sample of 1,264 12-16 year olds, and the relationship between both of these and adolescents' coping strategies. In doing so consideration was

Thriving, Surviving, or Going Under: Coping with Everyday Lives, 3–24
Copyright © 2004 by Information Age Publishing

given not only to how often strategies were used but also how effective they were perceived to be by the individuals using them. Significant relationships were noted between the usage and effectiveness of a range of strategies and well-being and dysfunction. For nonproductive strategies both well-being and dysfunction related more closely to usage than to perceived effectiveness. In contrast when productive strategies were considered, boys' perception of a strategy's usefulness was more closely related to well-being than was the frequency with which the strategy was used. The implications of these findings are discussed.

INTRODUCTION

Stress and coping have arguably been the most well researched areas in the field of psychology in the past two decades. In the psychology literature alone there have been 49,758 references to stress and coping between 1982 and 1992 and 34,018 in the following decade. This has been matched by increasingly frequent references in the education literature (6,758 between 1982 and 1992 and 8,334 between 1992 and 2002). At the beginning of the twenty-first century leading psychologists such as Seligman and Csickszentimihalyi (2000) steered the interest of both practitioners and researchers to focus on the positive aspects of human endeavor and to consider our capacities rather than our deficits. In light of these developments it is most appropriate to invest our resources into understanding how we move from survival to thriving and how we avoid the likelihood of going under.

Psychology, overall, for much of the twentieth century has focused on deficits and the field of coping has been no exception. Although some studies examine the relationship between coping and emotional or physical well-being, most studies that consider coping as a predictor of a psycho-social outcome generally focus on negative outcomes such as depression (Ebata & Moos, 1994), low self-esteem (Brodzinsky, Elias, Steiger, Gill, & Hitt, 1992), poor academic performance (Band & Weisz, 1988), suicidal ideation (Asarnow, Carlson, & Guthrie 1987; Spirito, Francis, Overholser, & Frank, 1996), or substance abuse (Wills, 1986). Additionally, well-being is generally interpreted as the absence of these negative indicators. For example, the adolescent component of a national survey of mental health and well-being, the largest study of child and adolescent mental health conducted in Australia, and one of the few national studies conducted in the world, appears to characterize well-being as the absence of "mental disorders" (Sawyer, Kosky, Gratez, Arney, & Zubrich, 2000).

A few studies have investigated the relationship between coping and indicators of both dysfunction and well-being (see for example Ebata &

Moos, 1991; Holahan & Moos, 1990, 1991). The present study examines the relationship between coping strategies associated with dysfunction and those associated with well-being. The hypothesis that well-being and dysfunction are polar opposites of the one continuum will also be explored.

COPING

To date much of the coping research in the child and adolescent area has been predicated on the theorizing of Folkman and Lazarus. They emphasize the context in which the coping actions occur, the attempt rather than the outcome, and the fact that coping is a process that changes over time, as the person and the environment are continuously in a dynamic, mutually influential relationship (Folkman & Lazarus, 1988b; Lazarus & Folkman, 1984). This is generally known as the transactional model of coping.

Folkman (1997) made modifications to the original theoretical model of stress and coping proposed by Lazarus and Folkman (1984), so as to accommodate positive psychological states. Transactions with the environment are appraised as threatening, harmful, or challenging and, according to the model, stress is regulated by emotion-focused strategies designed to reduce the distress or manage the problem. These may lead to a favorable resolution, nonresolution, or an unfavorable resolution. According to this model, emotion is generated at three phases, at the appraisal phase, the coping phase, and the outcome phase. There are three pathways. The first is directed by positive psychological states that give meaning to the situation and lead to "revising goals and planning goal-directed problem-focused coping" (Folkman, 1997, p. 1216). The second pathway is the response to the distress rather than the condition that created it. This accounts for the co-occurrence of both negative and positive states where the negative states, while they may be a result of enduring distress, may lead to the individual striving to find (consciously or unconsciously) positive meaning in the event. Such interpretations may then lead to the use of resources such as hope, social support, and self-esteem. The third pathway derives from the positive psychological states that result from coping processes per se and can help the person re-motivate, re-energize and re-engage in goal-directed activities. This formulation of stress and emotion is yet to be tested on young people but it would appear that, at least for adolescents, the search for meaning and the subsequent impact on mood state is likely to hold true. For example, Muldoon (1996), following the analysis of interview responses of 9-10 year olds, found that primary appraisal, that is, assessing whether a situation is one of harm or loss, is an important determinant of children's coping. This is a view that has been readily accepted, but rarely demonstrated in the literature relating to stress in childhood and adolescence.

EFFECTIVENESS OF COPING

Although it is difficult to determine what constitutes effective coping skills, general research in the field of coping has identified characteristics that make an adolescent an effective coper, and thus better able to deal with stress. These have been found to include temperament, optimism, perceived personal control, familial factors (such as family cohesion, shared values, loving parents, and a relationship with at least one parent figure), flexibility, and the availability of social support (Frydenberg & Lewis, 2002; Luthar & Zigler, 1991).

In a study of well-being, Ebata and Moos (1991) compared 190 young people aged between 12 and 18 years, with behavioral, psychological, and physical problems with a control group of healthy adolescents. A 48-item instrument reflecting active coping (approach threat) and passive coping (avoid threat) was administered. Perceived happiness and self-worth were used as measures of well-being. Results indicated that higher levels of well-being were related to greater use of active coping responses (positive appraisal, guidance/support, problem solving, and alternate rewards) and lower use of passive coping, namely resigned acceptance. In general, the results suggest that young people are likely to be better adjusted if they actively engage in a problem solving approach, "look at the bright side," and do not get caught up in rumination and resignation.

STUDIES USING THE ADOLESCENT COPING SCALE (ACS)

A number of studies have employed the ACS (Frydenberg & Lewis, 1993a) to investigate the relationships between coping and theoretically related characteristics associated with young people's well-being (for example, self-concept, self-efficacy, achievement). The ACS is a 79-item scale that elicits ratings of young people's use of 18 coping strategies, each of which reflect a coping response, plus an open-ended question, which asks the young person to write down anything they do to cope that is not described in the preceding 79 items. Coping styles are obtained using standardized scores from the 18 different scales.

Self-efficacy

In a study of Year 8 students the relationship between coping and self-efficacy was examined (Jenkin, 1997). The 135 students (81 male and 54 female) surveyed were participants in a school-initiated Outward Bound (rugged, outdoor camping) program. The Specific Long Form of the ACS and a physical self-efficacy measure (Ryckman, Robins, Thornton, & Cantrell, 1982) were used. The results indicated that active coping strategies, namely, focus on the positive, focus on solving the problem, and work hard to achieve, were the best predictors that distinguished between high and low self-efficacy. Moreover, for 70% of students, a combination of these strategies accurately predicted low or high self-efficacy (top and bottom quartiles). However, while students in the low efficacy group could be correctly identified by their lesser use of these strategies, predicting students in the high efficacy group was less successful. That is, active coping strategies are used less frequently by students with low self-efficacy, whereas, students high in self-efficacy do not necessarily use more of these strategies.

Academic Well-being

Other studies have used the ACS to examine the relationship between achievement and coping. For example, in a study of 374 boys in years 9, 10, and 11 at a Melbourne independent boys school, overachieving students (those that achieved better than would be expected on the basis of ability alone), were compared with other students. The results suggested that overachieving students were less likely to declare that they did not have the strategies to cope than were the other students (Parsons, Frydenberg & Poole, 1996). Additionally, boys who achieved more than would have been on the basis of ability alone used more hard work to achieve, more problem solving, and more social support.

Similarly, in a study of 90 girls in years 9, 10, and 11 (Noto, 1995), significant positive correlations were reported between active coping strategies (namely, work hard and achieve, focus on solving the problem, seek social support and focus on the positive), and academic achievement. Measures were the ACS, an intelligence test (ACER Higher Test), and academic achievement based on final grades from the previous year. Noto compared these data with data from the Parsons, Frydenberg, and Poole (1996) study, using partial correlations with gender and IQ being controlled. While there was a positive relationship between coping and achievement, significant negative correlations were reported for three avoidant strategies, namely, not cope, tension reduction, and ignoring the problem. Furthermore, use of the strategy, invest in close friends, was negatively associated with academic achievement.

Sex and Coping

In conceptualizing an investigation into adolescents' coping responses it is important to note that there are differences in how boys and girls cope. Sex differences tend to be consistent across studies (see Frydenberg, 1997, for a summary of studies). Girls are generally more affiliative and use more social support than do boys. For example, Bird and Harris (1990) found that females use more social support and males use more ventilation, while Patterson and McCubbin (1987) found that males use more humor whereas females are more focused on interpersonal relationships with siblings, parents, friends, and other adults. Copeland and Hess (1995), using Patterson and McCubbin's A-Cope as the measure of coping, found that females used more proactive orientation and catharsis, whereas the males tended more to avoid problems and to use physical diversions. In another study boys were found to be less open and sociable, but evaluated problems more optimistically and were less inclined to withdraw resignedly. However, when a more serious problem occurred which could not be solved readily they did resort to alcohol and other drugs (Seiffge-Krenke, 1995). Gender-based relationships between the use of particular strategies and outcomes, to date, remain relatively unexplored.

THE STUDY

The study reported here examines the relationship between the various coping strategies and measures of both dysfunction and well-being with a view to highlighting the efficacy of a range of coping responses. The analysis was conducted independently for boys and girls to determine the extent to which the efficacy of strategies is gender related.

To examine the relationship between general coping responses and states of well-being two questionnaires were administered to a sample of 1,264 12-16-year-old secondary school students in Metropolitan Melbourne, Australia. Of these, 37% were in Year 7, 30% in Year 8, and 33% in Year 9. In general half the sample were girls as the proportion of girls in Years 7, 8, and 9 was 40, 45, and 56% respectively.

The first questionnaire administered was a slightly modified version of the Short Form of the ACS (Frydenberg & Lewis, 1993a). The other was a State of Being scale (Reynolds, 2001), which comprises 12 items. With regard to the ACS, the not cope item was omitted due to the overlap with the concept of dysfunction and the belong item (improve my relations with others) was also omitted due to perceived overlap with the friends item (spend good time with a friend). Three new strategies which have been derived from the responses to the open question, "What else do you do to cope?" on the ACS in previous studies (Frydenberg & Lewis, 1993b, 1994, 1996, 1999a, 2000) were included. These assess acting out (act up), the use of humor (humor) and accepting that it was not possible to do more than had been done (accept). In total there were 23 coping items, each describing a coping response. Students indicated whether, in response to their general concerns, they used the strategy hardly ever or never, a few times, sometimes, often or nearly always.

The State of Being scale contained a mixture of two kinds of items. Approximately half appear to assess the likelihood of well-being (e.g., I felt good about myself, I felt that everything was OK in my life) and the other half indicated dysfunction (e.g., I felt depressed or sad, I had trouble concentrating). Students indicated how frequently, in the last 6 months, the item described them. The response alternatives were never, hardly ever, some of the time, most of the time, and nearly all of the time. For both the coping and the State of Being items responses were coded 1-5 respectively.

To examine the structure of this State of Being scale a factor analysis was performed. Because any potential factors would be likely to be related, an oblique rotation was performed (Oblimin). Table 1.1 reports the factor pattern matrix. The solution provided two factors with Eigen values greater than 1 that explain a total of 49% of variance. All but two items load significantly (> .3) on only one factor. The seven items loading positively on Factor 1 refer to recent experiences which may be termed dysfunctional, and include reference to loneliness, tension, nervousness, depression and sadness, difficulty falling asleep, feeling like crying, and difficulty in concentrating. In contrast, the five items loading positively on Factor 2 refer to well-being, for example enjoying the company of friends and family, being comfortable in the company of new people, and feeling good about oneself and life in general. It is interesting to note that the factor intercorrelation is a moderate −.35, which supports the two-factor structure and indicates that dysfunction and well-being are not polar opposites of the one continuum.

The statistical significance of the correlation is primarily due to the fact that very few respondents express high levels of both well-being and dysfunction. In general, higher levels of well-being are associated with lower levels of dysfunction and vice versa. The reason for the moderate magnitude of the correlation is the number of respondents who score low on both the dysfunction and well-being scales. That is, although it is unlikely

Table 1.1.   Factor Structure of the Well-being Items

Item	Factor 1	Factor 2
I felt depressed or sad	.803	.008
I felt like crying for no reason	.748	.003
I felt very tense	.712	−.067
I was very lonely	.691	−.089
I had trouble concentrating	.657	.089
I had trouble falling asleep	.629	.066
I felt nervous	.582	.033
I felt that everything was OK in my life	−.475	.368
I had fun with friends	.032	.759
I enjoyed getting together with my friends and family	.046	.750
I felt comfortable meeting new people	.032	.639
I felt good about myself	−.340	.496
Eigenvalue	4.43	1.42
Percent of variance	37%	12%

that respondents will profess to be experiencing both dysfunction and well-being, they may report very little of both.

To test the reliability of the scales containing these two sets of items, Cronbach alpha coefficients of internal consistency were computed. For the seven well-being items the alpha was an acceptable .70 and it was .82 for the five dysfunctional items. Before considering the connection between these scale scores and the students' responses to the modified ACS, it was necessary to resolve a problem. As noted above, the well-being scale contained some items that noted how frequently in the last 6 months students "enjoyed getting together with friends and family," "had fun with friends," and "felt comfortable meeting new people." However some of the coping strategy measures referred to the frequency with which students "looked for support and encouragement from others" (social support strategy) and spent "more time with a good friend" (friends). It was recognized in this study that overlap of this kind may lead to tenuous conclusions when associations were sought between well-being and some coping strategies. Consequently a scale was constructed from the two, more general, well-being items "I felt that everything was OK in my life" and "I felt good about myself." This two-item scale had an alpha coefficient of .70 and was labeled General Well-being.

Detailed inspection of the factor loadings in Table 1.1 indicates that only 2 of the 12 items load substantially ($>.3$) and positively on one factor and negatively on the other. Ten of the 12 items display a significant positive loading on one factor and an almost zero loading on the other. These results provide additional reason to question the bipolar characterization of dysfunction and well-being.

To examine the relationship between coping and well-being and dysfunction, Pearson correlations were computed between the 23 coping strategies and the measures of dysfunction (negative items on the well-being scale), well-being (positive items on the well-being scale) and general well-being items (two items on the well-being scale—see above). For this analysis scaling was converted to ensure a positive correlation reflected a positive relationship. Correlations were utilized rather than regression analysis on the understanding that just as coping strategies may affect well-being, the opposite is also arguable. As noted above, the boys' and girls' data were examined separately to determine the extent to which relationships between coping and outcomes were gender related. Table 1.2 reports these correlations.

Table 1.2. Statistically Significant Associations between Coping Scales, Dysfunction, and Well-being

	Boys (N = 395)			Girls (N = 485)		
Scale	Well-being	General Well-being	Dysfunction	Well-being	General Well-being	Dysfunction
1 Social Support	.10	.08	.02	.20	.16	-.07
2 Work Hard	.17	.19	-.00	.21	.21	-.10
3 Worry	-.03	-.09	.37	-.14	-.16	.22
4 Tension Reduce	-.07	-.10	.25	-.19	-.24	.32
5 Wish Think	-.01	-.08	.19	-.12	-.18	.21
6 Social Act	-.06	-.01	.11	.09	.02	.05
7 Self Blame	-.25	-.24	.36	-.32	-.36	.43
8 Keep Self	-.06	-.06	.28	-.27	-.22	.25
9 Spirit	-.03	-.02	.12	-.03	-.02	.12
10 Focus Positive	.29	.25	-.11	.27	-.28	-.21
11 Prof Help	.15	.20	.01	.02	.02	.02
12 Phys Recreation	.22	.19	-.04	.20	.18	-.11
13 Act Up	-.16	-.15	.23	.23	-.25	-.26
14 Humor	.09	-.09	-.06	.07	.06	.05
15 Accept	.24	.27	-.06	.22	.24	-.15
16 Ignore	-.06	-.04	.31	-.21	-.22	.23
17 Friends	.27	.14	-.01	.13	.01	-.02
18 Solve Problem	.18	.19	-.01	.24	.19	-.10
19 Relax	.18	.22	-.16	.14	.12	-.04

All correlations > .14 for boys and .12 for girls; $p < .01$.

As has been noted elsewhere a number of coping responses reported in Table 1.2 are associated with dysfunction (Frydenberg & Lewis, 1999b). These are generally avoidant or nonproductive strategies such as worry, tension reduction, self-blame, wishful thinking, keep to self, act up, and ignore. In contrast, strategies such as focus on the positive, physical recreation, and acceptance are identified as productive.

Using a significance level of 0.01, boys' coping strategies were grouped into five major categories on the basis of their associations with well-being and dysfunction. For the boys, all the correlations greater than 0.14 were significant at the 0.01 level. Seven coping strategies related positively with well-being but had no significant association with dysfunction (work hard, friends, seek professional help, accept, focus on the positive, physical recreation, and solve the problem). Five associated positively with dysfunction but had no significant correlation with well-being (worry, ignore, keep to self, wishful thinking, and tension reduction). Two strategies correlated negatively with well-being and positively with dysfunction (self-blame and act up) and one strategy did the opposite (relax). Finally, four failed to relate significantly to either dysfunction or well-being (seek spiritual support, and social support, engage in social action, and humor).

To interpret adolescent boys' state of being it is useful to talk in terms of thriving, surviving, or going under whereby thriving denotes a state of well-being and contentment and going under indicates distress and dysfunction. Surviving suggests a lack of dysfunction as well as a lack of well-being. Consequently adolescents who are surviving report low levels of both distress and well-being.

From Table 1.2 and Figure 1.1 it can be seen that some strategies associate only with boys' thriving, that is, the use of such strategies relates to the relative presence or absence of contentment or well-being. Their relative absence however is not related to any indication of dysfunction, only a lack of contentment.

For male adolescents, working hard, seeking out the company of friends, seeking professional help, accepting their best efforts, focusing on the positive, engaging in physical recreation, and attempting to solve the problem can be argued to relate to the difference between surviving and thriving. That is, boys who use more of these strategies are more likely to be those who are thriving. Nevertheless, boys who are going under are not more likely to be using less of these strategies than are other male adolescents.

As indicated above, going under is a measure of distress. When a strategy is said to discriminate on the basis of dysfunction, greater or lesser usage of the strategy is associated with greater or lesser distress respectively, but the extent of reliance on the strategy fails to associate with levels of well-being. Consequently the strategies worry, ignore, keep to self,

Girls

Thriving   _____

Relax
Seek Social Support
Work hard
Physical Recreation
Solving the problem

Ignore
Self-blame
Acting up
Worry
Tension
Reduction
Wishful Thinking
Keep to Self
Accept
Focus on the
Positive

Surviving   _____

Going
Under   _____

Boys

Thriving   _____

Work hard
Solve the problem
Professional help
Accept best effort
Focus on the positive
Physical recreation
Friends

Self-blame
Acting up
Relax

Surviving   _____

Tension reduction
Worry
Keep to self
Ignore
Wishful thinking

Going
under   _____

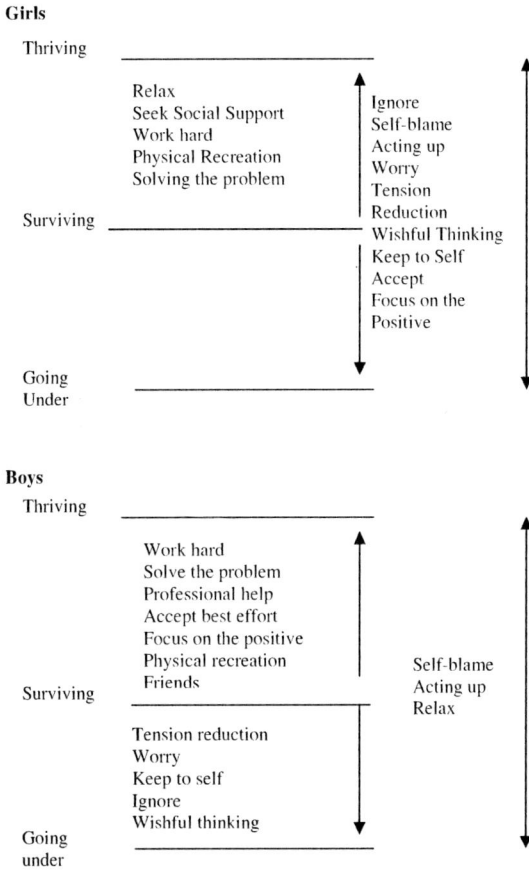

Figure 1.1. Strategies associated with either thriving, surviving, or going under or with all outcomes for boys and girls

wishful thinking, and tension reduction can be argued to relate to the difference between surviving and drowning. The increased presence of these strategies associates with going under, however their absence does not predict thriving.

Only three strategies (self-blame, act up, and relax) significantly associated with both thriving and going under. Lesser use of the strategies of self-blame and acting up is associated with thriving while greater use corresponds to drowning. In contrast, greater use of relaxing pastimes is reported by boys who are more likely to be thriving, whereas lesser use is associated with going under.

In summary, for boys, only three strategies associate with both thriving and going under. In contrast a total of 13 of the 19 considered relate to either thriving or going under but not both. Those associated with the former are generally described elsewhere as productive strategies whereas those described as nonproductive appear related to dysfunction. There are no strategies that show a significant negative relation with one outcome while remaining unrelated to the other. A reasonable characterization of boys' coping therefore is that, in general, use of productive strategies such as work hard, solve the problem, physical recreation and focus on the positive, associate with thriving but their avoidance does not appear to signal malfunction, but rather a failure to thrive. In addition, greater use of nonproductive strategies such as worry, ignore, keep to self, and wishful thinking associate with going under but lesser use does not relate to thriving.

Table 1.2 also reports the relationships between coping and both well-being and dysfunction for girls. Correlations of .12 or greater are statistically significant at the .01 level. Only 8 of the 20 coping strategies show a similar pattern of relationships for girls as they do for boys. These are social action, work hard, self-blame, seek spiritual support, physical recreation, act up, humor, and solve the problem. Whereas for boys only three strategies were related to both thriving and going under, for girls the number is nine. In addition to greater use of self-blame and act up, another five nonproductive strategies (worry, tension reduction, wishful thinking, keep to self, and ignore) associate positively with dysfunction and negatively with well-being. Further, two productive strategies (accept best efforts and focus on the positive) also associate with both thriving and going under. The remaining four gender-related findings indicate that for girls the seeking of professional help and the company of friends fails to relate to well-being (as it does for boys). Secondly, girls' use of social support does relate to well-being whereas for boys it does not, and finally, unlike for boys, girls' lack of use of relaxation fails to associate with dysfunction.

In characterizing the coping pattern for girls (see Figure 1.1) it can be argued that of the 14 coping strategies that show significant relationships with well-being and/or dysfunction, most relate to both. Nearly all of these are nonproductive strategies (worry, tension reduction, wishful think, self-blame, act up, keep self, and ignore). Two however are productive (focus on the positive and accept best efforts). Finally a number of productive strategies (relax, seek social support, work hard, physical recreation, and solving the problem) discriminate only between thriving and surviving.

In summary of the results reported so far in this chapter it can be concluded that most productive coping strategies are associated with thriving for both girls and boys, however the nonproductive strategies generally relate only to dysfunction for boys and not thriving, whereas for girls they appear to associate with both dysfunction and well-being. That is, boys do not thrive just because they avoid the use of nonproductive strategies.

Is it the Quality or the Quantity that Counts?

To further the analysis it was acknowledged that adolescents who find a particular strategy more effective are more likely to be using it. If so, this could provide a difficulty in analysis when examining the relationships between frequency of usage, and helpfulness, of various coping strategies, and states of being. If the use and effectiveness of a strategy were compounded it would be necessary to partial out the effect of one when examining the effect of the other. Consequently to examine the relationship between the quantity and quality of coping, and well-being and dysfunction, it was necessary to consider the degree to which the frequency of usage of a particular coping strategy was related to perceptions of its efficacy. Examination of the correlations between strategy use and perceptions of its helpfulness shows that they are statistically significant. They range from .14 to .60 with a median figure of .52 and with an arithmetical mean of .44. Consequently Table 1.3 provides partial correlations, which allow the consideration of strategy use and well-being and dysfunction independent of the perceived effectiveness of the strategy. These are recorded on the left hand side of Table 1.3.

Inspection of the partial correlations on the left-hand side of Table 1.3 allows an examination of the association between the use of a strategy and outcomes assuming all adolescents used the strategy equally effectively. On the right-hand side of Table 1.3 partial correlations are reported between the perceived helpfulness or efficacy of each of the strategies and both dysfunction and well-being, while controlling for the amount the strategy was used. This allows for an examination of the association between the efficacy of a strategy and outcomes independent of the frequency of usage of the strategy. Statistically significant correlations ($p < .001$) have been asterisked. This stringent level of probability was adopted as 184 correlations were being considered.

To explore the extent to which the reported relationships between the use of particular coping strategies and states of being were due to their association with the perceived effectiveness of the strategy, two analyses were undertaken. First, coping strategies most affected by the compounding of these two variables were identified. These were those for which the correlation between usage and either well-being or dysfunction changed by at least 0.1 when their respective usefulness was controlled. If a partial correlation, reported in the left-hand side of Table 1.3, was at least 0.1

Table 1.3. The Relationship between Strategy Use and Effectiveness and both Well-being and Dysfunction

| | Partial Correlations between Use (Effectiveness Controlled) and | | | | Partial Correlations between Effectiveness (Use Controlled) and | | | |
| | Boys (N = 298) | | Girls (N = 415) | | Boys (N = 298) | | Girls (N = 415) | |
Scale	General Well-being	Dysfunction	General Wellbeing	Dysfunction	General Well-being	Dysfunction	General Well-being	Dysfunction
1 Social support	-.04	.01	-.07	-.04	.17	-.06	.17	-.08
2 Recognize inability	-.07	.21	-.27	.20	.02	.14	.01	.03
3 Work	.09	.09	.16	-.07	.16	-.22	.07	-.04
4 Worry	-.17	.35	-.15	.21	.15	.01	.03	-.01
5 Acknowledge defeat	-.16	.24	-.13	.15	.16	.02	.06	.02
6 Tension reduction	-.15	.25	-.27	.29	.10	-.09	.11	-.06
7 Wishful thinking	-.20	.23	-.19	.20	.29	-.14	.06	-.05
8 Social act	-.09	.15	-.02	.08	.13	-.09	.05	-.03
9 Give up	-.15	.30	-.33	.29	.04	.02	.08	.09
10 Self-blame	-.28	.35	-.37	.42	.01	.10	.04	.01
11 Keep self	-.13	.24	-.22	.22	.03	.07	.05	.02
12 Spirit	-.04	.06	-.02	.12	.02	.02	.01	-.06
13 Focus positive	.16	-.00	.17	-.12	.06	-.09	.10	-.06
14 Professional help	-.12	.02	-.05	.07	.06	-.01	.09	-.06
15 Relax	.10	.03	.00	.02	.08	-.00	.13	-.10
16 Physical relaxation	.01	-.00	.09	-.09	.17	-.03	.05	.02
17 Act up	-.14	.20	-.23	.23	.08	.02	.02	.01
18 Humor	.02	.07	-.02	.06	.13	-.04	.08	-.05
19 Get sick	-.06	.32	-.28	.28	-.05	-.01	-.07	.02
20 Accept best effort	.16	.01	.10	-.07	.12	-.08	.11	-.04
21 Ignore	.08	.28	.23	.25	.09	-.03	.09	-.06
22 Friends	.08	.01	.02	.01	.05	-.01	.03	-.01
23 Solve problem	.00	.07	.06	.01	.24	-.13	.10	-.08

greater or less than the corresponding raw correlation in Table 1.2, an assumption of compounding of variables was accepted. That is, it was assumed that the raw correlation between strategy usage and states of being was artificially inflated or depressed due to the relationship of perceived effectiveness with both usage and well-being or dysfunction. Since the boys' and girls' data were examined independently there were 184 raw correlations considered. Of these, 10 measuring the relationship between usage and well-being changed by at least 0.1. Six were derived from the boys' data and four from the responses of the girls. Another three raw correlations between strategy usage and dysfunction, also changed by 0.1. These were all based on the boys' data.

In total, there were seven strategies for which the relationship between frequency of usage and well-being decreased by at least 0.1 once effectiveness of the strategy was controlled statistically. The first to be considered is the strategy solve the problem. When the usefulness of this strategy was held constant, the previously statistically significant raw correlations of .19 (for both boys and girls) between usage and well-being were replaced by corresponding partial correlations of .00 for boys and .06 for girls. Both partial correlations reflect a lack of statistically significant relationship. This indicates that if the perceived usefulness of problem solving is not controlled, its significant relationship with extent of usage artificially inflates the latter's apparent association with well-being. It is of interest to note that inspection of the relationship between perceived helpfulness of problem solving and well-being, with frequency of usage controlled, is significant for boys ($r = .24$, $p < .001$) but not for girls ($r = .10$, $p > .05$). Consequently one may argue that when it comes to boys trying to solve problems, it is not a matter of how often they try to use the strategy that associates with well-being but rather how effectively it is seen to work.

A similar result is observed for the strategies "accept one's best efforts" and "relax." If these strategies' respective effectiveness is taken into account, the raw coefficients that quantify the relationship between the frequency of usage and well-being are replaced by partial coefficients, which are at least 0.1 less in magnitude. The only relationship to remain statistically significant once effectiveness is controlled is that between boys' use of accepting their best efforts and their well-being.

The other strategies for which usefulness appears to play a substantial role in inflating the extent of relationship between usage and well-being differ for girls and boys. For the latter, they are work hard and seek physical recreation. For each of these strategies the relationship between usage and well-being drops by .10 and neither remains statistically significant.

In addition, inspection of the right-hand side of Table 1.3 shows that once levels of usage have been controlled, boys' perceptions of the usefulness of both work hard ($r = .16$) and physical recreation ($r = .17$) are both significantly associated with well-being. Consequently for these productive strategies, the perceived helpfulness of the strategy appears to be a better predictor of well-being than the extent of usage.

In summary, from the analysis so far it can be concluded that, particularly for boys, the frequency of usage of strategies such as problem solve, relax and work hard, quantity (that is, the extent of usage of the strategy) is less important than quality (that is, how well the strategy is seen to work) in explaining any relationship between coping strategies and well-being.

The second analysis to be undertaken involved scanning the correlations in Table 1.3 for patterns of statistically significant results. This provided a broader overview of the findings with regard to the role that quality and quantity of coping might play in explaining the relationships between coping strategies and well-being or dysfunction.

Some strategies, like self-blame, generally exhibit significant partial correlations between use and outcomes when effectiveness was controlled, but not between effectiveness and outcomes when usage is controlled. Most of these (worry, recognize inability, acknowledge defeat, give up, get sick, tension reduction, self-blame, keep to self, act up) appear to be strategies described elsewhere as nonproductive (Frydenberg & Lewis, 1996). In each case increased use of the strategy generally associates positively with dysfunction and negatively with well-being. In contrast, a few strategies display statistically significant relationships between perceived effectiveness and outcomes (with usage controlled). Those that do generally have only moderate correlations, that is, less than 0.2. Nevertheless it is of interest that as far as boys are concerned, the perceived effectiveness of four productive strategies (social support, work hard, physical recreation, solve the problem) associates significantly with their well-being even though the extent of usage of these strategies does not. It can therefore be argued that for boys, it is generally the quality of productive strategies that relate to well-being not the quantity.

In conclusion, the major findings of the second phase of the analysis suggests, first, that the frequency of adolescents' usage of nonproductive coping strategies generally relates more closely to both well-being and dysfunction than does their perceived effectiveness. Second, when boys' use of the productive strategies is considered, perceived effectiveness generally relates more closely to well-being than does extent of usage. However, in considering the validity of boys evaluations of the effectiveness of their coping strategies it should be noted that an earlier study by Seiffge-Krenke (1995) found that boys evaluated problems more optimistically and when a more serious problem occurred which could not be solved readily they did resort to alcohol and other drugs. Thus, although boys appear pragmatic in their use of coping strategies, in that they will use strategies that they deem to be helpful, when things do not work out they resort to substance abuse and other unhelpful activities.

In general, these results support an argument that when one is evaluating the value of coping responses, it is not sufficient to focus *only* on the frequency of usage of a particular strategy, although it is most defensible when the coping strategies of interest are those labeled as nonproductive. These appear to relate to both well-being and dysfunction. The frequency of usage of the more productive strategies however generally fails to relate to either dysfunction or well-being. It is a different story when the efficacy of usage of different coping strategies is considered. The perceived usefulness of most of the nonproductive strategies appears unrelated to dysfunction and, with the exception of worry and wishful thinking for boys, they are also unrelated to well-being. When it comes to nonproductive strategies the key element appears to be how often they are used. In contrast, with regards to productive strategies frequency is not important but the ability to use them well is.

These data show that the strategy problem solving relates not only to thriving but also unlike the earlier conclusion, it also relates to going under when one focuses on the effectiveness with which the strategy is implemented rather than the frequency of usage.

One implication of these findings, which needs at this stage to be seen as tentative, is that evaluations of coping programs which report as criterion measures less dysfunction or more well-being may need to examine separately the impact of increased usage of particular coping strategies and the effectiveness of the implementation of these strategies. It is possible that equating increased, ineffective, usage of a strategy with increased, effective, usage of a strategy may lead to tenuous findings. For example, if a program led to an increase in the quantity of problem solving attempts without improving the quality of problem solving, the frustration experienced may result in an associated increase in self-blame or wishful thinking. Any increased usage in these nonproductive strategies may be expected to associate with increased dysfunction and less wellness. For the productive strategies it may not only be how often young people use them, but also how well they use them. This can be seen from the drop in magnitude of the relationship between the frequency of use of these strategies and well being, once the self-perceived effectiveness (how often it was helpful) is taken into account.

IMPLICATIONS FOR EDUCATIONAL PRACTICE

Overall young people who are at risk of "going under" need to be brought to a situation where they can confidently have the skills to survive. This can be done by having them develop an awareness of the negative consequences of their reliance on strategies of worry, ignore, keep to self, wishful thinking, and tension reduction. While use of these strategies is not harmful in all circumstances, there needs to be an awareness of the potential for excessive and inappropriate use. When it comes to self-blame and acting up, the less these strategies are used the greater the likelihood that young people will thrive and greater use is likely to be associated with going under. In contrast, decreased reliance on worry, ignore, keep to self, wishful thinking, and tension reduction does not guarantee thriving. Young people need to be encouraged to use strategies such as working hard to solve problems, seeking professional help and seeking social support. Boys, in particular need to reflect on how effective their problem solving strategies are and how to improve them.

When it comes to implementation of programs to enhance coping skills it is important to first tackle the strategies which will save young people from going under in order that they can be brought to a level of survival. The next task is to bring those who are surviving to a level of thriving. When this approach is taken in the context of educating for coping it cannot be assumed that absence of dysfunction implies the presence of well-being. There needs to be a focus on both thriving and surviving. For example, it is possible that reducing worry or ignore will decrease levels of dysfunctionality but there appears little chance of an increase in well-being. In general, well-being is achieved by increasing productive strategies that are perceived to be helpful to the individual and reducing the reliance on nonproductive coping strategies. Since we know that some students use nonproductive strategies even if they are not found to be helpful (see Chapter 2 by Lewis & Frydenberg, this volume) it is even more important to help these young people to understand the benefits of some strategies (that is, those associated with thriving), the minimal survival attributes of others (surviving) along with the recognition of the damaging effects of others (going under).

The implications of the findings in this chapter are not restricted to clinicians working with adolescents. As indicated earlier, researchers attempting to establish the productivity of various coping responses frequently infer a relationship between a particular coping strategies and well being by demonstrating its negative relationship with dysfunction. However, depending on the strategy such an inference may be unreasonable. As shown in this chapter most of the coping strategies that associate significantly with thriving fail to relate to going under, and vica versa. For boys, only three of the 23 strategies investigated support the above inference. Although, for girls there were nine such strategies, they still form a minority of those investigated. Consequently before one can equate a positive relationship between a coping strategy and less dysfunction with a negative relationship between that strategy and well-being, both the gender of the adolescent and the specific coping strategy need to be considered.

Finally the findings in this chapter have implications for the evaluations of programs designed to improve the coping effectiveness of youth. Commonly, such evaluations compare the frequency of use of a range of coping strategies before and after exposure to a program. Increased usage of productive strategies such as, problem-solving and working hard, are then assumed to provide support for the program's effectiveness. However, this may not be a reasonable assumption if it is not the quantity of usage of such strategies that associates with well-being but the effectiveness with which they are used. For example, any program that increases adolescents' usage of problem solving without improving its perceived effectiveness may not be assumed useful. Further, as indicated above, before such program evaluation can be predictably linked to strategy use, the nature of the dependent variable in the evaluation will need to be specified in terms of both well-being and dysfunction, and the gender of the adolescents participating in the program will need to be taken into account.

In conclusion, it appears clear that the findings in this chapter may have serious implications for those attempting to identify productive and nonproductive coping strategies in order to promote the usage of the former while reducing reliance on usage of the latter. Consequently, further research is encouraged in this area to replicate these findings.

REFERENCES

Asarnow, J. R., Carlson, G. A., & Guthrie, D. (1987). Coping strategies, self-perceptions, hopelessness, and perceived family environments in depressed and suicidal children. *Journal of Consulting and Clinical Psychology, 55*, 361-366.

Band, E. B., & Weisz, J. R. (1998). How to feel better when it feels bad: Children's perspectives on coping with everyday stress. *Developmental Psychology, 24*, 247-253.

Bird, G. W., & Harris, R. L. (1990). A comparison of role strain and coping strategies by gender and family structure among early adolescents. *Journal of Early Adolescence, 10*, 141-158.

Brodzinsky, D. M., Elias, M. J., Steiger, C., Gill, S. J., & Hitt, J. C. (1992). Coping scale for children and youth: Scale development and validation. *Journal of Applied Developmental Psychology, 13*, 195-214.

Copeland, E. P., & Hess, R. S. (1995). Differences in young adolescents' coping strategies based on gender and ethnicity. *Journal of Early Adolescence, 15*, 203-219.

Ebata, A. T., & Moos, T. (1991). Coping and adjustment in distressed and healthy adolescents. *Journal of Applied Developmental Psychology, 12*, 33-54.

Ebata, A. T., & Moos, R. H. (1994). Personal, situational, and contextual correlates of coping in adolescence. *Journal of Research on Adolescence, 4*, 99-125.

Folkman, S. (1997). Positive psychological states and coping with severe stress. *Social Psychology Medicine, 45*, 1207-1221.

Folkman, S., & Lazarus, R. (1988a). *Ways of Coping Questionnaire Test Booklet.* Palo Alto, CA: Consulting Psychological Press.

Folkman, S., & Lazarus, R. S. (1998b). Coping as a mediator of emotion. *Journal of Personality and Social Psychology, 54*, 466-475.

Frydenberg, E. (1997). *Adolescent coping: Research and theoretical perspectives.* London: Routledge.

Frydenberg, E., & Lewis, R. (1993a). *Manual: The Adolescent Coping Scale.* Melbourne: Australian Council for Educational Research.

Frydenberg, E., & Lewis, R. (1993b). Boys play sport and girls turn to others: Age gender and ethnicity as determinants of coping. *Journal of Adolescence, 16*, 252-266.

Frydenberg, E., & Lewis, R. (1994). Coping with different concerns: Consistency and variation in coping strategies used by adolescents. *Australian Psychologist, 29*, 45-48.

Frydenberg, E., & Lewis, R. (1996). The Adolescent Coping Scale: Multiple forms and applications of a self report inventory in a counselling and research context. *European Journal of Psychological Assessment, 12*, 216-227.

Frydenberg, E., & Lewis, R. (1999a). Adolescent coping: The role of schools in facilitating reflection. *The British Journal of Educational Psychology, 69*, 83-96.

Frydenberg, E., & Lewis, R. (1999b). Academic and general wellbeing: The relationship with coping. *Australian Journal of Guidance and Counselling, 9*, 19-36.

Frydenberg, E., & Lewis, R. (2000). Teaching coping to adolescents: When and to whom. *American Educational Research Journal, 37*, 727-745.

Frydenberg, E., & Lewis, R. (2002). Adolescent wellbeing: Building young people's resources. In E. Frydenberg (Ed.), *Beyond coping: Meeting goals, vision and challenges.* Oxford, England: Oxford University Press.

Holahan, C. J., & Moos, R. H. (1986). Personality, coping and family resources in stress resistance. A longitudinal analysis. *Journal of Personality and Social Psychology, 51*, 389-395.

Holahan, C. J., & Moos, R. H. (1987). Personal and contextual determinants of coping strategies. *Journal of Personality and Social Psychology, 52*, 946-955.

Holahan, C. J., & Moos, R. H. (1990). Life stressors, resistance factors, and improved psychological functioning: An extension of the stress resistance paradigm. *Journal of Personality and Social Psychology, 58*, 909-917.

Holahan, C. J., & Moos, R. H. (1991). Life stressors, personal and social resources, and depression: A 4-year structural model. *Journal of Abnormal Psychology, 100*, 31-38.

Jenkin, C. (1997). *The relationship between self-efficacy and coping: Changes following an Outward Bound Program.* Unpublished master's of educational psychology project, University of Melbourne, Melbourne, Australia.

Lazarus, R. S., & Folkman, S. (1984). *Stress, appraisal and coping.* New York: Springer.

Luthar, S. S., & Zigler, E. (1991). Vulnerability and competence: A review of research on resilience in childhood. *American Journal of Orthopsychiatry, 61*, 6-22.

Muldoon, O. T. (1996). *Stress, appraisal and coping: A psychosocial approach.* Unpublished doctoral thesis, The Queens University, Belfast.

Noto, S. S. (1995). *The relationship between coping and achievement: A comparison between adolescent males and females.* Unpublished master's of educational psychology project, University of Melbourne, Melbourne, Australia.

Patterson, J. M., & McCubbin, H. I. (1987). Adolescent coping style and behaviors: Conceptualization and measurement. *Journal of Adolescence, 10*, 163-186.

Parsons, A., Frydenberg, E., & Poole, C. (1996). Overachievement and coping strategies in adolescent males. *British Journal of Educational Psychology, 66*, 109-114.

Reynolds, W. M. (2001). *Reynolds Adolescent Adjustment Screening Inventory.* US: Psychological Assessment Resources.

Ryckman, R. M., Robins, M. A., Thornton, B., & Cantrell, P. (1982). Development and validation of a self-efficacy scale. *Journal of Personality and Social Psychology, 42*, 891-900.

Sawyer, M. G., Kosky, R. J., Graetz, B. W., Arney, F., & Zubrick, P. B. (2000). The national survey of mental health and wellbeing: The child and adolescent component. *Australian and New Zealand Journal of Psychiatry, 34*, 214-220.

Seiffge-Krenke, I. (Ed.). (1995). Conceptual approach for studying stress, coping and relationships in adolescence. In *Stress, coping and relationships in adolescence* (pp. 26-43). Mahwah, NJ: Erlbaum.

Seligman, M. E. P., & Csikszentmihalyi, M. (2000). Positive psychology. *The American Psychologist, 55*, 5-14.

Spirito, A., Francis, G., Overholser, J., & Frank, N. (1996). Coping, depression, and adolescent suicide attempts. *Journal of Clinical Child Psychology, 25*, 147-155.

Wills, A. T. (1986). Stress and coping in early adolescence: Relationships to substance use in urban school samples. *Health Psychology, 5*, 503-529.

CHAPTER 2

STUDENTS'
SELF-EVALUATIONS
OF THEIR COPING

How Well Do They Do It?

Ramon Lewis
La Trobe University, Australia

Erica Frydenberg
University of Melbourne, Australia

ABSTRACT

In order to assist adolescents to cope at their optimum, it is helpful to understand how they evaluate the effectiveness of their coping strategies. This chapter reports 1,229 students' evaluations of the effectiveness of their coping responses using the short form of the Adolescent Coping Scale. It addresses the question: Are adolescents' evaluations consistent with research findings that show that some strategies result in nonproductive outcomes whereas others are more effective in either solving a problem or accommodating to it? In general both age and gender appear to influence strategies defined as useful although the students' evaluations are generally consistent

Thriving, Surviving, or Going Under: Coping with Everyday Lives, 25–43
Copyright © 2004 by Information Age Publishing
All rights of reproduction in any form reserved.

with reported research. They identify as most productive, strategies such as solve the problem, seek relaxing diversions, work hard, focus on the positive, seek social support, spend time with friends, and physical recreation. Similarly their less positive evaluations of self-blame, give up, worry, and wishful thinking are equally consistent with research outcomes. Nevertheless there is still a substantial minority of adolescents who are prepared to provide support for less helpful strategies. Implications for intervention are considered.

EFFECTIVE AND INEFFECTIVE COPING: STUDENTS' SELF-EVALUATIONS

An expanding body of literature suggests that inadequate responses to coping with stress in children of school age contributes to a range of psychosocial problems, including poor academic performance, conduct problems, anxiety, depression, suicide, eating disorders, and violence (Kovacs, 1997; Matheny, Aycock, & McCarthy, 1993). When young people are distressed, their energy is directed away from the learning process, thereby interfering with optimal school performance and age-appropriate psychosocial development (Compas & Hammen, 1996; Kovacs, 1997). In the Australian context, it is estimated that anywhere from 15% to 40% of children and adolescents currently in the school system could potentially benefit more from their education in both the social and academic domain if they were more psychologically resilient (Cunningham & Walker, 1999; Dadds, Spence, Holland, Barrett & Laurens, 1997; Roberts, 1999; Shochet & Osgarby, 1999). Additionally, many more students might benefit at some time in the future if they acquired a wider range of skills and competencies that enabled them to respond to future stressful and challenging situations in ways that were adaptive to their own emotional well-being.

The growing awareness of the long-term negative consequences of psychosocial risks on children's development has resulted in governments increasingly looking to schools as settings for promoting effective coping in young people.

SEX AND COPING

Sex differences in coping have been reported consistently in the literature. For a summary of studies see Frydenberg (1997). Girls generally use the support of others and focus on interpersonal relationships with siblings, parents, friends, and other adults (Bird & Harris, 1990; Copeland & Hess, 1995; Frydenberg & Lewis, 1999a, 2000; Patterson & McCubbin,

1987). Males, in contrast, resort more to ventilation (Bird & Harris, 1990) and humor (Patterson & McCubbin, 1987). There are some inconsistencies among studies, however. For example, Copeland and Hess (1995), using Patterson and McCubbin's (1987) A-Cope as the measure of coping, found that females used more proactive orientation and catharsis, whereas the males tended more to avoid problems and use physical diversions.

AGE AND COPING

Age-related differences in coping have been reported frequently, and sometimes there are different patterns of variation for boys and girls. In a general sense there is some evidence that productive or functional coping decreases with age (Compas, Malcarne, & Fondacaro, 1988; Frydenberg & Lewis, 1999a, 2000; Seiffge-Krenke & Shulman, 1990) while emotional coping increases with age (Compas et al., 1988). Further, older adolescents generally use more tension-reducing strategies than do younger adolescents (Compas et al., 1988; Frydenberg & Lewis, 1993a, 1999a, 2000). For example, in a study of 673 students (12 to 17 years), drawn from five secondary schools in metropolitan Melbourne, Australia, where age-related responses were evaluated (Frydenberg & Lewis, 1993a), young people in the early years of post-primary schooling reported using more work-related and less tension-reducing strategies than did students at higher levels. In contrast, the older students (16 year olds) were least likely to use hard work and most likely to rely on tension reduction and self-blame.

One study reported on the long-term effects of using social support (Feldman, Fisher, Ransom & Dimiceli, 1995). In that study, 169 adolescents were interviewed once at 13 and again 5 to 6 years later when they were adults. For boys, turning to religion and to friends during adolescence was each associated with poor adaptation as young adults, whereas for girls they were each associated with good adaptation. This led the authors to conclude that what is "good for the goose is not necessarily good for the gander." That is, the prognostic value of specific adolescent coping behaviors for adult adaptation is not identical for boys and girls. Turning to friends may work differently for boys than for girls. Moreover, social support may be used by boys and girls to manage different problems.

In other studies boys and girls are reported as coping differently according to a variation related to both age and sex. Both boys and girls report using "active distraction" techniques such as sports and exercise. However, girls reduce their use of this strategy in the senior years of high school but increase the use of "passive distraction" which includes behaviors such as reading, listening to music, and sleeping (Groër, Thomas, & Shoffner, 1992). In another cross-sectional study, Matheney, Aycock, and McCarthy (1993) reported an increase in emotion-focused coping over the school years.

Two recent studies by Frydenberg and Lewis (1999a, 2000) report age-related findings. The first examined cross-sectional data for a sample of 829 students aged 11-18 years, and the second tracked 168 adolescents over 5 years. Both reported that older adolescents use more nonproductive strategies and that this was more particularly the case for girls. In contrast, a study by Ebata and Moos (1994), which tracked young people for a 1-year period found that older adolescents were less likely to try avoiding their problems but were more active, appraised the focal stressor as controllable and as a challenge, and had more ongoing social resources.

SELF-REFLECTION

Self-consciousness is an integral part of self-regulation so it can be assumed that it is essential as part of personal and cognitive development. Thus the avoidance of reflection could be deemed to be a risk factor for psychological ill health (Schwarzer, 1996). Further, Hoyer and Klein (2000) have identified not only extremely low self-reflection as a risk factor for psychological maladjustment but also extremely high self-reflection. Thus the role of schools in facilitating the social and emotional development of youth by having young adolescents reflect on their coping behavior as a precursor to self-stimulated change is important as long as reflection is encouraged at an appropriate level. The act of learning through reflection on one's current beliefs is consistent with a number of developments in the field of psychology and education. In the area of psychology it is consistent with the current emphasis on positive psychology, which focuses on strengths and abilities rather than pathology and disability (Seligman & Csikszentmihalyi, 2000). In line with this approach is the importance of self-evaluation in stimulating self- and/or counselor-initiated behavioral change. More recently we have been cautioned against an overly optimistic self-evaluation by construing self-evaluations as "mindfulness." This involves attempts to be flexible, creative in our solutions, and to be embedded in the present rather than in the past (Langer, 2002). Similarly, self-efficacy or "believing that you can" is a cornerstone for setting goals and meeting challenges. A belief in one's own ability to cope is based on positive outcomes from prior self-evaluations.

There are two main views of education that are pertinent to the development of self-reflection, namely metacognition (White & Gunstone, 1992) and constructivism (Watzlawick, 1984; Fensham, Gunstone, & White, 1994; Gardner, 1991). While researchers in the area of secondary school science learning initially pursued these views, their interpretations of how learning occurs have been found to be of general relevance. In brief, according to proponents of constructivist education, learners develop schemas or frameworks for dealing with their experiences. Historically, to facilitate change in learners' understanding, students have been given a description of the correct way to understand it and were also told why their current understanding was incorrect. As a result, the learner adopted the new schema, and may have even applied it consistently. However, the old schema was often not discarded but only temporarily suppressed, and as time passed this old schema frequently resurfaced and replaced the new one.

It has been argued that to effect permanent change to a learners' schema, several components are essential. Primarily, learners are required to reflect on their currently held paradigm, understand it, find it unsatisfactory in the light of new information or observations, adapt their view, act in the light of these adaptations, and judge their new behavior as satisfactory. If not, modifications made in a learner's schema will, in many cases, be temporary. It is this constructivist, reflective approach to learning that is being adapted in the area of coping, where notions of correct understanding do not readily apply and are best replaced by notions of young people seeking alternate ways of understanding their circumstances and their actions. For example, in learning to cope, adolescents can be encouraged to reflect on their current coping repertoire as well as the coping strategies of others.

COPING

Coping refers to the behavioral and cognitive efforts used by individuals to manage the demands of a person-environment relationship (Frydenberg & Lewis, 2000). An individual's access to available resources, styles, and strategies subsequently influences the coping process (Frydenberg & Lewis, 2002). Strategies may vary across time and context depending on the stressor (Compas, 1987), and include aspects of both the self, such as problem-solving skills and self-esteem, and the social environment (i.e., supportive social network).

Coping styles are methods of coping that characterize individuals' reactions to stress either over time or across different situations. They may partially reflect the ways of coping preferred by individuals because they are consistent with personal values, beliefs, and goals. One of the most widely used models of coping, the transactional model, proposes that coping can be defined in terms of two global coping styles: problem-focused (or behavioral) coping and emotion-focused (or cognitive) coping (Folkman, 1982; Lazarus & Folkman, 1984). Other researchers have found that the strategies can best be grouped to characterize three coping styles that represent two functional and one dysfunctional aspect of coping (Frydenberg & Lewis, 1991; Seiffge-Krenke & Shulman, 1990).

Functional coping styles represent direct attempts to deal with the problem, with or without reference to others. Dysfunctional coping styles relate to the use of nonproductive strategies, such as worry and self-blame. While productive coping has generally been associated with positive adaptation (Ebata & Moos, 1991), the use of the terms functional and dysfunctional styles do not refer to "good" or "bad" styles, as styles of coping are largely context dependent.

Studies examining the link between coping and well-being have identified characteristics associated with more effective coping in adolescence. These characteristics include temperament, optimism, perceived personal control, familial factors (such as family cohesion, shared values, loving parents, and a relationship with at least one parent figure), flexibility, and the availability of social support (Luthar & Zigler, 1991; Frydenberg & Lewis, 2002).

Research has found that coping strategies that focus on problem solving and positive cognitions are related to less emotional, behavioral, and substance use problems (Compas, Malcarne, & Fondacaro, 1988; Ebata & Moos, 1991). In contrast, avoidant or nonproductive coping is generally associated with poor adaptation and more mental health problems in adolescents (Ebata & Moos, 1991; Frydenberg & Lewis, 1999b; Sandler, Wolchik, MacKinnon, Ayers, & Roosa, 1997).

THE ROLE OF APPRAISAL

The concept of appraisal is one of the basic tenets of Lazarus' theory. It is an important part of the coping process and has explicatory power. Cognitive appraisal is what a person does to evaluate whether a particular encounter is relevant to his or her well-being. In each encounter two forms of appraisal are said to take place: *primary appraisal*, where the question "What is at stake in terms of potential harm or benefit?" is asked, and *secondary appraisal*, where the question is asked "What can be done about the situation or what are the options or resources available?" (Lazarus, Kanner, & Folkman, 1980; Lazarus & Folkman, 1984; Folkman, Lazarus, Dunkel-Schetter, DeLongis, & Gruen, 1986; Folkman, Lazarus, Gruen &

DeLongis, 1986). The appraisals may initiate a chain of activity and coping actions to manage a situation.

Researchers, such as Stone and Neale (1984), have developed their own measures of coping and found that appraisal is associated with the type and amount of coping. Manzi (1986) found that students assessed what is stressful in a work situation according to whether they regarded the situation as one of loss, threat, or challenge. In relationship to stressful academic and social events in a school environment, appraisal played a part, in that the severity of the stress was assessed according to whether individuals felt that they could do something constructive to deal with the problem (Fahs, 1986). According to Muldoon (1996), who examined the interview responses of 9-10 year olds, events that are harmful or loss inducing are perceived by children as most stressful and when asked to describe an event that is stressful children spontaneously described a harmful event.

The model posits that coping is a function of the situational determinants and the individual's characteristics, perception of the situation, and coping intentions. The individual brings a host of biological dispositional, personal and family history, and family climate characteristics. It is how these impact the perception of the situation that is of interest. Following an appraisal of the situation, the individual assesses the likely impact of the stress, that is, whether the consequences are likely to lead to "loss," "harm," "threat," or "challenge," and what resources (personal or interpersonal) are available to the individual to deal with the situation. The intent of the action along with the action determines the outcome. Following a response, the outcome is reviewed or reappraised (*tertiary appraisal* or *reappraisal*) and another response may follow. There may be a subsequent development in an individual's coping repertoire. Thus the circular nature of the process illustrates the fact that strategies are likely to be tried again or rejected from future use, and retaining a strategy is consequent on the coping experience of the individual.

If the encounter is amenable to change, problem-focused strategies are frequently used. Where the situation is assessed as unchangeable, emotion-focused strategies are more likely to be used (Folkman & Lazarus, 1980).

As stated above, whether or not a stressor is controllable is an important factor in how one copes. A study by Compas, Malcarne, and Fondacaro (1988) found that academic stressors were assessed as more controllable than interpersonal stressors; and generally more problem-focused strategies than emotion-focused strategies were used to deal with the academic rather than the interpersonal stressors. It was also found that in general when there was low perceived control of the stressor, there was greater use of emotion-focused coping whereas when there was high perceived control, there was greater use of problem-focused coping. Another interesting finding was that in those cases where the self-reports and maternal reports indicated that emotional or behavioral problems existed, there was higher usage of emotion-focused coping, and where there were no emotional or behavioral problems, there was a higher usage of problem-focused coping.

Lazarus emphasizes the central role of cognitions in emotional outcomes, asserting that when people experience situations as a "hassle," it is the meaning that they give to a transaction and whether they appraise the situation as threatening, harmful, or challenging, that may have an impact on the emotion generated and the coping reaction (Folkman, Lazarus, Pimley, & Novacek, 1987). That is what is meant by the "perception of the situation." For example, males tend to appraise "hassles" in terms of a challenge and employ problem-focused strategies, while females are more inclined to appraise situations as threatening or harmful and are more inclined to use emotion-focused coping (Ptacek, Smith, & Zanas, 1992).

Psychological stress resides neither in the person nor in the situation, but depends on the transaction between the two, that is, how the person appraises the event and how he or she adapts to it. Thus to some young people, each exam, public occasion or interview may be stressful, while to others it is perceived as part of the excitement of living and an opportunity to move forward.

THE MEASUREMENT OF COPING

As stated earlier, the most common categorization of approaches to coping is the dichotomous grouping of strategies by Lazarus and Folkman (Lazarus, 1993; Lazarus & Folkman, 1984), which identifies problem- and emotion-focused coping. Alternative categorizations range from groupings of 8 to 10 strategies or scales (e.g., Stark, Spirito, Williams, & Guevremont, 1989), to the specificity of 18 strategies that make up the Adolescent Coping Scale (Frydenberg & Lewis, 1993a). Strategies have often been grouped to characterize coping styles that represent functional and dysfunctional aspects of coping (Cox, Gotts, Boot, & Kerr, 1985; Frydenberg & Lewis, 1991; Seiffge-Krenke & Shulman, 1990). The functional styles represent direct attempts to deal with the problem, with or without reference to others, whereas the dysfunctional styles relate to the use of nonproductive strategies, such as self-blame and wishful thinking.

While there are numerous coping strategies that individuals use to manage their concerns, grouping these according to similarity in action facilitates the study of adolescent coping. In Australia a profile of adolescent coping has been developed by generating young people's description of their coping and grouping their responses on the basis of similarity of idea or action. These descriptions (which included 2,014 coping behaviors) provided the basis for the development of the Adolescent Coping Scale (ACS) (Frydenberg & Lewis, 1993b), an 80-item checklist used to identify 18 commonly used coping strategies.

To distinguish between coping in general and coping with a specific issue, a Specific and General Form were developed. Both forms contain the same items, differing only in the wording of the instructions. The Specific Form elicits responses to either a particular self-nominated or administer-nominated concern, whereas the General Form elicits responses to coping with concerns in general. For both forms, coping styles can be identified based on the combination of items. As stated earlier, we have found support for categorizing coping into three areas, namely dealing with the problem, reference to others and nonproductive coping (Frydenberg & Lewis, 1993b, 1996).

METHODOLOGY

To gather information on adolescents' coping responses and how effective they perceived these to be, a questionnaire was designed based on the short form of the ACS. The instrument contained items assessing the 18 coping strategies measured by the ACS plus five extra items. Two of these were taken from the not cope scale of the long form of the ACS. These were added since one aim of the study was to determine how acceptable the least productive coping responses may be to adolescents. Two additional items, "Act up and make life difficult for those around me" and "Accept things as they are because I've done my best," were also added. These items were derived from responses to the open question, "What else do you do to cope?" on the ACS in previous studies (Frydenberg & Lewis, 1993b, 1994, 1996, 1999a, 2000).

Each item on the questionnaire was accompanied by two response formats. One requested an indication of how often the coping response was used. The other addressed how useful the response was when used. In each case the response alternatives were Hardly ever or Never, A few times, Sometimes, Often and Nearly always. These were coded from 1 to 5 respectively. After completing the 23 items on the questionnaire, students were invited to identify, in writing, which four strategies were least useful.

They were then asked to report if these strategies were ever helpful and if so, in what situations.

SAMPLE

In total, a sample of 1,264 students were drawn from 11 schools in the Melbourne Metropolitan region of Victoria, Australia. The schools represented a convenience sample but included both larger and smaller schools situated in a range of socioeconomic regions of Melbourne (southeastern and northwestern suburbs). Unfortunately in one school, students refrained from reporting their sex or year levels. Consequently some analyses included these 276 adolescents and some did not. Thirty seven percent of the sample was in Year 7, 30% in Year 8, and 33% in Year 9. In general half the sample were girls as the proportion of girls in Years 7, 8, and 9 was 40, 45, and 56% respectively.

To investigate students' evaluations of the 23 coping responses on the short form of the augmented ACS, item means were computed and items ranked. In addition, the proportion of respondents rating the strategy as often or nearly always helpful was determined. Finally the proportion of students (in percentages) rating the strategy as sometimes helpful was added in parentheses. These data are recorded in Table 2.1.

Inspection of the data in Table 2.1 indicates that the majority of respondents report that five strategies are often or always helpful. These involve staying socially connected (Strategy 4) and remaining relaxed (1) and healthy (2), while working at solving the problem (5, 3). There are another three coping strategies which three quarters of respondents identify as at least sometimes useful. These include focusing on the positive (7), accepting that one has done one's best (6), and seeking social support (8).

The remaining 15 strategies are on average seen by respondents as useful less than "sometimes." The least useful strategies are nevertheless claimed by approximately one third of students to be helpful at least sometimes. This reflects the notion that there is great difficulty associated with generalizing the idea of productive and nonproductive coping strategies to all individuals.

In summary, the students' evaluations are generally consistent with reported research in identifying as most productive, strategies such as problem solve, relax, work hard, focus on the positive, social support, friends, and physical recreation. Similarly their less positive evaluations of self-blame (21), give up (19, 20), worry (16) and wish think (14) are equally consistent with research outcomes. The evaluation of the tension reduction strategy (9) seems to be more positive than might have been

Table 2.1.   Percentage of Students Rating a Strategy as Often or Nearly Always Helpful (or Sometimes Helpful in Brackets)

Strategy	Mean	Often/ Always Helpful (Sometimes)
1. Relax, e.g., watch TV, play computer games, go for a walk	4.00	70 (20)
2. Keep fit and healthy, e.g., play sport	3.90	66 (21)
3. Work hard	3.84	65 (20)
4. Spend time with a good friend	3.83	64 (23)
5. Work out a way of dealing with the problem	3.53	53 (28)
6. Accept things as they are, because I've done my best	3.39	47 (33)
7. Look on the bright side of things and think of all that is good	3.27	43 (33)
8. Look for support and encouragement from others	3.20	39 (39)
9. Find a way to let off steam: for example, cry, scream, drink	3.01	29 (24)
10. Try to be funny	2.91	31 (33)
11. Ask a teacher or other professional person for help	2.87	35 (26)
12. Accept that I have no way of dealing with the situation	2.67	22 (36)
13. Don't let others know about my problem	2.61	22 (31)
14. Wish a miracle will happen to make things turn out well	2.51	24 (22)
15. Shut myself off from the problem so I can try and ignore it	2.49	19 (30)
16. Worry about what will happen to me	2.47	21 (25)
17. Join with others to deal with the problem (e.g., organize a petition, attend a meeting)	2.39	23 (22)
18. Pray for God to look after me	2.30	24 (15)
19. Tell myself there is nothing I can do, so I don't do anything	2.20	15 (22)
20. I just give up	2.19	18 (18)
21. Blame myself	2.09	13 (20)
22. Act up and make life difficult for those around me	2.08	14 (17)
23. I get sick	1.99	13 (17)

expected but overall there is a great deal of consistency between outcomes-based evaluations of alternative strategies and the evaluations provided by adolescents. In short, the latter seem to agree with prior research on which strategies work best and which do not. Nevertheless, as noted above, there is still a substantial minority of adolescents who are prepared to provide support for less helpful strategies. For example, get sick (23), the strategy rated on average as least helpful, is evaluated as always helpful by 7% of the sample (84 adolescents), helpful often by another 6% (N = 66), and helpful sometimes by a further 17% (N = 201).

PERCEIVED HELPFULNESS OF
COPING STRATEGIES BY SEX AND YEAR LEVEL

To determine what factors may be associated with the perceived helpfulness of strategies, a two-way MANOVA was computed in which the 23 coping strategies were the dependent variables and respondents' sex and year level were the independent variables. Both year level (Multivariate F (46, 1,422) = 2.17, p < .00) and sex ($F(23, 710)$ = 4.68, p < .000) were statistically significant so univariate results were then inspected. Since there were 23 separate analyses to be considered a conservative significance level of .01 was used. At this level four strategies showed significant associations with year level and seven with sex. With regard to the former, year level was significantly associated with the perceived helpfulness of work hard (F = 5.24, p = .005), worry (F = 6.64, p = .001), wish think (F = 4.87, p = .008) and focus on the positive (F = 5.59, p = .004). Inspection of the comparisons of means for respondents at Years 7, 8, and 9 (Sheffé test) shows no significant difference between any pair for work hard. However respondents in Year 7 rated worry as less helpful and focus on the positive as more helpful than did the older respondents. They also rated wish think as more useful than did Year 9 students.

As stated above, there were seven strategies seen by girls and boys to be differentially effective. Girls perceived sharing (seek social support and fitting in with friends) and letting off steam (tension reduction) as more helpful than did boys. Boys in contrast reported that relax and physical recreation were more useful than did girls. Boys were also more likely than girls to note the usefulness of acting up and attempting to ignore the problem.

HELPFULNESS AND USE OF COPING STRATEGIES

In a bid to explore potential incongruence in perceptions of usefulness of respective coping strategies and the extent of their usage, two categories of strategies were identified. The first comprised those where at least 10% of the sample (approximately 100 adolescents) indicated that they used the strategy sometimes, often, or nearly always, even though they rated it as never helpful. There were eight strategies in this group. The second category consisted of strategies which were hardly ever or never utilized by at least 10% of the sample, even though they were found to be often, or nearly always helpful when they were employed. No such strategies were found. Table 2.2 records the number of respondents who rated strategies as never helpful yet used them at least sometimes. In each case the number of adolescents concerned is included in parentheses.

Table 2.2.   Coping Strategies Used at Least Sometimes Although Never Helpful

Strategy	Percent used at least Sometimes but never helpful (N)
Don't let others know about my problem	13 (157)
Tell myself there is nothing I can do, so I don't do anything	10 (118)
I just give up	11 (130)
Blame myself	18 (220)
Act up and make life difficult for those around me	10 (118)
I get sick	18 (211)
Wish a miracle will happen to make things turn out well	17 (208)
Worry about what will happen to me	17 (205)

Three of the eight strategies in Table 2.2 effectively describe giving up, giving in, and going under (acknowledge defeat, give up, and get sick), and have been nominated elsewhere as indicators of an inability to cope (Frydenberg & Lewis, 1993b). Nevertheless, as indicated earlier (see Table 2.1), there are substantial numbers of students who view these strategies as sometimes, often, or always helpful. Some of the explanations offered to the open-format question on the survey suggests that these can act as a circuit breaker, prevent more negative outcomes, and reduce the pressure from self and others, for example "it gives you a rest," "either give up or get stressed," "I knew that if I kept going I would get hurt," "Everybody went away."

Justification for the usefulness of the remaining five strategies were also given by respondents, verbatim examples of which are reproduced in Table 2.3.

Table 2.3.   Justifications for Using Least Helpful Strategies

Strategy	Justification
Worry	Keeps me working Makes me more careful
Wishfully Think	Allows an escape Not to crack under pressure
Self-blame	Didn't take it out on anyone else People blame me less
Act up	Forgot problems Showed them how I felt so they were more considerate toward me
Keep to Self	Don't want people's sympathy and all of the other crap they say Didn't want them telling others

From Table 2.3 it can be seen that there is justification, in certain circumstances for worry, wishful thinking, self-blame, acting up, and keeping to oneself.

DISCUSSION

In general, adolescents' evaluations of the helpfulness or effectiveness of their coping responses are consistent with the results of studies into the relationship between coping and outcomes (Frydenberg & Lewis, 1999b). The strategies viewed as most helpful address staying physically fit, relaxed, socially connected, focusing on the positive, and problem solving. If the problem cannot be solved, accepting one's best effort was seen as effective. All of these strategies are rated, on average, as at least "sometimes" to be of benefit.

In contrast, strategies referred to in previous publications as nonproductive are seen by adolescents as least helpful (Frydenberg & Lewis, 1999a). These primarily comprise strategies such as worry, get sick, wishfully think, give up, self-blame, and ignore. In addition, adolescents' evaluation of social action, acting up, and prayer to a deity indicated that they were seen to be of limited benefit.

The fact that in some circumstances the use of nonproductive strategies is justified can readily be understood. First, for example, worry can be helpful as a way to energize the individual, as before an examination or an important performance. This has elsewhere been referred to as a source of eustress[1] (Selye, 1976). Although wishful thinking is a strategy which in some circumstances has been construed as an unrealistic reliance on an external force, it can also be a source of hope (Snyder, 1994) and a useful way of averting despair and negative thinking (Frydenberg & Lewis, 2002). Second, although self-blame is generally unhelpful as a strategy of choice, in some circumstances it can be justified as a way of taking responsibility on the self, rather than blaming others. The blaming of others, as an external locus of control activity, however, is found to be nonproductive in its own right. Third, although acting up is generally a form of inappropriate conduct, in this study it has been justified on some occasions as a form of assertive behavior. Finally keeping one's problems to oneself is not helpful when it is a form of withdrawal from others as it avoids the opportunity to gain support or assistance from others. Nevertheless, in this study it has been justified as a form of self-reliance, which may be appropriate, although it is difficult to determine whether this is the case from the comments provided by students in this investigation.

Further to these general findings, some gender and age related differences were noted. Younger adolescents found worrying less helpful, and both focusing on the positive and wishfully thinking more helpful than did older youth. In addition, girls reported more value in sharing and letting off steam, whereas boys saw more benefit in acting up, relaxing and keeping fit. This is somewhat consistent with earlier findings where girls' usage of social support and tension reduction and boys' reliance on relaxation and utilization of physical recreation has been noted (Frydenberg & Lewis, 1999b). Additionally it has been reported that girls increasingly resort to tension reduction and self-blame as they grow older (Frydenberg & Lewis, 2000).

In general, the more effective a strategy was evaluated, the more it was used. Nevertheless, between approximately 100 and 200 adolescents reported using eight strategies at least sometimes even though they identified them as never helpful. The willingness of a substantial minority of adolescents to use strategies, which both they and reported research indicate have very limited usefulness, is a cause for concern. Prior research has demonstrated associations between strategies such as self-blame, worry, keep to self, and wishful thinking and a range of dysfunctional outcomes, ranging from homesickness to anorexia and depression (Frydenberg & Lewis, 1999b). Most recently there has been evidence that in the presence of nonproductive coping strategies such as self-blame, worry, keep to self, and wishful thinking, the effectiveness of more productive strategies such as social support, problem-solving, keeping fit, and working hard appears inhibited (Lewis & Frydenberg, 2002).

In conclusion, the data reported above provide evidence for practitioners working with adolescents that adolescents in general are aware of what coping strategies are effective. Too many, however, are prepared to use strategies that they recognize as unhelpful. The implications are that it is up to practitioners working with adolescents to counsel them to reduce their reliance on strategies that they know themselves to be ineffective and to facilitate greater use of strategies which they know to be effective (see Chapter 1 by Lewis & Frydenberg, this volume). Furthermore, practitioners need to determine why it is that young people maintain reliance on nonproductive strategies that are perceived by youth to be ineffective. For example, a reliance on self-blame could be a reflection on family roles such as being the oldest sibling who is hard on him or herself when things go wrong (Adler, 1963). Alternatively, it could be the result of the power of social learning, in that young people are mirroring the use of nonproductive strategies, for example self-blame, by significant adults in their lives, such as parents or teachers. Another explanation could be a well-developed conscience or superego (Freud, 1946, 1961) or because there is a heightened sense of concern and fair play regarding the world around them, and they correspondingly take responsibility for the grief or ills of others (Frydenberg & O'Mullane, 2000).

Personality factors may also play a part. For example anxious children are more likely to use nonproductive strategies to cope (see Chapter 5 by Jones & Frydenberg, this volume). Having explored and understood the factors that maintain the use of nonproductive strategies in the face of a perceived lack of helpfulness, practitioners can engage in the task of discouraging their use. This needs to be complemented by strengthening the adolescents' resolve to increase use of productive coping strategies.

There is a likelihood that those who evaluate nonproductive strategies as acceptable as well as those who evaluate them as not helpful, may be drawing on a poorer resource pool (see Chapter 4 by McKenzie & Frydenberg, this volume). Thus, augmenting young people's resource pool, especially their coping resources, should prove to be helpful in reducing reliance on nonproductive strategies.

Within a framework of positive psychology we can foster a belief in young people's ability to cope and foster mindful self-reflection that is not overly optimistic and which acknowledges the individual's capacity to be flexible and to focus on the present rather than to dwell on the past. This is likely to assist young people to thrive. Additionally we need to foster attempts to increase productive coping and to decrease reliance on nonproductive coping strategies.

NOTE

1.   Eustress is a positive stress set off by a positive event on one' s life.

REFERENCES

Adler, A. (1963). *The problem child*. New York: Capricorn Books. (Original work published 1930)

Bird, G. W., & Harris, R. L. (1990). A comparison of role strain and coping strategies by gender and family structure among early adolescents. *Journal of Early Adolescence, 10,* 141-158.

Compas, B. (1987). Coping with stress during childhood and adolescence. *Psychological Bulletin, 101, 393-403.*

Compas, B. E., & Hammen, C. L. (1996). Child and adolescent depression: Covariation and comorbidity in development. In R. J. Haggerty & L. R. Sherrod (Eds.), *Stress, risk, and resilience in children and adolescents: Processes, mechanisms, and interventions* (pp. 225-267). New York: Cambridge University Press.

Compas, B. E., Malcarne, V. L., & Fondacaro, K. M. (1988). Coping with stressful events in older children and adolescents. *Journal of Consulting and Clinical Psychology, 56,* 405-411.

Copeland, E. P., & Hess, R. S. (1995). Differences in young adolescents' coping strategies based on gender and ethnicity. *Journal of Early Adolescence, 15*, 203-219.

Cox, T., Gotts, G., Boot, N., & Kerr, J. (1985). Physical exercise, employee fitness and the management of health at work. *Work and Stress, 2*, 71-77.

Cunningham, E., & Walker, G. (1999). Screening for at-risk youth: Predicting adolescent depression from coping styles. *Australian Journal of Guidance and Counselling, 9*, 37-46.

Dadds, M. R., Spence, S. H., Holland, D. E., Barrett, P. M., & Laurens, K. R. (1997). Prevention and early intervention for anxiety disorders: A controlled trial. *Journal of Consulting and Clinical Psychology, 65*, 627-635.

Ebata, A. T., & Moos, R. H. (1994). Personal, situational, and contextual correlates of coping in adolescence. *Journal of Research on Adolescence, 4*, 99-125.

Fahs, M. E. (1986, April). *Coping in school: Correlations among perceptions of stress, coping styles, personal attributes and academic achievement in inner-city junior high school students.* Paper presented at the Annual Meeting of the American Educational Research Association, San Francisco.

Feldman, S. S., Fisher, L., Ransom, D. C., & Dimiceli, S. (1995). Is "What is good for the goose good for the gander?" Sex differences in relationships between adolescent and adult adaptation. *Journal of Research on Adolescence, 5*, 333-336.

Fensham, P., Gunstone, R., & White, R. (1994). *The content of science*. London: The Falmer Press.

Folkman, S. (1982). An approach to the measurement of coping. *Journal of Occupational Behaviour, 3*, 95-107.

Folkman, S., & Lazarus, R. S. (1980). An analysis of coping in a middle-aged community sample. *Journal of Health and Social Behavior, 21*, 219-239.

Folkman, S., Lazarus, R. S., Dunkel-Schetter, C., DeLongis, A., & Gruen, R. J. (1986). Dynamics of a stressful encounter: Cognitive appraisal, coping and encounter outcomes. *Journal of Personality and Social Psychology, 50*, 992-1003.

Folkman, S., Lazarus, R. S., Gruen, R. J., & DeLongis, A. (1986). Appraisal, coping, health status, and psychological symptoms. *Journal of Personality and Social Psychology, 50*, 571-579.

Folkman, S., Lazarus, R. S., Pimley, S., & Novacek, J. (1987). Age differences in stress and coping processes. *Psychology and Aging, 2*, 171-184.

Freud, A. (1946). *The ego and the mechanisms of defense*. New York: International Universities Press. (Original work published 1936)

Freud, S. (1961). The unconscious. In J. Strachey (Ed.), *The standard edition of the complete psychological works of Sigmund Freud* (Vol. 14). London: Hogarth Press (Original work published 1915)

Frydenberg, E. (1997). *Adolescent coping: Research and theoretical perspectives*. London: Routledge.

Frydenberg, E., & Lewis, R. (1991). Adolescent coping styles and strategies: Is there functional and dysfunctional coping? *Australian Journal of Guidance and Counselling, 1*, 1-8.

Frydenberg, E., & Lewis, R. (1993a). Boys play sport and girls turn to others: Age, gender and ethnicity as determinants of coping. *Journal of Adolescence, 16*, 252-266.

Frydenberg, E., & Lewis, R. (1993b). *The Adolescent Coping Scale: Practitioners manual.* Melbourne: Australian Council for Educational Research.

Frydenberg, E., & Lewis, R. (1994). Coping with different concerns: Consistency and variation in coping strategies used by adolescents. *Australian Psychologist, 29,* 45-48.

Frydenberg, E., & Lewis, R. (1996). The Adolescent Coping Scale: Multiple forms and applications of a self report inventory in a counselling and research context. *European Journal of Psychological Assessment, 12,* 216-227.

Frydenberg, E., & Lewis, R. (1999a). Adolescent coping: The role of schools in facilitating reflection. *The British Journal of Educational Psychology, 69,* 83-96.

Frydenberg, E., & Lewis, R. (1999b). Academic and general well-being: The relationship with coping. *Australian Journal of Guidance and Counselling, 9,* 19-36.

Frydenberg, E., & Lewis, R. (2000). Teaching coping to adolescents: When and to whom. *American Educational Research Journal, 37,* 727-745.

Frydenberg, E., & O'Mullane, A. (2000). Nurturing talent in the Australian context: A reflective approach. *Roeper Review, 22,* 78-85.

Gardner, H. (1991). *The unschooled mind: How children think and how schools should teach.* London: Fontana Press.

Groër, M. W., Thomas, S. P., & Shoffner, D. (1992). Adolescent stress and coping: A longitudinal study. *Research in Nursing and Health, 15,* 209-217.

Hoyer, J., & Klein, A. (2000). Self-reflection and well-being: Is there a healthy amount of introspection. *Psychological Reports, 86,* 135-141.

Kovacs, M. (1997). Depressive disorders in childhood: An impressionistic landscape. *Journal of Child Psychology and Psychiatry, 38,* 287-298.

Langer, E. (2002). Mindfulness versus positive evaluation. In C. R. Snyder & S. J. Lopez (Eds.), *Handbook of positive psychology* (pp. 215-230). New York: Oxford University Press.

Lazarus, R. S. (1993). From psychological stress to the emotions: A history of changing outlooks. *Annual Review of Psychology, 44,* 1-21.

Lazarus, R. S., & Folkman, S. (1984). *Stress, appraisal, and coping.* New York: Springer.

Lazarus, R. S., Kanner, A. D., & Folkman, S. (1980). Emotions: A cognitive phenomenological analysis. In R. Plutchick & S. Kellerman (Eds.), *Emotion-theory research and experience: Theories of emotion* (Vol. 1, pp. 189-217). New York: Academic Press.

Lewis, R., & Frydenberg, E. (2002). Concomitants of failure to cope: What we should teach adolescents. *British Journal of Educational Psychology, 72,* 419-431.

Luthar, S. S., & Zigler, E. (1991). Vulnerability and competence: A review of research on resilience in childhood. *American Journal of Orthopsychiatry, 61,* 6-22.

Manzi, P. A. (1986). Cognitive appraisal: Stress and coping in teenage employment. *The Vocational Guidance Quarterly, 34,* 161-170.

Matheney, K., Aycock, D., & McCarthy, C. (1993). Stress in school-age children and youth. *Educational Psychology Review, 5,* 109-134.

Muldoon, O. T. (1996). *Stress, appraisal and coping: A psychosocial approach.* Unpublished doctoral thesis, The Queens University, Belfast.

Patterson, J. M., & McCubbin, H. I. (1987). Adolescent coping style and behaviors: Conceptualization and measurement. *Journal of Adolescence, 10*, 163-186.

Ptacek, I., Smith, R., & Zanas, J. (1992). Gender, appraisal and coping: A longitudinal analysis. *Journal of Personality and Social Psychology, 60*, 747-769.

Roberts, C. M. (1999). The prevention of depression in children and adolescents. *Australian Psychologist, 34*, 49-57.

Sandler, I. N., Wolchik, S. A., MacKinnon, D., Ayers, T. S., & Roosa, M. W. (1997). Developing linkages between theory and intervention in stress and coping processes. In S. A. Wolchik & I. N. Sandler (Eds.), *Handbook of children's coping: Linking theory and intervention* (pp. 3-40). New York: Plenum Press.

Schwarzer, R. (1996). Thought control of action: Interfering self-doubts. In I. G. Sarason & G. R. Pierce (Eds.), *Cognitive interference: Theories, methods, and findings* (pp. 99-115). Mahwah, NJ: Erlbaum.

Seiffge-Krenke, I., & Shulman, S. (1990). Coping style in adolescence. A cross cultural study. *Journal of Cross-Cultural Psychology, 21*, 351-377.

Seligman, M. E. P., & Csikszentmihalyi, M. (2000). Positive psychology. *The American Psychologist, 55*, 5-14.

Selye, H. (1976). *Stress in health and disease*. Reading, MA: Butterworth.

Shochet, I., & Osgarby, S. (1999). The Resourceful Adolescent Project: Building psychological resilience in adolescents and their parents. *The Australian Educational and Developmental Psychologist, 16*, 43-64.

Snyder, C. R. (1994). *The psychology of hope: You can get there from here*. New York: Free Press.

Stark, L. J., Spirito, A., Williams, C. A., & Guevremont, D. C. (1989). Common problems and coping strategies I: Findings with normal adolescents. *Journal of Abnormal Child Psychology, 17*, 203-212.

Stone, A. A., & Neale, J. M. (1984). New measure of daily coping: Development and preliminary results. *Journal of Personality and Social Psychology, 46*, 892-906.

Watzlawick, P. (Ed.). (1984). *The invented reality: How do we know what we believe we know? Contributions to constructivism*. New York: Norton.

White, R. T., & Gunstone, R. S. (1992). *Probing understanding*. London: Falmer.

CHAPTER 3

CHILDREN LIVING WITH PARENTAL MENTAL HEALTH PROBLEMS

Do Young People Adopt Their Parents' Coping Style?

Nicola Cogan, Sheila Riddell, and Gillian Mayes
University of Glasgow, United Kingdom

ABSTRACT

Children of parents with mental health problems (MHPs) have been reported to be "at risk" of diagnosable psychopathology, as well as for impairment in cognitive, social, and school functioning. This chapter reports on a study that builds on earlier work documenting the mechanisms of risk and identification of protective factors that increase children's resilience toward adversity. The coping styles used by affectively ill parents and their children (aged 12-17 years) were compared with "well" parents and their children using the Adolescent Coping Scale and the Coping Scale for Adults and semistructured interview schedules. Analysis revealed that affectively ill parents and their children were more likely to adopt the nonproductive coping style and were less likely to seek external support to help them cope with their family situation compared to "well" parents and their children. This was largely due to the fear, secrecy, and stigma surrounding MHPs in the family, which prevented them from seeking effective advocacy and support. Although a familial association in parents' and their children's coping styles were found for both affected and comparative families, this was particular evident for the affectively ill parents and their children. This may be due to the lack of external support networks available to families, which limited the range of elements influencing their choice of coping styles. Researchers, service providers, and policymakers who have the common goal of developing the human potential of children "at risk" are encouraged to make use of these findings.

THE NEGATIVE IMPACTS ON CHILDREN

The impact on children affected by parental mental health problems is a growing concern across a number of disciplines. It has implications that are at once medical, psychological, economic, political, and social. Children of parents with MHPs are a diverse group and how they are affected will be mediated by person-environment interdependencies (Silberg & Rutter, 2002). Children bring individual predispositions and attributes into family interactions, which in unspecified ways may be expressive of a potential genetic component involved in the transmission of MHPs (Ashman & Dawson, 2002; Craddock & Jones, 1999; Moldin, 1999; Rutter, Silberg, O'Connor, & Simonoff, 1999; Warner, Weissman, Mufson, & Wickramaratne, 1999). The social context in which children lead their lives (Hammen, 1997, 2002), the behavior of parents with MHPs (Compas, Phares, Banez, & Howell, 1991; Field, Healy, Goldstein, & Perry, 1988; Gordon et al., 1989; Harnish, Dodge, & Valente, 1995; Johnson, Cohen, Kasen, Smailes, & Brook, 2001) and the actions of "other" family members (Downey & Coyne, 1990; Garley, Gallop, Johnston, & Pipitone, 1997; Phares, Duhig, & Watkins, 2002) are some of the factors which may also contribute toward the outcomes for children.

Nevertheless, extensive clinical research and ample statistical evidence has shown that children of parents with MHPs may be "at risk" of a wide range of direct, indirect, and long-term negative impacts (Beardslee et al., 1988; Beardslee, Versage, Gladstone, & Tracy, 1998; Beck, 1999; Downey & Coyne, 1990; Gross, 1984; Jaenicke et al., 1987; McDaniel, 1990; Ruppert & Bagedahl-Strindlund, 2001). Children of parents with MHPs have been found to be at greater risk of health (Billings & Moos, 1986; Kramer et al., 1998), cognitive (Coghill, Caplan, Alexandra, Robson, & Kumar, 1986; Sharp et al., 1995), psychological (Beardslee, Bemporad, Keller, & Klerman, 1983; Beardslee, Keller, Lavori, Staley, & Sacks, 1993; Field et al., 1988; Sharp et al., 1995; Warner, Mufson, & Weissman, 1995) and social difficulties (Dierker, Merikangas, & Szatmari, 1999; Hipwell, Gossens, Melhuish, & Kumar, 2000; Murray, Fiori-Cowley, Hooper, & Cooper, 1996) compared with children of "well" parents.

An array of studies utilizing different theoretical perspectives have been conducted, however, the body of conventional theorizing on children of parents with MHPs has come from an individual pathological perspective. Quantitative studies using standardized instruments to measure the adverse consequences for children have primarily featured, with little reference to potential positive outcomes. While helpful results and ample statistical evidence of problematic child outcomes exist, little research has explored the social, financial, and contextual factors associated with the living circumstances of parents with MHPs and their children (Newman, 2003). The way that parental MHPs affect children is highly complex in that various aspects of the child's situation interact with each other to produce different levels and time-scales of impact (Goodman & Gotlib, 2002). Many factors, including the child's age (Aldwin, 1991), gender (Sharp et al., 1995), socioeconomic status (Bradley & Corwyn, 2002), ethnicity (Guarnaccia & Parra, 1996), family environment (Shiner & Marmorstein, 1998) and access to external support systems (Elliott, 1992) act as potential mediators in determining how children are affected by parental MHPs (Goodman & Gotlib, 2002).

INCREASING CHILDREN'S RESILIENCE TOWARD ADVERSITY

In contrast to the negative effects, some researchers have identified a number of roles that may be thought to typify the responses of children, some of which have positive or mixed connotations. They include "young carer" (Aldridge & Becker, 1993), "stress-resistant children" (Garmezy, 1985), "superkids" (Kaufman, Grunebaum, Cohler, & Gamer, 1979) and "invulnerable children" (Anthony & Cohler, 1987). These studies have reported on children who appear resilient to adverse family situations and have attempted to shed light on the processes that may underlie protective factors (Conrad & Hammen, 1993; Gilligan, 2000; Gilligan & James, 2001; Radke-Yarrow & Brown, 1993; Rutter, 1979, 1985).

The concept of resilience, which has been quite uniform across studies, was described by Masten and colleagues as a process, capacity, or outcome of successful adaptation despite challenges or threatening circumstances (Masten, Best, & Garmezy, 1990). Rutter (1985) viewed resilience similarly but emphasized more the individual's sense of self-esteem, self-confidence, and the ability to deal with change and adaptation. In some respects, the concept of the resilient child has changed, in that children are viewed as being "vulnerable but invincible" where dysfunction and adaptation is dependent on the child's ability to work within themselves and in their environments (Werner, 1989; Werner & Smith, 2001). Factors which have been identified as contributing toward resiliency in children include positive temperament in infancy, good peer relations, good achievement in school, positive self concept, assertiveness, and independence (Gilligan, 2000; Gilligan & James, 2001; Masten et al., 1990; Radke-Yarrow & Brown, 1993; Rutter, 1985, 1993; Tebes, Kaufman, Adnopoz, & Racusin, 2001; Werner, 1989; Werner & Smith, 2001). Emphasis is also placed on their methods or strategies of dealing with stress and adversity (Tebes et al., 2001; Werner & Smith, 2001).

COPING WITH PARENTAL MENTAL HEALTH PROBLEMS

An interest in the impact of parental MHPs on children inevitably means a concomitant interest in the coping process. Over the last 30 years, researchers in many fields have theorized and researched the concept of coping. The growing body of research reflects attempts to move from a focus on pathology and the ways in which people mismanage their lives, to one that attempts to make sense of human ability and development (Frydenberg, 1997, 1999). Coping can be regarded as the cognitive and behavioral efforts to master, tolerate, or reduce external and internal demands and the conflicts between them. Coping is viewed as being what an individual does in a given situation and how changes in the situation influence what the individual does (Folkman & Lazarus, 1985; Folkman, Lazarus, Dunkelschetter, Delongis, & Gruen, 1986; Lazarus, 1991; Lazarus, Delongis, Folkman, & Gruen, 1985; Lazurus & Folkman, 1984).

There is little data on the topic of coping among parents with MHPs and their children (Hammen, 1997). One of the few cross-sectional studies examining coping with maternal depressed affect and depression (Klimes-Dougan & Bolger, 1998) drew comparisons between adolescent children, aged 13-17 years, of: (1) mothers with unipolar affective illness ($n = 66$), (2) mothers with bipolar affective illness ($n = 24$) and (3) "well" mothers ($n = 28$). Two children were selected as participants from each family. Children were assessed using the Maternal Affectivity Coping Scale which was based on a modified version of the Self Report Coping Scale (Causey & Dubow, 1992). This measure was designed to explore children's responses to maternal negative affect and/ or depression. An open-ended semistructured interview schedule was also administered to examine children's level of awareness of depressed family members and how they coped with depression in the family. Researchers "blind" to the parents' diagnostic status then coded children's narrative responses regarding their mother's depression.

The results revealed that mothers' current psychological distress was weakly related to young adolescents' coping patterns. For children of depressed mothers, if the mother was distressed, the children tended to respond by taking it out on others (e.g., yelling, throwing things) and rarely responded by attempting to alleviate the problem. This style of coping has been found to be associated with increased incidence of psychopathology in children (Billings & Moos, 1984). An association was also found between adolescents' coping styles and the type of depressive symptoms the mother exhibited. That is, adolescents were more likely to use maladaptive coping strategies when the mothers directed their distress primarily toward themselves (e.g., sadness, worry, vegetative symptoms) rather than when they directed their distress to others (e.g., irritability, anger). Although some evidence was found for unique coping strategies that may be necessary to cope with a depressed mother, the lack of robust findings was consistent with previous work (Kriss, 1987).

However, this study was limited by problems with the methods used to assess children's coping. The analysis focused on two concepts from a measure of children's coping that are labeled internalizing (e.g., crying about a problem) and externalizing (e.g., ventilating one's anger about a problem) coping (Causey & Dubow, 1992). Both of these concepts measure symptoms of emotional and behavioral problems and neither represents the regulation or modulation of cognition, emotion, or behavior (Compas, Langrock, Keller, Merchant, & Copeland, 2002). As a consequence, it is not surprising that these studies did not identify coping responses to parental depression that may have been adaptive.

Different results were reported in a longitudinal study of children of depressed parents which explored both adaptive and maladaptive coping methods (Radke-Yarrow, 1998). The coping efforts of children, aged 13 years, dealing with (1) maternal unipolar depression ($n = 42$) and (2) maternal bipolar depression ($n = 26$) were examined. A semistructured interview schedule addressing children's experiences of family life was administered. Children's responses were audio recorded and coded quantitatively by researchers "blind" to the parents' mental health status. Analyses revealed a wide variety of reactions, multiple methods of coping, and similarity of methods across gender and age. Children of depressed parents were found to have made explicit attempts to avoid, both physically and psychologically, the problems of the family. Children described difficulties in coping with parental MHPs. Rumination about the mothers' illness, wondering about its causes, and worrying about their own role as potential contributors to their parents' distress were frequent descriptions by both boys and girls. Caregiving to the depressed mother, in the sense of providing emotional support or comfort, and caregiving in the instrumental sense of taking on household or child care responsibilities were also described equally often by boys and girls. In line with earlier work (Garley, Gallop, Johnson, & Pipitone, 1997), children turned to themselves and invested in goals or activities that brought them self-satisfaction, such as high academic achievement, artistic expression, or gaining support from a substitute relationship (i.e., friend, sibling, other relative, pet). In many instances, children failed to recognize certain behaviors as patterns of coping. That is, children did not use the term "coping" to classify certain behaviors or acts. Instead they illustrated how they coped through examples of how they dealt with difficult family situations.

The results supported previous research indicating that children convey a level of awareness concerning some of the impacts of parental MHPs on themselves (Garley, Gallop, Johnson, & Pipitone, 1997; Landells & Pritlove, 1994). However, the study failed to explore the coping methods of children of "well" mothers, in order to establish whether they are unique or different from those of children of parents with MHPs. Also, the lack of standardized format used in the assessment of children's coping behavior creates difficulties in evaluating the findings in the context of previous work examining how children cope with diverse family stressors. Perhaps if a broader range of research tools had been used to examine the coping behavior of parents with MHPs and their children, a clear picture of the extent to which certain coping methods were used, and family patterns of coping could have been explored.

A PHENOMENOLOGICAL APPROACH TO COPING

Research utilizing a phenomenological approach to understanding the coping process advocates that the concept of coping and its validity is best addressed through a methodology that is "grounded" in people's everyday activities and concerns. Coping behavior is seen as a function of the person, situation, and most importantly, the personal perception of each problematic situation (Compas et al., 2002; Frydenberg, 1997, 1999). People are viewed as active agents, selectively perceiving problematic situations and developing coping strategies through past experiences, observing others, perceptions of one's own biological disposition, societal standards, and so forth (Frydenberg, 1999; Frydenberg & Lewis, 1998). Thus, coping is conceived as a reciprocal dynamic process and may be effective or ineffective in terms of the stressor.

How adolescents cope with stress has been examined for some time from an adult-centric orientation (Frydenberg, 1989) but in recent years there have been attempts to develop instruments that reflect more accurately adolescent coping behavior. Frydenberg and Lewis (1993a) developed the Adolescent Coping Scale (ACS) which not only measures 18 different coping strategies but also three coping styles (productive, reference to others, and nonproductive coping) which encapsulate the different strategies adolescents adopt. The standardized format of the ACS enables the measurement of coping behaviors, which might not spontaneously come to mind in less structured approaches. At the same time it does not preclude respondents from nominating other ways of coping with their concerns which might not be covered by the items in the questionnaire as it has an open-ended question included for this purpose. An adult version of the scale has also been developed which consists of 19 conceptually and empirically distinct coping strategies (Frydenberg & Lewis, 1997). The Coping Scale for Adults (CSA) identifies four distinct coping styles (dealing with the problem, optimism, sharing, and nonproductive coping). The ACS and the CSA can be used to offer insights into family patterns of coping.

Studies utilizing this approach have examined how children cope with different family concerns including living in separated and in intact families (Frydenberg, 1996), perceptions of the family climate (Fallon, Frydenberg, & Boldero, 1993) and stress in the family (Frydenberg & Lewis, 1993b). Overall, these studies reveal that the picture that presents is one where, if family life is experienced as functioning well, adolescent children make use of productive strategies in the process of coping with daily life. In contrast, where family dysfunction exists, adolescent children are more likely to adopt nonproductive coping strategies.

One explanatory framework to understanding such processes is that the behavior of parents serves as a model for adolescent coping behavior (Shulman, 1993). The family's role in children's coping has been identified as a major socializing influence (Stern & Zevon, 1990). Maternal coping style that minimizes or ignores a daughter's distress has been found to be associated with the use of avoidant coping strategies by daughters. Equally, mothers who use problem-focused responses in helping their children deal with problems were more likely to have daughters who used constructive coping strategies (Eisenberg, Fabes, & Murphy, 1996). In contrast, Lade and colleagues (1998) found that most coping strategies appear to be determined by elements outside the home, including the influence of adolescent friendships. Further research is needed to examine the relationship between the coping styles used by parents with MHPs and their children (Lade, Frydenberg, & Poole, 1998).

A NEW STUDY OF THE COPING STYLES USED BY PARENTS WITH MENTAL HEALTH PROBLEMS AND THEIR CHILDREN

The current study draws on quantitative data collected from parents with MHPs and their children (affected families) and "well" parents and their children (comparative families) using the short versions of the ACS and CSA. Qualitative data collected using the semistructured interview schedules exploring how parents and their children cope with family life are also presented. The research aimed to, first, examine how the affected families coped with their family situation and how this differed from the comparative families. Second, to determine whether there was a relationship between the coping styles used by affected and comparative parents and their children.

While recognizing that "a truly representative sample is an abstract ideal unachievable in practice" (Coolican, 1996) obtaining a representative sample became of secondary consideration, first, because it was difficult to determine what a representative sample would be and, second, due to the difficulties in identifying parents with MHPs with dependent children. It was clear even in the planning stages of the research that one of the most challenging factors to be overcome would consist of recruiting an appropriate research sample in order to make meaningful statistical comparisons. However, contacting the research sample proved more difficult than anticipated. As Renzetti and Lee (1993) note "The more sensitive or threatening the topic under examination, the more difficult sampling is likely to be, because potential participants have greater need to hide involvement" (Renzetti & Lee, 1993).

Parents with MHPs and their children offer a prime example of the need to hide involvement and thus offer a substantial challenge to any researcher attempting to locate an appropriate sample. In studies of relatively innocuous issues, complete sampling frames are often available that allow for random sampling and a sound estimate of sampling bias (Herzberger, 1993). This is rarely the case in studies of sensitive topics such as research examining how children cope with parental MHPs.

Instead, a purposive sample following inclusion/exclusion criteria was sought. Although there are different definitions and understandings of what constitutes a MHP within and across cultures (Guarnaccia & Parra, 1996), the parents with MHPs recruited for the study were identified as having received an ICD-10 diagnosis of an affective illness (World Health Organization, 1992). The affected group were eligible if: (1) the parent was using psychological/psychiatric services at the time of the investigation, (2) they were of households that included both the biological parent and their child(ren), (3) they had at least one adolescent child (aged 12-17 years old) living within the family home, (4) the child was still living with the parent(s) so that they could provide fresh commentaries on their family situation, and (5) they were English speaking. Families affected by alcohol and drug misuse/abuse were to be excluded from the study.

Identical criteria were used for the comparative group with the exception that no family members were to have received an ICD-10 diagnosis of a MHPs and/or be using mental health services provided by community mental health teams (CMHTs). An attempt was made to match the comparative families with the affected families on a number of variables: (1) age, (2) sex, (3) education, (4) ethnicity, (5) the family's socioeconomic level, and (6) the marital status of the parent (single parent or two parents). It was envisaged that there might be difficulties in constructing a comparison group, since it was difficult to determine with any great certainty as to whether MHPs existed within the family, as they may have gone unreported. Checks were made with the family support workers through which the comparative families were recruited in order to establish whether they were aware of MHPs in the family.

After a lengthy period of extensive networking and negotiation the research samples were recruited. Since recruitment of the affected families was through CMHTs who identified parents with affective illnesses who also had dependent children (aged 12-17 years) and excluded children in care, the sample was skewed toward the serious end of MHPs. The most extreme cases where parental MHPs had contributed to long-term substitute care were excluded. The comparative families were identified through family centers, lone-parent groups, and voluntary organizations developed to support families living on low incomes. Fewer difficulties were evident in this stage of recruitment and families were identified with greater ease than was the case for the affected families.

Power analysis was performed (Bond, 1999) using a two sample, unequal variances model to determine the power for the sample size. The power calculation determined that the power was .9178, therefore, sufficient to address the aims of the work. Meaningful statistical comparisons could be made between the two groups of families, while allowing for sufficient time for a more in-depth exploratory analysis of the qualitative data.

ANALYSIS AND RESULTS

The quantitative data collected using the short versions of the coping scales (ACS & CSA) were managed using SPSS computer package and analyzed using descriptive and inferential statistics. The qualitative data stemming from the transcripts were managed with the software program NUD*IST (N5), which facilitates the online storage, analysis and retrieval of textual information (Richards & Richards, 1994). The interactive model of Huberman and Miles (1994) was used to analyze the data set. The subprocesses of this model are: (1) data reduction, (2) data display, and (3) conclusion drawing and verification. Data reduction consisted of a cycle of deductive verification and inductive identification. For example, numerical data derived from the deductive analysis of the quantitative data taken from the standardized measures served as a guidepost to direct more in-depth and focused approach to analyzing the qualitative data. Many accounts of this approach to data analysis demonstrate that there are multiple tactics at work (Chesler, 1987; Fischer & Wertz, 1975) rather than one central aim. In this sense, data transformation took place as information was condensed, coded, and ranked over time (Gherardi & Turner, 1987).

Household Characteristics

Although family members from the affected and comparative families selected only one "focus child" from the family to be interviewed, household characteristics were gathered using the Household Demographic Questionnaire (Cogan, 1999). Households varied in size from 2 to 6 family members, however chi-square analysis revealed that a significant difference emerged between the two groups in terms of the total number of household members ($\chi^2 = 3.85$, $df = 1$, $p < .05$). The comparative families ($m = 3.95$, $SD = .88$) had significantly more household members than the affected families ($m = 3.25$, $SD = 1.25$). The number of children per household ranged from 1 to 4, however, the majority of both affected and comparative families had two children. Chi-square analysis showed that there was no significant difference between the two groups in terms of the number of children per household ($\chi^2 = 2.92$, $df = 1$, $p < .087$). Over two thirds of the affected and comparative households contained lone parents: the rest being two-parent households (see Table 3.1). No significant difference was found between the affected and comparative parents' marital status ($\chi^2 = 1.62$, $df = 1$, $p < .202$).

Although, in-depth inquiries were not made regarding family household income, both the affected and comparative families had been raised or were on the margins of poverty, since in over three quarters of the families, nobody was in paid employment. This applied particularly to the affected families, as only 2 of the 20 families (10%) included a wage earner, whereas 5 of the 20 families (25%) in the comparative families included a wage earner, however, this difference was not statistically significant ($\chi^2 = 1.51$, $df = 1$, $p < .218$). Most of the families were reliant on state benefits and all lived in a Social Inclusion Partnership (SIP) area representing an area of designated deprivation. All of the families were of White Scottish origin. A participant identification code (PIC) was given to each participant who took part in the research. The PICs were as follows: (1) AP1 to AP20 refer to parents with MHPs (affected parents), (2) CP21 to CP40 refer to "well" parents (comparative parents), (3) AA1 to AA20 refer to adolescent children of parents with MHPs (affected adolescents), and (4) CA21 to CA40 refer to children of "well" parents (comparative adolescents). The PICs are used after the presentation of quotations from the affected and comparative families' accounts and provide supportive evidence for the qualitative research findings.

Parents' and their Adolescent Children's Characteristics

Twenty parents (male = 8, female = 12) with an affective illness (affected parent) and 20 "well" parents (male = 6, female = 14) (comparative parent) took part in the study. In all cases the "focus child" interviewed in the study was living with the affected parent at the time of the research investigation. It was apparent through interviewee's statements that in two of the families in the affected group, both parents had MHPs. In one such case, one of the affected parents was no longer living with the family and had minimal contact with the children (on average two parental visits per year) and in the other, the coparent had been imprisoned and was currently homeless and had no contact with the family. Therefore a decision was made to include the families in the sample. Affected parents' ages ranged from 36 to 55 years old (mean age = 42.14, SD = 4.99) and the comparative group of parents' ages ranged from 36 to 47 (mean age = 40.35, SD = 3.51). Chi-square analysis revealed that there were no significant differences between the affected and comparative families in terms of the parents' age (χ^2 = 1.704, df = 1, p = 1.92) and gender (χ^2 = .429, df = 1, p < .5213).

The "focus" adolescents (male = 10, female = 10) of the parents with an affective illness (affected adolescents) and the adolescents (male = 10, female = 10) of "well" parents (comparative adolescents) were also recruited. Affected adolescents' ages ranged from 12 to 17 years old (mean = 13.8, SD = 1.74) and the comparative group of adolescent's ages ranged from 13 to 17 (mean age = 14.7, SD = 1.63). Chi-square analysis revealed that there were no significant differences between the affected and comparative adolescents in terms of their age (χ^2 = 2.73, df = 1, p < .098), gender (χ^2 = .00 df = 1, p < .624) and educational level (χ^2 = 2.15, df = 1, p < .1.42).

Coping Styles Used by Parents

Comparisons were made between the coping styles used by the affected and comparative parents. Dealing with the problem coping style encompasses working hard and solving the problem while maintaining a social dimension characterized by relaxing and indulging in humorous diversions and physical recreation as well as attempting to improve significant relationships. It also includes the use of techniques that aim to maintain one's self esteem. The sharing coping style entails gaining support from others in order to cope with problems, including gaining professional help, social action, seeking social support, and not keeping the problem to oneself. The nonproductive coping style is associated with not coping, for example, worrying, keeping the problem to oneself, self blame, wishful thinking, ignoring the problem, and tension reduction. Lastly, the optimism coping style is comprised of strategies such as focusing on the positive, seeking relaxing diversions, seeking spiritual support, and wishful thinking.

Examining the relative usage of the different coping styles used by the affected parents, analysis shows that they were most likely to use the nonproductive ($M = 3.52$, $SD = .385$) coping style, followed by optimism ($M = 2.36$; $SD = .447$), dealing with the problem ($M = 2.35$, $SD = .438$) and, lastly, sharing ($M = .912$, $SD = .557$) coping style. In terms of the coping styles used by the comparative parents, they were most likely to use the dealing with the problem ($M = 2.74$, $SD = .347$) coping style, followed by optimism ($M = 2.58$, $SD = .399$), nonproductive coping ($M = 2.52$, $SD = .409$) and, finally, sharing ($M = 1.33$, $SD = .453$) coping style.

Independent samples t tests were performed to examine differences between affected and comparative parents on the coping styles data. Analysis showed that there were significant differences between the two groups of parents for dealing with the problem ($t = -3.08$, $df = 38$, $p < .004$), sharing ($t = 2.64$, $df = 38$, $p < .012$), and nonproductive ($t = 7.891$, $df = 38$, $p < .001$) coping styles. There was no significant difference between the two groups in terms of the optimism ($t = -1.67$, $df = 38$, $p < .102$) coping style.

Dealing with the Problem

The affected parents stressed the importance of their relationship with their children; they were significantly less likely than comparative parents to be dealing effectively with their family situation ($t = 3.08$, $df = 38$, $p < .004$). Some of the affected parents described instances where they had tried to cope effectively, for example, commenting "I try and do my best for my kids" (AP1) and "sometimes things are great, we can be really close, I try and play a game of bingo with the weans (children) if I feel up to it" (AP3). However, many of the affected parents experienced problems in coping with their family situation during severe depressive episodes, as one affected parent explained:

> I can be doing really well and the kids are out to school and I will try and have their dinner ready when they come home and do all the housework but some mornings I just can't get up, you know, it's hard enough drawing the curtains, I feel so depressed (AP10).

In contrast, the majority of the comparative parents described how they tried to find effective ways of coping with their family situation. Although many of the comparative parents also experienced difficulties bringing up their children, they were more likely to have outlets to help them cope. For example, one comparative parent remarked, "Sometimes you need time out, you know, a break away from all the hassles that teenagers bring (laughs). I like to just go up to my room and watch television and they know not to disturb me" (CP32).

Sharing

Affected parents were significantly less likely than comparative parents to share their family concerns with others ($t = 2.64$, $df = 38$, $p < .012$). That is, few of the affected parents made reference to other people who could help them to cope with their MHPs and parenting role. Many of the affected parents emphasized their fear of discussing their family situation with others. At the same time, they spoke of how social work and other statutory agencies only became involved with their families when they reached "crisis point" (AP15). For example, affected parents explained "The only time they (social workers) will react is when you can't cope, it's not about actually having good contact and good relationships" (AP8) and "It was a crisis point, I obviously knew I had mental (health) problems but I never went for any support or anything until I just couldn't take any more and I phoned the (psychiatric) hospital and that was it" (AP14). One affected parent pointed to the difficulties she experienced gaining support to help her in her parenting role:

> Our family just broke down. Does it have to get to that? I mean does (son) have to get picked up by the police or does he have to go and do something that he wouldn't have done in the first place if we had a little help. I know it's our children but everybody needs a little help now and then. It's not a crime to get help, you know, but it's very hard cos they ask you "what do you want a social worker for?" and you go "just forget it" it makes you feel stupid and you feel that size (indicates small using hand gesture), you know what I mean (AP11).

Some of the affected parents also discussed how they felt there were few resources available to help prevent their family from reaching a "breakdown point" (AP19), as one affected parent explained:

> The social work department and all the rest of it, no one wants to know you, they turn round and say they haven't got the resources or nothing but when it comes to a big disaster they are just like flies, you know what I mean, we are here to help you and all the rest of it, as soon as it reaches crisis point, as soon as you reach breakdown point and it's really bad, they are all there and they are like "we can do this" and "we can do that" but as soon as things change a tiny bit everything is dragged away and you are left to cope alone (AP19).

While a few of the comparative parents also pointed to instances where they had found it difficult to discuss family problems with other people, including professionals, the majority of them discussed how they had gained support from informal support networks in order to deal with family concerns. One comparative parent said "I don't know what I would do without (Sadie) (neighbor), I mean she is always popping in and out the house, you know, she helps me a lot with the weans (children) as well" (CP37) and "a lot of my family live close by so they are there for me if I need help, like my sister, she will go down the street for my messages (shopping), she's a great help" (CP26).

Nonproductive Coping

Affected parents were significantly more likely than comparative parents to be using avoidance strategies associated with an inability to cope with their family situation ($t = 7.891$, $df = 38$, $p < .001$). Eleven of the 20 affected parents described their experiences of psychiatric hospitalization and the difficulties this caused for their families. For example, one affected parent said "They (doctors) want to put you in (psychiatric) hospital as soon as you're not well, to take you away from your family, but I don't see that as the answer" (AP10) and another remarked:

> You don't know at what age it's going to affect you, I mean I was 12 when I was first hospitalized, it's even more stressful now cos of my children, it's a constant worry, what if I end up back in that place (psychiatric hospital)? What will happen to (Mark) (son)? (AP15).

In most instances, affected parents drew attention to the problems and distressing occurrences they experienced during periods of psychiatric hospitalization. One affected parent remarked "When I was in (psychiatric) hospital there were about eight people who took their lives (suicide), and people cut themselves (self harm)" (AP6) and others said "I think the nurses know about it but they are turning a blind eye but there are people that shouldn't be in there (psychiatric hospital), it's not safe in there, you feel worse when you come out" (AP15) and "if you go into somewhere that's bright and cheerful you are gonna feel a 100% better. You should take a look at Parkhead (psychiatric) hospital, it's terrible, I hate it in there" (AP8).

Dissimilarly, the comparative parents were more inclined to describe how they found ways of dealing with family stresses and strains, as one comparative parent commented "I just have to get on with it, I mean I hate living on benefits, I've never got any money for me and the weans (children)" and another remarked "It can be a struggle but we get by, I mean I just have to think of the things we have got, a lot of people are worse off than us, like homeless people or druggies (people with drug dependency). We get by cos we've got each other" (CA32).

These findings suggest that parents with MHPs were significantly more likely to adopt nonproductive coping strategies and less likely to use adaptive strategies compared to "well" parents. It was apparent that for many of the affected parents the difficulties they experienced in coping with their family situation were largely due to the lack of appropriate services or support available to help them in their parenting role. Psychiatric hospitalization further exacerbated the difficulties both the parents with MHPs and their children experienced in coping with their family situation. In terms of comparative parents' accounts, they were less likely to convey an inability to cope with family concerns compared to affected parents. This was largely a consequence of their access and usage of informal support networks, which assisted them in their parenting roles, and alleviated some of the stresses and strains associated with raising a family on a low income.

Coping Styles Used by Adolescent Children

Comparisons were made between the coping styles used by affected and comparative adolescent children. The first of these styles, productive coping is characterized by attempting to solve the problem while remaining physically fit and socially connected. The second style is reference to others, which represents an attempt to deal with the problem by drawing on the support and resources of others. The third is called nonproductive coping, a style that does not lead to a solution to the problem but at best relieves the tension.

Inspection of the data for the affected children indicated that the most commonly used style was nonproductive coping ($M = 3.07$, $SD = .321$), followed by productive coping ($M = 2.87$, $SD = .545$) and the least used style was reference to others ($M = 1.96$; $SD = .284$). For the comparative children the most commonly used style was productive coping ($M = 3.05$; $SD = .456$), followed by nonproductive coping ($M = 2.75$; $SD = .420$) and, lastly, reference to others ($M = 2.25$; $SD = .550$) coping style.

Independent samples t tests were conducted to determine whether significant differences existed between the coping styles used by the affected and comparative children. Analysis showed that significant differences existed between the two groups of children on two of the three coping styles: reference to others ($t = -2.077$, $df = 38$, $p < .05$) and nonproductive ($t = 2.725$, $df = 38$, $p < .01$) coping style. No significant difference was found between the two groups on the productive ($t = -1.154$, $df = 38$, $p < .256$) coping style.

Nonproductive Coping

Affected children were significantly more likely to use avoidance strategies, which were associated with an inability to cope with their family concerns than comparative children ($t = 2.725$, $df = 38$, $p < .01$). For example, affected children commented, "I don't know what to do, so I don't do anything. I just try and pretend it's not happening" (AA11), "I sometimes think it's my fault, I blame myself for the way my dad is feeling, even though he tells me it's not" (AA9) and "I just bottled it all up and then one day I just lost my temper (pauses), I just totally burst my top! It's the worst thing you can ever do, is just let it all build up inside" (AA7). For many of the affected children living with parental MHPs had a significant impact on their schoolwork in a multitude of different ways. Although a couple of the affected children described positive school experiences, for example commenting "school gives me a chance to think about something else and see my pals" (AA1) and "I like school, most of my teachers are alright" (AA3), the majority of the affected children emphasized the detrimental impact their parents' MHPs had on their ability to get their school work done. Thirteen of the 20 affected children stressed how they experienced difficulties completing schoolwork in the classroom setting. For example, one affected child said "when I'm trying to do my (school) work I'm worried cos ma mum can't go out her house and she doesn't like being by herself, I can't concentrate on ma (school) work" (AA16) and others explained "It's hard to listen to the teacher when I'm thinking about if my mum is OK" (AA17) and "I was falling asleep in school and all that cos of my dad's illness. We (family) had been up the night before" (AA18).

Fourteen of the 20 affected children described how they experienced difficulties in completing homework. One affected child commented "when I was going through my exams, doing my studying and everything, everyone (family members) was arguing all the time, I could never get homework done" (AA8) and another child said "I have found it quite hard to do homework, cos I keep on wondering if dad is having a bad day" (AA5). Five of the 20 affected children also discussed how they "missed school" (AA4) and/or were "late for school" (AA5). A few of the children pointed to the lack of a family routine and time framework within the home as contributing toward the difficulties they experienced in attending school, as one affected child said "I can't get up to go (to school) sometimes cos there isn't anyone else getting up in the morning" (AA14).

In contrast, the comparative children were less likely to be using the nonproductive coping style and were more likely to be trying to deal effectively with their family concerns than the affected children. For example, one comparative child said "If I'm worried about something, I'll ask my mum, that helps sometimes" (CA27) and another remarked "I try and not get into trouble at school, cos I know that's the last thing my mum needs when she's stressed out" (CA40). Although 13 of the 20 comparative children felt that they would not be able to discuss family issues with their schoolteacher, describing this as "private and personal" (CA40), few of them felt that their family situation impacted on their ability to get their schoolwork done.

Reference to Others

Affected children were significantly less likely to make reference to others, whether peers, professionals or deities in a bid to deal with their family situation than comparative children ($t = -2.077, df = 38, p < .05$). This was largely due to other people's negative attitudes toward people with MHPs and their fear of being removed from their parents' care. Affected children remarked, "some of my pals have asked me "what's happening in your house?" but I can't tell them. I just say "can you leave it, I don't want anyone to know about my dad's (mental health) problems" (AA2) and "I don't want the social workers coming around again. Last time I ended up going to foster parents (pause), I hated it" (AA16). One affected child described how his mother found it difficult discussing her MHPs with other people, in particular, professionals, because she felt that they did not understand what she was experiencing:

> My mum has always said to me "you can't tell them (professionals) your problems," you can't tell the doctor your problems or the social worker your problems cos they haven't went through what you've went through, they don't know what it's like to live with it (AA7).

Despite the fact that their family situation may have interfered with their progress at school, many of the affected children emphasized how they feared discussing family issues with schoolteachers, instead prefer-ring to keep such issues a secret. Affected children commented "well I don't generally tell anyone about it [parental MHPs] cos I want to keep it a secret from them cos I don't want to tell them about my dad's [mental health] problems" (AA18) and "I don't like talking to teachers about ma family, about what's going on in ma house and all that [pauses], it just gets to me" (AA5). One affected child who confided in a teacher explained how the consequential action was that of informing a social worker of his family situation:

> Sometimes you might be able to talk to some teachers but not other ones cos some teachers can take it too far, you know, you just want to go to them for advice and then they take it too far and then they phone other people up and then it goes too far, like the social [social workers] end up coming out [pause]. That happened to me but it made things worse (AA4).

Four of the 20 affected children had discussed their family situation with a guidance teacher, however, still conveyed fears of disclosure, as one affected child commented "my guidance teacher was alright to talk to but I still worry that she might tell other teachers" (AA9). Only three of the affected children had been consulted by a health professional or informed that their parent had MHPs by a mental health worker. Instead, many of the affected children had to rely on their own judgments, their parents informing them of their MHPs, or relying on an older sibling to provide them with information. One affected child remarked:

> I think the doctor should try and explain in the best way possible what has happened ... not too much cos I wouldn't have understood. I think schools should give some more education about it cos we have only ever had like one lesson about it [MHPs] and I don't think that's enough, no one really understood it at all (AA16).

Although some of the comparative children also emphasized how they found it difficult to discuss family problems with other people, many of them described instances where they had gained support from others. For example, comparative children said "it's hard talking about your family, especially to someone who doesn't know you that well, it can help though" (CA30) and "I've got ma pals to talk to, [Sharon, friend] is always there for me, she tells me all her problems as well" (CA38).

Overall, the affected children were significantly more likely to use the nonproductive coping style and were less likely to seek support from oth-ers compared to children of "well" parents, largely due to the fear, stigma and secrecy surrounding MHPs in the family.

Table 3.1. Pearson's Correlations for Affected and Comparative Parents and their Children's Coping Styles

Coping Styles	Adult Dealing with the Problem		Adult Sharing		Adult Nonproductive Coping		Adult Optimism	
	Affected Families	Comp. Families	Affected Families	Comp. Families	Affected Families	Comp. Families	Affected Families	Comp. Families
Adolescent Productive Coping	.525**	.325	.472*	.338	.457	.153	.056	.182
Adolescent Reference to Others	.051	.108	.063	.409	.068	.092	.345	.180
Adolescent Nonproductive Coping	.100	.004	.363	.155	.503**	.536**	.134	.094

Note. Data collected using the ACS and the CSA.
*$p < .05$. **$p < .01$.

FAMILIAL ASSOCIATIONS IN CHILD/PARENT COPING STYLES

Pearson's correlational analysis was performed to examine whether there was a relationship between parent's and children's scores on the CSA and ACS. Table 3.1 presents the correlations for affected and comparative parents and their children on the coping styles data. First, analysis revealed that, for the affected families, there was a significant positive correlation between adult dealing with the problem and child productive coping style ($r = .53$). This finding suggests that parents with MHPs who used effective strategies for coping with their family situation were more likely to have children who used productive coping strategies, which helped them to deal with family problems.

In terms of adult sharing coping style, a significant positive correlation was found with reference to others coping style for children ($r = .47$). This result shows that parents with MHPs who were more likely to seek external support from other people in a bid to cope with their family situation were also more likely to have children who gained support from external others. Examining adult nonproductive coping style, a significant negative correlation was found with productive coping for children ($r = -.46$) and a positive significant correlation with nonproductive coping for children ($r = .50$). Parents with MHPs who used avoidance coping strategies, which were associated with an inability to cope with their family situation were significantly less likely to have children who used effective coping strategies and were more likely to use avoidance strategies were significantly more likely to have children who used avoidance strategies in trying to cope with family concerns.

Analysis revealed that for the comparative families, a significant positive correlation was found between the adult nonproductive coping and nonproductive coping for children ($r = .54$). This result indicates that "well" parents who were more likely to use avoidance coping strategies which were associated with an inability to cope with their family concerns also had children who were significantly more likely to use such ineffective coping strategies. There were no other significant correlations between "well" parents and their children's coping styles, indicating that for the affected families there were more similarities in terms of the coping styles they adopted than was found for the comparative families. This may be due to the lack of external and informal support networks available to the affected families, which limited the range of elements influencing their coping repertoires.

DISCUSSION

In moving away from the individual pathological model of understanding how children are affected by parental MHPs, researchers have directed attention toward looking at more adaptive ways in which children deal with adversity. The concept of coping has been reported as being a potential mediating and/or protective factor which may increase children's resilience toward difficult family problems (Beardslee & Poderefsky, 1988; Radke-Yarrow & Brown, 1993; Rutter, 1987; Werner & Smith, 2001). A comparative study (affected and comparative families) was used to, first, examine how parents with MHPs coped with their family situation and how this differed from "well" parents.

Parents with MHPs were significantly more likely to have used the nonproductive coping style compared to "well" parents and were significantly less likely to have used the dealing with the problem and sharing coping styles. Many of the affected parents experienced difficulties in coping during severe depressive episodes and they often described the fear they experienced in discussing their family situation with others. In particular, they drew attention to their negative experiences of social work and other statutory agencies that had been involved with their families upon reaching "crisis point." Distressing and negative experiences associated with psychiatric hospitalization was a prevalent theme among the accounts of parents with MHPs. These findings provide supportive evidence for research stressing the importance of early intervention and preventative work with families affected by MHPs (Blanch, Nicholson, & Purcell, 1994; Close, 1999; Goode, 2000; Hugman & Phillips, 1993; Tanner, 2000).

No significant differences were found between the affected and comparative parents on the optimism coping style. However, it should be noted that the relative usage of this coping style, for both affected and comparative parents, was a good deal lower than that reported in previous work (Frydenberg & Lewis, 1997, 1998). Perhaps the stressors associated with raising a family on a low income impacts on parents' coping resources to the extent that they are more inclined to adopt a less hopeful outlook on life and how they cope with family stressors.

In terms of the coping styles used by adolescent children, in support of research indicating that children of parents with MHPs use maladaptive coping strategies (Garley et al., 1997; Klimes-Dougan & Bolger, 1998; Radke-Yarrow & Brown, 1993), affected children were found to be significantly more likely to convey an inability to cope with their family situation compared to children of "well" parents. It could be argued that children of parents with MHPs are often vulnerable, partly because they may not receive adequate support and partly because they feel stigmatized by their parents' MHPs (Sargent, 1985). Either way, inspection of the affected children's accounts revealed that they were more likely to blame themselves for the difficulties their parents experienced compared to the children of "well" parents. Indeed, earlier research has reported that children of affectively ill parents see themselves as responsible for their parents' MHPs (Garley et al., 1997). These findings emphasis the importance of providing children with age appropriate information about the etiology of MHPs in order to assist them in coping more effectively with their parents' MHPs.

Affected children were significantly less likely to make reference to others whether it be friends, professionals, or deities in a bid to try and cope with their family situation and were significantly more likely to use the nonproductive coping style compared to children of "well" parents. This was largely due to the fear, secrecy, and isolation surrounding MHPs in the family, which prevented them from seeking effective advocacy and/or support. While previous studies have suggested that teachers have a key role as confidants, mentors, and guarantors of children's welfare (Gilligan, 1998, 2000), both groups of children described how they feared discussing family concerns with their school teacher, indicating that they felt such issues were private and personal and to be kept within the family. Although, schools may be the first point of contact with "vulnerable" children who are experiencing difficulties in getting their school work done as a consequence of adverse family situations, it is important to recognize the difficulties children might experience in communicating with teaching staff. Perhaps a nonteaching member of staff, for example, a school counselor or psychologist, would more adequately fulfill the mentoring role and reduce children's fear of discussing such issues.

Children were rarely consulted about the nature and consequences of living with parental MHPs. At the same time, it seemed that children were quite literally seen but not heard. The picture to emerge was one of exclusion rather than inclusion, where children had access to few support networks. These findings provide supportive evidence for research on children living with parental MHPs which has pointed to the neglect of such children by welfare professionals from both children's and adults' services (Banks et al., 2001, 2002; Blanch et al., 1994; Close, 1999; Cowling, 1996; Cowling, McGorry, & Hay, 1995; De Chilo, Matorin, & Hallahan, 1987; Elliott, 1992; Goode, 2000; Grunbaum & Gammeltoft, 1993; Heatherington & Baistow, 2001; Luntz, 1995; Ostman & Hansson, 2002). Such inattention could be accounted for by the contemporary nature of children affected by parental MHPs as a welfare issue. Nonetheless, key policy and legislative changes have since occurred in the United Kingdom to address these oversights, underlining the need for more holistic, family-based approaches to service provision (Aldridge & Becker, 2003).

Although no significant difference was found between the affected and comparative children in terms of the productive coping style, both groups of children were least likely to use this coping style compared to the nonproductive and reference to other coping styles. This may be due to the difficulties facing children who have to cope with family concerns in the context of living within a deprived area. There is research evidence to suggest that the usage of productive coping strategies decreases among economically disadvantaged adolescents (Choe, 2001) and that adolescents' responses to stressors are influenced by their family environment (Stern & Zevon, 1990)

Finally, familial associations between the parents and children's coping styles were also found for the affected and comparative families. Parents with MHPs who used productive strategies and shared their family concerns with others (albeit these coping styles were used less than the nonproductive coping style) were more likely to have children who used such coping styles. Parents with MHPs who used avoidance strategies that were associated with an inability to cope with their family situation were less likely to have children who used effective coping methods. Instead, parents with MHPs who were more likely to use avoidance strategies were also significantly more likely to have children who used nonproductive methods of coping. These findings are in contrast to previous work reporting that familial associations in coping strategies are relatively weak (Lade, Frydenberg, & Poole, 1998). The "well" parents who were more likely to use avoidance strategies (although this was the coping style least used by the comparative parents) also had children who were more likely to deal ineffectively with family concerns, however, this was the only significant association found for the comparative families. Perhaps, this was due to the fact that "well" parents and their children described how they had more outlets to external and informal support networks compared to the affected families, therefore a broader range of elements influencing their choice of coping styles. Nevertheless, if parents are not coping well children are less likely to cope effectively.

The limitations of the current study that should be considered for further research relate to the fact that data are based on the accounts of parents and their "focus" children. Perhaps a more holistic perspective could have been achieved if the perspectives of the whole family unit (e.g., siblings, spouses, grandparents) had been included. In addition, this study examined the coping styles used by parents with severe affective illnesses and their children. While rich and informative data have been presented, it is difficult to make generalizations from the current study's findings in terms of the coping styles used by parents with other MHPs (e.g., schizophrenia, personality disorder). Incorporating the perspectives of parents with a wide range of MHPs and the perspectives of their children is critical to the development of relevant and effective strategies for mental health promotion programs (Armstrong, Hill, & Secker, 2000; Imiela, 1993; Secker, 1998; Secker, Grove, & Seebohm, 2001). This is particularly pertinent in the light of a recent U.K. statistical survey which found that attitudes toward people with mental illness have become slightly worse between 2000 and 2003 (Department of Health, 2003). De-stigmatization programs may reduce some of the social and attitudinal barriers experienced by families affected by MHPs.

CONCLUSION AND IMPLICATIONS FOR EDUCATIONAL PRACTICE

The indications from this study are that parents with MHPs and their children are more likely to use nonproductive coping styles and are less likely to seek support from others compared to "well" parents and their children. Yet, rather than describing wholly negative family experiences, affected families often stressed the importance of their relationship with one another and how it helped to allay some of the difficulties associated with their family situation. In this respect the need for some children to remain in parental care, out of choice, should be acknowledged, and flexible, sensitive interventions should be made available to those families who request support. Providing age appropriate information about MHPs, for example, would benefit children and it may also help alleviate their anxieties while they are in school or away from home. De-stigmatization campaigns and mental health promotion in schools would also help children when coping with their family situations.

However, it is undoubtedly the case that children's relationships with their parents can be adversely affected by the symptomatic outcomes and behaviors of their parents when they experience severe depressive episodes. This is more likely to be the case when parents are inadequately or ineffectively treated or supported. Also, during times when the continuity of parent-child relationships are compromised, for example, by psychiatric hospitalization, child protection procedures, and/or family separation.

School counselors, psychologists, teachers, child welfare workers, and mental health social workers need to take into account the rights and needs of both parents with MHPs and their children as well as the costs and benefits of maintaining these relationships. Children "at risk" who have received adequate support and encouragement have been found to go on and do well in life (Beardslee, 1989; Beardslee & Poderefsky, 1988; Gilligan, 1998, 2000). Education intervention involving parents with MHPs and their children in decisions that impact on their lives may improve the acceptability of services provided and enable an infrastructure of family support to be developed.

REFERENCES

Aldridge, J., & Becker, P. (1993). *Children who care: Inside the world of young carers.* Leicestershire, UK: Loughborough University.

Aldridge, J., & Becker, S. (2003). *Children caring for parents with mental illness.* Bristol, UK: Policy Press.

Aldwin, C. M. (1991). Does age affect the stress and coping process? Implications of age differences in perceived control. *Journal of Gerontology, 46,* 174-180.

Anthony, E., & Cohler, B. (1987). *The invulnerable child.* New York: Guilford Press.

Armstrong, C., Hill, M., & Secker, J. (2000). Young people's perceptions of mental health. *Children and Society, 14,* 60-72.

Ashman, S. B., & Dawson, G. (2002). Maternal depression, infant psychobiological development and risk for depression. In I. H. Gotlib (Ed.), *Children of depressed parents* (pp. 37-58). Washington, DC: American Psychological Society.

Banks, P., Cogan, N., Deeley, S., Hill, M., Riddell, S., & Tisdall, K. (2001). Seeing the invisible children and young people affected by disability. *Disability and Society, 16,* 797-814.

Banks, P., Cogan, N., Deeley, S., Hill, M., Riddell, S., & Tisdall, K. (2002). Does the covert nature of caring prohibit the development of effective services for young carers? *Journal of Guidance and Counselling Psychology, 30,* 231-245.

Beardslee, W. R. (1989). The role of self understanding in resilient individuals: The development of a perspective. *American Journal of Orthopsychiatry, 59,* 266-278.

Beardslee, W. R., Bemporad, J., Keller, M. B., & Klerman, G. L. (1983). Children of parents with a major affective disorder. *The American Journal of Psychiatry, 140*, 825-832.

Beardslee, W. R., Keller, M. B., Lavori, P. W., Klerman, G. R., Dorer, D. J., & Samuelson, H. (1988). Psychiatric disorder in adolescent offspring of parents with affective disorder in a nonreferred sample. *Journal of Affective Disorder, 15*, 313-322.

Beardslee, W. R., Keller, M. B., Lavori, P. W., Staley, J., & Sacks, N. (1993). The impact of parental affective disorder on depression in offspring: A longitudinal follow up in a nonreferred sample. *Journal of the American Academy of Child and Adolescent Psychiatry, 32*, 723-730.

Beardslee, W. R., & Poderefsky, D. (1988). Resilient adolescents whose parents have serious affective and other psychiatric disorders: importance of self understanding and relationships. *American Journal of Psychiatry, 145*, 63-69.

Beardslee, W. R., Versage, E. M., Gladstone, M. A., & Tracy, R. G. (1998). Children of affectively ill parents: A review of the past 10 years. *Journal of the American Academy of Child and Adolescent Psychiatry, 37*, 1134-1141.

Beck, C. T. (1999). Maternal depression and child behaviour problems: A meta-analysis. *Journal of Advanced Nursing, 29*, 623-629.

Billings, A. G., & Moos, R. H. (1984). Coping, stress, and social resources among adults with unipolar depression. *Journal of Personality and Social Psychology, 46*, 877-891.

Billings, A. G., & Moos, R. H. (1986). Children of parents with unipolar depression: A controlled 1 year follow up. *Journal of Abnormal Child Psychology, 14*, 149-166.

Blanch, A. K., Nicholson, J., & Purcell, J. (1994). Parents with severe mental illness and their children: The need for human services integration. *Journal of Mental Health Administration, 21*, 388-396.

Bond, J. (1999). *General power calculator* [On-line]. Available: http://www.stat.ucla.edu/cgi-bin/textbook/powercalc/

Bradley, R. H., & Corwyn, R. F. (2002). Socio-economic status and child development. *Annual Review of Psychology, 53*, 371-399.

Causey, D., & Dubow, E. (1992). Development of a self report coping measure for elementary school children. *Journal of Clinical Child Psychology, 21*, 47-59.

Chesler, M. (1987). Professionals' views of the dangers of self help groups. In A. Arbor (Ed.), *CRSO Paper 345*. MI: Center for Research on Social Organisation.

Choe, J. H. (2001). Coping strategies as mediators and moderators of the relationship between stress and negative psychological outcome among economically disadvantaged African American adolescents. *Dissertation Abstract International: Section B: The Sciences and Engineering, 61*, 4395.

Close, N. (1999). Drowning not waving: The parent as co-ordinator of inter-agency support for a child with mental health problems. *Journal of Mental Health, 8*, 551-554.

Cogan, N. (1999). *Demographic questionnaire*. Glasgow, UK: Strathclyde Centre for Disability Research, University of Glasgow.

Coghill, S. R., Caplan, H. L., Alexandra, H., Robson, K. M., & Kumar, R. (1986). Impact of maternal postnatal depression on cognitive development of young children. *British Medical Journal Clinical Research, 292*, 1165-1167.

Compas, B., Langrock, A. M., Keller, G., Merchant, M. J., & Copeland, M. E. (2002). Children coping with parental depression: processes of adaptation to family stress. In S. H. Goodman (Ed.), *Children of depressed parents* (pp. 227-252). Washington, DC: American Psychological Association.

Compas, B., Phares, V., Banez, G. A., & Howell, D. C. (1991). Correlates of internalizing and externalizing behaviour problems: Perceived competence, causal attributions and parental symptoms. *Journal of Abnormal Child Psychology, 19*, 197-218.

Conrad, M., & Hammen, C. (1993). Protective and resource factors in high and low risk children: A comparison of children with unipolar, bipolar, medically ill and normal children. *Development and Psychopathology, 5*, 593-607.

Coolican, H. (1996). *Introduction to research methods and statistics in psychology*. London: Hodder and Stroughton.

Cowling, V. R. (1996). Meeting the support needs of families with dependent children where the parent has a mental illness. *Australian Institute of Family Studies, 45*, 22-25.

Cowling, V. R., McGorry, P. D., & Hay, D. A. (1995). Children of parents with psychotic disorders. *Medical Journal of Australia, 163*, 119-120.

Craddock, N., & Jones, I. (1999). Genetics of bipolar disorder. *Journal of Medical Genetics, 36*, 585-594.

De Chilo, N., Matorin, S., & Hallahan, C. (1987). Children of psychiatric patients: Rarely seen or heard. *Health and Social Work, Fall*, 296-302.

Department of Health. (2003). *National statistics on adults' attitudes to mental illness in Great Britain*. London: Stationery Office.

Dierker, L. C., Merikangas, K. R., & Szatmari, P. (1999). Influence of parental concordance for psychiatric disorders on psychopathology in offspring. *Journal of the American Academy of Child and Adolescent Psychiatry, 38*, 280-288.

Downey, G., & Coyne, J. C. (1990). Children of depressed parents: An integrative review. *Psychological Bulletin, 108*, 50-76.

Eisenberg, N., Fabes, R. A., & Murphy, B. C. (1996). Parents' reactions to children's negative emotions: Reactions to children's social competence and comforting behaviour. *Child Development, 67*, 2227-2247.

Elliott, A. (1992). *Hidden children: A study of ex young carers of parents with mental health problems in Leeds*. Leeds: Mental Health Development Section, Leeds Social Work Services Department.

Fallon, B., Frydenberg, E., & Boldero, J. (1993). *Perceptions of family climate and adolescent coping*. Paper presented at the 28th Annual Conference of the Australian Psychological Society, Gold Coast, Australia.

Field, T., Healy, B. T., Goldstein, R. B., & Perry, S. (1988). Infants of depressed mothers show "depressed" behaviour even with nondepressed adults. *Child Development, 59*, 1569-1579.

Fischer, C., & Wertz, F. (1975). Empirical phenomenological analyses of being criminally victimized. In A. Giorgi (Ed.), *Phenomenology and psychological research* (pp. 135-158). Pittsburgh, PA: Duquesne University Press.

Folkman, S., & Lazarus, R. S. (1985). If it changes it must be a process—study of emotion and coping during 3 stages of a college-examination. *Journal of Personality and Social Psychology, 48*, 150-170.

Folkman, S., Lazarus, R. S., Dunkelschetter, C., Delongis, A., & Gruen, R. J. (1986). Dynamics of a stressful encounter—cognitive appraisal, coping, and encounter outcomes. *Journal of Personality and Social Psychology, 50*, 992-1003.

Frydenberg, E. (1989). *Concerns of youth and how they cope: A study of Australian adolescents.* Unpublished doctoral dissertation, La Trobe University, Melbourne, Australia.

Frydenberg, E. (1996). The coping strategies used by adolescents in intact and in separated families. *Australian Journal of Guidance and Counselling, 6*, 87-97.

Frydenberg, E. (1997). *Adolescent coping: Theoretical and research perspectives.* London: Routledge.

Frydenberg, E. (Ed.). (1999). Understanding coping: Towards a comprehensive theoretical framework. In *Learning to cope: Developing as a person in complex societies* (pp. 9-30). New York: Oxford University Press.

Frydenberg, E., & Lewis, R. (1993a). *Adolescent Coping Scale.* Melbourne: Australian Council for Educational Research.

Frydenberg, E., & Lewis, R. (1993b). *Stress in the family: How adolescents cope.* Paper presented at the 28th Annual Conference of the Australian Psychological Society, Gold Coast, Australia.

Frydenberg, E., & Lewis, R. (1997). *Coping Scale for Adults.* Melbourne: Australian Council for Educational Research.

Frydenberg, E., & Lewis, R. (1998). Age, gender and profession: A study of coping among managers. *Australian Journal of Psychology, 50*, 85.

Garley, D., Gallop, R., Johnston, N., & Pipitone, J. (1997). Children of the mentally ill: A qualitative focus group approach. *Journal of Psychiatric and Mental Health Nursing, 4*, 97-103.

Garmezy, N. (1985). Stress-resistant children: The search for protective factors. In J. Stevenson (Ed.), *Aspects of current child psychiatry research.* Oxford: Pergamon Press.

Gherardi, S., & Turner, B. (1987). *Real men don't collect soft data.* Trento, Italy: Universita di Trento.

Gilligan, R. (1998). The importance of schools and teachers in child welfare. *Child and Family Social Work, 3*, 13-25.

Gilligan, R. (2000). Adversity, resilience and young people: The protective value of positive school and share time experiences. *Children and Society, 14*, 37-47.

Gilligan, R., & James, A. (2001). Promoting resilience: A resource guide on working with children in the care system. *British Journal of Social Work, 31*, 514-515.

Goode, S. (2000). Researching a hard-to-access and vulnerable population: Some considerations on researching drug and alcohol-using mothers. *Sociological Research Online, 5*, U105-U120.

Goodman, S. H., & Gotlib, I. H. (2002). *Children of depressed parents: Mechanisms of risk and implications for treatment.* Washington, DC: American Psychological Association.

Gordon, D., Burge, D., Hammen, C., Adrian, C., Jaenicke, C., & Hiroto, D. (1989). Observations of interactions of depressed women with their children. *American Journal of Psychiatry, 146*, 50-55.

Gross, D. (1984). Relationships at risk: Issues and interventions with a disturbed mother-infant dyad. *Perspectives in Psychiatric Care, 22*, 159-164.

Grunbaum, L., & Gammeltoft, M. (1993). Young children of schizophrenic mothers: Difficulties of intervention. *American Journal of Orthopsychiatry, 63*, 16-27.

Guarnaccia, P. J., & Parra, P. (1996). Ethnicity, social status and families experiences of caring for a mentally ill family member. *Community Mental Health Journal, 32*, 243-260.

Hammen, C. (1997). Children of depressed parents: The stress context. In I. N. Sandler (Ed.), *Handbook of children's coping: Linking theory and intervention. Issues in clinical child psychology*. New York: Plenum Press.

Hammen, C. (2002). Context of stress in families of children with depressed parents. In I. H. Gotlib (Ed.), *Children of depressed parents* (pp. 175-199). Washington, DC: American Psychological Association.

Harnish, J., Dodge, K. A., & Valente, E. (1995). Mother child interaction quality as a partial mediator of the roles of maternal depressive symptomology and socioeconomic status in the development of child behaviour problems. *Child Development, 66*, 739-753.

Heatherington, R., & Baistow, K. (2001). Supporting families with a mentally ill parent: European perspectives on interagency cooperation. *Child Abuse Review, 10*, 351-365.

Herzberger, S. D. (1993). Designing research on sensitive topics. In R. M. Lee (Ed.), *Researching sensitive topics*. London: Sage.

Hipwell, A. E., Gossens, F. A., Melhuish, E. C., & Kumar, R. (2000). Severe maternal psychopathology and infant mother attachment. *Development and Psychopathology, 12*, 157-175.

Huberman, M. A., & Miles, M. B. (1994). Data management and analysis methods. In Y. S. Lincoln (Ed.), *Handbook of qualitative research*. Thousand Oaks, CA: Sage Publications.

Hugman, R., & Phillips, N. (1993). "Like bees round the honey pot" social work responses to parents with mental health needs. *Practice, 6*, 193-205.

Imiela, F. (1993). How to make mental disease better known, understood and accepted. *Soins*, 56-58.

Jaenicke, C., Hammen, C., Zupan, B., Hiroto, D., Gordon, D., Adrian, C., & Burge, D. (1987). Cognitive vulnerability in children at risk for depression. *Journal of Abnormal Child Psychology, 15*, 559-572.

Johnson, J. G., Cohen, P., Kasen, S., Smailes, E., & Brook, J. (2001). Association of maladaptive parental behaviour with psychiatric disorder among parents and their offspring. *Archives of General Psychiatry, 58*, 453-460.

Kaufman, C., Grunebaum, H., Cohler, B., & Gamer, E. (1979). Superkids: Competent children of psychotic mothers. *American Journal of Psychiatry, 136*, 1398-1402.

Klimes-Dougan, B., & Bolger, A. K. (1998). Coping with maternal depressed affect and depression: Adolescent children of depressed and well mothers. *Journal of Youth and Adolescence, 27*, 1-15.

Kramer, R. A., Warner, V., Olfson, M., Ebanks, C. M., Chaput, F., & Weissman, M. M. (1998). General medical problems among the offspring of depressed parents: A 10-year follow-up. *Journal of the American Academy of Child and Adolescent Psychiatry, 37*, 602-611.

Kriss, M. R. (1987). Children of depressed mothers: Psychiatric status, adjustment and coping behaviour. *Dissertation Abstract International, 48*, 266-267.

Lade, E., Frydenberg, E., & Poole, C. (1998). Daughters don't merely imitate their mothers coping styles: A comparison of the coping strategies used by mothers and their daughters. *The Australian Educational and Developmental Psychologist, 15*, 62-69.

Landells, S., & Pritlove, J. (1994). *Young carers of a parent with schizophrenia*. Leeds: Leeds City Council.

Lazarus, R. S. (1991). *Emotion and adaptation*. New York: Oxford University Press.

Lazarus, R. S., Delongis, A., Folkman, S., & Gruen, R. (1985). Stress and adaptational outcomes—the problem of confounded measures. *American Psychologist, 40*, 770-779.

Lazarus, R. S., & Folkman, S. (1984). *Stress, appraisal and coping*. New York: Springer.

Luntz, J. (1995). The invisible dimension in mental health—children whose parents suffer from a serious mental illness. *Australian Social Work, 48*, 19-27.

Masten, A. S., Best, K. M., & Garmezy, M. (1990). Resilience and development: Contributions from the study of children who overcome adversity. *Development and Psychopathology, 2*, 425-441.

McDaniel, J. E. (1990). At risk: Children of the mentally ill. *Journal of Psychosocial Nursing Mental Health Service, 2*, 5.

Moldin, S. (1999). Report of the NIMH's genetic workgroups: Summary of research. *Biological Psychiatry, 45*, 559-602.

Murray, L., Fiori-Cowley, A., Hooper, R., & Cooper, P. (1996). The impact of postnatal depression and associated adversity on early mother-infant interactions and later infant outcome. *Child Development, 67*, 2512-2526.

Newman, T. (2003). *Children of disabled parents: New thinking about families affected by disability and illness*. Dorset, England: Russell House Publishing.

Ostman, M., & Hansson, L. (2002). Children in families with a severely mentally ill member. Prevalence and needs for support. *Social Psychiatry Psychiatric Epidemiology, 37*, 243-248.

Phares, V., Duhig, A. M., & Watkins, M. M. (2002). Family context: Fathers and other supports. In I. H. Gotlib (Ed.), *Children of depressed parents* (pp. 203-226). Washington, DC: American Psychological Society.

Radke-Yarrow, M. (1998). *Children of depressed mothers: From early childhood to maturity*. Cambridge, England: Cambridge University Press.

Radke-Yarrow, M., & Brown, E. (1993). Resilience and vulnerability in children of multiple risk families. *Development and Psychopathology, 5*, 581-592.

Renzetti, C., & Lee, R. (1993). *Researching sensitive topics*. Newbury Park: Sage.

Richards, T. J., & Richards, L. (1994). Using computers in qualitative research. In Y. S. Lincoln (Ed.), *Handbook of qualitative research* (pp. 445-462). London: Sage Publications.

Ruppert, S., & Bagedahl-Strindlund, M. (2001). Children of the parapartum mentally ill mothers: A follow up study. *Psychopathology, 34,* 174-178.

Rutter, M. (1979). Protective factors in children's response to stress and disadvantage. In N. H. Hanover (Ed.), *Primary prevention of psychopathology.* Lebanon, NH: University Press of New England.

Rutter, M. (1985). Resilience in the face of adversity. Protective factors and resistance to psychiatric disorder. *British Journal of Psychiatry, 147,* 598-611.

Rutter, M. (1987). Psychosocial resilience and protective mechanisms. *American Journal of Orthopsychiatry, 57,* 316-331.

Rutter, M. (1993). Resilience: Some conceptual considerations. *Journal of Adolescent Health, 14,* 626-631.

Rutter, M., Silberg, J., O'Connor, T., & Simonoff, E. (1999). Genetics and child psychiatry: II Empirical research findings. *Journal of Child Psychology and Psychiatry, 40,* 19-55.

Sargent, K. L. (1985). Helping children cope with parental mental illness through use of children's literature. *Child Welfare, 64,* 617-628.

Secker, J. (1998). Current conceptualizations of mental health and mental health promotion. *Health Education Research, 13,* 57-66.

Secker, J., Grove, B., & Seebohm, P. (2001). Challenging barriers to employment, training and education for mental health service users: The service user's perspective. *Journal of Mental Health, 10,* 395-404.

Sharp, D., Hay, D. F., Pawlby, S., Schmucker, G., Allen, H., & Kumar, R. (1995). The impact of postnatal depression on boys intellectual development. *Journal of Child Psychology and Psychiatry and Allied Disciplines, 36,* 1315-1336.

Shiner, R. L., & Marmorstein, N. R. (1998). Family environments of adolescents with lifetime depression: Associations with maternal depression history. *Journal of the American Academy of Child and Adolescent Psychiatry, 37,* 1152-1160.

Shulman, S. (1993). Close relationships and coping behaviour in adolescence. *Journal of Adolescence, 16,* 267-283.

Silberg, J., & Rutter, M. (2002). Nature-nurture interplay in the risks associated with parental depression. In I. H. Gotlib (Ed.), *Children of depressed parents* (pp. 13-36). Washington, DC: American Psychological Society.

Stern, M., & Zevon, M. A. (1990). Stress, coping and family environment: The adolescent's response to naturally occurring stressors. *Journal of Adolescent Research, 5,* 3, 290-305.

Tanner, D. (2000). Crossing bridges over troubled waters? Working with children of parents experiencing mental distress. *Social Work Education, 19,* 287-297.

Tebes, J. K., Kaufman, J. S., Adnopoz, J., & Racusin, G. (2001). Resilience and family psychosocial processes among children of parents with serious mental disorder. *Journal of Child and Family Studies, 10,* 115-136.

Warner, V., Mufson, L., & Weissman, M. M. (1995). Offspring at high and low risk for depression and anxiety: Mechanisms of psychiatric disorder. *Journal of the American Academy of Child and Adolescent Psychiatry, 34,* 786-797.

Warner, V., Weissman, M. M., Mufson, L., & Wickramaratne, P. J. (1999). Grandparents, parents, and grandchildren at high risk for depression: A three-generation study. *Journal of the American Academy of Child and Adolescent Psychiatry, 38,* 289-296.

Werner, E. E. (1989). High-risk children in young adulthood: A longitudinal study from birth to 32 years. *American Journal of Orthopsychiatry, 59,* 72-81.

Werner, E. E., & Smith, S. (2001). *Journeys from childhood to midlife: Risk, resilience and recovery.* New York: Cornell University Press.

World Health Organization. (1992). *International classification of diseases 10.* Geneva: Author.

PART II

RESOURCES AND COPING WITH PREVALENT PROBLEMS

The resources model of stress and coping is introduced in this section. Since we know that those who are higher on resources cope more effectively than those who are resource poor the model highlights the importance of developing young people's coping resources, especially where young people are resource poor. Early and appropriate identification of problems assists with the development of interventions. For example, anxiety is prevalent in children and often predicts anxiety related problems in adulthood. The capacity to identify those at risk of developing anxiety disorders holds promise for helping young people avoid the debilitating disorder in later life so that they can cope effectively. In a similar vein, the ability to distinguish two types of aggression in young people enables us to help particular groups of vulnerable young people to cope more effectively

CHAPTER 4

YOUNG PEOPLE AND THEIR RESOURCES

Vicki McKenzie and Erica Frydenberg
University of Melbourne, Australia

ABSTRACT

The resources young people bring to the tasks of managing stress are considered to be key factors in coping with their circumstances. Development of a measurement instrument is necessary in the study of these resources. Steven Hobfoll, in research on the Conservation of Resources theory, developed the Conservation of Resources Evaluation to measure the resources of his adult respondents in numerous studies. This instrument was modified to investigate its applicability to young people in an Australian school context. The modified resource measure was validated and a relationship was found between the degree to which students held the resources considered, and the coping styles the students used. The young people high in resources tended to use productive coping strategies, while those low in resources tended to use nonproductive coping strategies. It appears that those low in resources were also likely to report that they did not have the skills required to cope with their difficulties. The implications of the findings are considered for educators involved in programs directed at the social and emotional needs of young people.

Thriving, Surviving, or Going Under: Coping with Everyday Lives, 79–108

INTRODUCTION

In this chapter, theories of stress and coping are examined with particular reference to an application of the Conservation of Resources (COR) theory (Hobfoll, 1988) to the utilization of coping skills by adolescents.

The mental health of young people in communities around the globe has become a concern in recent years, stimulating considerable research interest. This is evident in Australia with the investigation of the Youth Suicide Task Force study (1997), and the concern aroused by the rising rates of depression in youth (Victorian Suicide Prevention Task Force, 1997, Commonwealth Department of Health and Aged Care, CDHAC, 2000). Alongside this there has been substantial interest in the promotion of mental health and well-being (Eckersley, 1998; Shochet & Osgarby, 1999), the study of how young people cope (Cunningham & Walker, 1999; Bailey & Dua, 1999; Bugalski & Frydenberg, 2000, Frydenberg, 1997, Frydenberg & Lewis, 1993b, 1996b, 1999a; Fuller, McGraw, & Goodyear, 1999; Natvig, Albrektsen, & Anderssen, 1999; Parsons, Frydenberg, & Poole, 1996; Shmotkin, Lomranz, Eyal, & Zemach, 1999), programs for teaching coping skills to young people (Brandon, Cunningham, & Frydenberg, 1999; Christenson, Sinclair, Thurlow, & Evelo, 1999; Shatte, Reivich, Gillham, & Seligman, 1999), and development of resilience in youth (Australian Health Promoting Schools Association, 2000; Butler, Godfrey, Glover, Bond, & Patton, 2000; D'Imperio, Dubow, & Ippolito, 2000; Fuller et al., 1999; Phillips, 2000).

The focus on youth issues rests within the broader context of a vast body of psychological research into the study of stress, and the individual coping methods used in its management. Studies reflect the belief that stress is a major factor affecting the way people manage their lives, is intimately tied to mental health, and is very possibly linked with problems of physical health (Dorian & Garfunkel, 1987; Frydenberg, 1999; Hobfoll, Schwarzer, & Chon, 1996). However, research has not as yet generated a unitary theory of coping or stress (Frydenberg, 1999).

STRESS

Two general approaches to stress and coping direct the content of the study reported. The *transactional model* proposes that in stress creating circumstances, the person and the environment are in an interaction, and a key determinant of the stressful nature of the stimulus will be the judgment or *appraisal* the individual makes about the situation (Lazarus & Folkman, 1984). In *primary appraisal* the individual assesses whether the situation presents danger or a threat to his/her resources or well-being. In *secondary appraisal* an assessment is made by the individual as to whether he/she possesses the coping resources to manage the threat, in which case, it will not be seen as stressful (Lazarus & Folkman, 1984). Hence, coping becomes the actions people take to manage stress, and their resources lie in their capacity to prepare and direct these actions (Lazarus & Folkman, 1984). This theoretical approach has stimulated research into types of coping strategies used, and their effectiveness.

Resource-based theories move the focus from the stressors to the impact resources have on the management of the stress process (Hobfoll, 1998b). Resource models focus on the resources of the individual and the relationship with demands made on them. Stress occurs when there is a mismatch between these factors, that is, the demands exceed the resources (Frydenberg, 1999), and resilience derives from an adequate resource-demand fit. Hobfoll (1988) has developed the Conservation of Resources theory (COR) emphasizing the role of interacting resources. This model offers a general theory of psychological stress, bridging the gap between environmental and cognitive viewpoints. It maintains that individuals are motivated to acquire and conserve social and personal resources as tools in achieving their goals. These are actively sought in order to maximize coping capacity and limit vulnerability to psychological distress. Financial security, friends, personal confidence, and social connections are highly valued resources due to their capacity to generate continued receipt of rewards over time. Hobfoll sees the search for these resources as biologically determined, part of the struggle for survival. In this paradigm, those holding fewer resources are likely to experience reduced coping options, leaving them more vulnerable to resource loss and distress. Hobfoll suggests that stress occurs when resources are lost, threatened with loss, or unsuccessfully invested (Hobfoll, 1988, 1989; Hobfoll & Lilly, 1993; Hobfoll, Schwarzer, & Chon, 1996). Historically, because resource loss meant a threat to survival, and because of social conflict and issues of territoriality, humankind, Hobfoll argues, is biologically tuned to defend resources and fear their loss. Stress in this framework is part of the continual struggle to maintain physical and psychological integrity, while coping, becomes a strategic exercise in maximizing gain of resources and minimizing their loss (Hobfoll, 2000).

In COR theory, loss of resources is a powerful, centrally motivating mechanism, which can operate with a spiral effect, with loss cycles having more power and rapidity than cycles of resource gain (Hobfoll & Lilly, 1993, Hobfoll & de Vries, 1995). When loss occurs it is more resource depleting than gain which is resource generating (Hobfoll, 1998b; Wells, Hobfoll, & Lavin, 1999), because the resource bank has been weakened for future combating of stress (Hobfoll, 1998b). Gain of resources on the other hand becomes important when the individual is faced with loss, in order to rebuild resources to deal with the consequent stress (Hobfoll & Lilly, 1993). Even so, gain cycles are shorter in life and less meaningful than loss cycles (Hobfoll, 1998b). Resources are categorized into four types: the object resources which are tangible commodities, condition resources which are the conditions surrounding the person (e.g., a supportive group), personal resources such as skills or attributes, and energy resources in terms of enabling factors such as finances.

Conservation of Resources theory attempts to explain patterns of resource allocation and use in which resources sit within an ecological context that includes family, friends, and social structures (Hobfoll, 1998a). These resources are not then individually determined, but are a product of social conditions and culture. Hobfoll and his associates have used this theory in a wide range of studies: in disaster situations (Hobfoll, 1991; Hobfoll, Dunahoo, & Monnier, 1995); in AIDS sufferers (Hobfoll, 1998a; Hobfoll, Freedy, Green, & Solomon, 1996); in anger, chronic illness, and social support (Lane & Hobfoll, 1992); in burnout with nurses (Freedy & Hobfoll, 1994); in undergraduate and community samples (Ennis, Hobfoll, & Schroder, 2000; Hobfoll & Lilly, 1993); and in women recently having given birth and their use of social support (Hobfoll, Ritter, & Shoham, 1991).

COPING

Snyder and Dinoff (1999) describe coping as "a response aimed at diminishing the physical, emotional, and psychological burden that is linked to stressful life events and daily hassles" (p. 5). *Coping strategy* then refers to the actions taken to manage the stress, in other words, the way one deals with a problem. Coping can be conceived as a process involving actions or cognitions used to deal with an internal or external difficulty, and which may involve reassessment of appropriate action as the difficulty proceeds (Lazarus, 1991). It is therefore process-related, not a function of the specific traits of the individual, but an interaction (transaction) between the individual and the environment.

Coping is essentially a dynamic phenomenon, which may involve solving the problem, or accommodating to the concern without bringing about a solution (Frydenberg, 1997). The effectiveness of coping depends on the reduction of immediate distress, as well as the provision of the long-term outcomes of well-being and prevention of disease (Snyder & Dinoff, 1999). Problem-focused coping describes efforts to deal with the sources of the stress, and emotion-focused coping strategies are attempts at managing emotional responses (Lazarus, 1991). Both strategies play a part when an individual deals with a situation; it is a matter of using the specific strategy or set of strategies that suits the context. An alternative method of conceptualizing coping responses is the approach-avoidance distinction, where approach strategies involve direct efforts to alter the stressful situation, whereas avoidance strategies involve making no effort to alter the situation (such as avoid, deny, give up) (Griffith, Dubow, & Ippolito, 2000).

Frydenberg and Lewis (1993a) grouped strategies in three *coping styles*, which categorize the strategies as either functional or dysfunctional. Functional or productive coping styles attempt to deal with the problem directly with or without the help of others, while dysfunctional styles relate to the use of nonproductive strategies such as avoidance, wishful thinking, and self-blame.

A range of tools has been developed for the measurement of coping over recent years (Frydenberg, 1997). The Adolescent Coping Scale (ACS) developed by Frydenberg and Lewis (1993a), measures coping strategies and styles. There may be individually preferred approaches to coping (similar to a trait approach) and situational specific coping (similar to a state approach) (Frydenberg & Lewis, 1994). These approaches are titled General and Specific.

ADOLESCENCE

It is evident that adolescence presents young people with a range of developmental and situational challenges: the changes deriving from normal growth and development, alongside the new social forces such as changes in the family, and in the community. Young people deal with the onset of puberty, the increasing need for independence, the influence of peers, parental and societal expectations of achievement, vocational choices and opportunities, and other critical factors. Most adolescents manage this period from childhood to adulthood without significant difficulties, but in recent years studies have aroused concern about mental health issues impacting on young people.

Figures indicate that almost 20% of all children, including adolescents, in Australia are affected by mental health problems, and at least half of those show impaired schooling and social development (CDHAC, 2000). There is evidence that the incidence of stress-related problems in teenagers has increased over the last 17 years (Eckersley, 1998; Frydenberg, 1997). One study of the incidence of depression suggests that up to 10% of children had developed clinical depression before age 14, and up to 20% of adolescents had experienced a major depressive episode before the end of their high school years (Shatte et al., 1999).

Studies show the main stressors experienced by adolescents to be in the day-to-day hassles category, in particular in problems with family relationships, school achievement, and peer relationships (Fanshawe & Burnett, 1998; Lohman & Jarvis, 2000). Frydenberg and Lewis (1990) identified a trend for girls to report a greater number of stressful events than boys. Prinz, Shermis, and Webb (1999) showed that an accumulation of stressful experiences increases adolescents' vulnerability to maladjustment, as stress was found to impact on school functioning, social relationships, and behavior.

There is evidence that the way young people cope may vary with the age of the person. It has been found that older adolescents cope differently from younger adolescents (Frydenberg & Lewis, 1993b, 1996b, 1999a, 2000; Griffith et al., 2000). Functional coping has been reported to decrease with age, whereas emotional coping increased (Frydenberg & Lewis, 1993b). Frydenberg and Lewis found that during the early years of secondary school, students reported using more work-related and less tension-reducing strategies than did students at other levels. Older students reported using the least "work hard and achieve," and the most "tension reduction" and "self-blame" strategies of all students surveyed. Similarly, Hobfoll and Lilly (1993) found age variation in resource orientation. Students concentrated around issues of identity whereas finances and family health were more primary for the community sample. Adolescents may well also present different emphases in their valuing of resources.

In studies of young people, there have been consistent findings that there are gender differences in the way coping behavior is reported and the strategies that are used (Frydenberg & Lewis, 1993b, 1999b, 2000; Frydenberg, 1997; Griffith et al., 2000). Age and socioeconomic background also influence choice of coping strategy (Frydenberg & Lewis, 1999b, 2000).

ADJUSTMENT

Coping style has been shown to be related to academic outcomes (Parsons et al., 1996) and to adjustment (Frydenberg, 1997; Griffith et al, 2000; Taris, 1999). Nonproductive coping style has been linked to depressive syndromes (Cunningham & Walker, 1999). The primary source of stress for adolescents in one study tended to be chronic interpersonal and nonsocial problems and the problems presented by daily hassles were responded to by unproductive, avoidant, and blaming responses (Prinz et al., 1999). Dumont and Provost (1999) replicated the finding that daily hassles are perceived to be more severe and tend to create greater distress for adolescents than they do for adults.

On the other hand some resources have been shown to moderate the impact of stress on adjustment, such as social support and problem solving abilities (Natvig et al., 1999; Printz et al., 1999; Sim, 2000). Printz and colleagues (1999) also found that family support was more powerful in their study than support from friends.

COPING RESOURCES

Hobfoll, Freedy, et al. (1996) present the view that coping research has concentrated on the process of coping, and not on the effectiveness of the outcomes. Because of the inherent difficulties in determining effectiveness of outcome, they maintain that there have been few attempts to look at the long-term and the short-term efficacy of coping, intervention has tended to focus on what people do to cope, how to strengthen coping resources, and methods of encouraging alternative interpretations of events. Hobfoll has been keen to ground practice in theory, by developing a research tool from which predictions could be made and tested. The COR Evaluation (COR-E) is used to identify the resources important to adults, and has been used in a large number of studies on resources, including studies evaluating the effects of resource loss and gain (Hobfoll, 1988).

Despite the recent research interest in adjustment in young people, there has been little understanding of how findings from stress and adjustment studies can be applied to intervention in the area of adolescent health and well-being (Printz et al., 1999). While efforts have been made to develop adult models of stress and coping processes, there are few models for adolescents (Printz et al., 1999), and there has been little discussion as to whether adult models are appropriate, and how the adult models might be adapted if they are relevant.

It was in this context that the COR-E, developed for study with adult populations, was considered in relation to the resources of adolescents. There has been little analysis of the way young people view their resources, and the way resources relate to the capacity of young people to cope with their circumstances. Adolescents are at a crucial time in building up their resources. In the period between childhood and independent adulthood, the young person is required to develop a repertoire of resources in knowledge and social behavior, which include building the personal strengths to cope with adulthood, dealing with cultural expectations, and preparing for and making decisions about career choices. As Snyder and Dinoff (1999) write, "[coping] not only is basic for survival, but it also relates to the quality and the ensuing constructive meaning of our own lives" (p. 5). Resources theory has the potential to increase our understanding of the methods young people use to manage to cope with these stresses and challenges.

Hobfoll and Lilly (1993) suggest that prevention of resource loss should be a primary focus for research and intervention. Adolescents are in a stage of growth and development that requires accumulating resources. However they are also in a vulnerable stage of their lives where they remain dependent on their families and the community for the extension of these resources. Loss of resources for this age group may be more crucial as the young person's approach to coping may be in a formative stage.

RESOURCES AND COPING STYLE

The relationship between resources and coping style is worthy of investigation. Coping has been variously categorized into problem versus emotion focused (Lazarus & Folkman, 1984), active or passive, prosocial or antisocial (Monnier, Stone, Hobfoll, & Johnson, 1998) and these styles impact and are impacted by resources. This has been demonstrated in an adult context (Hobfoll, Dunahoo, Ben-Porath, & Monnier, 1994; Monnier et al., 1998).

In understanding methods of dealing with the stresses of life, as well as its daily hassles, any model must manage the intra-individual, the interpersonal, and the situational factors involved in coping. The theoretical and research work completed by Hobfoll with adult groups invites replication with a younger age group. It is important to develop our knowledge of the ways young people view and develop their resources, in order to assist them extend their capacity to cope—with their ever-changing world, with the effects of the negative accumulation of stresses, with limiting negative outcomes, and with the task of building the resources that are needed.

THE STUDY

Conservation of Resources theory is used as a tool to explore the way adolescents deal with the demands made on them. It considers what resources adolescents in the Australian context value, and explores the relationship between the holding of resources and the use of particular coping strategies.

The four specific aims of the study were:

1.   To develop an adapted version of the COR-E (Hobfoll, 1989) that establishes resources that young people in the study sample consistently identify as important to them.

2.   To establish to what extent the students in the sample believe they hold these resources.

3.   To examine how young people evaluate the impact of loss and gain of these resources.

4.   To examine the relationship between the reported resources held, and the coping strategies of the student.

METHODOLOGY

The Study Sample

The study sample was taken from three coeducational secondary schools, which span different socioeconomic areas in the northern suburbs of Melbourne, Australia. One hundred seventy-two students completed the questionnaires, 43.6% male, 56.4% female, 32.6% in the 11-13 age group, 27.9% in the 14-15 age group, and 39.5% in the 16-18 age range. No further demographic information was collected. Informed consent was gained from those who participated, resulting in a 50% response rate. A random selection of 24 students participated in the 3 focus groups, consisting of seven Year 7 students, nine Year 9 students, and eight Year 11 students. There were 17 females and 7 males due to the poor rate of return of consent from male students at that stage.

Research Instruments

The Conservation of Resources Evaluation

Conservation of Resources Evaluation is an assessment tool, developed by Hobfoll (1988) to test the Conservation of Resources theory, which identifies the resources individuals report to have available to them. Through a series of group processes, Hobfoll asked groups from the university and the community to nominate important resources in their lives, creating a list of 74 resources, that were considered comprehensive although not exhaustive (Hobfoll & Lilly, 1993). The COR-E allows the respondent to identify which resources they have recently gained and lost and to what extent. It also asks respondents to rank these resources in importance. Hobfoll and Lilly reported that test-retest for the recent loss and gain measures ranged from .55 to .64 and for the loss and gain during the past year measures ranged from .64 to .67. These figures suggest that the COR-E is a reasonable research tool, as reliable and valid as other commonly used life-event measures.

In developing the instrument for the current study, the 74 items were considered as the starting pool for the adolescent instrument. The aim was to adapt the COR-E for use with adolescents. The 74 items were scrutinized for applicability to an adolescent age group, by discussion with a small group of young people prior to more comprehensive discussions with the focus groups. A range of items was omitted due to their clear relevance primarily to an adult population, and items, which overlapped, were consolidated into one item. The following items were added or altered to be more applicable to the developmental stage of adolescents: "support from parents" was added, "support from teachers" replaced "understanding from my employer/boss," and "status/seniority at work" was replaced by "having leadership responsibilities."

Following focus group discussions, additional revisions were made in some of the terms used, however students accepted all items as important except for: "access to a computer" and "access to the Internet." As these were the only two items challenged, and they were items in widespread use by young people, it was decided to leave them in the questionnaire. The following items were added as a result of suggestions or comments from the students: "being able to go out with friends," "playing sport," "being able to speak up for yourself," "having fashionable clothing" (replaced "more clothing than I need"). The final questionnaire contained 48 items (see Table 4.1).

The COR-E asks respondents to evaluate the impact of loss and gain of resources. The questionnaire developed for this study asked the following questions:

- Are these items (resources) important in your life? 3-point scale;
- How much of this item (resource) do you have? 5-point scale;
- How stressful would it be to lose this item (resource)? 5-point scale;
- If you gained on this item (resource) what effect would it have? 5-point scale.

Measurement of Coping

The Adolescent Coping Scale (ACS) was chosen because it has been validated on Australian adolescent samples (Frydenberg & Lewis, 1993b, 1996a). Developed from the responses of 643 Australian adolescents, aged from 12 to 18 years, this self-report questionnaire requires responses to 79 statements describing coping behaviors, rating how far the statement applies to the respondent on a 5-point Likert-style scale. The Gen-

**Table 4.1.   The Revised COR-E Items Used in the
Resources for Adolescents Questionnaire**

1. Believing that I am successful	25. Being able to go out with friends
2. Having adequate clothing	26. Having support from teachers
3. Feeling that I am valuable to others	27. Playing sport
4. Having a stable family life	28. Having fashionable clothing
5. Being close to one or more members of my family	29. Having support from parents
6. Having a sense of pride in myself	30. Being able to speak up for yourself
7. Having time to work	31. Having support from other adults
8. Feeling that I am accomplishing my goals	32. Feeling that I know who I am
9. Having free time	33. Feeling independent
10. Having a feeling of hope	34. Being self-disciplined
11. Having the necessary items to achieve at school	35. Feeling that my life has meaning or purpose
12. Being able to keep going without giving up	36. Having friends
13. Having a positively challenging routine	37. Belonging to organized groups (church, clubs, ...)
14. Achieving at school	38. Knowing where I am going with my life
15. Believing my future success depends on me	39. Feeling affection from others
16. Finding a positive way to look at things	40. Having a positive feeling about myself
17. Having adequate food	41. Having companionship
18. Having an adequate home	42. Knowing people I can learn from
19. Having a sense of humor	43. Having money for transportation
20. Feeling I have control over my life	44. Having money for my needs
21. Having the ability to communicate well	45. Having a job
22. Having the ability to organize tasks	46. Having leadership responsibilities
23. Being close with at least one friend	47. Access to a computer
24. Having the motivation to get things done	48. Access to the internet

eral form of the instrument asks respondents to indicate how they cope generally, and the Specific form of the instrument asks respondents to indicate how they cope with a specific self-nominated concern. The Specific scale was used.

The 18 coping strategies in this scale are: seek social support, focus on solving the problem, work hard and achieve, worry, invest in close friends, seek to belong, wishful thinking, not cope, tension reduction, social action, ignore the problem, self-blame, keep to self, seek spiritual support, focus on the positive, seek professional support, seek relaxing diversions, and physical recreation. (For an exemplar of these coping strategies see Chapter 8, this volume) These 18 strategies cluster into three general coping styles. The productive coping style consists of items referring to problem solving, working hard, belonging, positive thinking, relaxation and physical recreation. The coping style of reference to others contains strategies for seeking social support from friends, professionals and spirituality. The third style, nonproductive coping, is comprised of items relating to worry, wishful thinking, not coping, tension reduction, ignoring the problem, keeping to oneself, and self-blame. In essence, this style reflects an inability to deal with, or avoidance of, the concern.

Procedure

A psychologist conducted the focus groups and at the end of the discussion a pilot of the adapted questionnaire was administered. These groups were asked a number of questions about their understanding of resources, the resources they believed were most important to young people, and how they managed when their resources were lost. Ten days later this group of students completed the same resources questionnaire to provide an indication of the reliability of the measure. Information gained in focus groups was analyzed and arranged into content areas and themes.

The questionnaire was then completed incorporating the suggested variations to the valuation made by the focus groups. Following this, a pretest was given to a group of ten Year 11 students to enable consideration of the time required, the effectiveness of layout, the phrasing of questions, and to determine whether additional items were required.

Slight modifications were made to layout as a result, although all questions were retained. On a later occasion, students completed the questionnaires in their schools. All testing was completed over a 10-week time span.

RESULTS

Focus Group

Students in focus groups identified resources as a complex collection of thoughts, actions, and possessions. Factors external to themselves such as school, teachers, family, and friends, were mentioned, as well as positive experiences, and facilities like libraries and computers. Some referred to self-reflective activities such as meditation and keeping a diary. Participants identified friends and family, involvement in activities such as school, music, sport, and debating, and the internal behaviors of setting goals, restating problems in a manageable form, self-reliance, determination, and having confidence in their abilities. The younger students tended to mention support from home and friends, whereas the older students tended to focus more on the inner resources of self-esteem, motivation, ambition, and effective goal setting.

When asked how they build up resources, students reported that they built connections (make friends, involve myself in things, ask my family, listen to people, learn at school, get mum to ring the school), used internal effort (tell yourself to ignore the problems, make jokes, meditate, pray, cry, scream, sleep, talk to myself), and took action (sing and dance, involve myself in as many things as I can, do things that I am good at, work to get experience and money, or mix with a range of people).

In considering loss of resources, the tendency was for focus group respondents to concentrate on losing a friend or failure at school. Again students identified internal actions (feel sad and depressed, use self-talk, block it out, review decisions, justify things), and external actions (go back to people I know, stay in contact with old friends, depend on other resources, work harder, get a tutor, talk to a friend). Younger students were quick to refer to the experience of transition, describing how they managed loss of primary school. Older students were more focused on loss of a friend or failing to achieve at school.

All age groups asserted strongly the themes of family, friends, and school being key aspects of their resource pool. The groups also reviewed the amended resources questionnaire, as described in the methodology section. It was concluded from the focus groups, that the concept of resources has meaning and relevance to the young people interviewed.

Qualitative Data Collected in the Open-Ended Questionnaire Section

The final question on the Resources Inventory asked "Are there any other things that help you that are missing?" A small number of students (17) responded to this question with suggestions of resources to include. They were pets (3), good looks (2), self-confidence (2), time to self (2), religion (2), creative outlets (1), drugs (1), backup plans (1), popularity (1), hobbies (1), and goals (1). The Resources Inventory tapped some of these elements, such as, goals (item 8), self-confidence (item 6, 30), time (item 9), and religion (item 37), however the other points could be incorporated in a future study to further develop a more complete understanding of the resources young people see as useful.

The ACS also contains an open-ended question asking for respondents to describe their main concern. One hundred sixty-two students listed concerns which included future directions (25%), school work/achievement (21%), family (19%), friendship (19%), feeling positive (5.5%), job/money (4.3%), time (2.4%), and global issues (1.9%). These concerns are

reflected in the resources items. The concerns were similar to those identified by Frydenberg and Lewis (1996b), which indicates that this cohort
was a typical group of young people, valuing achievement and relationships.

At the conclusion of the ACS, students were asked to "list any *other*
things you do to cope with your main concern." The 49 coping actions
listed were: distract/enjoy oneself (13), talk (7), reflect (7), eat (5), work
harder (4), keep quiet (3), write (3), play music (3), exercise (2), sleep (1),
and take it out on others (1).

Questionnaire Results

The Importance of Resources

As predicted when presented with the adapted version of the COR-E
(Hobfoll, 1989), groups of Australian adolescents consistently rated the
resources listed as important. On a scale from 3 to 1, the overall mean was
2.53, with a standard deviation of 0.16. The highest scoring items were:
Having friends (mean 2.88, 90% always), being close with at least one
friend (2.78, 82% always), parent support (2.77, 78% always), adequate
home (2.77, 82% always), adequate food (2.69, 76% always), being able to
speak up for yourself (2.68, 71% always), and stable family (2.67, 70%
always). The lowest mean was 2.14, SD 0.72 (34% always) for belonging to
organized groups such as church and clubs.

On the whole, students indicated that the resources in the inventory
were of importance to them, and in particular they valued friends, family,
and adequacy in the basics (home, food), and their own skill in being able
to present their needs.

The 48 items on the importance scale were then used in a principal
component analysis, to investigate whether there were groupings or factors inherent in the items. Factor analysis showed that one factor was sufficient to explain a considerable degree of the variance. Fourteen of the
unrotated factors showed eigenvalues of 1 or more. The first variable
explained 20.7% of the variance, the second 6.2%, the third 5.5%, the
fourth 4.6%, and the fifth 4.0%.

The first general factor, which can be identified as "resources,"
appeared to be most useful in understanding the importance ratings. In
examining the scree plot, it is clear that eight factors could have been
explored; however as this study focused on Having resources, this was not
taken further. The reliability analysis, with the 172 cases and 48 items,
gave an alpha of 0.91. Results indicated that all items were worth retaining as they had scores of .24 and above, except for item 45, Having a job
(.02).

The Have Resources Scale

Students on the whole saw themselves as having resources, the mean occurring between "a good amount" and "some." On a scale of 5 to 1, the mean for the scale was 3.84 with a standard deviation of .51. The minimum score was 2.44 and the maximum was 4.96.

The items that students had reported as most important to them tended to fairly closely match the items that they reported having, with a few exceptions. The highest and lowest rating resources on *importance* compared with *have* are listed in Table 4.2. The comparison between the scales indicates that the resources that students rate as important are in most cases the resources that they believe they have.

A reliability analysis was completed on the have scale, with 172 cases and 48 items, the reliability coefficient (alpha) was .93. As in the importance scale, only Item 45 was a candidate for exclusion (.08), which raised the reliability of the alpha coefficient to .94. It was the only one omitted from the later scoring. All other items were above .27 on item total correlation, which supports the use of the total have resources score.

Table 4.2.   Similarity of Student Rating of items on the Importance of the Resource compared with their Ratings of Having the Resource

Importance	*Have*
The 10 highest ratings on each scale	
*36. Having friends	47. Access to a computer
*23. Being close with at least one friend	*36. Having friends
*18. Having an adequate home	*17. Having adequate food
*29. Having support from parents	*18. Having an adequate home
*17. Having adequate food	*23. Being close with at least one friend
30. Being able to speak up for yourself	*29. Having support from parents
*4. Having a stable family life	*19. Having a sense of humor
33. Feeling independent	*4. Having a stable family life
44. Having money for my needs	2. Having adequate clothing
*19. Having a sense of humor	11. Having the necessary items to achieve at school
The 3 lowest rating items on each scale	
*45. Having a job	*37. Belonging to organized groups
13. Having a positively challenging routine	46. Having leadership responsibilities
*37. Belonging to organized groups	*45. Having a job

*The asterisks indicate items rated similarly on both scales.

When a principal component analysis was undertaken on the have resources scale, the scree plot revealed a rapid decline after the fourth value, suggesting four factors. Thirteen variables showed eigenvalues of 1 or more. The first variable explained 26.7% of the variance, the second 6.1%, the third 4.3%, and the fourth 4.1%. Factor scores were calculated by salient items with loadings greater than .30.

A rotated factor matrix revealed that all items except Item 45 had some substantial loadings on one or other of the four factors. Salient items were those considered to define each factor, representing shared relevance not held in common with items on other factors. Factor 1 can be summarized as a purpose factor, involving a sense of direction, because most items relate to achievement, independence, and a sense of moving forward with the support and guidance of teachers, adults, and others. Factor 2 items are concerned with friends or socializing with friends, having money, and access to computers and the Internet. This factor was labeled friends, which appeared to capture most of the items, although some have more to do with having the means to socialize. Factor 3 is concerned with self-satisfaction, items that involve fundamental needs such as feeling well established, having adequate home and food, regarding oneself positively, and self-esteem; and Factor 4 contains items which relate to family and affiliation. As in Factor 2, there are some items, such as playing sport and having the necessary items to achieve at school, which do not appear to directly relate to family support, although they loaded together. There may well be a family support component in these items. These factor scores were significantly correlated, with correlations from .50 to .63, $p <$ .001.

Items that loaded on more than one factor were placed where they held the highest loading. One item, number 45, "having a job," was not included in any factor, although it did show signs of being related to Factor 2 (.20). It may be influenced by the age of the student, as it is only relevant for students who were over 15 years. When the factor means are compared, the highest mean was for self-satisfaction (4.07, SD .53), the next friends (4.02, SD .59), the third family (3.89, SD .66), and the lowest Purpose (3.68, SD .64). The difference between these means was calculated using a paired samples test. There was a significant difference at the $p < .001$ or $p < .01$ levels between all factors, with the exception of the factors of friends and self-satisfaction.

The substantial correlation between the factors suggests that there may be some validity in using a single total score to indicate the respondents' overall perception of resource availability. Here the four-factor version made possible a more detailed study of what the students regarded as their main resources.

The have factors were analyzed on a paired t test according to gender. The only statistically significant difference between the means for males and females was a tendency for boys to report higher levels of "self-satisfaction" (M male $= 4.17$, M female $= 4.00$, $p < .05$).

The Impact of Loss and Gain on Resources

When the highest ranking items in importance and stress due to loss were compared, the items students rated as likely to cause them great stress corresponded to a substantial degree with those items which they valued.

Consistently students reported similar ratings on resources in terms of their importance to them, the degree to which they had them, and the cost to them in stress if they were to lose them. The 10 highest scoring items on importance to the student compared with loss only varied on Item 14, achieving at school (third highest stress on loss rating), Item 20, feeling I have control over my life (ninth highest) and Item 9, having free time (10th highest).

The mean for stress on loss of resources was 3.62, while the mean for impact of gain of resources was 3.87. The two sets of results share a similar pattern, indicating that the questions were tapping similar issues. The results confirm that the students were keen on having these resources, and

Table 3. Comparison of Student Rating of Stress on Anticipation of Loss and Gain of Resources

Loss	Gain
The 10 highest scoring items	
*36. Having friends	*36. Having friends
*18. Having an adequate home	*23. Being close with at least one friend
*14. Achieving at school	*14. Achieving at school
4. Having a stable family life	*20. Feeling I have control over my life
*23. Being close with at least one friend	*18. Having an adequate home
*29. Having support from parents	25. Being able to go out with friends
17. Having adequate food	*29. Having support from parents
*44. Having money for my needs	*44. Having money for my needs
*20. Feeling I have control over my life	21. Having the ability to communicate well
9. Having free time	24. Having the motivation to get things done
The 3 lowest scoring items	
*46. Having leadership responsibilities	*46. Having leadership responsibilities
*37. Belonging to organized groups (church, clubs, ...)	*13. Having a positively challenging routine
*13. Having a positively challenging routine	*37. Belonging to organized groups (church, clubs, ...)

*The asterisks indicate commonly occurring items.

would suffer greatly if they were lost. There was no further measure of loss of resources in this study.

The Relationship between Having Resources and the Coping Styles and Strategies of the Student

The Adolescent Coping Scale Specific version of the long form in this study gained a reliability alpha of .82. The responses on the ACS gave scores on the response styles of productive coping (alpha .76), nonproductive coping (alpha .84) and reference to others (alpha .68), which were then correlated with the scores on the have resources measure using Pearson's product-moment correlation coefficients accompanied by a two-tailed test of significance. As predicted, there was a significant positive correlation between productive coping style and have resources (.45, $p <$ .001), a significant negative correlation between nonproductive coping and have resources (−.20, $p < .01$), and a positive correlation between Reference to others and have resources (.19, $p < .05$).

Because the relationship between reference to others and have resources was small, it was decided to calculate partial correlations for productive and nonproductive coping with have resources. Controlling for nonproductive coping, the have resources and productive coping correlation was significant (.55, $p < .001$). When controlling for productive coping, the partial correlation coefficients also show a clear negative correlation (−.41, $p < .001$) between have resources and nonproductive coping.

When the specific strategy items making up productive coping were examined, there was significant correlation with have resources between all items except for "belong."

When the items making up nonproductive coping were considered, there was significant negative correlation between five out of the eight nonproductive coping strategies and have resources.

Table 4.4.   Correlations between Having Resources and Reporting Use of Particular Coping Strategies

Productive		Nonproductive	
Strategies (N = 172)	Have Resources	Strategies	Have Resources
Solve the problem	.33***	Worry	−.16*
Relax	.25**	Time with friends	.16*
Physical recreation	.31***	Wishful thinking	.02
Belong	.03	Not cope	−.26**
Work hard	.44***	Ignore	.01
Focus on the positive	.35***	Tension reduction	−.27***
		Keep to oneself	−.28***
		Self-blame	−.28***

***$p < .001$. **$p = .001$ (Pearson 2-tailed test of significance).

As "ignore the problem" and "wishful thinking" are relatively passive activities, they may not relate to having resources. "Time with friends" related positively to having resources, which throws into question its identification as a nonproductive strategy. For those with resources, contact with friends might be seen as genuinely helpful.

The factors identified by using the have scale were correlated with the ACS results. A positive, significant ($p < .001$) correlation was found between productive coping and having the resources of purpose (.43), friends (.35), self-satisfaction (.31) and family (.35). It appears that those respondents who use productive coping have resources in all facets measured by the adapted resources inventory. On the other hand having resources in purpose and family were significantly negatively correlated with nonproductive coping (purpose $-.22$, $p = .005$, and family $-.25$, $p = .001$). This supports the view that those who have resources use productive coping, and do not use nonproductive coping. Those who use nonproductive coping are less likely to have resources in the category of purpose and family. Reference to others has a significant positive correlation with have/purpose (.21, $p = .006$), and have/family (.22, $p = .004$). The respondents in this sample who have resources in the purpose and family domains, also are likely to use reference to others as well as productive coping.

The factors derived from the have scale were then correlated with scores on anticipated stress from loss and gain of resources. Productive copers rated the stress involved in loss of purpose or family as highly stressful, and they highly valued gain in all resources factors (significant at the $p < .001$ level). There were no significant correlations between nonproductive coping and the factors when related to the loss or gain of resources. Nor were there any significant correlations between reference to others and the factors, except for gain of resources with family.

Modest intercorrelations were found (.33, .34, .33, $p < .001$) between the coping styles. Although there is support for three styles, this interrelation needs to be noted.

Further Analysis of the Have Scale and Coping Styles Results

The have scale data was split into categories according to reported holding of resources. Three groups were identified: Group 1 was the lowest 27.6% ($N = 46$) on have resources, Group 2 a middle band ($N = 80$), and Group 3 the highest 26.7% ($N = 46$). A discriminant function analysis was completed in which two functions were found: (1) productive coping style and (2) nonproductive coping style. Most of the separation of the three groups was a result of function one, productive coping ($p < .001$) accounting for 27% of the variance. Group 3, the high have resources group were relatively positive on function one (.76 compared with .08 for the middle group and −.92 for the low resourced group), the middle group (Group 2) higher on function two (.05 compared with −.04 for the low resource group, and −.05 for the high resource group), and the low have resources group (Group 1) did not score positively on either function (−.92 for function 1 and −.04 for function 2).

The high have resources group tended to use productive coping, the low haves neither used nonproductive nor productive coping. The middle group used nonproductive coping more than either of the two more extreme groups and made only moderate use of productive coping.

To check on the validity of the conclusions from the analysis using the coping styles, the same form of analysis was undertaken using the 18 coping strategies. Results showed a pattern that is generally in agreement with the results for the styles. When the item "not cope" was isolated and compared with the three have resources groups, significant differences were found between the three groups on not cope, the relationship being a linear one.

The mean of the low resources group was 2.76, SD of .76, the mid resources group mean was 2.40, SD of .73 and the high resources group mean was 2.17, SD of .61. The differences between the three group means on "not cope" were statistically significant (F = 8.16, df = 2,169, $p < .001$). The lower the students described their possession of resources, the greater the likelihood that they would use "not cope" as a way of managing concerns.

A further analysis was then completed using the coping strategy scores of the three have resources groups. The variables that discriminated between the three groups were "work hard to achieve" (F = 13.8, df = 2,169, $p < .001$), "keep to self" (F = 11.17, df = 2,169, $p < .001$), and "seek social support" (F = 9.82, df = 2,169, $p < .001$).

In summary, the high have resources group cope by working hard and avoiding nonproductive strategies, while those respondents low on resources cope by keeping to themselves and make little use of "work hard to achieve." The middle have resources group do not fit neatly between the high and low groups, as their way of coping is to "seek social support" and they tend to make more use of the nonproductive coping strategies than might be expected.

DISCUSSION

The Value of Resources to Young People

The importance of resources scale and the have resources scale were shown to be reliable measures as evidenced by the focus group responses, the responses to the questionnaires and the reliability correlations. The importance and have scales have excellent internal reliability. The method used to establish the adapted COR list supports its content validity.

The results indicate that all of the resources in the adapted version of the COR-E were valued to a substantial extent (between "sometimes" and "all the time") by the respondents. Furthermore the respondents rated themselves as well supplied with the resources that they valued. The resource themes identified by the focus groups were reflected in the factors that were developed from the have resources questionnaire responses—purpose, friends, self-satisfaction, and family. The most commonly valued resources on the adapted COR questionnaire were frequently the highest scoring items in terms of possession, and the lowest scoring resources on importance were those items ranked lowest on possession.

The highest scoring of specific resources on both value and ownership were friends, support of parents, and adequate home and food. Given the dependent circumstances of young people of school age, the high ranking of these resources is not surprising. The students ranked lowest having a job, belonging to organized groups, having leadership responsibilities, and having a positively challenging routine. Having a job may not be relevant to the school-attending adolescent age group, except those students who are over 15 years of age. The low rating of belonging to an organized group may well be a reflection of community changes with many young people attending fewer organized activities such as church and youth groups. This question used the examples of church and clubs, and could be extended to sporting groups, scouts, and guides, in case these had been overlooked. The focus groups asserted the value of the resources listed on the questionnaire and had few additional resources to add. This was supported by the questionnaire results, where the average percentage ratings of resources as *always* important was 58%, *sometimes* important 36%, and 5% *never* important.

Resources and Coping Strategies

The study shows that young people who report that they have resources on the adapted COR-E, also report that they use productive coping strategies, which comprise "solving the problem," "relaxing," "physical recreation," "working hard," and "focusing on the positive" (Frydenberg & Lewis, 1993a).

The coping strategies could be regarded as the resources that Hobfoll (1988) calls personal characteristics. The one productive coping strategy that did not correlate with resources was seek to belong. This scale on the ACS consists of items such as: make a good impression on others, worry about my relationships with others, try to fit in with my friends, improve my relationships, and do as my friends want. These items might be seen as less positive and less problem solving oriented than the other productive strategies. Having resources also correlated significantly ($p < .05$) with the coping style of reference to others. It appears that having resources builds the readiness and confidence to enable the individual to reach out to others for assistance.

A negative correlation was found between having resources and use of a nonproductive coping style, comprising worry, belong, wishful thinking, not cope, ignore the problem, tension reduction, keep to self, and self-blame. Those students who reported not having resources also said they used methods of coping that are not productive, such as the strategy of not cope. This type of coping serves to lower psychological distress, but makes no attempt at resolving the problem.

When assessing the factors identified in the have resources scale, a significant positive correlation was found between having the four resource factors of purpose, friends, self-satisfaction, and family, and the productive coping strategies. nonproductive coping was significantly negatively correlated with have factors of purpose and family. This may indicate that for those students who score highly on nonproductive coping, the resources involved in having a sense of purpose or direction, and in having the support that comes from family are less available. Both of these factors are important in school achievement. Without the motivation to work and the back-up from family the student may then turn to nonproductive coping.

When the sample was divided into those who were high, moderate, and low scoring on have resources, the high have students were found to use productive coping strategies, the moderate Have students used more nonproductive coping, and the low have students used neither productive nor nonproductive coping. Detailing this further, it emerged that the low Have students were students who did not use seek social support, did not report use of work hard to achieve, and were likely to use keep to self. The moderate group did not see themselves as particularly well-resourced, and tended to use seek social support. Instead of attending to their achievement, one might speculate that they are more likely to turn to others for support than focus on school attainment. This may reflect a need for, or dependence on others, a lack of motivation, or may represent a capacity for seeking assistance.

The groups that may present as requiring intervention are the moderate have resources group, who may need further encouragement to persist with working hard to achieve their goals. The low have resources group are of concern to the educator and welfare oriented professional as they perceive themselves as low in resources, which were well valued by the total sample. This group reports that they use not cope and keep to self to cope, which are unlikely to create positive outcomes.

Some resources on the inventory relate to contextual factors that are difficult to alter. However the educator has the capacity to impact on the student's personal resources. Students in this study highly valued such personal resources as being able to speak up for yourself and being able to communicate well, both skill areas that can be targeted in educational programs. The low-resourced group may well benefit from attention to the resources that they have (and may not acknowledge), and to the training of new behaviors and skills that can serve as gained resources.

This study also confirmed that family and friends are resources that are highly valued by young people. Laible, Carlo, and Raffaelli (2000) found that that the adolescents scoring highly on both peer and parent attachment were the best adjusted, and those low on both were the least well adjusted. Lohman and Jarvis (2000) found that family dynamics were linked with high levels of functional coping. Prinz et al. (1999) also found that support from family was more vital than support from friends, and suggested that peers may serve as a secondary resource when parental support is not available. These studies are supported by numerous others (Helsen, Vollebergh, & Meeus, 2000; Richman, Rossenfeld, & Bowen, 1998; Van Beest & Baerveldt, 1999; Vandervoort, 1999), which assert the value of social support as a resource, which is extremely valuable in stressful circumstances. Fuller et al. (1999) found that young people identified peer connectedness, fitting in at school, feeling loved by family and an interested adult, as of greatest importance in their well-being. Similarly Resnick et al. (1997), in a large U.S. study, found connection with family and school to be protective factors.

Following COR theory, young people will be motivated to protect and enhance their resources as they manage the challenges that come with their life experiences. When young people are faced with loss or potential loss of resources, they will be primed to protect their resources and minimize their depletion. The greater the resource pool, the more buffered the adolescent will be to manage the effects of loss. Those young people with fewer resources will be at greater risk, and this study suggests that these may be the young people who have fewer productive coping strategies in their resources repertoire. The potential damage can then be exacerbated by the possibility of entering a loss spiral. Following COR theory, this is a crucial point for intervention based on injecting resources, since, in the context of loss, resource gain has more effect than it would otherwise (Hobfoll, 1998b). A COR orientation would encourage the helping professional to assess the available resource pool (including under-utilized resources), the degree of loss, and the particular resources required to assist a young person to cope and break the loss cycle.

Resource theory encourages the treating agent to look for resources in a number of areas, not only in the cognitive appraisal of the circumstances. It reminds us that a complex set of factors may be involved and that many practical points of assistance may buffer the individual, averting a loss spiral. The current study suggests that the young people at risk may benefit from a focus on improving their productive coping strategies, and reducing their tendency to retreat and not cope. There is also evidence in this sample that many young people may benefit from such interventions, for the middle range group (46.5% of the sample) compared with the highly resourced group did not score strongly on productive coping. In the development of coping skills programs, there may be value in attending to the issue of resources. One might ask what resources are needed before productive coping can be used. Working hard depends on resources. If they are unavailable, the young person may not be able to use that coping strategy, or might need to protect other resources. It may be that the middle group does not have the confidence that working hard will pay off for them. Instead they seek support of others more than hard work, because working hard might present them with loss (of face, of self-esteem) should they not achieve the results. In teaching this group coping skills, it would be important to demonstrate that there are gains to be made from working hard to solve problems.

IMPLICATIONS FOR EDUCATIONAL PRACTICE

Schools and teachers offer a wealth of resources to adolescents. The focus group respondents mentioned the school as a key resource, particularly in offering access to social interaction with friends. Schools also offer, in addition to intellectual development and skills, interpersonal and life skills both incidentally and through direct teaching of programs. The teaching of coping skills, conflict management, communication, and personal development all address the development of a pool of social resources for the students that may be used in tackling threats of resource loss as they arise.

The questionnaire responses in both the Importance and the Have scales, rated the item "Having support from teachers" as 43 out of 48, and 44 out of 48 respectively. It was highly ranked in Factor 1, purpose, which was negatively related to nonproductive coping, as was Factor 4 family. This might suggest that those students who see themselves as not having support from teachers and/or family use nonproductive coping, and may be left without support from those who may be able to offer it from a position of maturity and experience. Richman et al. (1998) found that the receipt of social support related to positive school outcomes, and that at-risk students perceived their parents and teachers as their primary sources of support, not their peers. Perhaps the students high in nonproductive coping did not have the social resources to recognize or access the support they needed. Building the social resources of the student, particularly of the at-risk students, is then an important strategy for enhancement of school outcomes. This is further supported by the results of a coping skills teaching program reported by Bugalski and Frydenberg (2000), which increased the subjects' Reference to others coping style, and reduced their use of nonproductive coping.

The challenge for schools is to find methods to assist those who use nonproductive coping strategies to engage students more effectively so as to help them to enhance their resources. Nonproductive coping strategies may well serve to protect the few resources these young people have. This could emerge as poor behavior, given the lack of resources and the possible defensive position needed to protect the resources the student has. It also may emerge as withdrawal and keeping to oneself, which may also be considered a counterproductive defense strategy.

This study is one of the first attempts to empirically measure the resources of young people; hence further work is needed to see if the items in the measurement tool adequately cover the range of resources that are important for adolescents. Examination of which resources have greatest power for adolescents would also be useful in future studies. Hobfoll, Dunahoo et al. (1995) discuss the difference between "robust" resources, used in a variety of circumstances, and "circumscribed" resources, used only in a restricted domain, as well as the effects of the strength of resources. Conservation of Resources theory maintains that having resources is a key to adjustment, and examines the role in this of loss and gain of resources. This study addressed having resources, but it was outside its scope to assess the contextual circumstances relating to the resources, in particular, whether the resources had been held or not held over time, or were recently acquired or lost. Although the comparative value of specific resources in stress reduction by young people was not considered in the study reported in this chapter, it is clearly an important area to investigate. Additionally, cross-cultural factors along with causal factors need to be considered

It would also be beneficial to study the acquisition of resources, understanding the impact of what having and not having resources can have, and to follow up in greater detail the aspects of the relationship between resources and coping which have been flagged by this study. Extended profiles of the productive and nonproductive copers' resource bases may offer professionals guidance in the appropriate strategies that should be presented in preventative training programs. Further analysis of the resources and coping skills may show how to minimize nonproductive coping in those young people low in resources, and indicate which resources are most productive in specific circumstances, extending the emphasis from distress to success and satisfaction with outcomes.

In summary, this study has shown that the COR-E can be adapted to identify the resources of adolescents. Students indicated that they valued all the resources in the COR adapted version to some extent and rated themselves as well provided for on those resources. A relationship was found between resources and coping strategies. Those students identified as high on resources, were the students who used the coping styles of productive coping and reference to others, and the strategy of "work hard to achieve." On the other hand those students who reported they did not have resources tended to use few coping strategies and were most likely to use the strategy of "keep to self." Four factors were found to be operative in the have resources scale: self-satisfaction, family, friends, and a sense of purpose. Finally, the educational and clinical applications of the findings were described, giving consideration to the value of combining a resources approach with an understanding of the coping methods used by young people.

REFERENCES

Australian Health Promoting Schools Association. (2000). *A national framework for health promoting schools (2000-2003)*. Sydney, Australia: Author.

Bailey, F. J., & Dua, J. (1999). Individualism-collectivism, coping styles, and stress in international and Anglo-Australian students: A comparative study. *Australian Psychologist, 34*, 177-182.

Brandon, C. M., Cunningham, E. G., & Frydenberg, E. (1999). Bright Ideas: A school-based program teaching optimistic thinking skills in pre-adolescence. *Australian Journal of Guidance and Counselling, 9*, 147-157.

Bugalski, K., & Frydenberg, E. (2000). Promoting effective coping in adolescents "at risk" for depression. *Australian Journal of Guidance and Counselling, 10*, 111-132.

Butler, H., Godfrey, C., Glover, S., Bond, L., & Patton, G. (2000, April). The Gatehouse Project: What do students' perceptions of school tell us about our methods of reform? *Australian Guidance and Counselling Association Newsletter, 1*, 15-19.

Christenson, S. L., Sinclair, M. F., Thurlow, M. L., & Evelo, D. (1999). Promoting student engagement with school using the check and connect model. *Australian Journal of Guidance and Counselling, 9*, 169-184.

Commonwealth Department of Health and Aged Care. (2000). *National action plan for promotion, prevention and early intervention for mental health 2000*. Canberra, Australia: Author.

Cunningham E. G., & Walker, G. (1999). Screening for at-risk youth: Predicting adolescent depression from coping styles. *Australian Journal of Guidance and Counselling, 9,* 37-46.

D'Imperio, R. L., Dubow, E. F., & Ippolito, M. F. (2000). Resilient and stress-affected adolescents in an urban setting. *Journal of Clinical Child Psychology, 29,* 129-142.

Dorian, B., & Garfinkel, P. E. (1987). Stress, immunity and illness—A review. *Psychological Medicine, 17,* 393-407.

Dumont, M., & Provost, M. A., (1999). Resilience in adolescents: Protective role of social support, coping strategies, self-esteem, and social activities on experience of stress and depression. *Journal of Youth and Adolescence, 28,* 343-364.

Eckersley, R. (1998). Rising psychosocial problems among young people. *Family Matters, 50,* 50-52.

Ennis, N. E., Hobfoll, S. E., & Schroder, K. E. E. (2000). Money doesn't talk, it swears: How economic stress and resistance resources impact inner-city women's depressive mood. *American Journal of Community Psychology, 28,* 149-173.

Fanshawe, J., & Burnett, P. (1998). School-related stressors in adolescents. *Australian Journal of Guidance and Counselling, 8,* 1-8.

Freedy, J. R., & Hobfoll, S. E. (1994). Stress inoculation for reduction of burnout: A Conservation of Resources approach. *Anxiety, Stress, and Coping, 6,* 311-325.

Frydenberg, E. (1997). *Adolescent coping: Theoretical and research perspectives.* London: Routledge.

Frydenberg, E. (Ed.). (1999). *Learning to cope: Developing as a person in complex societies.* Oxford, England: Oxford University Press.

Frydenberg E., & Lewis, R. (1990). How adolescents cope with different concerns: The development of the Adolescent Coping Checklist (ACC). *Psychological Test Bulletin, 3,* 63-73.

Frydenberg, E., & Lewis, R. (1993a). *The Adolescent Coping Scale administrator's manual.* Melbourne, Australia: ACER.

Frydenbery E., & Lewis, R. (1993b). Boys play sport and girls turn to others: Age, gender and ethnicity as determinants of coping. *Journal of Adolescence, 16,* 252-266.

Frydenberg E., & Lewis, R. (1994). Coping with different concerns: Consistency and variation in coping strategies used by adolescents. *Australian Psychologist, 29,* 45-48.

Frydenberg, E., & Lewis, R. (1996a). A replication study of the structure of the Adolescent Coping Scale: Multiple forms and applications of a self-report inventory in a counselling and research context. *European Journal of Psychological Assessment, 12,* 224-235.

Frydenberg, E., & Lewis, R. (1996b). The coping strategies used by adolescents in intact and in separated families. *Australian Journal of Counselling and Guidance, 6,* 87-97.

Frydenberg, E., & Lewis, R. (1999a). Things don't get better just because you're older: A case for facilitating reflection. *British Journal of Educational Psychology, 69,* 81-94.

Frydenberg, E., & Lewis, R. (1999b). Academic and general well-being: The relationship with coping. *Australian Journal of Guidance and Counselling*, 9, 1-18.

Frydenberg, E., & Lewis, R. (2000). Teaching coping to adolescents: When and to whom? *American Educational Research Journal*, 37, 727-745.

Fuller, A., McGraw, K., & Goodyear, M. (1999). Bungy jumping through life: What young people say promotes well-being and resilience. *Australian Journal of Guidance and Counselling*, 9, 159-168.

Griffith, M. A., Dubow, E. F., & Ippolito, M. F. (2000). Developmental and cross-situational differences in adolescents' coping strategies. *Journal of Youth and Adolescence*, 29, 183-204.

Helsen, M., Vollebergh, W., & Meeus, W. (2000). Social support from parents and friends and emotional problems in adolescence. *Journal of Youth and Adolescence*, 29, 319-333.

Hobfoll, S. E. (1988). *The ecology of stress.* New York: Hemisphere.

Hobfoll, S. E. (1989). Conservation of Resources: A new attempt at conceptualizing stress. *American Psychologist*, 44, 513-524.

Hobfoll, S. E. (1991). Traumatic stress: A theory based on rapid loss of resources. *Anxiety Research*, 4, 187-197.

Hobfoll, S. E. (1998a). Ecology, community, and AIDS prevention. *American Journal of Community Psychology*, 26, 133-144.

Hobfoll, S. E. (1998b). *Stress, culture, and community.* New York: Plenum Press.

Hobfoll, S. E. (2000). *The influence of culture, community, and the nested-self in the stress process: Advancing Conservation of Resources theory.* Manuscript submitted for publication.

Hobfoll, S. E. & de Vries, M. W. (Eds.). (1995). *Extreme stress and communities: Impact and intervention.* Dordrecht, The Netherlands: Kluwer Academic.

Hobfoll, S. E., Dunahoo, C. L., Ben-Porath, Y., & Monnier, J., (1994). Gender and coping: The Dual-Axis Model of Coping. *American Journal of Community Psychology*, 22, 49-82.

Hobfoll, S. E., Dunahoo, C. L., & Monnier, J. (1995). Conservation of Resources and traumatic stress. In J. R. Freedy & S. E. Hobfoll (Eds.), *Traumatic stress: From theory to practice* (pp. 29-47). New York: Plenum Press.

Hobfoll, S. E., Freedy, J. R., Green, B. L., & Solomon, S. D. (1996). Coping in reaction to extreme stress: The roles of resource loss and resource availability. In M. Zeidner & N. S. Endler (Eds.), *Handbook of coping* (pp. 322-349). New York: Wiley

Hobfoll S. E., & Lilly, S. (1993). Resource Conservation as a Strategy for community psychology. *Journal of Community Psychology*, 21, 128-148.

Hobfoll, S. E., Ritter, C., & Shoham, S. B. (1991). Women's satisfaction with social support and their receipt of aid. *Journal of Personality and Social Psychology*, 61, 332-341.

Hobfoll, S. E., Schwarzer, R., & Chon, K. (1996). Disentangling the stress labyrinth: Interpreting the meaning of the term stress as it is studied. *Japanese Health Psychology*, 4, 1-22.

Laible, D. J., Carlo, G., & Raffaelli, M. (2000). The differential relations of parent and peer attachment to adolescent adjustment. *Journal of Youth and Adolescence*, 29, 45-59.

Lane, C., & Hobfoll, S. E. (1992). How loss affects anger and alienates potential supporters. *Journal of Consulting and Clinical Psychology, 60*, 935-942.

Lazarus, R. S. (1991). *Emotion and adaptation.* New York: Oxford University Press.

Lazarus, R. S., & Folkman, S. (1984). *Stress, appraisal and coping.* New York: Springer.

Lohman, B. J., & Jarvis, P. A. (2000). Adolescent stressors, coping strategies, and psychological health studied in the family context. *Journal of Youth and Adolescence, 29*, 15-43.

Monnier, J., Stone, B. K., Hobfoll, S. E., & Johnson, R. J. (1998). How antisocial and prosocial coping influence the support process among men and women in the U.S. Postal Service. *Sex Roles: A Journal of Research, 39*, 1-20.

Natvig, G. K., Albrektsen, G., & Anderssen, N. (1999). School-related stress and psychosomatic symptoms among school adolescents. *The Journal of School Health, 69*, 362-8.

Parsons, A., Frydenberg, E., & Poole. C. (1996). Overachievement and coping strategies in adolescent males. *British Journal of Educational Psychology, 66*, 109-114.

Phillips, N. (2000, April). The development and application of the concept of resilience. *Australian Guidance and Counselling Association Newsletter, 1*, 8-14.

Prinz, B. L., Shermis, M. D., & Webb, P. M. (1999). Stress-buffering factors related to adolescent coping: A path analysis. *Adolescence, 34*, 715-734.

Resnick, M. D., Bearman, P. S., Blum, R. W., Bauman, K. E., Harris, K. M., Jones, J., Tabor, J., Beuhring, T., Sieving, R. S., Shew, M., Ireland, M., Bearinger, L. H., & Udry, J. R. (1997). Protecting adolescents from harm: Findings from the National Longitudinal Study on Adolescent Health. *Journal of the American Medical Association, 278*, 823-832.

Richman, J. M., Rosenfeld, L. B., & Bowen, G. L. (1998). Social support for adolescents at risk of school failure. *Social Work, 43*, 309-324.

Shatte, A. J., Reivich, K., Gillham, J. E., & Seligman, M. E. P. (1999). Learned optimism in children. In C. R. Snyder (Ed.), *Coping: The psychology of what works* (pp. 165-179). New York: Oxford University Press.

Shmotkin, D., Lomranz, J., Eyal, M., & Zemach, M. (1999). The contribution of personal resources to physical and mental health: Looking into age and gender effects. *Genetic, Social, and General Psychology Monographs, 125*, 5-26.

Shochet, I., & Osgarby, S. (1999). The Resourceful Adolescent Project: Building psychological resilience in adolescents and their parents. *The Australian Educational and Developmental Psychologist, 16*, 46-65.

Sim, H. (2000). Relationship of daily hassles and social support to depression and antisocial behavior among early adolescents. *Journal of Youth and Adolescence, 29*, 647-660.

Snyder, C. R., & Dinoff, B. L. (1999). Coping: Where have you been? In C. R. Snyder (Ed.), *Coping: The psychology of what works* (pp. 3-16). New York: Oxford University Press.

Taris, T. W. (1999). The mutual effects between job resources and mental health: A prospective study among Dutch youth. *Genetic, Social, and General Psychology Monographs, 125*, 433-450.

Van Beest, M., & Baerveldt, C. (1999). The relationship between adolescents' social support from parents and from peers. *Adolescence*, *34*, 193-202.

Vandervoort, D. (1999). Quality of social support in mental and physical health. *Current Psychology*, *18*, 205-222.

Victorian Suicide Prevention Task Force. (1997). *Suicide prevention task force report*, Melbourne, Australia: Victorian Government.

Wells, J. D., Hobfoll, S. E., & Lavin, J. (1999). When it rains, it pours: The greater impact of resource loss compared to gain on psychological distress. *Personality and Social Psychology Bulletin*, *25*, 1172-1182.

CHAPTER 5

ANXIETY IN CHILDHOOD

How Do Children Cope?

Barbara Jones and Erica Frydenberg
University of Melbourne, Australia

ABSTRACT

Anxiety experienced by children is real, frightening, and often debilitating. The behavior of anxious children can be mistakenly seen as disruptive, attention seeking, and manipulative. Anxiety during development is normal, however for some children anxiety can become so severe that they may be at risk of developing anxiety disorders. Early identification of children who are at risk of developing anxiety disorders is imperative so that they can be taught how to cope effectively with anxious thoughts and feelings that interfere with their daily functioning. In this chapter the nature of childhood anxiety is examined with a particular focus on the traditionally recognized trait anxiety, which refers to a predisposition to respond to threatening stimuli in a certain way; and a recently recognized construct, anxiety sensitivity which is essentially the fear of anxiety-related bodily sensations. Evidence in the research literature indicates that adults with a high level of both trait anxiety and anxiety sensitivity reported a significantly higher incidence of anxiety disorders. Based on these findings a recent study was conducted to determine whether the same may be the case for

Thriving, Surviving, or Going Under: Coping with Everyday Lives, 109–133

children. Results of the study are reported in this chapter. Furthermore, how children cope with anxiety is discussed and ways of encouraging children to adopt effective coping strategies to manage their anxiety are also outlined.

> *I have often thought that few people know what secrecy there is in the young under terror. No matter how unreasonable the terror so that it be terror.*
>
> —Pip (Great Expectations)

INTRODUCTION

Anxiety in children at particular times during development is normal, however, some children experience anxiety so severe that it interferes with their day-to-day functioning and psychosocial development (Fonseca & Perrin, 2001). If severe anxiety is left untreated a significant proportion of children will face long-term impairment and may develop an anxiety disorder (Dadds, Spence, Holland, Barrett, & Laurens, 1997). The characteristic features of anxiety disorders are intense feelings of anxiety and avoidance of situations that are likely to bring on these feelings (American Psychiatric Association, 1994). Anxiety disorders are the most common childhood emotional disorders (Spence & Dadds, 1996) and include separation anxiety, social anxiety, generalized anxiety disorder, obsessive compulsive disorder, panic disorder, agoraphobia, and posttraumatic stress disorder (American Psychiatric Association, 1994). Depression, which is often a reaction to severe anxiety, is frequently reported by young people. In two thirds of major depressive disorder cases, anxiety was recorded as having preceded the depression (Kovacs, Gatsonia, Paulauskas, & Richards, 1989). Children who are anxious are more likely to develop depression than children who are not anxious, and as adolescents are more likely to become involved in substance abuse (Dacey & Fiore, 2000).

Prevalence rates for anxiety disorders in children are between 2.5% and 9% in the general population and between 20% and 30% among clinically referred children (Anderson, 1994; March, 1995). Therefore it is likely that teachers will have children in their classroom who experience severe anxiety and who may be at risk of developing anxiety disorders. Girls are at a slightly higher risk of developing anxiety disorders than boys (Anderson, 1994; Verhulst, 2001); and anxiety disorders are more prevalent in older than younger children (Verhulst, 2001). It is also recognized that anxiety disorders in adults have their genesis in childhood (Mattison, 1992; Rapee & Barlow, 1993; Spence, 1996).

Anxiety disorders in children can be treated. An age-appropriate cognitive behavioral therapeutic approach has been found to be extremely effective and is most often used in treating anxiety disorders in children (Rapee, Wignall, Hudson & Schniering, 2000). If children who experience a high level of anxiety—those who may be "drowning in anxiety"—those who are at risk of developing an anxiety disorder are identified, they can be taught to cope effectively with their anxious thoughts and feelings, and to cope effectively when they are in anxiety provoking situations using this approach (Dacey & Fiore, 2000). It is also important for parents, teachers, and health professionals to be educated and informed about the factors which contribute to high levels of anxiety so that intervention is provided at the earliest possible time to avoid the onset of a more disabling anxiety disorder.

In this chapter the nature of childhood anxiety is examined with a particular focus on two anxiety constructs—the traditionally recognized trait anxiety which refers to an individual's predisposition to respond or react to threatening stimuli in a particular way (Spielberger, 1966), and a recently recognized construct, anxiety sensitivity. Anxiety sensitivity is essentially the fear of anxiety-related bodily sensations and is based on beliefs that anxiety symptoms have harmful consequences; that anxiety symptoms cause illness, embarrassment, and additional anxiety which increases worry about becoming more anxious (Reiss & McNally, 1985). It has been found that a high level of both trait anxiety and anxiety sensitivity result in more anxiety symptoms in children and therefore may act as a predictor of the development of anxiety disorders in childhood and adolescence (Jones & Frydenberg, 2003).

How anxious children cope with the anxiety experience and associated symptoms varies. Children who report a high level of anxiety commonly use nonproductive coping strategies (Dacey & Fiore, 2000). However, if given the opportunity to learn about and understand their own coping, children can expand their repertoire of coping strategies and as a consequence cope more effectively with their anxiety (Frydenberg, 1997). The coping strategies utilized by children who experience a high level of anxiety are examined in this chapter and ways of encouraging anxious children to adopt more effective coping strategies to deal with their anxiety are outlined.

Having an understanding of the factors involved in the anxiety process, as well as understanding how trait anxiety and anxiety sensitivity contribute to the development of anxiety disorders, is useful when trying to identify children at risk. Furthermore, the fact that children cope with their anxiety in various ways is an important consideration in the treatment of anxious children and essential to the development of anxiety management and coping skills programs for children.

ANXIETY—THE PROCESS

Anxiety is "the tense anticipation of a threatening but vague event, a feeling of uneasy suspense" (Rachman, 1998, p. 2). Anxiety is described as being diffuse, objectless, unpleasant, persistent, and pervasive and anxious individuals often have difficulty in identifying the cause of their anxiety (Rachman, 1998; Sheehan, 1983). Anxiety includes a cognitive, physiological, and behavioral component.

A cognitive appraisal process commences when potentially threatening information is perceived. The potential consequences of the imminent event are evaluated (Lazarus, 1966); straight away the physiological component or the "fight or flight" response (a response triggered by the nervous system to suppress feelings of anxiety to protect the individual) is activated. Hormones are released into, and circulated by the bloodstream to increase heart rate and respiratory action and to inhibit digestion, salivation, and muscle tension. Such activation allows for an increase in an individual's strength and endurance to physically deal with the threat (Kleinknecht, 1991). The behavioral component involves observable physical responses such as attempts to avoid or to escape the threatening situation. If escape or avoidance is not possible then the anxiety may manifest as trembling, shaky, or stammering speech, sweating, restlessness, or agitation (Kleinknecht, 1991). To some extent these three components act independently, although they do interact with one another during an anxiety-provoking situation, although the portion of each of the three components may vary relative to the situation (Kleinknecht, 1991).

Anxiety is a necessary and normal part of life. However, some individuals experience responses such as those described above, when there is no apparent evidence of real threat or danger; the anxiety can become pathological and typically prevents the individual from functioning normally. In some cases an anxiety disorder develops whereby distressing symptoms that have severe anxiety as a dominant disturbance manifest as a high level of negative affect, a frightening physiological response, a sense of uncontrollability, hypervigilance, and an inability to concentrate (Rosen & Schulkin, 1998). As a result of the distressing anxiety symptoms, depression often develops (Kovacs et al., 1989; Rapee & Barlow, 1993).

An anxiety disorder is a function of biological, psychological, and environmental factors (Nelles & Barlow, 1988; Spence, 1996). Biological factors refer to a genetic predisposition to developing an anxiety disorder. Inherited personality and temperament characteristics affect biological processes in the brain associated with adrenaline levels and fear circuits (Dacey & Fiore, 2000; Rosen & Schulkin, 1998). Psychological factors include anxiety sensitivity, which is basically the fear of anxiety symptoms

(Reiss & McNally, 1985); distorted or faulty cognitions, whereby an individual misinterprets bodily sensations associated with anxiety; as well as factors associated with learning processes through which an individual acquires anxiety as a result of conditioning (Kendall, 1994; Rachman, 1998). Environmental factors include parenting styles, parental conflict, separation or divorce, death in the family, family size, socioeconomic status, and parental psychopathology (Spence, 1996).

Trait Anxiety

Trait anxiety is an acquired disposition that predisposes an individual to respond or react to threatening stimuli in a particular way (Spielberger, 1966). Generally, individuals with high trait anxiety perceive the environment as more dangerous or threatening, and experience anxiety in a range of situations with more intense levels of anxiety, usually disproportionate in intensity to the magnitude of the objective danger than individuals experience who have low trait anxiety (Rachman, 1998; Spielberger, 1966). Children with high trait anxiety are constantly alert to anticipated danger, they focus excessively on negative outcomes that may occur, experience somatic complaints, and tend to avoid threatening situations (Dacey & Friore, 2000; Rapee et al., 2000).

Anxiety Sensitivity

Anxiety sensitivity is a recently identified construct that has become part of the conceptualization of anxiety. Anxiety sensitivity is essentially the fear of anxiety symptoms based on beliefs that the symptoms have harmful consequences, that the anxiety symptoms cause illness, embarrassment, and additional anxiety, which increases worry about becoming more anxious (Reiss & McNally, 1985). For example, a child with high trait anxiety who hears noises in the house at night will react with intense anxiety. As part of the anxiety process the child will experience a physiological reaction that may manifest as palpitations, breathlessness, sweating, feeling hot or dizzy, and so forth. The physiological reactions are unpleasant for the child, but will pass. However, if the child also has high anxiety sensitivity a cognitive reaction to the physiological symptoms will occur. The child's anxiety is heightened as he/she believes that he/she will stop breathing, that there is something wrong with his/her heart, that he/she is going to faint or is extremely ill, which intensifies the anxiety and prolongs the reaction. The physiological reactions become the anxiety provoking stimuli.

EMPIRICAL RESEARCH—ANXIETY

Anxiety is the most frequently reported type of psychopathology across the child and adolescent lifespan and although the prevalence of any anxiety symptom is constant, how the anxiety manifests varies with age (Kashani & Orvaschel, 1990) (e.g., an individual experiencing separation anxiety in childhood may experience panic disorder as an adult). There is an abundance of evidence in the research literature describing the problems children experience as a result of elevated anxiety. Children who experience nightmares have a significantly higher level of anxiety than children who do not, and there is also a relationship between nightmare distress and trait anxiety (Mindell & Barrett, 2002). High trait anxiety has been found to be associated with higher levels of negative self-talk (Lodge, Harte, & Tripp, 1998); and performance during experimental tasks (Gaskell, Walls, & Calam, 2001). Children with a high level of anxiety are more fearful of failure and criticism than children with low anxiety (King, Gullone, & Ollendick, 1992); high anxiety is significantly associated with lower academic achievement (Ialongo, Edelsohn, Werthamer-Larsson, Crockett, & Kellam, 1994); and conduct problems have been found to be positively associated with trait anxiety (Frick, Lilienfeld, Ellis, Loney, & Silverthorn, 1999).

To date most of the research relating to anxiety sensitivity has focused on anxiety sensitivity as a contributing factor to the development of anxiety disorders in adults although it is proposed in the literature that anxiety disorders in adults have their genesis in childhood (Mattison, 1992; Rapee & Barlow, 1993; Spence, 1966). Anxiety sensitivity is an important measure for investigating the development of anxiety disorders in children (Weems, Hammond-Laurence, Silverman, & Ginsburg, 1998). Minimal research has been undertaken on anxiety sensitivity in children however consistent with research findings in relation to adults anxiety sensitivity distinguishes children with anxiety disorders from children with no anxiety disorders (Silverman & Weems, 1999). It was found among clinical samples that anxiety sensitivity was higher for children with anxiety diagnoses compared to children with externalizing disorder diagnoses (Rabin, Peterson, Richters, & Jensen, 1993) and children who did not meet diagnostic criteria for a psychological disorder (Vasey, Daleiden, Williams, & Brown, 1995). Furthermore anxiety sensitivity distinguished children meeting the criteria for panic disorder from children with other anxiety disorders (Kearney, Albano, Eisin, Allan, & Barlow, 1997; Lau, Calamari, & Waraczynski, 1996) indicating that anxiety sensitivity is higher in the children who have panic disorder. Furthermore in a study of adolescents a significant relationship between anxiety sensitivity and symptoms associated with panic disorder and agoraphobia, as well as depression was found (Muris, Schmidt, Merckelbach, & Schouten, 2001).

Anxiety is a process influenced by various factors, however, two constructs that appear to underlie the development of anxiety symptoms are trait anxiety and anxiety sensitivity. There is evidence to suggest that there is a relationship between both forms of anxiety and the number of anxiety symptoms experienced by children.

Coping is also a process influenced by various factors. In the management of anxiety in children the utilization of effective coping strategies is extremely important.

COPING

Coping is a dynamic process whereby cognitive and behavioral strategies are utilized to deal with everyday demands (Frydenberg, 1997). Furthermore, it is a process used by individuals to manage specific external or internal demands that are appraised as taxing or exceeding their personal environmental resources (Lazarus & Folkman, 1984). Coping is influenced not only by the objective and perceived nature of the situation but also by individual differences in gender, socioeconomic states, ethnicity, anxiety, depression, and self-efficacy (Frydenberg & Lewis, 1993a; Lazarus & Folkman, 1984; Zeidner, 1994).

In order to understand children's coping resources, it is also important to consider the level of dependence that the child has on adults for survival (Leiderman, 1983), the developmental stage of the child and the relationship between the child's social context and environment (Compas, 1987). Children's health and emotional well-being are strongly influenced by the degree of exposure to stress and their ability to cope with stress (Compas, Connor-Smith, Saltzman, Thomsen, & Wadsworth, 2001). The ability to cope depends on a child's psychological and biological preparedness to respond to stress (Compas, 1987) (e.g., temperament) as well as cognitive and social factors, such as self-perception, self-efficacy, self-control, attributions of cause, friendships, and parental relationships (Bandura, 1981; Compas, 1987; Harter, 1983; Macoby, 1983; Ruble & Rholes, 1981).

Individuals use two major coping styles, problem-focused coping and emotion-focused coping. Problem-focused coping is concerned with task orientation and changing the unstable relationship between the person and the environment. Ideally to manage a problem, the problem is defined, alternative solutions are generated and weighted in terms of their costs and benefits, the best solution is selected, and finally action is taken to deal with the problem (Endler & Parker, 1990; Lazarus & Folkman, 1984). Emotion-focused coping is person oriented and is concerned with changing the meaning of the situation and lessening emotional distress (Endler & Parker, 1990; Folkman & Lazarus, 1985). Emotion-focused coping dominates when a stressful situation is appraised as unmanageable and difficult to change while problem-focused coping dominates when a stressful situation is appraised as controllable by action (Lazarus, 1990).

Recognizing this dichotomy researchers have described these coping styles in many different ways, "productive/nonproductive" (Frydenberg & Lewis, 1991), "approach/avoid" (Suls & Fletcher, 1986), and "primary control/secondary control" (Band & Weisz, 1988). Different terms are used and different aspects are emphasized, but the common theme of either addressing or avoiding the stressors prevails.

When children believe that they can deal with the stressor they will use problem-focused coping (productive, approach, or primary control coping). Alternatively, when children perceive that the stressor will be enduring, emotion-focused coping (nonproductive, avoidance, and secondary control coping) will predominate (Boekaerts, 1996).

Children use a wide range of coping responses; they use different coping responses for different domains; and the coping responses can be grouped into coping strategies that are relatively stable over time. The most salient coping strategies are a form of active coping such as danger control and seeking social support, as well as various forms of internal coping such as planned problem solving, active and passive distraction. The least salient coping strategies are self-destruction, aggression, withdrawal, relaxation, and anxiety control, such as controlling one's breathing (Boekaerts, 1996)

In this chapter the terms "problem-focused coping" and "emotion-focused coping" will be used to describe the dichotomous coping styles when reviewing empirical research.

EMPIRICAL RESEARCH—COPING

Children were asked to recall stressful episodes in different situations (e.g., separation, medical stress, and school failure) and describe how they responded in each instance (Band & Weisz, 1988). Generally, children coped with everyday stress, however, children's coping style was influenced by situational constraints (controllable situations versus less familiar situations) and cognitive development. With regard to stress associated with school failure, children reported high levels of problem-focused coping, while with medical stress children reported high levels of emotion-focused coping (Band & Weisz, 1988). In a similar study, Brown (2000) explored children's coping with situational stressors in relation to parents/

family, siblings, or peer/interpersonal. Children's patterns of coping depended on the situation. Although problem-focused coping was most frequently used, children also used strategies associated with emotion-focused coping, particularly wishful thinking and emotional regulation.

In relation to postwar stress, children's coping behaviors were examined during a scud missile attack which occurred in the Persian Gulf War. Contrary to expectations, emotion-focused coping in this rare and unusual situation such as avoidance and distraction strategies were found to be associated with less postwar stress reactions than problem-oriented strategies (Bar-Ilan, 1993). In a study that focused on coping and anxiety Muris, Merkelbach, Gadet, and Meesters (2000) investigated the relationship between monitoring, a problem-focused coping strategy according to Suls and Fletcher (1986), anxiety disorder symptoms, and trait anxiety in a group of nonreferred children. Monitoring refers to the extent to which an individual scans for or attends to threatening information. A significant positive relationship was found between monitoring and anxiety disorder symptoms as well as between monitoring and trait anxiety. As monitoring is viewed as a problem-focused coping strategy, the high level of anxiety disorder symptoms in high monitors seems anomalous. However, as has already been noted, anxious children are particularly vigilant.

The examples of children's coping as outlined above illustrate that although the problem-focused/emotion-focused dichotomy dominates there does not appear to be universally consistent outcomes. Like all things involving individuals the issues are both complex and demanding of further investigation. When an individual is confronted with stressful circumstances coping processes are adopted to manage the situation "there may be no universally good or bad coping processes, though some might often be better or worse than others" (Lazarus, 1990, p. 235)

A common theme apparent in each of the studies described above indicates that most children make an effort to cope regardless of the stressors they are confronted with. Furthermore, even though biological, psychological, and developmental factors affect the acquisition of coping resources, it is reassuring to know that children make attempts to cope rather than relinquish control of the situation by surrendering, or simply not coping effectively.

GENDER DIFFERENCES—ANXIETY AND COPING

For children in the general population, girls are at a higher risk of developing an anxiety disorder than boys (Anderson, 1994; Verhulst, 2001) and for girls with both anxiety and depression in childhood there is an increased risk of adolescent anxiety disorders (March, 1995). Anxiety disorders are more common in girls than boys (Rapee et al., 2000) and are reported approximately four times more frequently (Fergusson, Horwood, & Lynskey, 1993). However, with regard to specific diagnoses gender differences seem to evaporate except for global measures of "any anxiety disorder" (March, 1995). In an attempt to explain the gender difference it has been suggested that when being evaluated for anxiety, girls are more open about their anxiety than boys and girls are more aware of their feelings than boys (Dacey & Fiore, 2000). In relation to anxiety sensitivity in children, girls reported a higher level than boys (Rabin et al., 1993; Silverman, Fleisig, Rabin, & Peterson, 1991).

With regard to coping "Boys turn to sport, girls turn to others" (Frydenberg & Lewis, 1993a, p. 253). The title of the paper reflects the findings on adolescent coping that at least in the Australian context boys are more private in that they keep their concerns to themselves, ignore the problem, and are more involved in physical recreation than girls, while girls use social support, tension reduction, self-blame and worry more than boys (Frydenberg & Lewis, 1991).

Minimal information has been reported on gender differences in children's coping. In examining coping efficacy in a medical situation it was revealed that boys and girls were equally likely to cope effectively at ages 6 and 9 years however at age 12 years efficacy in coping for girls was significantly greater than that of boys (Band & Weisz, 1988). Seeking social support protected victimized girls from social problems but was associated with lower peer preference for victimized boys (Kochenderfer-Ladd, 2002). Girls reported higher levels of the monitoring coping strategy than boys in a study investigating the relationship between monitoring coping style and anxiety disorder symptoms (Muris et al., 2000).

AGE DIFFERENCES—ANXIETY AND COPING

Age affects children's anxiety patterns (Dacey & Fiore, 2000). Children aged 6 to 7 years are typically anxious about loud noises, supernatural beings, being separated from parents, being alone at night, going to school, or being physically harmed or rejected by specific individuals at school. Children aged 7 to 8 years are anxious about the dark and real life catastrophes suggested by television, movies, and books. For children in this age group, not being liked, being late for school, or left out of school take on a greater focus. Also, fear of physical harm or rejection by specific individuals at school become more prevalent. Children aged 9 to 11 years become anxious about personal humiliation, failure in school, play, or sports, being the victim of physical violence, parents fighting, parents separating, being hurt, or becoming sick, specific animals, heights, and sinister people. Between the age of 11 to 13 years children become anxious about failure in school, sports or social popularity, looking and acting "strange," death or life-threatening illness or disease, sex (attracting or repelling others or being attacked) and fear of losing possessions or being robbed (Dacey & Fiore, 2000).

Age-related anxiety patterns are linked to children's cognitive development. Children's cognitive abilities proceed from a vague to a specific awareness of their environment until early adolescence when concrete thinking is replaced by the capacity for more abstract thought. As children's thinking develops they are able to anticipate the future and deal with increasingly complex tasks including being able to imagine the possibility of unpleasant events. It is at this stage that normal fears become associated with exaggerated expectations (Dacey & Fiore, 2000). Hence some children become progressively more anxious as they approach adolescence and it seems that age may only differentiate children with regard to causes of anxiety such as loud noises or separation from parents. There is minimal information available with regard to age differences in relation to anxiety sensitivity but one study by Weems et al. (1998) found no significant difference between age groups.

With regard to age differences in coping there is evidence to suggest that problem-focused coping decreased as age increased (Compas, Mcfarlane, & Fondarcaro, 1988; Frydenberg & Lewis, 1999) while emotion-focused coping increased with age as older adolescents used more tension-reduction strategies than younger adolescents (Compas et al. 1988; Frydenberg & Lewis, 1993b, 1999). Children between 6 and 12 years of age take account of situational constraints when selecting a coping strategy; older children were more aware than younger children that when avoidance is not possible, partial avoidance can be achieved; and as children get older they have more access to their own thoughts and strategies which can help them expand their repertoire of coping strategies (Altshuler & Ruble, 1989; Band & Weisz, 1988). As children develop cognitively and emotionally they learn to apply coping strategies differently to cope with different stressors.

In teaching children with heightened anxiety to cope effectively it is important to recognize coping as a "dual purpose" process. It is necessary to teach children how to cope effectively with anxiety and associated symptoms, just as it is necessary to teach children how to cope effectively with a threatening situation. As a result of an interaction between the duality it is likely that an anxious child would eventually develop effective coping strategies. Therefore, it is important that children with anxiety disorder symptoms understand their own coping and, be taught how to cope effectively with anxiety symptoms. As a result of being able to cope better with anxiety, young people's abilities to deal with everyday problems and stressors are also likely to improve.

The inclusion of an exemplar will illustrate how severe anxiety can develop into an anxiety disorder, how important it is for anyone involved with or working with children to understand the nature of anxiety in childhood, the importance of early identification and intervention for anxious children, and the importance of acknowledging the fact that for some children anxiety is debilitating rather than being part of a normal developmental stage.

AMY'S STORY—ANXIETY THROUGHOUT CHILDHOOD

Amy's anxious thoughts and feelings associated with a fear of death developed during her kindergarten year. These thoughts would come and go. Throughout her primary school years she would become extremely anxious when she heard about someone who had died. She often reported feeling like she was going to throw up at these times. A fear of contracting a serious illness also developed which caused her considerable distress and extreme anxiety. She required constant reassurance that she was healthy.

In her final year of primary school Amy became anxious about her parents and was convinced that something terrible would happen to them when they went out. She experienced severe anxiety symptoms such as shortness of breath, racing heart, a choking feeling in her throat to the extent that she was unable to swallow her food; she often felt dizzy, hot and shaky, and thought that she was going crazy. She also experienced disturbed sleep as she became anxious about the anxiety symptoms and believed that the anxiety symptoms would cause her death. A psychologist informed Amy's parents that she was suffering from separation anxiety and that her behavior maybe somewhat manipulative. Strategies for dealing with her behavior were recommended to her parents and Amy was instructed to challenge her anxious thoughts and to try and control her anxiety.

Amy became withdrawn and isolated herself from her friends. Between the age of 11 and 13 years medical opinion was often sought about her many physical complaints but she was always given the all clear. In her second year of high school Amy began to have panic attacks and eventually developed agoraphobia. An opinion was sought from another psychologist who proposed Amy's anxiety was due to an extremely close relationship that she had with her parents, particularly her mother and that a change in family dynamic was necessary. Amy did not improve, her panic attacks became more severe and her agoraphobia prevented her from attending school.

A third psychologist acknowledged that Amy's anxiety was real and frightening and that Amy had developed panic disorder. Amy attended weekly sessions for one year. A cognitive behavioral therapeutic approach (combined with antidepressant medication early in the treatment) was adopted and proved to be effective in treating her panic disorder. Over time

Amy learned how to cope effectively with her anxiety and eventually made a good recovery.

When reflecting on Amy's story the following questions were raised: What distinguished Amy's anxiety from normal developmental anxiety? What factors associated with Amy's anxiety may have identified her as being at risk of developing an anxiety disorder? Would Amy have developed an anxiety disorder if there had been earlier recognition of possible predictors of anxiety disorders and early intervention implemented? If an effective treatment had been provided at the earliest possible time and she was taught effective coping strategies to deal with her anxiety and associated symptoms would an anxiety disorder have developed?

Early identification of children who are at risk of developing an anxiety disorder is imperative so that intervention can be implemented at the earliest possible time. A study recently undertaken by Jones and Frydenberg (2003) was concerned with identifying children who may be at risk of developing an anxiety disorder. This study was based on findings in the research literature in relation to anxiety disorders in adults. It has been found that adults who have a high level of anxiety sensitivity reported a significantly higher incidence of anxiety disorders (Silverman & Ginsburg, 1998). Furthermore, anxiety sensitivity is elevated across all anxiety disorders (e.g., Amundson, Norton, Lanthier, & Cox, 1996; Peterson & Reiss, 1987; Rapee, Ancis, & Barlow, 1988; Taylor, Koch, McNally, & Crockett, 1992; Telch, Lucas, & Nelson, 1989), except for phobias (Rachman, 1998). Participants in the all of the above mentioned studies also reported high trait anxiety.

The primary aim of the study by Jones and Frydenberg (2003), and reported again here to demonstrate the nature of anxiety in children, was to determine whether children with high levels of both trait anxiety and anxiety sensitivity manifested more anxiety symptoms and were therefore at a greater risk of developing anxiety disorders than others. Also, acknowledging the fact that children who report a high level of anxiety do not use effective coping strategies (Dacey & Fiore, 2000), a key aspect of the Jones and Frydenberg study was to examine the coping strategies used by children who reported experiencing a high level of either trait anxiety or anxiety sensitivity or both, and to compare their use of coping strategies to children who did not report a high level of either trait anxiety or anxiety sensitivity.

THE STUDY

Trait anxiety, anxiety sensitivity, anxiety symptoms, and coping were measured in a study designed to identify those children who reported experiencing both high trait anxiety and high anxiety sensitivity. The coping strategies of children who reported high levels on the anxiety measures were compared to the coping strategies of children who did not report high levels on the anxiety measures.

Participants

Participants included 455 primary school children (241 males and 214 females) from 27 primary school located in metropolitan, regional, and country areas of Victoria, Australia. The mean age of the children was 9.68 years ($SD = 1.23$).

Measures

The A-Trait scale of the State-Trait Anxiety Inventory for Children (STAIC) (Spielberger, 1973) includes 20 item statements that ask children how they generally feel and measures children's tendency to experience anxiety on a three-point scale (1 = hardly ever, 2 = sometimes, 3 = often). Trait anxiety scores range from a minimum of 20 to a maximum of 60 with higher scores reflecting higher levels of trait anxiety.

The Childhood Anxiety Sensitivity Index (CASI) (Silverman, Fleisig, Rabin, & Peterson, 1991) is an 18-item, self-rating scale which requires children to rate their fear of anxiety related sensations on a three-point scale (1 = none, 2 = some, 3 = a lot). The total score ranges from 18 to 54 with higher scores reflecting high levels of anxiety sensitivity.

The Anxiety Symptoms Checklist for Children (ASCC) is a 26-item checklist of anxiety symptoms adapted for use with children from the Sheehan Patient Rated Anxiety Scale (Sheehan, 1983). Anxiety symptoms are measured on a three-point scale (1 = never, 2 = sometimes, 3 = a lot). The range for this checklist is 26 to 78 with higher scores reflecting a greater number of anxiety symptoms.

Coping styles and strategies were measured using the Coping Scale for Children–General Form adapted as a children's version of the Adolescent Coping Scale (Frydenberg & Lewis, 1993) (see Chapter 8, this volume). The CSC–G is a self-report inventory comprising 79 items (78 structured and one open-ended question) which reliably assess 18 conceptually and empirically distinct coping strategies which are included in three coping styles. The three coping styles are: solving the problem, reference to others, and nonproductive coping. Each item asks children to describe how they cope in general circumstances and rate how often the response is used on a three-point scale (1 = never, 2 = sometimes, 3 = a lot). Some examples of items are "I talk to others to see what they would do," "I cry and scream," and "I just give up." Scores for coping styles and strategies are derived by summing relevant items.

Procedure

The purpose of the research, the data collection procedure, and issues of confidentiality were explained to the children. Questionnaires were administered to children in a group and took approximately 30 minutes to complete.

Results

Anxiety

Of the 455 primary school children who participated in the study, 280 (62%) children did not report a high level of anxiety sensitivity or trait anxiety (NOTHIGH group). However, 78 (17%) children reported high anxiety sensitivity together with high trait anxiety (HASHTA group); 42 (9%) reported a high level of anxiety sensitivity only (HAS group); and 50 (11%) reported a high level of trait anxiety only (HTA group).

As expected the children who reported a high level of both anxiety sensitivity and trait anxiety (HASHTA), or reported a high level of either anxiety sensitivity only (HAS) or trait anxiety only (HTA) reported more anxiety symptoms than children who did not report a high level on either anxiety sensitivity or trait anxiety (NOTHIGH). Furthermore, the high anxiety sensitivity and high trait anxiety children reported more anxiety symptoms than the high anxiety sensitivity only children and the high trait anxiety only children.

Anxiety—Gender and Age Differences.   Generally, girls reported significantly more anxiety sensitivity and trait anxiety than boys. In relation to age differences, there was a significant age difference on each of the anxiety measures in the not high on trait anxiety and anxiety sensitivity group only. Children aged 8 and 9 years reported significantly more trait anxiety, anxiety sensitivity, and anxiety symptoms than children aged 11 and 12 years. However, age did not appear to be a discriminating factor for children in the high anxiety sensitivity and high trait anxiety, high anxiety sensitivity only or high trait anxiety only groups.

Anxiety Sensitivity and Trait Anxiety as Predictors of Anxiety Symptoms.
A statistical analysis determined that anxiety sensitivity and trait anxiety combined explained 46.5% of the variability in anxiety symptoms. Separately, anxiety sensitivity explained 39% and trait anxiety explained 41% of the variability in anxiety sensitivity.

Coping

In relation to coping styles, results revealed that the children in the high anxiety sensitivity and high trait anxiety group used significantly more nonproductive coping and significantly more reference to others coping than the children in the not high on trait anxiety and anxiety symptoms group. There was no significant difference between the groups on solve the problem coping style.

With regard to coping strategies, results revealed that there was a significant difference between the not high on trait anxiety and anxiety sensitivity group and the high anxiety sensitivity and high trait anxiety, high anxiety sensitivity only and high trait anxiety only groups on 13 of the 18 coping strategies (see Table 5.1).

Table 5.1   Group Differences on Coping Strategies and Coping Styles

Coping Strategies	F Value (3,451)	Group Differences
Worry	28.503**	1 < 2, 3 & 4; 2 > 3
Invest in close friends	4.448*	1 > 4
Seek to belong	3.023*	1 < 2
Wishful thinking	10.022**	1 < 2
Not cope	12.155**	1 < 2; 2 > 3 & 4
Tension reduction	9.722**	1 < 2 & 4
Social action	2.909*	1 < 3
Self blame	22.640**	1 < 2, 3 & 4
Keep to self	9.765**	1 < 2; 2 < 3
Seek spiritual support	6.538**	1 < 2
Focus on positive	2.683*	1 < 2
Seek professional help	3.802*	2 < 4
Physical recreation	4.135**	1 > 4
Coping Styles		
Reference to others	4.860*	1 < 2
Nonproductive coping	7.778**	1 < 2; 2 > 4

1 = NOTHIGH group; 2 = HASHTA group; 3 = HAS group; 4 = HTA group.
Group differences significant at .05 level.
*p < .05. **p < .01.

Coping—Gender and Age Differences.   There was no significant gender difference between and within the groups—not high on trait anxiety and anxiety sensitivity, high anxiety sensitivity and high trait anxiety, high anxiety sensitivity only, and high trait anxiety only groups on coping styles. In relation to coping strategies there was a significant gender difference on six coping strategies in the not high on trait anxiety and anxiety sensitivity group only. Girls used more seek social support and social action than boys; and boys used more ignore the problem, keep to self, seek relaxation diversion, and physical recreation than girls. Gender did not appear to be a discriminating factor in the use of coping strategies in the high anxiety sensitivity and high trait anxiety, high anxiety sensitivity only and high trait anxiety only groups.

No significant age difference was found between and within the groups on coping styles. However, a significant age difference was found in the not high on trait anxiety and anxiety symptoms group in relation to the coping strategies with younger children using more seek social support, worry, seek to belong, social action, self-blame, seek spiritual support, focus on the positive, and seek professional help than older children. A significant age difference was also found in the high anxiety sensitivity and high trait anxiety group in relation to some of the coping strategies with younger children using more seeking social support, focus on solving the problem, social action, keep to self and seek relaxation diversions than older children. There was no significant age difference in relation to the use of coping strategies in the high anxiety sensitivity only and high trait anxiety only group.

DISCUSSION

Children who reported a high level of either anxiety sensitivity or trait anxiety, or both anxiety sensitivity and trait anxiety reported a significantly greater number of anxiety symptoms than the children who did not report a high level on one or both of the anxiety measures. The anxiety symptoms reported by children with heightened anxiety included sleeping difficulties (i.e., trouble getting to sleep and waking during the night), feelings of tiredness, weakness, dizziness, and shakiness. It seems that high anxiety in any form can produce anxiety symptoms that are problematic and are likely to interfere with children's normal functioning. However, the children who reported a high level of both anxiety sensitivity and trait anxiety reported significantly more anxiety symptoms related to bodily sensations such as increased heart rate, headaches, nausea, as well as more concentration difficulties and worrying thoughts than any of the other children.

The constructs of anxiety sensitivity and trait anxiety combined predicted more anxiety symptoms than the number of anxiety symptoms predicted by anxiety sensitivity and trait anxiety separately.

There is a unique constellation of symptoms predicted by the combined anxiety constructs when compared with the anxiety constructs separately. Of particular interest is the fact that symptoms concerned with anxiety-related bodily sensations were predicted by anxiety sensitivity and trait anxiety combined and also by anxiety sensitivity only. Further investigation of the anxiety constructs is required to determine how reliable they are as predictors for developing anxiety disorders. However, the evidence to date is a guide to the importance of the anxiety sensitivity as a separate and important factor when examining the nature of anxiety in children.

When comparing the coping strategies used by the children who reported heightened anxiety to those children who did not report heightened anxiety there were significant differences between the groups in the use of coping styles and strategies. The children in the not high on trait anxiety and anxiety sensitivity group used significantly less reference to others coping and significantly less nonproductive coping than the children in the high anxiety groups. Significant differences were particularly evident between the not high on trait anxiety and anxiety sensitivity group and the high anxiety sensitivity and high trait anxiety group in relation to coping strategies. Children who reported both high anxiety sensitivity and trait anxiety used significantly more worry, seek to belong, wishful thinking, not cope, tension reduction, self-blame, keep to self, and seek spiritual support than children who did not report a high level on the two anxiety measures.

Age did not discriminate children in the high anxiety groups however in the not high on trait anxiety and anxiety sensitivity group younger children reported higher levels on each of the anxiety measures which may be associated with the anxiety patterns and cognitive development as suggested by Dacey and Fiore (2000). Gender did not appear to be a discriminating factor in the use of coping styles and strategies in the high anxiety groups. In the not high on trait anxiety and anxiety sensitivity group results were consistent with previous research, in that girls reported significantly more anxiety than boys (e.g., Anderson, 1994; Verhulst, 2001). With regard to coping, results indicate that the trend is similar to that found in the adolescent population that "boys turn to sport, girls turn to others" (Frydenberg & Lewis, 1993a, p. 253).

It is important to be mindful of the fact that the results of the present study (Jones & Frydenberg, 2003) relied completely on children's self-report of anxiety sensitivity, trait anxiety, anxiety symptoms, and coping. To determine whether a child meets the criteria for an anxiety disorder a thorough clinical interview should be undertaken with the child and his/

her parents. Accepting the limitations of the study it is reasonable to assert that together, anxiety sensitivity and trait anxiety could be used as a screen for identifying children who are experiencing a significant number of anxiety symptoms and are therefore at risk for developing anxiety disorders in childhood, adolescence, and adulthood.

The results of the present study also revealed that young children with heightened anxiety use coping strategies associated with a nonproductive coping style; thus it seems that children's coping is influenced by anxiety and in turn influences anxiety. Therefore it is important that anxious children are taught effective coping strategies to deal with their anxious feelings and thoughts to empower them with the skills and motivation to cope productively and effectively. The findings of the study have implications for parents, teachers, and other individuals who work with children.

IMPLICATIONS

Most children at some stage during their development become distressed at times of separation from their parents or due to a fear of the dark, fear of storms, animals, strangers, or similar concerns. If a child is predisposed to a high level of trait anxiety and/or has a high level of anxiety sensitivity then the anxiety experience will be of a greater magnitude than for other children. Anxiety experienced by a child is real, frightening and often debilitating. Anxiety symptoms can be mistakenly seen as disruptive, attention seeking, and manipulative behavior. Of paramount importance to an anxious child is reassurance and understanding, but most of all it is important that their anxiety is taken seriously. It is likely that most parents and teachers have been in a situation when a child they care for has expressed fear and worry about an anxiety-provoking situation or threatening circumstance. In most cases a parent or teacher's response may have been something like, "there's no need to worry," "don't be silly," "there's nothing to be afraid of," "you'll be OK." For children who are not highly anxious, reassurance such as this will help them cope with the threatening stimuli. However, for a highly anxious child, particularly a child who has high trait anxiety and high anxiety sensitivity such a response will make them feel inadequate, weak, and cowardly. The feelings associated with the response are often internalized and over time will have a detrimental affect on a child's self-esteem, self-confidence, self-efficacy, and sense of adequacy, and of course will eventually impact on their emotional well-being as anxiety symptoms increase. Therefore, it is vital for parents and teachers to be informed and educated about the nature of childhood anxiety so they can identify children who are predisposed to developing anxiety disorders and react to their behavior in an appropriate positive and constructive manner.

It is also essential for children to be educated and informed about the nature of anxiety, and to also be encouraged to accept their anxiety, that it is OK to be anxious; being anxious does not make them bad, or is not a sign of weakness, it is just how they are. Furthermore, children need to be taught how to cope effectively with their anxious thoughts and feelings and how to cope effectively with threatening situations. Parents and teachers also need to be aware of effective intervention strategies. Life for Amy may not have been so difficult if she had been educated about her anxiety and taught how to cope effectively with her anxious thoughts and feelings. Life may not have been so difficult for Amy if her parents, teachers, and health professionals had been educated about anxiety and had been alert to the predictors for developing an anxiety disorder.

Behavior therapy is an effective treatment for anxiety disorders particularly for young children where children are gradually exposed to the anxiety-provoking stimulus or situation while engaged in an incompatible response, usually relaxation or controlled breathing techniques. The gradual exposure is continued until the fear is extinguished. For older children a most effective approach is a cognitive behavioral therapeutic (CBT) approach which is designed to assist children to learn how their thoughts and feeling affect their behavior. Children can use the thoughts and feelings as cues for managing their anxiety and to help them cope more effectively with their anxiety. Sometimes, as was the case with Amy antidepressant medication may be required to lower the anxiety level and to reduce the associated depression before CBT can have a therapeutic effect. However, if a child at risk of developing an anxiety disorder is provided with intervention at the earliest possible time it is likely that medication will not be necessary.

As children become more able to deal with their anxiety and learn to take control of their anxiety, rather than allowing the anxiety to control them, they develop increased self-confidence and self-esteem which enables them to cope more effectively. In the case of children with both high anxiety sensitivity and high trait anxiety it would seem that such a task becomes two fold. Fortunately, the CBT approach can be applied to reduce levels of both forms of anxiety.

It is apparent that children with high trait anxiety and high anxiety sensitivity report a significantly greater number of anxiety symptoms and utilize more nonproductive coping strategies than other children. An intervention focusing on the development of productive coping strategies that act to reduce reliance on nonproductive coping strategies would be useful to anxious children. Such an intervention would assist anxious children in managing their anxiety and to cope generally in more effective and productive ways.

CONCLUSION

Anxiety is a process which includes a cognitive, physiological, and behavioral component and is a function of biological, psychological, and environmental factors. Anxious children cope in various ways, however, those children with heightened anxiety generally use nonproductive coping, therefore it is important to encourage them to adopt more effective copings strategies to deal with their anxiety.

Processes by which highly anxious children can be identified at an early age and information concerning the prevalence and nature of childhood anxiety, and information about the availability of treatment and resources for anxious children, their parents, and teachers needs to be disseminated throughout the community. With early diagnosis and intervention children can be relieved of debilitating anxiety. They will be given the opportunity to thrive!

REFERENCES

American Psychiatric Association. (1994). *Diagnostic and statistical manual of mental disorders* (4th ed.).Washington, DC: Author.

Amundson, G. J. G., Norton, G. R., Lanthier, N. J., & Cox, B. J. (1996). Fear of anxiety: Do current measures assess unique aspects of the construct? *Personality and Individual Differences, 20*, 607-612.

Anderson, J. C. (1994). Epidemiological issues. In T. H. Ollendick, N. J. King, & W. Yule (Eds.), *International handbook of phobic and anxiety disorders in children and adolescents* (pp. 43-66). New York: Plenum Press.

Altshuler, J. L., & Ruble, R. N. (1989). Developmental changes in children's awareness of strategies for coping with uncontrollable stress. *Child Development, 60*, 1337-1349.

Band, E. B., & Weisz, J. R. (1988). How to feel better when if feels bad: Children's perspectives on coping with everyday stress. *Developmental Psychology, 24*, 247-253.

Bandura, A. (1981). Self referent thought: A developmental analysis of self-efficacy. In J. H. Flavell & L. Ross (Eds.), *Social cognitive development: Frontiers and possible futures* (pp. 200-239). Cambridge, England: Cambridge University Press.

Bar-Ilan, U. (1993). Coping of school-age children in the sealed room during scud missile bombardment and postwar stress reactions. *Journal of Consulting and Clinical Psychology, 61*, 462-467.

Boekaerts, M. (1996). Coping with stress in childhood and adolescence. In M Zeidner & N. S. Endler (Eds.), *Handbook of coping—theory, research and applications* (pp. 452-484). New York: John Wiley & Sons.

Brown, U. (2000). Patterns of children's coping with life stress: Implications for clinicians. *American Journal of Orthopsychiatry, 70,* 351-359.

Compas, B. E. (1987). Coping with stress during childhood and adolescence. *Psychological Bulletin, 101,* 393-403.

Compas, B. E., Mcfarlane, V. L., & Fondacaro, K. M. (1988). Coping with stressful events in older children and adolescents. *Journal of Consulting and Clinical Psychology, 56,* 405-411.

Compas, B. E., Connor-Smith, J. K., Saltzman, H., Thomsen, A. H., & Wadsworth, M. E. (2001). Coping with stress during childhood and adolescence: Problems, progress and potential in theory and research. *Psychological Bulletin, 127,* 87-127.

Dacey, J. S., & Fiore, L. B. (2000). *Your anxious child: How parents and teachers can relieve anxiety in children.* San Francisco: Jossey-Bass.

Dadds, M. R., Spence, S. H., Holland, D. E., Barrett, P. M., & Laurens, K. R. (1997). Prevention and early intervention for anxiety disorder: A controlled trial. *Journal of Consulting and Clinical Psychology, 65,* 627-635.

Endler, N. S., & Parker, J. D. A. (1990). State and trait anxiety, depression and coping styles. *Australian Journal of Psychology, 42,* 207-220.

Fergusson, D. M., Horwood, L. J., & Lynskey, M. T. (1993). Prevalence and comorbidity of DSM-111-R diagnoses in a birth cohort of 15 year olds. *Journal of the American Academy of Child and Adolescent Psychiatry, 32,* 1127-1134.

Folkman, S., & Lazarus, R. S. (1985). If it changes it must be a process: Study of emotion and coping during three stages of a college examination. *Journal of Personality and Social Psychology, 48,* 150-170.

Fonseca, A. C., & Perrin, S. (2001). Clinical phenomenology, classification and assessment of anxiety disorders in children and adolescents. In W. K. Silverman & P. D. A. Treffers (Eds.), *Anxiety disorders in children and adolescents, research, assessment and intervention* (pp. 126-158). United Kingdom: Cambridge Press.

Frick, P. J., Lilienfeld, S. O., Ellis, M., Loney, B., & Silverthorn, P. (1999). The association between anxiety and psychopathy dimensions in children. *Journal of Abnormal Child Psychology, 27,* 383-392.

Frydenberg, E. (1997). *Adolescent coping: Theoretical and research perspectives.* London: Routledge.

Frydenberg, E. (1999). *Learning to cope developing as a person in complex societies.* New York: Oxford University Press.

Frydenberg, E., & Lewis, R. (1991). Adolescent coping: The different ways in which boys and girls cope. *Journal of Adolescence, 14,* 119-133.

Frydenberg, E., & Lewis, R. (1993a). Boys play sport and girls turn to others: Age gender and ethnicity as determinants of coping. *Journal of Adolescence, 16,* 252-266.

Frydenberg, E., & Lewis, R. (1993b). *Adolescent coping scale—administrator's manual.* Australia: The Australian Council for Educational Research.

Frydenberg, E., & Lewis, R. (1999). Things don't get better just because you're older: A case for facilitating reflection. *British Journal of Educational Psychology, 69*, 83-96.

Gaskell, S. L., Wells, A., & Calam, R. (2001). An experimental investigation of thought suppression and anxiety in children. *British Journal of Clinical Psychology, 40*, 45-56.

Harter, S. (1983). Developmental perspective on the self system. In P. H. Mussen & E. M. Hetherington (Eds.), *Handbook of child psychology: Socialisation, personality and social development* (Vol. 4., pp. 275-385). New York: Wiley.

Ialongo, N., Edelsohn, G., Werthamer-Larsson, L., Crockett, L., & Kellam, S. (1994). The significance of self reported anxious symptoms in first grade children. *Journal of Abnormal Child Psychology, 22*, 441-456.

Jones, B., & Frydenberg, E. (2003. Anxiety in children—the importance of the anxiety sensitivity factor. *Australian Journal of Guidance and Counselling, 13*(2), 145-158.

Kashani, J. H., & Orvaschel, H. (1990). A community study of anxiety in children and adolescents. *American Journal of Psychiatry, 147*, 313-318.

Kearney, C. A., Albano, A. M., Eisen, A. R., Allan, W. D., & Barlow, D. H. (1997). The phenomenology of panic disorder in youngsters: An empirical study of a clinical sample. *Journal of Anxiety Disorders, 11*, 49-62.

Kendall, P. C. (1994). Treating anxiety disorders in children: Results of randomized clinical trials. *Journal of Consulting and Clinical Psychology, 62*, 100-110.

King, N. J., Gullone, E., & Ollendick, T. H. (1992). Manifest anxiety and fearfulness in children and adolescents. *Journal of Genetic Psychology, 153*, 63-73.

Kleinknecht, R. A. (1991). *Mastering anxiety the nature and treatment of anxious conditions*. New York: Plenum Press

Kochenderfer-Ladd, B. (2002). Children's coping strategies: Moderators of the effects of peer victimization. *Developmental Psychology, 38*, 267-278.

Kovacs, M., Gatsonia, C., Paulauskas, S. L. & Richards, C. (1989) Depressive disorders in childhood, IV: A longitudinal study of comorbidity with the risk for anxiety disorders. *Archives of General Psychiatry, 46*, 776-783.

Lau, J. J., Calmari, J. E., & Waraczynski, M. (1996). Panic attack symptomatology and anxiety sensitivity in adolescents. *Journal of Anxiety Disorders, 10*, 355-364.

Lazarus, R. S. (1966). *Psychological stress and the coping process*. New York: McGraw-Hill.

Lazarus, R. S. (1990). Theory-based stress measurement. *Psychological Inquiry, 1*, 3-13.

Lazarus, R. S., & Folkman, S. (1984). *Stress, appraisal and coping*. New York: Singer.

Leiderman, P. H. (1983). Social ecology and childbirth. The newborn nursery as environmental stressor. In N. Carmezy & M. Rutter (Eds.), *Stress, coping and development in children* (pp. 133-159). New York: McGraw-Hill.

Lodge, J., Harte, K. K., & Tripp, G. (1998). Children's self talk under condition of mild anxiety. *Journal of Anxiety Disorders, 12*, 153-176.

Macoby, E. E. (1983). Social emotional development and response to stressors. In N. Garmezy & M. Rutter (Eds.), *Stress, coping and development in children* (pp. 217-234). New York: McGraw-Hill.

March, J. S. (Ed.) (1995). *Anxiety disorders in children and adolescents*. New York: Guilford Press.

Mattison, R. E. (1992). Anxiety disorders. In S. R. Hooper, G. W. Jynd, & R. E. Mattison (Eds.), *Child psychopathology: diagnostic criteria and clinical assessment* (pp. 179-202). Hillsdale, NJ: Lawrnece Erlbaum Associates.

Mindell, J. A., & Barrett, P. M. (2002). Nightmares and anxiety in elementary-aged children: Is there a relationship. *Child care, health and development, 28,* 317-322.

Muris, P., Merckelbach, H., Gadet, B., & Meesters, C. (2000). Monitoring and anxiety disorders symptoms in children. *Personality and Individual Differences, 29,* 775-781.

Muris, P., Schmidt, H., Merckelbach, H., & Schouten, E. (2001). Anxiety sensitivity in adolescents: Factor structure and relationship to trait anxiety and symptoms of anxiety disorders and depression. *Behavior Research Therapy, 39,* 89-100.

Nelles, W. B., & Barlow, D. H. (1988). Do children panic? *Clinical Psychology Review, 8,* 359-372.

Peterson, R. A., & Reiss, S. (1987). *Test manual for the anxiety sensitivity index.* Orland Park, IL: International Diagnostic Systems.

Rabin, B., Peterson, R. A., Richters, J., & Jensen, P. S. (1993). Anxiety sensitivity among anxious children. *Journal of Clinical Child Psychology, 22,* 441-446.

Rachman, S. (1998). *Anxiety*. United Kingdom: Psychology Press.

Rapee, R., & Barlow, D. H. (1993). Generalized anxiety disorder, panic disorder and the phobias. In P. B. Sutker & H. E. Adams (Eds.), *Comprehensive handbook of psychopathology* (2nd ed., pp. 109-127). New York: Plenum Press.

Rapee, R. M., Ancis, J. R., & Barlow, D. H. (1988). Emotional reactions to physiological sensations: Panic disorder patients and non-clinical subjects. *Behavior Research and Therapy, 26,* 265-269.

Rapee, R. M., Wignall, A., Hudson, J. L., & Schniering, C. A. (2000). *Treating anxious children and adolescents. An evidence-based approach.* Oakland, CA: New Harbinger Publications.

Reiss, S., & McNally, R. J. (1985). The expectancy model of fear. In S. Reiss & R. R. Botzin (Eds.), *Theoretical issues in behavior therapy* (pp. 101-121). New York: Academic Press.

Rosen, J. B., & Schulkin, J. (1998). From normal fear to pathological anxiety. *Psychological Review, 105,* 325-350.

Ruble, D. N., & Rholes, W. S. (1981). The development of children's perceptions and attributions about their social world. In J. H. Harvey, W. Ickes, & R. F. Kidd (Eds.), *New directions in attribution research* (Vol. 3., pp. 1-36). Hillsdale, NJ: Erlbaum.

Sheehan, D. V. (1983). Sheehan patient rated anxiety scale. *The anxiety disease.* New York: Scribner Book.

Silverman, W. K., Fleisig, W., Rabin, B., & Peterson, R. A. (1991). Childhood anxiety index. *Journal of Clinical Psychology, 20,* 162-168.

Silverman, W. K., & Ginsburg, G. S. (1998). Anxiety disorders. In T. H. Ollendick & M. Hersen (Eds.), *Handbook of child psychopathology* (3rd ed., pp. 239-268). New York: Plenum.

Silverman, W. K., & Weems, C. F. (1999). Anxiety sensitivity in children. In S. Taylor (Ed.), *Anxiety sensitivity theory, research and treatment of the fear of anxiety* (pp. 239-268). Mahwah, NJ: Lawrence Erlbaum Associates.

Spence, S. (1996). The prevention of anxiety disorders in childhood. In P. Cotton & H. Jackson (Eds.), *Early intervention and prevention in mental health* (pp. 87-107). Australia: The Australian Psychological Society.

Spence, S. H., & Dadds, M. R. (1996). Preventing childhood anxiety disorders. *Behavior Change, 13*, 241-249.

Spielberger, C. C. (Ed.). (1966). *Anxiety and behavior*. New York: Academic Press.

Spielberger, C. D. (1973). *State-trait anxiety inventory for children*. Palo Alto: CA: Consulting Psychologists Press.

Suls, J., & Fletcher, B. (1986). The relative efficacy of avoidant and non-avoidant coping strategies: A meta analysis. *Health Psychology, 4*, 249-288.

Taylor, S., Koch, W. J., McNally R. J., & Crockett, D. J. (1992). Conceptualisations of anxiety sensitivity. *Psychological Assessment, 4*, 245-250.

Telch, M. J., Lucas, J. A., & Nelson, P. (1989). Non-clinical panic in college students: An investigation of prevalence and symptomatology. *Journal of Abnormal Psychology, 98*, 300-306.

Vasey, M. W., Daleiden, E. L., Williams, L. L., & Brown, L. (1995). Biased attention in childhood anxiety disorders: A preliminary study. *Journal of Abnormal Child Psychology, 23*, 267-279.

Verhulst, F. (2001). Community and epidemiological aspects of anxiety disorders in children. In W. K. Silverman & P. D. A. Treffers (Eds.), *Anxiety disorders in children and adolescents, research, assessment and intervention*. United Kingdom: Cambridge Press.

Weems, C. F., Hammond-Laurence, K., Silverman, W. K., & Ginsburg, G. (1998). Testing the utility of the anxiety sensitivity construct in children and adolescents referred for anxiety disorders. *Journal of Clinical Child Psychology, 27*, 69-77.

Zeidner, M. (1994). Personal and contextual determinants of coping and anxiety in an evaluative situation: A prospective study. *Personality and Individual Differences, 16*, 899-918.

CHAPTER 6

TWO TYPES OF AGGRESSION AND THE RELATIONSHIP WITH COPING

Implications for Educational Practice

Geraldine Larkins and Erica Frydenberg
University of Melbourne, Australia

ABSTRACT

Aggression is a widespread problem in our communities in general and in our educational communities, in particular. While there are many approaches to addressing this problem it is helpful to recognize that aggression manifests itself in different ways in different people. Furthermore we are now able to identify two types of aggression in young people. An ability to distinguish the characteristics of the two types of aggressive young people, including their use of coping skills allows us to develop appropriate intervention strategies to help them cope more productively and to reduce the negative impact of aggression on the educational community. A study of 206 fifth and sixth grade students from rural, Catholic schools in Victoria, Australia who completed three surveys: the Children's Coping Scale, the Children's Automatic Thoughts Scale, and Beck's Youth Inventory of Anger

Thriving, Surviving, or Going Under: Coping with Everyday Lives, 135–163
Copyright © 2004 by Information Age Publishing

validated the two forms of aggression. There was a significant difference found between reactive aggression and nonreactive aggression on some of the scales. The finding supports the theory that there are two distinct aggressive groups who cope differently. The implications for different types of treatment approaches are discussed.

WHY STUDY AGGRESSION?

The problem of aggression has been theorized and researched since the early days of psychology. Therefore, there is a vast amount of research and literature available on the topic. So why is there a need for more research in this area? The need to continue to address the issue of aggression comes out of the human and financial cost to society. As pointed out by Lorenz (1967) and Bandura (1973), technological advances in weaponry have increased the destructive potential of aggression. Mass killings by students in America, and more recently in Germany, highlight the need for a greater understanding of aggression. United States Department of Justice statistics show that juvenile arrests for murder have doubled since 1984 (Ciampi, 2001). Similarly, figures from the Australian Institute of Criminology show an increase in juvenile homicide and violent crime in Victoria from 1,495 offenders, processed in 1991-1992 to 1947 in 1995-1996.

Many studies have shown the negative outcomes for children with aggression. It appears to be stable over the lifespan with 29 out of 50 convicted males in Farrington's (1991) 40-year longitudinal study having been aggressive as children. They were also more likely to be substance abusers, not own their own home, have more marital conflict, and not have a job. In other studies childhood aggression predicted later delinquency, dating violence, drug use, and irritability (Brendgen, Vitaro, Tremblay, & Lavoie, 2001; Brook, Whiteman, & Finch, 1992; Caspi, Elder, & Bem, 1987). As well as problems in the future, aggressiveness is the single most likely reason for a child to be rejected by peers (Coie, Underwood, & Lochman, 1991; Henington, Hughes, Cavell, & Thompson, 1998).

Most children with behavioral and aggression problems are educated in mainstream schools. This is particularly so in rural areas where there are no available special schools for behavior disordered students. This means that teachers are required to manage these students themselves. Although teachers experience negative feelings of anger, irritation, and indifference toward students with behavioral difficulties, including aggression, they want to help them and favor the use of positive techniques (Poulou & Norwich, 2000). Therefore, there is a need for more understanding about these students in order to inform educational practice. Teachers are seeking support in the management of these children, with behavioral issues and aggression problems accounting for 25% of student referrals from Catholic primary schools in Northern Victoria (School Community Services Data Base, 2002).

These children are referred for behavior and social problems but do not all present with the same difficulties or respond to the same treatments (Kendall, Ronan, & Epps, 1991). For example, of two students referred to the school counselor for aggression problems, one gets angry easily and strikes back when he thinks he has been teased or threatened. When a peer accidentally hurts him by bumping into him, he assumes that they meant to do it and then overreacts with anger and fighting. Whenever there is a fight, he always claims that other children are to blame and feels that they started the whole trouble. The other child uses or threatens to use physical force in order to dominate other children. She threatens or bullies other children in order to get her way and gets other children to gang up on peers she does not like. Do these children both have the same underlying problems? Will the same treatment be effective with both of them? Or are there different aggressive groups that need to be treated differently?

WHAT IS AGGRESSION?

Aggression is defined as "any physical or verbal behavior intended to hurt or destroy, whether done out of hostility or as a calculated means to an end" (Myers, 1998, p. 631). Aggression is used to describe a wide variety of acts involving attack and hostility. The definition however depends on the theoretical orientation of the person using the term.

In psychological terms aggression has been variously described as: a basic death drive displaced as aggression toward others (Freud, 1933), an instinct for survival (Lorenz, 1967), a motivational drive resulting from frustration (Dollard, Doob, Miller, Mowrer, & Sears, 1939), and a response to external and internal stimuli (Berkowitz, 1978). In social learning theory, it is proposed that aggression is learned through direct experience with natural reinforcers and by modeling (Bandura, 1973).

Anger and aggression are also seen as resulting from cognition. The way a person interprets a situation will have an effect on his or her emotional response. In cognitive theory a person may become angry because of direct intentional physical or psychological harm, indirect harm which affects a person's self-esteem or causes loss of face, and behaviors which violate a person's code of laws, rules, principles, and standards even if they do not directly affect the person (Beck, 1976). Cognitive-behavioral theory incorporates beliefs, emotions, cognitions, and arousal in understanding and managing aggressive behavior. Treatment effects last longer and are more global if cognition is included (Meichenbaum, 1977).

Most of these theories are more helpful in explaining the aggression of the first child in the example above who is acting out of fear or anger. The behavior of the second child who deliberately uses aggression for power and gain is best explained by social learning theory. None of these theories adequately explains the behavior of both children.

The social information-processing model of children's social adjustment attempts to summarize all of the ideas about how children understand and respond in social situations. In this model, a child brings to each new experience their memories of experiences and their capabilities. In each experience, the child receives a number of cues both internal and external. These cues are interpreted and encoded. They are then used to clarify or select a goal. Next, the child either recalls possible responses or creates new possible responses. These responses are then evaluated and one is chosen and enacted (Crick & Dodge, 1994). This is still a response-based theory and as such, it better explains the aggression of the first child but not of the second child who tends to create situations rather than respond to them.

Two Types of Aggression

The two types of aggression are referred to as "reactive" and "proactive" (Dodge, 1991). These two groups have specific qualities and etiology. Reactive aggressors are described as *troubled by others*; their aggression is affective and usually occurs as a response to anger or fear. These children have often experienced trauma or life-threatening danger in their early years or had poor early relationships with primary caregivers. They often view the world as a hostile place, from which they have to protect themselves. Proactive aggressors are described as *troubling to others* and their aggression is instrumental and purposeful. These children develop in families where aggressive behavior is accepted and even rewarded. Aggressive heroes and models are valued and there is significant modeling of aggression on television, in the neighborhood, and in the family (Dodge, 1991).

Various studies support the theory of two types of aggression through identification of different characteristics for the two groups. The reactive and proactive aggressive groups performed differently on measures of leadership, "bothersomeness," and sense of humor (Dodge & Coie, 1987). Students identified as reactive aggressive, have attention problems, impulsivity, and a background of physical abuse and harsh discipline.

Reactive aggressive children are three and a half to four times more likely to suffer peer rejection, have more social problems, greater problems attending to relevant social cues, and generate a higher proportion of aggressive responses than nonaggressive children. Children identified as proactive aggressive show no indication of abuse and their early experiences do not differ from average children. They are no more rejected than nonaggressive children. They expect more positive consequences from aggression for themselves and think it would be easier for them than other children to be aggressive. Those children identified with a combination of reactive and proactive aggression have abusive backgrounds and suffer more peer rejection than proactive aggressive children (Dodge, Lochman, Harnish, Bates, & Pettit, 1997).

Differences have also been found in the friendship patterns of the two distinct groups of aggressive boys. Boys identified as proactive aggressors had friends who were also identified as proactive aggressors. These boys were proactively aggressive prior to their friendship and their aggression did not become more similar over time suggesting that the friendships were the result of mutual selection on the grounds of proactive aggression. This pattern was not found for boys with reactive aggression (Poulin & Boivin, 2000).

Schwartz's (2000) findings gave support to the notion that there are distinctly different groups of aggressive children. He specifically examined the attributes of aggressive victims. These children would probably fit the classification of combined proactive and reactive aggressive as Salmivalli and Nieminen (2002) found their bully-victim group to be high in both proactive and reactive aggression. The aggressive victims of Schwartz's (2000) study were found to have poorly regulated affect and behavior, and poor academic performance. They had high scores for hyperactivity and impulsive behavior and were overly reactive. Aggressive victims reported feelings of depression and anxiety. These children were also found to be unpopular with peers.

Children described as "nonvictimized aggressors" who would equate to Dodge's proactive aggressors also had poor social skills and poor academic performance. They were disliked by peers but were not as rejected as the "aggressive victims." They did not appear to have the same difficulties with affect regulation. This group of children use aggression in a controlled way to obtain what they want and to dominate peers (Schwartz, 2000). Bullies scored high on both reactive and proactive aggression but also could be reactive only and proactive only. Victims unexpectedly were found to be more reactively aggressive than the control group (Salmavilli & Nieminen, 2002).

Different types of early aggression have been linked to different types of later violence and different parenting qualities. There is a relationship between proactive aggression, delinquency related violence, and low parental monitoring, whereas reactive aggression is related to dating violence and lack of mother's warmth and care giving (Brendgen et al., 2001).

Distinctions have been made between boys who are aggressive-rejected, just aggressive, and just rejected. Some aggressive students are rejected, while others are not, which lends further support for the view that there are distinct groups within aggressive students. Both aggressive and aggressive-rejected boys have higher levels of physical aggression than the other boys, but the aggressive-rejected boys have the highest levels of verbal aggression, hyperactivity, and rule violation. The conduct problems of just aggressive boys were fewer than those of aggressive-rejected boys (Bierman, Smoot, & Aumiller, 1993).

Although there has been much support for the theory of two types of aggression put forward by Dodge (1991), a meta-analysis of research about conduct disorder and oppositional defiant disorder by Hill (2002), suggests the need for a broader specification of aggression similar to the concept of adult personality disorder.

COPING

There are two main approaches that describe coping. The first is the transactional theory of Richard Lazarus (1966, 1991) and the second is the Conservation of Resource (COR) theory (Hobfoll, 1988, 1998). The former focuses on an individual's appraisal of a situation as one of threat, harm, or challenge, and the latter emphasizes that an individual's coping is reliant on their resources, whether they be instrumental (able to achieve ends), personal, or relational. These theoretical approaches, mainly developed with adult populations, have been extended to measurement and application with young people. For example, the transactional model has been incorporated into the work of Frydenberg and Lewis (see Chapters 1 and 2, this volume) and the resources model has been extended to research with young people in the Australian context (see Chapter 4 by McKenzie & Frydenberg, this volume). Essentially, if young people are resource rich, including personality characteristics such as esteem, language skills, and emotional regulation, they are likely to cope differently than those who are resource poor.

AGGRESSION AND COPING

Some research suggests that aggressive children may have a maladaptive coping style. The fact that stressful events in the lives of young people and their parents lead to increases in emotional and behavioral problems (Compas, Howell, Phares, Williams, & Giunta, 1989), tends to suggest that they are not coping with these events or are using maladaptive coping strategies. An accumulation of stressful experiences was found to lead to increased vulnerability to maladjustment (Compas et al., 1989; Printz, Shermis, & Webb, 1999). The build up of minor daily events was more stressful than isolated major events. Students coped better with stress if they felt they had social support and problem solving abilities and this perception was more important than actual abilities (Printz, Shermis, & Webb, 1999).

According to Garmezy (1985), much can be learned from studying children who are at risk for disorder but who develop adaptive functioning. There are three main protective factors for children at risk; they are the child's personality, a supportive family, and an external support system, all of which may encourage productive coping. Some children who are at risk do develop maladaptive functioning (Garmezy, 1985). These children develop verbally and physically aggressive behaviors (Compas et al., 1989), supporting the link between aggression and nonproductive coping.

There are no firm conclusions regarding the potential harm or benefit of externalizing coping, but girls who use an aggressive coping style are more likely to be rejected by their peers. Social problems, low popularity, and loneliness also occur more often in girls who express their anger (Kochenderfer-Ladd & Skinner, 2002). Aggressive coping must however be considered with other coping strategies because it is not a unique predictor of adjustment problems for girls (Kochenderfer-Ladd & Skinner, 2002). The rejection of angry girls may be related to findings that females tend to use more interpersonal support coping (Frydenberg & Lewis, 1993b; Greenglass, 2002). Anger and aggression may interrupt this social support for girls and lead to rejection. A decrease in social support was also found in patients whose anger increased because of an increase in losses and symptoms associated with disease (Lane & Hobfoll, 1992). That is, patients tended to use anger as a maladaptive means of coping with their disease. While aggression was not used to a significantly different extent by boys and girls in Olafsen and Viemero's (2000) study, some differences were found. Girls tended to use more stress-recognition strategies, while boys used more self-destruction strategies. Children classified as bully/victims used more aggressive strategies than other children, and bully victim boys used more self-destructive strategies. These results suggest that children who bully tend to employ negative coping strategies.

Aggressive children with attention problems may use an avoidant strategy that involves disengaging from a threatening situation rather than looking for ways to relieve the problem through coping options (Hill, 2002). Verbal deficits have also been linked to a lack of coping strategies to manage anger and aggression. It is thought that children who are not able to assert themselves or reason verbally may use aggression to solve social problems (Green, Sullivan, & Eichberg, 2001; Hill, 2000). In the children studied by Green and colleagues (2001), anxiety and depression were also present. They found that these children experienced family violence, spousal abuse, alcoholism, and marital problems, supporting the connection between reactive aggression and nonproductive coping. Teachers felt that victimized boys, whose externalizing behavior included aggression, displayed more anxious-depressed symptoms (Kochenderfer-Ladd & Skinner, 2002).

Coping has traditionally been defined in terms of reaction, that is, how people respond after or during a stressful event, which seems to relate to reactive aggression. But more recently just as aggression has been defined in terms of reactive and proactive, coping is being defined more broadly to include reactive coping, anticipatory coping, preventive coping, and proactive coping (Schwarzer & Taubert, 2002). Proactive coping, described by Greenglass (2002) as future oriented, has the main features of planning, goal attainment and the use of resources to obtain goals. The proactive coper takes initiative, uses others and takes the credit for successes, but does not blame his or her self for failures. The proactive leader is driven by values, choosing actions according to their values and imagining the future (Schwarzer & Taubert, 2002). The profile of the proactive aggressor is very similar to the proactive coper in that he or she also uses aggression to obtain goals and makes a deliberate choice of action. While proactive coping is seen as positive and proactive aggression is seen as negative there may be some underlying characteristics, which are the same but are manifested differently in the proactive copers and proactive aggressors.

AGGRESSION AND ANGER

"Anger refers to an unpleasant emotion ranging in intensity from irritation or annoyance to fury or rage. Angry affect, the subjective or experiential component of this emotion, is typically accompanied by physiological arousal, characteristic facial expression, and activation of action tendencies or impulses toward aggression" (Smith, 1994, p. 25). Anger is also related to a person's perception of events and may increase if they think they are being subjected to illegitimate or unfair treatment or harm (Lazarus, 1991). The likelihood of a child becoming angry in social situations is increased by encoding biases and hostile attributions (Hill, 2002). Hill (2002) believes that Dodge's (1991) social information processing theory "implies a lower threshold for anger" for aggressive children.

Focusing on an object of anger increased anger in boys whereas distraction, passive waiting and information gathering decreased anger (Gilliom, Shaw, Beck, Schonberg, & Lukon, 2002). Boys who used distraction and passive waiting at three years of age received lower teacher ratings for aggression and delinquent behaviors at six years of age; while those who focused attention on the frustrating object were described by teachers as less cooperative and more aggressive.

Examination of anger-in (suppression) and anger-out (expression) coping styles in relation to perceived social support, found that an anger-in style of coping has a negative effect on social support but social support does not seem to be related to an anger-out coping style (Palfai & Hart, 1997). This contradicts the findings of Schwartz (2000), where reactive aggressive children were more rejected than their peers and thus less likely to receive support. Palfai and Hart (1997) point out that their findings were in relation to perceived rather than actual social support. This would then support the idea that angry or aggressive children are not very good at recognizing and understanding social interactions (Dodge & Newman, 1981), so they may not realize that they are being rejected. Anger appears to be more related to characteristics of reactive than proactive aggression. Therefore, it would be expected that the reactive aggressive group and the combined group would obtain higher scores on the measure of anger than the proactive aggressive group.

AGGRESSION AND COGNITION (AUTOMATIC THOUGHTS)

Automatic thoughts are described as the stream of thoughts a person has about what they are doing, which is referred to as an individual communicating with him or herself. Whenever a person has an emotional response they are able to identify some thoughts, which occur just prior to the emotion and because these appear to emerge rapidly and automatically, they are named "automatic thoughts" (Beck, 1976). Many people describe their automatic thoughts. These thoughts are specific and discrete, occur in telegraphic style, do not occur after deliberation, reasoning, or reflection, and there are no logical sequence of steps, they "just happen." They appear to be autonomous and difficult to control in disturbed patients (Beck, 1976).

People who approach problems negatively do not cope as well with stress. A person's attitude to their problem-solving ability may be more important than the ability itself with cognitive factors limiting effective coping. Young people who feel that they have an overwhelming number of daily hassles may practice avoidance, shifting causal attributions to factors beyond their control, and adopting irrational beliefs (Printz et al., 1999).

Aggressive boys have been found to have a hostile attributional bias (Dodge & Newman, 1981). This means that they attribute hostility to peers in ambiguous encounters. Aggression correlated with both a quicker response, which did not give attention to social cues, and selective recollection of hostile cues over nonhostile cues. This finding supports Dodge's (1980) proposal that aggressive boys behave aggressively because they expect others to behave in a hostile way toward them. Their peers then respond aggressively to their aggressive behavior, which reinforces aggressive children's expectations of hostile behavior from their peers. Other studies found that boys' hostile attributional bias only related to behavior directed at them not interactions they observed as an onlooker, that the reactive but not the proactive aggressive students had an attributional bias and that the reactive aggressive students also thought of more aggressive responses to ambiguous situations (Dodge & Coie, 1987; Dodge & Frame, 1982). Children with reactive aggression were more likely to attribute hostile intent to peer interactions. Although unexpected, the proactive aggressive children also had hostile attributional biases, but this seemed to be related to the shared variance with reactive aggression. When this was partialled out in statistical analysis the proactive aggressive children did not demonstrate hostile attributional bias (Dodge, Price, Bachorowski, & Newman, 1990).

Many of the treatment approaches for aggressive students use a cognitive behavioral approach. According to Leung and Poon (2001), aggression has rarely been included in studies of cognitive distortions in psychopathology, compared with depression and anxiety. Apart from the works by Dodge and colleagues on attributional bias, very little research considers cognitive distortions in relation to aggression. Leung and Poon (2001) point out that there are different distortions of cognitions, which are related to specific emotional and behavioral problems. They found that aggressive young people had an external attribution and their irrational beliefs tended to be related to hostility, injustice, and immediate gratification. Likewise the anger of chronically ill people has been attributed to their cognitive processes. People become angry when they interpret their loss as damaging self-esteem, an insult, a threat to their current lifestyle, or failed expectancy (Lane & Hobfoll, 1992). Similarly, aggressive children may be interpreting events in a way which leads them to feel anger and display aggression.

One of the reasons for limited research in the area of cognitive distortions among aggressive children may be the lack of measurement instruments. Schniering and Rapee (2001) found that there were few self-report questionnaires to measure negative thinking in children. The Children's

Automatic Thoughts Scale (Schniering & Rapee, 2001) was developed to fill this gap. The scale has four factors: physical threat, social threat, personal failure, and hostile intent. The hostility factor discriminates behavior-disordered children from other groups. In their study of children's automatic thoughts, the authors concluded that self-esteem did not appear to be a significant factor for aggressive children, with scores on the personal failure scale not distinguishing this group from other groups of children. However, the behavior-disordered group was not divided by aggression type and the two different aggressive groups may have different negative beliefs. The girls had higher scores for social threat while the boys scored the highest for hostile intent. Schniering and Rapee (2001) suggest that knowing the cognitive content has direct relevance for therapy. The finding that different clinical populations, anxious, depressed, and externalizing, had different negative beliefs highlights the need to tailor therapy to specific groups.

Although Zwemer and Deffenbacher (1984) used university students for their study rather than children, it is one of the few studies which looked specifically at cognition in relation to anger. They found that angry students were more likely to score highly on personal perfection, anxious over concern, blame proneness, and catastrophizing. All these factors except blame proneness were shared by anxious students.

Aggressive and depressed children have social skill deficits and faulty thinking in relation to conceptions of relationships (Rudolph & Clark, 2001). It is suggested that therapy should focus on changing cognitive distortions and developing social skills, but the particular cognitive distortions and skills deficits vary across children and need to be targeted to specific subgroups (Rudolph & Clark, 2001).

INTERVENTIONS FOR AGGRESSION

When children are referred for the treatment of aggression there are several interventions available based on the different theoretical explanations of aggression. However, if none of the theories adequately explain the behavior of both groups of children then it would be expected that a treatment based on any one theory would not support the needs of both groups of children. As cognitive and behavioral factors have been implicated as features of childhood aggression, it would be expected that a cognitive-behavioral approach would be more appropriate in helping children to change their behavior. Some improvement in self-control and prosocial behavior has resulted from cognitive-behavioral treatments for aggression which included learning about feelings, self-evaluation, rewards, modeling, role-plays, and empathy through perspective taking

(Kendall et al., 1991). However, these gains were not maintained and the treatment was not highly successful with conduct-disordered youth.

A social skills program, which included anger management and problem solving, was successful in improving the behavior of young children with conduct disorder and oppositional defiant disorder (Webster-Stratton, Reid, & Hammond, 2001). One reason suggested for the success of this program where others have had limited success was the young age of the participants, who were four to eight years old.

Another approach to treatment is a social skills training program based on social learning theory: Children are taught problem solving, understanding feelings, listening, following instructions, joining in, self-control, responding to teasing, and keeping out of fights (Pepler, King, & Byrd, 1991). Although this program appeared to address all the identified deficits of aggressive children, it was not highly successful. One explanation for the results given by Pepler et al. (1991) was that the program did not take into account the different types of aggression. The group work nature of the program may not have allowed for the fact that children who act aggressively do not all have the same deficits.

There is substantial overlap in the problems and behaviors of children with behavioral, emotional, and cognitive problems. It is recommended that treatment programs cover the range of problems and not just focus on one area (Garnefski & Diekstra, 1997). The limited success of treatment programs combined with recommendations that programs target specific difficulties indicates that aggression may not be a single construct.

Different treatments have been recommended for the different types of aggression. Three different treatment approaches have been identified: those that focus on the overt behavior, those that focus on relationships between the child and others, and those that focus on the child's cognition (Dodge, 1991). Treatments for reactively aggressive children need to redirect attention away from threatening cues, teach social role-taking and understanding others' thoughts and feelings, and may also include forming a close interpersonal relationship. For a proactive child Dodge (1991) recommends consistent punishment of aggressive behaviors and positive reinforcement of nonaggressive behaviors. As proactive children see aggression as having a favorable outcome they may need help to focus on its negative consequences and the possibility of nonaggressive actions meeting needs just as well, without the negative consequences. The theory of two types of aggression seems to best explain the differences in behavior of the two students in the opening example.

Many studies have dealt with the etiological and social factors relating to aggression. Research in the area of childhood aggression has looked at the formation of friendships (Poulin & Boivin, 2000), developmental histories (Dodge, 1991), social-information processing (Dodge & Coie, 1987;

Dodge & Frame, 1982), and moderating effects of parental involvement (Brendgen et al., 2001), however, there is little research which explicitly endeavors to explore the underlying coping skill deficits, anger and negative thinking of aggressive children.

A greater understanding of the coping skills, negative thinking, and anger related to aggression could contribute to therapeutic approaches and management of aggressive children. Frydenberg and Lewis (2002) recommend focusing on the reduction of nonproductive strategies while increasing productive coping and emphasize the need to teach the skills of cognitive appraisal. Programs such as "Bright Ideas" (Brandon & Cunningham, 1999a, 1999b) have been found to increase psychological control, and thus promote productive coping (Brandon, Cunningham, & Frydenberg, 1999). If nonproductive coping skills and negative automatic thoughts are found to be factors in aggression they may offer a more accessible treatment than those needed for already implicated familial, biological, and environmental factors found in Compass, Howell, Phares, Williams, and Giunta (1989), Dodge (1991), McCabe, Hough, Wood, and Yeh (2001), and Olweus (1991).

RESEARCH DIRECTIONS

It could be asserted that the modeling of aggressive behavior as a way of problem solving, lack of warmth and involvement, permissiveness for aggressive behavior, and power-assertive child rearing practices described by Olweus (1991), lead to the development of negative thinking and nonproductive coping skills for proactively aggressive children. Reactively aggressive children are also expected to develop negative thinking and nonproductive coping skills, because of early traumas, experiences of abuse and/or poor early relationships, but these will probably be different to those of the proactive aggressive children.

From the research findings above, it is expected that reactive aggressive children will have inadequate coping skills and will score high on physical threat, and personal failure on the automatic thoughts scale and high on Beck's anger scale. It is expected that proactive aggressive children will have inadequate coping skills, will be high on hostile intent on the automatic thoughts scale, and will score average to low on Beck's anger scale.

If aggressive students demonstrate a particular coping style or poor coping skills, which is different to the nonaggressive population, this may point to the need for providing aggressive students with the opportunity to participate in a coping skills program. Similarly, if it is possible to identify the automatic thoughts of aggressive children these may be able to be addressed with a cognitive behavioral approach to therapy, which targets the identified automatic thoughts.

THE STUDY

Participants

Twenty-two country Catholic schools in Victoria, Australia were invited to participate in the study. Of these, 15 were able to participate. From these schools 206 grade five and six students out of a possible 787 (25%) had parental permission and volunteered to participate. These students ranged in age from 9 years to 13 years (M = 10.98, SD = 0.75). The grade five students comprised 44% of the sample (n = 91) and 56% of the sample were in grade six (n = 115). There were 110 females (54%) and 96 males (46%). Most of the students were from Anglo-European and middle to low socioeconomic backgrounds.

Materials

Children's Coping Scale

This is a relatively new 78-item scale developed from the Adolescent Coping Scale of Frydenberg and Lewis (1993a). The Children's Coping Scale is a self-report inventory which requires students to respond to 78 items about how they cope with problems at school. Students rate the frequency that they employ each coping strategy, using a three-point scale: 0 = never, 1 = sometimes, and 2 = a lot. Generally, the scale is very similar to the Adolescent Coping Scale except that the wording has been simplified to suit younger children. Item 27, "Make myself feel better by taking alcohol, cigarettes, or other drugs (not medication)" and item 80, asking students to list other things they do to cope have been omitted. Using this instrument, there is support for a two-factor model of coping described as nonproductive and productive coping (Cunningham, 2002). The nonproductive factor is comprised of worry, self-blame, not coping, tension reduction, and keep to self, while the productive coping factor is comprised of focus on solving the problem, focus on the positive, work hard to achieve, and seek recreational diversions. In the current study the Cronbach alpha coefficient for the total scale was .89.

Beck's Youth Inventory of Anger

This is a new 20-item scale published in 2001. Students are asked to respond to questions about being angry on a four-point scale from 0 = never to 3 = always. Beck, Beck, and Jolly (2001) report internal consistency coefficients for the anger scale from .87 to .92 over age and gender. The manual reports a test retest reliability over a week of .74 and .87 for females and males in the 7-10 age group and .84 for both genders in the

11-14 age group. Scores of a clinical sample were compared with matched controls and it was found that the clinical sample had a significantly higher mean score than the matched control group. In the current study the Cronbach alpha coefficient was .92.

Children's Automatic Thoughts Scale

This new 40-item scale has a test retest correlation coefficient of .79 at 1 month and .76 at 3 months, and is considered to be adequate. The authors point out that the scale has been developed with children at each stage, from item generation onward, and is not simply a modified scale for adults (Schniering & Rapee, 2001). The results of the Schniering and Rapee (2001) study indicate that the scale is psychometrically sound and valid and its factor structure has been replicated. In this study, the Cronbach's alpha coefficient was .96.

This scale asks children to indicate, on a five-point scale ranging from 0 = not at all to 4 = all the time, how often they have had a range of negative thoughts in the last week. It is scored for the four factors of physical threat, social threat, personal failure, and hostile intent. Each factor is made up of 10 items. Physical threat has items relating to the students or those they are close to being hurt. Social threat relates to students thinking others are making negative evaluations of them. Personal failure relates to students making negative evaluations of themselves and hostile intent relates to both a view that people are against them and that they have a right to take revenge on those who hurt them.

Procedure

To categorize children according to aggressiveness, teachers were asked to answer six questions about each child prior to questionnaires being administered. The teachers' questions came from a study by Dodge and Coie (1987).

Reactive aggression items included:

- When this child has been teased or threatened, he/she gets angry easily and strikes back.
- When a peer accidentally hurts this child (such as bumping into him/her) this child assumes that the peer meant to do it and then overreacts with anger and fighting.
- This child always claims that other children are to blame in a fight and feels that they started the whole trouble.

Proactive aggression items included:

- This child uses or threatens to use physical force in order to dominate other children.
- This child threatens or bullies other children in order to get his/her way.
- This child gets other children to gang up on a peer he/she does not like.

The findings of the Dodge and Coie (1987) study supported the discriminant validity of the teacher-rating measures. Teacher-rated behavior was also shown to have adequate construct validity through comparison with peer-rated behavior and direct observation (Achenbach, McConaughy, & Howell, 1987). A study in aggression by Henington et al. (1998) found that teacher ratings of aggression were similar to peer ratings of aggression.

Students were allocated to a group if their score was above six for reactive aggression and above four for proactive aggression: these scores were one standard deviation above the mean for the total group. Responses from the teachers' checklists were used to identify children as reactive aggressive, proactive aggressive, or nonaggressive. Of the total 206 students, 146 were identified as nonaggressive, 17 as reactive only, 13 as proactive only, and 30 as both reactive and proactive aggressive.

Students were asked to complete the three questionnaires during school time in one 40-minute session, by arrangement with the classroom teacher. All participating students at each school completed the surveys together. The questions were read to the students but they could choose to work ahead. The order of the surveys was from longest to shortest. The Children's Coping Scale was introduced by asking the children to circle the number that shows the things that they do whenever they are feeling nervous or worried in school because of something that has happened at school. The Children's Automatic Thoughts Scale was introduced with the instructions: "Listed below are some thoughts that children and adolescents have said pop into their heads. Please read each thought carefully and decide how often if at all, each thought popped into your head over the past week." Beck's Youth Inventory of Anger was introduced with the instructions: "Here is a list of things that happen to people and that people think or feel. Read each sentence carefully and circle the one word that tells about you best." After completing the surveys the teacher or the researcher wrote the reactive and proactive scores on the front of each child's set of surveys.

Data Analysis

The data were analyzed using a $2 \times 2 \times 2$ multivariate analyses of variance (MANOVA). The three factors were reactivity with two levels, low and high, proactivity with two levels, low and high, and gender, male, and female. Tests of between-subjects effects were conducted to examine differences between the groups on each of the significant measures.

The data were screened and most scales had homogeneous variance. Some scales were skewed because of the nature of the questions but a MANOVA was still used because the distributions were a similar shape. To compensate for variance, heterogeneity, and nonnormality of some scales, the confidence level was set at .025 as recommended by Keppel (1991) and Tabachnick and Fidell (1996). Where .05 is used assumptions about variance, heterogeneity, and nonnormality have been met.

The data were also screened for missing data. Two subjects were removed because they had more than five missing data points. The other missing item scores were replaced with the mean of the scale to which they belonged. No individual survey had more than four missing scores and no scale had more than one missing score.

Results

Children's Coping Scale

To determine if there were any differences in the coping strategies of children in the different aggression groups, the children completed the Children's Coping Scale. A $2 \times 2 \times 2$ multivariate analysis of variance (MANOVA) was performed on the two main factors, adaptive and non-adaptive coping, and the 18 subscales. Main effects were found for students in the reactive aggressive group, for nonproductive coping and social action, for the proactive group on tension reduction and for gender on social support, tension reduction, and physical recreation. An interaction effect was found between reactive and proactive aggression for relax.

The group of children identified by their teachers as reactive aggressive obtained a higher score on nonproductive coping ($M = 18.6$, $SD = 8.36$) than the nonreactive group ($M = 16.53$, $SD = 6.47$). Tests of between subjects effects indicated a main effect of $F(1, 196) = 6.650, p < .025$, for reactive aggression. The mean score for the reactive group on nonproductive coping was higher than all the other groups as seen in Table 6.1. Of the factors underlying the nonproductive scale, not coping $F(1, 196) = 7.696, p < .025$ and tension reduction $F(1, 196) = 6.742, p < .025$, were significant. The reactive aggressive group also obtained a higher mean for social action ($M = 2.0$, $SD = 1.82$) than the nonreactive

Table 6.1.   Means and Standard Deviations (SD)
for the Children's Coping Scale

	Nonaggressive (n = 146)	Reactive Only (n = 17)	Nonreactive (n = 159)	Proactive Only (n = 13)	Nonproactive (n = 163)	Combined (n = 28)
Nonproductive Coping						
Female	17.75	20.5	17.6	16.0	17.88	17.07
	(6.25)	(5.69)	(6.25)	(6.44)	(6.22)	(9.93)
Male	15.42	19.77	15.06	10.6	16.17	18.5
	(6.3)	(7.93)	(6.53)	(8.44)	(6.76)	(8.23)
Tension Reduction						
Female	3.04	5.0	2.97	2.25	3.13	2.86
	(1.81)	(1.83)	(1.81)	(1.67)	(1.85)	(2.28)
Male	2.42	2.85	2.36	1.6	2.49	2.86
	(1.72)	(1.68)	(1.78)	(2.51)	(1.71)	(1.51)
Not Coping						
Female	3.71	4.25	3.66	3.13	3.74	3.93
	(1.65)	(1.26)	(1.63)	(1.46)	(1.63)	(2.4)
Male	3.11	4.46	3.03	2.0	3.35	3.79
	(1.77)	(2.22)	(1.8)	(2.12)	(1.91)	(1.58)
Social Action						
Female	1.65	2.5	1.63	1.37	1.69	1.93
	(1.8)	(1.73)	(1.77)	(1.51)	(1.8)	(1.77)
Male	1.34	2.38	1.28	0.6	1.52	1.57
	(1.47)	(2.26)	(1.44)	(0.89)	(1.66)	(1.51)
Social Support						
Female	5.85	6.25	5.75	4.75	5.86	4.57
	(1.93)	(2.5)	(1.99)	(2.49)	(1.94)	(1.55)
Male	4.5	4.23	4.45	3.8	4.45	5.29
	(2.17)	(2.42)	(2.14)	(1.79)	(2.2)	(1.77)
Physical Recreation						
Female	6.11	5.5	6.15	6.63	6.08	6.64
	(1.49)	(2.38)	(1.5)	(1.59)	(1.53)	(1.59)
Male	6.65	6.85	6.7	7.2	6.68	6.93
	(1.16)	(1.41)	(1.14)	(.84)	(1.41)	(1.54)
Relax						
Female	3.36	3.0	3.3	2.75	3.34	3.64
	(.801)	(.82)	(0.82)	(.89)	(0.8)	(.633)
Male	3.44	3.23	3.4	3.0	3.4	3.64
	(.738)	(1.36)	(0.79)	(.71)	(0.87)	(.633)
Worry						
Female	4.74	3.25	4.65	3.75	4.67	3.93
	(2.12)	(2.63)	(2.14)	(2.25)	(2.15)	(2.37)
Male	4.0	5.08	3.88	2.4	4.19	4.5
	(2.13)	(2.29)	(2.18)	(2.51)	(2.18)	(3.28)
Friends						
Female	7.14	7.0	7.21	7.88	7.14	5.86
	(2.19)	(3.46)	(2.2)	(2.3)	(2.23)	(2.18)
Male	6.11	6.3	6.09	5.8	6.15	7.36
	(2.44)	(2.43)	(2.18)	(1.3)	(2.26)	(1.86)
Solve Problems						
Female	6.38	7.25	6.28	5.25	6.42	5.07
	(1.84)	(2.06)	(1.85)	(1.83)	(1.85)	(1.38)
Male	5.65	5.54	5.62	5.4	5.63	5.93
	(2.07)	(1.71)	(2.0)	(0.55)	(2.01)	(1.77)

group ($M = 1.48$, $SD = 1.65$). Social action was one of the strategies not included in either productive or nonproductive coping. In tests of between subject effects the difference between reactive and nonreactive aggression was significant $F(1, 196) = 4.961$, $p < .05$.

There was also a main effect for proactive $F(1, 196) = 5.199$, $p < .025$, and gender $F(1, 196) = 4.355$, $p < .05$, on tension reduction. As can be seen in Table 6.1 the proactive students had lower means than the other groups for tension reduction and the girls had higher means than the boys in all groups except combined.

There was a main effect for gender on social support, as expected $F(1, 196) = 3.792$, $p = .05$, and a trend toward an interaction effect between gender and proactive, although this was not significant $F(1, 196) = 2.86$, $p = .092$. Proactive females have lower scores ($M = 4.64$, $SD = 1.89$) than nonproactive females ($M = 5.86$, $SD = 1.94$) on social support but males scores are similar for both proactive ($M = 4.89$, $SD = 1.85$) and nonproactive ($M = 4.45$, $SD = 2.2$). As can be seen in Table 6.1, females have higher scores than males on social support in all groups except the combined group. There was also a main effect for gender on physical recreation $F(1, 196) = 4.581$, $p < .05$, with boys scoring higher across all the groups.

The only strategy which showed an interaction effect between reactive and proactive aggression was that of relax $F(1, 196) = 8.139$, $p < .025$. As can be seen in Table 6.1 the means for the combined group are higher than nonaggressive and the two aggressive groups.

Children's Automatic Thoughts Scale

It was expected that aggressive children would have negative thinking. This was assessed using the Children's Automatic Thoughts Scale. A $2 \times 2 \times 2$ MANOVA was conducted with the total score and the four subscales. There was a main effect for reactive on the total score and two of the scales and a main effect for gender on the scale of hostile intent. It was expected that the proactive group would have a higher mean score for hostile intent but there was no significant difference between the groups on this factor.

The reactive aggressive group was again found to be the only group with a higher mean for the total negative thinking scale, as seen in Table 6.2. This difference was statistically significant $F(1, 196) = 7.362$, $p < .025$. Two of the factors, which make up the total scale, were significant. On tests of between-subject effects $F(1, 196) = 9.864$, $p < .025$ the reactive aggressive group had a significantly higher score for physical threat ($M = 10.51$, $SD = 8.83$) than the nonreactive group ($M = 6.98$, $SD = 7.38$). The reactive group also had a higher score on personal failure (M

**Table 6.2.   Means and Standard Deviations (SD)
for the Children's Automatic Thoughts Scale**

	Nonaggressive (n = 146)	Reactive Only (n = 17)	Non-reactive (n = 159)	Proactive Only (n = 13)	Non-proactive (n = 163)	Combined Reactive and Proactive (n = 28)
Negative Thinking						
Female	39.96	70.25	39.91	39.37	41.34	42.71
	(29.02)	(36.56)	(29.18)	(32.94)	(29.83)	(31.97)
Male	39.29	54.23	38.69	31.2	41.88	55
	(27.11)	(37.94)	(26.57)	(18.94)	(29.53)	(29.2)
Physical Threat						
Female	7.33	17.25	7.32	7.13	7.78	8.14
	(7.45)	(12.31)	(7.58)	(9.4)	(7.91)	(6.37)
Male	6.76	10	6.52	3.6	7.32	11.43
	(7.31)	(10.38)	(7.13)	(3.51)	(7.94)	(8.23)
Personal Failure						
Female	8.89	15.75	8.98	9.87	9.21	10.93
	(8.87)	(9.43)	(9.01)	(11.04)	(8.95)	(11.43)
Male	6.27	13.77	6.02	2.8	7.57	11.5
	(6.76)	(12.85)	(6.61)	(3.12)	(8.52)	(9.05)
Hostile Intent						
Female	11.37	19.25	11.32	10.75	11.73	12.93
	(7.57)	(8.34)	(7.47)	(6.73)	(7.74)	(9.56)
Male	16.18	16	16.33	18.2	16.15	20.5
	(8.98)	(11.83)	(9.02)	(10.35)	(9.45)	(8.02)

$= 12.36$, $SD = 10.79$) than the nonreactive group ($M = 7.73$, $SD = 8.19$), which was statistically significant $F(1, 196) = 9.098$, $p < .025$.

On the between-subjects test there was a main effect for gender on hostile intent $F(1, 196) = 4.566$, $p < .05$ with boys scoring higher on the hostile intent factor ($M = 16.79$, $SD = 9.35$) than girls ($M = 11.72$, $SD = 7.8$).

Beck's Anger Inventory

Since an aspect of the reactive aggressive group is anger, it was expected that this group would score higher on Beck's Anger Inventory. This was found to be the case in tests of between-subjects effects with the reactive group being significantly higher than the other groups $F(1, 196) = 5.77$, $p < .025$. See Table 6.3 for a comparison of means.

Gender

When these groups were considered by gender, boys had a higher percentage of reactive (14%) and combined (15%) aggression, compared with

Table 6.3. Means and Standard Deviations (SD) for Beck's Youth Inventory of Anger

	Nonaggressive (n = 146)	Reactive Only (n = 17)	Nonreactive (n = 159)	Proactive Only (n = 13)	Nonproactive (n = 163)	Combined Reactive and Proactive (n = 28)
Female	18.61 (9.41)	27.75 (6.4)	18.45 (9.36)	16.75 (9.18)	19.02 (9.47)	20.43 (12.7)
Male	17.32 (10.57)	21 (12.16)	17.36 (10.32)	17.8 (7.16)	17.96 (10.87)	23.29 (8.75)

girls' reactive (4%) and combined (12%) aggression. Girls had a higher percentage of proactive aggression (8%) than boys (5%).

Combined Effect

A MANOVA performed with the variables of nonproductive coping, physical threat, social threat, personal failure, social action, relax, and anger was significant $F(7, 190) = 2.843$ $p < .025$ and produced a combined effect size of partial $\eta^2 = .095$ for reactive aggression.

DISCUSSION

The results indicate that there is a difference between the two groups of aggressive students in this study. While there was only one significant difference between the proactive and nonproactive students, the reactive students differed from the nonreactive students in a number of ways.

Coping

All groups reported using a similar number of productive coping strategies but the reactive group had a higher mean score for nonproductive coping strategies than the other groups. This suggests that they do know and use productive coping strategies but may also use nonproductive strategies. This supports recommendations for interventions to focus on reducing nonproductive coping strategies rather than just increasing productive coping strategies (Frydenberg & Lewis, 2002).

The two main nonproductive strategies used by the reactive group were tension reduction—trying to feel better by letting off steam—and not coping, which was giving up or not doing anything about the problem. Tension reduction included items such as: "cry or scream" and "take my frustrations out on others." Not coping included items such as: "there is nothing I can do about the problem so I just don't do anything" and "I get headaches and stomach aches." The proactive group reported using significantly fewer of these strategies than the nonproactive group. This supports a view of proactive children being in control and behaving in a purposeful way while reactive children act impulsively, responding aggressively to fear and anger (Dodge et al., 1997).

Negative Thinking (Automatic Thoughts)

The reactive students also obtained significantly higher scores on two of the factors of the automatic thinking scale. Reactive students were found to have more negative thinking about physical threat and personal failure than the other groups. Items on the physical threat scale include: "I'm going to get hurt" and "Something will happen to someone I care about." The personal failure scale had items such as: "I can't do anything right" and "I am a failure." The significantly higher score for physical threat is consistent with Dodge's (1980) theory of hostile attributional bias. The higher score for personal failure is a different finding to that of Schniering and Rapee (2001) but their research did not distinguish between the two types of aggression. It was expected that proactive aggressive children would have higher scores on hostile intent, however, this was not the case. This is either because they do not have hostile intent or they do not perceive themselves as having hostile intent. It may also be because the items of the hostile intent scale are a mixture of reactive, "I always get blamed for things that are not my fault," and proactive, "Some people deserve what they get."

Anger

As expected the reactive group had a significantly higher score on anger than the nonreactive group and was higher than all the other groups, while the proactive group scored similarly or below the nonaggressive children. This finding supports Dodge's (1991) view that reactive aggression is affective and a response to anger or fear unlike proactive aggression which is instrumental and not a response to anger. It also raises concerns about the appropriateness of providing proactive aggressive students with a treatment, which includes anger management.

Proactive Aggression

Although the findings for the reactive children were significant they were as expected. The interesting finding is that the results for the proactive children are not significantly different to those of the nonaggressive children. This may be because they are not different in the measures used in this study or it could be that they are less aware, less honest, or just perceive themselves differently to how others see them. Proactive students may not score differently from nonaggressive children on the coping scale because it focused on reactive coping. Children with proactive aggression may be more closely related to proactive coping with its emphasis on goals and control (Greenglass, 2002), which would imply that their proactive approach to life could be steered toward positive outcomes.

Gender

Although traditionally aggression has been attributed more to males than females there were almost equal numbers of aggressive boys and girls in this study. Gender differences identified in this study were congruent with previous research (Frydenberg & Lewis, 1993b; Greenglass, 2002; Schniering & Rapee, 2001). Girls used more tension reduction while the boys resorted to more physical recreation and hostile intent. Both aggressive groups of girls have lower scores for social support than nonaggressive girls. Social support has been identified in the coping literature (Frydenberg & Lewis, 1993b; Greenglass, 2002) as a commonly used coping strategy for girls. Not having this strategy available or choosing not to use this strategy may lead to aggression or being aggressive may reduce the availability of social support.

DIRECTIONS FOR EDUCATIONAL PRACTICE

Although actual treatment programs were not trialed in this study, the findings support and challenge the underlying assumptions of different treatment approaches. Since the profiles of the two aggressive groups appear to be different, the treatments should also be different. Aggression is a complex phenomenon, triggered by a range of situational determinants including a lack of resources. Helping children to manage their emotions and to develop coping skills, including positive self-talk, is likely to be of benefit. An approach that does not take into consideration all the underlying causes of the problem is unlikely to achieve the goal of enabling young people to thrive, although it may enable them to avoid "sinking."

Reactively aggressive students may be helped by coping skills programs which focus on reducing nonproductive coping and negative thinking. These children need help to recognize that using aggression or not doing anything does not solve problems and can often make the situation worse. While they appear to use some productive coping strategies, they may need help in selecting the best strategy for a given situation. These students could also benefit from anger management to help them control their anger. It would also allow them to address their hostile attributional bias by encouraging them to assume the best rather than the worst. Unfortunately reactively aggressive students' expectations about other people's hostility are often fulfilled because of the response they get from their own aggression, so teachers need to respond to these children in a calm, understanding way and encourage the other children in the class to do the same. Reactive children's aggression is a response to a perceived threat or injustice which needs to be acknowledged before addressing the poor choice of coping strategy by the child. Like any other deficit, the most productive way of managing aggression is through education.

This study does not add any new directions for the treatment of proactive aggression except to reinforce that anger management is not the most useful approach. Proactively aggressive students do not appear to be any angrier than nonaggressive students. As Schwarzer and Taubert (2002) describe the proactive leader as being value driven, it would be important to look at the values of proactive children who have been described by Dodge and Coie (1987) as having leadership qualities. Intervention with proactive aggressive children may need to focus more on values education and developing prosocial goals.

CONCLUSIONS

The study reported here supports previous findings of gender differences in the coping literature (Frydenberg & Lewis, 1993b). It also substantiates the findings of Dodge and colleagues' (Dodge & Coie, 1987; Dodge et al., 1997) that there are two types of aggression and has shed some light on the characteristics of reactive aggressive children. It has not identified any underlying differences in negative thinking between proactive aggressive children and nonaggressive children. A greater understanding of these children may be linked to the more recent coping literature which looks at proactive coping (Greenglass, 2002; Schwarzer & Taubert, 2002). While proactive coping is seen as a positive skill, the processes may be the same for proactive aggressive children but applied with faulty goals and values contrary to those which are socially acceptable. If coping strategies increase one's sense of psychological control (Frydenberg & Lewis, 2002) then proactive aggressive children who are already in control may be using effective, albeit socially inappropriate strategies.

Future research could include other factors that may affect aggression, such as irrational beliefs. As only limited information was gained about proactive aggression from this study, further research could address personality factors that may influence proactive aggression, such as having a lower than general response to anxiety producing situations. This is suggested by the lesser use of the coping strategy worry. Although not significant, the proactive group had a lower mean for worry than the other groups. The connection between proactive coping and proactive aggression could be explored further.

Finally this research also supports the need to identify the type of aggression being displayed by individual children and tailoring the treatment to suit both the aggression type and the gender of the child. While traditional anger management and cognitive behavioral strategies used with aggressive children appear to be appropriate for reactively aggressive children, there is no evidence in this study to support their use with proactively aggressive children. As this study looked at anger and negative thinking with self-report surveys it would be necessary to develop and trial different treatments for the reactive and proactive groups to test this finding.

This research has provided support for subgroups within aggression by its findings of different coping styles, negative thinking, and anger between the reactive aggressive group and the proactive aggressive group. While differences between the reactive and the nonreactive groups were found, only one significant difference between proactive and nonproactive groups was evident in this study. This highlights the importance of observing children's behavior, identifying the triggers and/or functions of the behavior, and determining whether their aggression is reactive or proactive in order that appropriate intervention interventions can be designed.

REFERENCES

Achenbach, T. M., McConaughy, S. H., & Howell, C. T. (1987). Child/adolescent behavioral and emotional problems: Implications of cross-informant correlations for situational specificity. *Psychological Bulletin, 101*, 213-232.

Bandura, A. (1973). *Aggression a social learning analysis.* Englewood Cliffs, NJ: Prentice Hall.

Beck, A. T. (1976). *Cognitive therapy and the emotional disorders.* Guilford, CT: International Universities Press.

Beck, J. S., Beck, A. T., & Jolly, J. B. (2001). *Manual for Beck youth inventories of emotional and social impairment*. San Antonio, TX: The Psychological Corporation.

Berkowitz, L. (1978). External determinants of impulsive aggression. In W. W. Hartup & J. De Wit (Eds.), *Origins of aggression*. The Hague, The Netherlands: Mouton.

Bierman, K. L., Smoot, D. L., & Aumiller, K. (1993). Characteristics of aggressive-rejected, aggressive (nonrejected), and rejected (nonaggressive) boys. *Child Development, 64*, 139-151.

Brandon, C. M., & Cunningham, E. G. (1999a). *Bright Ideas manual*. Melbourne: Oz Child Australia.

Brandon, C. M., & Cunningham, E. G. (1999b). *Bright Ideas workbook*. Melbourne: Oz Child Australia.

Brandon, C. M., Cunningham, E. G., & Frydenberg, E. (1999). Bright Ideas: A school-based program teaching optimistic thinking skills in pre-adolescence. *Australian Journal of Guidance & Counselling, 9*, 153-163.

Brendgen, M., Vitaro, F., Tremblay, R. E., & Lavoie, F. (2001). Reactive and proactive aggression: Predictions to physical violence in different contexts and moderating effects of parental monitoring and caregiving behavior. *Journal of Abnormal Child Psychology, 29*, 293- 308.

Brook, J. S., Whiteman, M. M., & Finch, S. (1992). Childhood aggression, adolescent delinquency, and drug use: A longitudinal study. *Journal of Genetic Psychology, 153*, 369-384.

Caspi, A., Elder, G. H., Jr., & Bem, D. J. (1987). Moving against the world: Life-course patterns of explosive children. *Developmental Psychology, 23*, 308-313.

Ciampi, D. (2001, September). Perpetrators of violence: Adolescents in America. *The Forensic Examiner*, 31-38.

Coie, J. D., Underwood, M., & Lochman, J. E. (1991). Intervention in the school setting. In D. J. Pepler & K. H. Rubin (Eds.), *The development and treatment of childhood aggression*. Mahwah, NJ: Lawrence Erlbaum Associates.

Compas, B. E., Howell, D. C., Phares, V., Williams, R. A., & Giunta, C. T. (1989). Risk factors for emotional/behavioral problems in young adolescents: A prospective analysis of adolescent and parental stress and symptoms. *Journal of Consulting and Clinical Psychology, 57*, 732-740.

Crick, N. R., & Dodge, K. A. (1994). A review and reformulation of social information-processing mechanisms in children's social adjustment. *Psychological Bulletin, 115*, 74-101.

Cunningham, E. G. (2002). Developing a measurement model for coping research in early adolescence. *Educational and Psychological Measurement, 62*, 147-163.

Dodge, K. A. (1980). Social cognition and children's aggressive behavior. *Child Development, 51*, 162-170.

Dodge, K. A. (1991). The structure and function of reactive and proactive aggression. In D. J. Pepler & K. H. Rubin (Eds.), *The development and treatment of childhood aggression*. Mahwah, NJ: Lawrence Erlbaum Associates.

Dodge, K. A., & Coie, J. D. (1987). Social-information-processing factors in reactive and proactive aggression in children's peer groups. *Journal of Personality and Social Psychology, 53*, 1146-1158.

Dodge, K. A., & Frame, C. L. (1982). Social cognitive biases and deficits in aggressive boys. *Child Development, 53*, 620-635.

Dodge, K. A., Lochman, J. E., Harnish, J. D., Bates, J. E., & Pettit, G. S. (1997). Reactive and proactive aggression in school children and psychiatrically impaired chronically assaultive youth. *Journal of Abnormal Psychology, 106*, 37-51.

Dodge, K. A., & Newman, J. P. (1981). Biased decision-making processes in aggressive boys. *Journal of Abnormal Psychology, 90*, 375-379.

Dodge, K. A., Price, J. M., Bachorowski, J., & Newman, J. P. (1990). Hostile attributional biases in severely aggressive adolescents. *Journal of Abnormal Psychology, 99*, 385-392.

Dollard, J., Doob, L. W., Miller, N. E., Mowrer, O. H., & Sears, R. R. (1939). *Frustration and aggression*. New Haven, CT: Yale University Press.

Farrington, D. P. (1991). Childhood aggression and adult violence: Early precursors and later life outcomes. In D. J. Pepler & K. H. Rubin (Eds.), *The development and treatment of childhood aggression*. Mahwah, NJ: Lawrence Erlbaum Associates.

Freud, S. (1933). *New introductory lectures on psycho-analysis*. London: The Hogarth Press.

Frydenberg, E., & Lewis, R. (1993a). *Manual: The Adolescent Coping Scale*. Melbourne: Australian Council for Educational Research.

Frydenberg, E., & Lewis, R. (1993b). Boys play sport and girls turn to others: Age, gender and ethnicity as determinants of coping. *Journal of Adolescence, 16*, 253-266.

Frydenberg, E., & Lewis, R. (2002) Adolescent wellbeing: Building young people's resources. In E. Frydenberg (Ed.), *Beyond coping: Meeting goals, visions and challenges*. New York: Oxford University Press.

Garmezy, N. (1985). Stress resistant children: The search for protective factors. In J. Stevenson (Ed.), *Recent research in developmental psychopathology*. Oxford, England: Pergamon.

Garnefski, N., & Diekstra, R. F. W. (1997). Comorbidity of behavioral, emotional and cognitive problems in adolescence. *Journal of Youth and Adolescence, 26*, 321-339.

Gilliom, M., Shaw, D. S., Beck, J. E., Schonberg, M. A., & Lukon, J. L. (2002). Anger regulation in disadvantaged preschool boys: Strategies, antecedents, and the development of self-control. *Developmental Psychology, 38*, 222-235.

Green, M., Sullivan, P. D., & Eichberg, C. G. (2001). What to do with the angry toddler. *Contemporary Pediatrics, 18*, 65-80.

Greenglass, E. R. (2002) Proactive coping and quality of life management. In E. Frydenberg (Ed.), *Beyond coping: Meeting goals, visions and challenges*. New York: Oxford University Press.

Henington, C., Hughes, J. N., Cavell, T. A., & Thompson, B. (1998). The role of relational aggression in identifying aggressive boys and girls. *Journal of School Psychology, 36*, 457-477.

Hill, J. (2002). Biological, psychological and social processes in the conduct disorders. *Journal of Child Psychology and Psychiatry, 43,* 133-164.

Hobfoll, S. E. (1988). *The ecology of stress.* New York: Hemisphere.

Hobfoll S. E. (1998). *Stress, culture, and community.* New York: Plenum Press.

Hobfoll S. E., & Lilly, S. (1993). Resource conservation as a strategy for community psychology. *Journal of Community Psychology, 21,* 128-148.

Kendall, P. C., Ronan, K. R., & Epps, J. (1991). Aggression in children/adolescents: cognitive-behavioral treatment perspectives. In D. J. Pepler & K. H. Rubin (Eds.), *The development and treatment of childhood aggression.* Mahwah, NJ: Lawrence Erlbaum Associates.

Keppel, G. (1991). *Design and analysis: A researcher's handbook* (3rd ed.). Engelwood Cliffs, NJ: Prentice Hall.

Kochenderfer-Ladd, B., & Skinner, K. (2002). Children's coping strategies: Moderators of the effects of peer victimization? *Developmental Psychology, 38,* 267-278.

Lane, C., & Hobfoll, S. E. (1992). How loss affects anger and alienates potential supporters. *Journal of Consulting and Clinical Psychology, 60,* 935-942.

Lazarus, R. S. (1966). *Psychological stress and the coping process.* New York: McGraw-Hill.

Lazarus, R. S. (1991). *Emotion and adaptation.* New York: Oxford University Press.

Leung, P. W. L., & Poon, M. W. L. (2001). Dysfunctional schemas and cognitive distortions in psychopathology: A test of the specificity hypothesis. *Journal of Child Psychology and Psychiatry, 42,* 755-765.

Lorenz, K. (1967). *On aggression.* London: Methuen & Co.

McCabe, K. M., Hough, R., Wood, P. A., & Yeh, M. (2001). Childhood and adolescent onset conduct disorder: A test of the developmental taxonomy. *Journal of Abnormal Child Psychology, 29,* 305- 322.

Meichenbaum, D. (1977). *Cognitive-behavior modification. An integrative approach.* New York: Plenum Press.

Myers, D. G. (1998). *Psychology.* New York: Worth.

Olafsen, R. N., & Viemero, V. (2000). Bully/victim problems and coping with stress in school among 10-12 year old pupils in Aland, Finland. *Aggressive Behavior, 26,* 57-65.

Olweus, D. (1991) Bully/Victim problems. In D. J. Pepler & K. H. Rubin (Eds.), *The development and treatment of childhood aggression.* Mahwah, NJ: Lawrence Erlbaum Associates.

Palfai, T. P., & Hart, K. E. (1997). Anger, coping styles and perceived social support. *The Journal of Social Psychology, 137,* 405-412.

Pepler, D. J., King, G., & Byrd, W. (1991). A social-cognitively based social skills training program for aggressive children. In D. J. Pepler & K. H. Rubin (Eds.), *The development and treatment of childhood aggression.* Mahwah, NJ: Lawrence Erlbaum Associates.

Poulin, F., & Boivin, M. (2000). The role of proactive and reactive aggression in the formation and development of boys' friendships. *Developmental Psychology, 36,* 233-240.

Poulou, M., & Norwich, B. (2000). Teachers' causal attributions, cognitive, emotional and behavioral responses to students with emotional and behavioral difficulties. *British Journal of Educational Psychology, 70,* 559-581.

Printz, B. L., Shermis, M. D., & Webb, P. M. (1999). Stress-buffering factors related to adolescent coping: A path analysis. *Adolescence, 34,* 715-730.

Rudolph, K. D., & Clark, A. G. (2001). Conceptions of relationships in children with depressive and aggressive symptoms: Social-cognitive distortion or reality? *Journal of Abnormal Child Psychology, 29,* 41-61.

Salmivalli, C., & Nieminen, E. (2002). Proactive and reactive aggression among school bullies, victims and bully-victims. *Aggressive Behavior, 28,* 30-44.

Schniering, C. A., & Rapee, R. M. (2001). *Development and validation of a measure of children's automatic thoughts: The children's automatic thoughts scale.* Unpublished manuscript. Macquarie University, Sydney.

School Community Services Data Base. (2002). Catholic Education Office, Sandhurst, Victoria, Australia.

Schwartz, D. (2000). Subtypes of victims and aggressors in children's peer groups. *Journal of Abnormal Child Psychology, 28,* 181-195.

Schwarzer, R., & Taubert, S. (2002). Tenacious goal pursuits and striving towards personal growth: Proactive coping. In E. Frydenberg (Ed.), *Beyond coping: Meeting goals, visions and challenges* (pp. 19-36). New York: Oxford University Press.

Smith, T. W. (1994). Study of anger, hostility and health. In A. W. Siegman & T. W. Smith (Eds.), *Anger, hostility and the heart.* Mahwah, NJ: Lawrence Erlbaum Associates.

Tabachnick, B. G., & Fidell, L. S. (1996). *Using multivariate statistics* (3rd ed.). New York: Harper Collins College.

Webster-Stratton, C., Reid, J., & Hammond, M. (2001). Social skills and problem-solving training for children with early-onset conduct problems: Who benefits? *Journal of Child Psychology and Psychiatry, 42,* 943-952.

Zwemer, W. A., & Deffenbacher, J. L. (1984). Irrational beliefs, anger and anxiety. *Journal of Counseling Psychology, 31,* 391-393.

PART III

TEACHING COPING SKILLS

The chapters in this section tackle the all important problem of how to teach young people to cope most effectively. The first chapter in this section addresses the importance of building resilience at an early age. This is proposed with a program developed for 4 year olds. Four further chapters address the development of coping skills in the adolescent years. First, a universal coping skills program is described and evaluated in a range of settings which overall demonstrate the benefits of teaching adolescents cognitive-based skills in coping. A coping skills program that helps performers overcome their performance anxiety is described and evaluated. A proactive approach to coping is taken in a chapter by Cinamon and Rich where they describe a program that prepares young people for the dual work-family roles that they are likely to encounter in their adult lives. The final chapter in this section presents the three keys to thriving, namely cooperative relationships, the capacity to resolve conflicts constructively, and finally the importance of civic values are presented as powerful tools for succeeding in life.

CHAPTER 7

SMALL KIDS AND BIG CHALLENGES

Resilience Promotion at a Young Age

Moshe Israelashvili
Tel Aviv University, Israel

ABSTRACT

Many young children are being exposed to daily hassles or to major stressors, which might influence their sense of security and well-being. This, in turn, might lower their level of resilience, as would be evident already at the time of elementary school entrance. Currently, most interventions to promote young children's resilience target parents only. The utility of leaving the children "aside" should be seriously questioned, both in terms of parents' collaboration with such programs, as well as their proper implementation of its instructions. This is due to their being seriously occupied with other problems, such as the daily stresses of living, taking care of other family members' problems, and so forth. In a trial to promote 4-year-old kindergarten children resilience, mentors of "The A.R.Y.A. Project" (Advancement of Resilience at a Young Age) indirectly teach children ways of coping by engaging them in activities related to animals' stress and coping. The major goal of the project is to foster in the children a feeling of "never give-up."

Thriving, Surviving, or Going Under: Coping with Everyday Lives, 167–187
167

The first point in which positive effects are supposed to be evident is upon entrance to first grade. The challenges of establishing additional programs to promote preschoolers' resilience, along with several challenges facing studies on preschoolers' resilience, are offered to the reader.

INTRODUCTION

Currently it is widely accepted that resilience is developed at a young age. Moreover, many young preschool-aged children are faced with various stressors, sometimes within their families and oftentimes outside their families (Barton & Zeanah, 1990; Field, McCabe, & Schneiderman, 1992; Karraker & Lake, 1991; Stanford & Yamamoto, 2001). Hence, more research is currently warranted to determine the best way to develop resilience in young people without detrimental effects on their sense of self (Frydenberg, 1999). Surprisingly, most interventions to promote resilience focus on grade school-age children and adolescents; little is known about the ways to promote younger children's resilience. Moreover, those interventions that have been designed to promote preschoolers' coping behavior and resilience usually address the adults in the children's lives, while devoting almost no resources to direct interaction with the children themselves.

This chapter will highlight the increasing need to address young children's resilience. Following that, the utility of current efforts to achieve a change in young children's resilience through change in their parents alone, will be questioned. This will be especially considered with regard to parents of at-risk children. As an alternative, an experimental new approach to advance young children's resilience, as developed at Tel Aviv University, will then be presented. The chapter will conclude by describing further theoretical and practical challenges still waiting for a thorough investigation in the area of young children's resilience.

THE NEED TO ADDRESS PRESCHOOLERS' RESILIENCE

Fascinated by the idea that some children are more resilient than others, since the late 1980s many researchers have sought to identify the antecedents of resilience, as well as the ways to promote it. Of the many findings that these studies have yielded, a common conclusion emerged regarding the importance of the infancy and preschool periods. Various studies demonstrated that differences between the resilient and nonresilient children can be traced back to almost the very first moments of life. For example, Cowen and colleagues (Cowen, Work, & Wyman, 1997; Wyman et al., 1999; Wyman, Cowen, Work, & Kerley, 1993) offer that attributes of the young child, the family milieu, and the transactions between the two would predict later resilience outcomes (see also Tschann, Kaiser, Chesney, Alkon & Boyce, 1996). Accordingly, Masten and colleagues (Masten, 2001; Masten & Coatsworth, 1998) conclude that the quality of parenting at a young age has a major implication on the child's resilience at a later age. These findings further encouraged researchers to try to better understand differences in young children's environments as a major step in uncovering the core of resilience (Horning & Rouse, 2002; Miliotis, Sesma, & Masten, 1999).

However, a review of the literature on resilience reveals that the focus of most studies has been on the prediction of resilience in adolescence and adulthood. The assessment of resilience in infancy and early childhood and its implications on preschoolers' behavior remained somewhat neglected. This is a troubling situation as even in infancy children are exposed to various kinds of significant stress. Besides the major stressors—such as societal armed conflict (Kapor-Stanulovic, 1999), poverty (Coleman & Karraker, 1998), parental divorce (Miller, Ryan, & Morrison, 1999), medical procedures (Zelikovsky, Rodriguez, Gidycz, & Davis, 2000), and so forth—many young children are also being exposed to daily hassles that might influence their sense of security and well-being (Field et al., 1992; Karraker, Lake, & Perry, 1994). Several examples of daily stressors are events such as: physical examination and inoculation (Lewis & Ramsay, 1995), maternal separation (Gunner & Brodersen, 1992), maternal depression (Cohn & Campbell, 1992), and extensive nonparental care (Belsky & Braungart, 1991). Some young children face these hassles in a skillful way, and succeed in managing both major stressors and minor hassles. Others manage their stresses poorly with all or some of the stress of the encounter, and this might make them to feel even less efficient at managing the various life events they are confronting. Thus, as a result of parental behavior, newborn characteristics, and various stress encounters, by the time children are getting ready for first grade, significant differences in their resilience are already evident (Del Gaudio Weiss & Fantuzzo, 2001).

In the long run, differences in preschoolers' resilience will turn out to be a major component (Gullo & Burton, 1992; Weir & Gjerde, 2002) in these children's encounters with the many stressors that occur during "normal" development (Israelashvili, 2001). Yet, in the near future, the first and maybe the most crucial implication of lower levels of resilience would be evident at the time of elementary school entrance.

RESILIENCE AND SCHOOL ENTRANCE

School represents a stressful situation for many students due to the many demands imposed upon them (Dickey & Henderson, 1989; Skinner & Wellborn, 1997) as early as entrance into first grade (Fox, Dunlop, & Cushing, 2002; Ramey, Lanzi, Phillips, & Ramey, 1998). Hence, to prevent school maladjustment, the issue of school readiness has been the focus of intensive studies (Blair, 2002), especially among socioeconomically disadvantaged children (Becker & Luthar, 2002). Over the years, parallel to the significant body of evidence regarding the importance of cognitive development and literacy for school readiness, gradually the social-emotional factors have gained a lot of attention as well. Findings of various studies demonstrate that social-emotional factors act as both risk and protective factors for school adjustment and academic success (Becker & Luthar, 2002). The reason for this can be traced to the fact that the child's class is an integrative social network that exposes first graders to intensive social interactions which must be managed efficiently in order to socially adjust (van den Oord & Van Rossem, 2002). Kellam, Ling, Merisca, Brown, and Ialongo (1998) supply one example of the relevance of socio-emotional factors to school adjustment. In their study, Kellam et al. followed a group of 1,084 children who entered first grade in 19 public elementary schools, through their middle school, 6 years later. Their findings indicated that the more aggressive first grade boys, who were in more aggressive first grade classrooms, were at markedly increased risk for being highly aggressive in middle school. Such a classroom aggression effect indicates the importance of teaching preschoolers how to socially and emotionally adjust to their future first grade. Poor management of these social interactions might lead to poorer academic achievement than what the child is capable of. Thus, a child's academic achievement and school success is shaped not only by that child's cognitive development but also by his/her management of environmental interactions. Blair (2002) connects this point to a child's capacity for emotion regulation. In his integration of cognitive, emotive, and neurobiological conceptualizations of children's functioning at school entry, Blair highlights that "from a neuroscientific and functional standpoint, emotional reactivity plays a key role in focusing selective attention and applying mental processes necessary for learning" (p. 118). Hence, Blair (2002) concludes that higher order cognitive processing might be inhibited by lack of regulation of emotions, such as anxiety and frustration (see also Prior, 1998).

Accordingly, a survey among kindergarten teachers (Lewit & Baker, 1995) revealed that these teachers believe that the essential characteristics to being ready to start kindergarten are: being able to communicate verbally (84%); being enthusiastic and curious (76%); and being able to follow directions and not be disruptive (60%). This means that kindergarten teachers are concerned with children's regulatory readiness more than with children's cognitive and academic competence. Awareness of the importance of socio-emotional functioning for school adjustment gained further support by Zigler, Styfco, and Gilman's (1993) conclusions regarding the Head Start project. Following a review of various evaluation studies of the Head Start project, these authors summarize by saying that Head Start contributed especially to the participating children's social skills, self-esteem, and sense of competence. Following that, Zigler, Styfco, and Gilman (1993) offered that these factors can contribute more than IQ to an individual's ability to succeed in school and work and to become an involved member of society.

The importance of paying more attention to preschoolers' socio-emotional state can be properly understood once the data about preschoolers' characteristics, upon first grade entrance, are taken into account. For example, Pianta and colleagues (Early, Pianta, Taylor, & Cox, 2001; Rimm-Kaufman, Pianta, & Cox, 2000) found that 46% of U.S. nationally representative sample of kindergarten teachers indicate that over half the children lack those social and emotive abilities and experiences that would enable them to function productively in the kindergarten class. Hence, the need to intervene among preschoolers, in order to promote their socio-emotional capability turns to be a major task for any educational system worldwide. Such a recommendation is relevant for all kids, but especially for children from disadvantaged areas. For low socioeconomic status children who are living in tough neighborhoods the need to utilize and build strength and resilience is not an option but rather a crucial component in their education (Arnold & Doctoroff, 2003; Jones & Zigler, 2002; National Institutes of Health, 2003). This is due to the fact that these children are more vulnerable to various maladaptive behaviors, such as school drop-out (Wyman et al., 1993), delinquency (Stouthamer-Loeber, Loeber, Wei, Farrington, & Wikstrom, 2002), and poverty (Arnold & Doctoroff, 2003). Thus, unless proper interventions among at-risk preschoolers are implemented, there is a high probability that many of them may have major adjustment problems with the transition to first grade. An indirect indication that many researchers share this conclusion can be found in the fact that the study of resilience has emerged not from studies on coping behavior in general but rather, from studies of children who perform well despite the stress that they are experiencing or have experienced/encountered throughout the years (Garmezy, 1993; Garmezy, Masten, & Tellegen, 1984).

Resilience is one of the qualifications that significantly correlated with early school adjustment (Prior, 1998). As mentioned above, there are indications that by the time children are getting ready for first grade, significant differences in their resilience are evident (Del Gaudio Weiss & Fantuzzo, 2001). Hence, it seems that the need to foster resilience as early as possible, in the course of life of especially at-risk children, is not a recommendation but rather a must.

FOSTERING RESILIENCE BY ENVIRONMENTAL INTERVENTIONS

When speaking of school readiness, usually it is the teachers' or the parents' perceptions that are investigated in order to understand the problem of transition to elementary school (e.g., Connell & Prinz, 2002); only seldom have preschool children's own perceptions and feelings been directly evaluated (Dockett & Perry, 1999). One reason might be the complexity of analyzing young children's reasoning (e.g., Sy, DeMeis, & Scheinfield, 2003). Accordingly, most programs for preschool education focus on either changing the kindergarten teachers' or the parents' behavior. As mentioned above, similar phenomena occurred with regard to preschoolers' resilience; that is, usually the parents are the subject of the studies and the target for intervention (e.g., Horning & Rouse, 2002). Those studies that addressed the children themselves usually focused on elementary or secondary school children, both in terms of exploring the nature of children's resilience (e.g., Luthar, Doernberger, & Zigler, 1993; Miliotis, Sesma, & Masten, 1999; Wyman, Cowen, Work, & Kerley, 1993) and in terms of how to intervene in order to promote resilience (e.g., Cowen, Wyman, Work, & Iker, 1995; Frydenberg, & Lewis, 2000; Rak & Patterson, 1996; Rollin, Anderson, & Buchner, 1999; Wang, Haertel & Walberg, 1997).

One example of an intervention to promote elementary school students' resilience is Cowen, Wyman, Work, and Iker's (1995) Rochester Child Resilience Project (RCRP). This project was designed to enhance resilience among fourth-sixth grade inner-city children who had experienced major life stress. In a 12-session school-based intervention, children participated in groups of five to eight co-led by school personnel. Themes of the curriculum were: understanding feelings in oneself and others, perspective taking, social problem solving, dealing with solvable and unsolvable problems, and building self-efficacy and self-esteem. Follow-up studies yielded positive evaluation of the project, with significant improvement among participating children on various teacher-rated and child-rated indices of learning problems, perceived self-efficacy, anxiety, and so forth. As previously mentioned, the RCRP, like most other projects on resilience promotion, focused on elementary school children. In light of Cowen and colleagues' own findings (1997) that resilience emerges in infancy, a question remains. That is, why wait until third grade? Alternatively, an earlier intervention could have prevented some of the damages that might have occurred to several children's self-, social, and familial perceptions as a result of their difficulties in adjusting to first grade.

An exceptional example of intervention that tries to promote preschoolers' resilience is Zeitlin and Williamson's (1994) approach. Following a comprehensive description of infants' stress and coping behaviors, Zeitlin and Williamson offered and initiated a workshop on "Early Intervention and Development." This "educational program" targets parents of young children. Parents were offered free babysitting so that they could attend a 90-minute meeting, one evening a week, over a 4-week period. The workshop addressed topics such as: identifying factors that may influence a young child's development; development of motor skills; understanding a young child's early communication and cognitive skills; and how children learn to cope and to adapt to "challenges of daily living." An additional workshop that was also offered to parents focused on helping the parent cope with the transition of their child to preschool placement. Though these workshops emerged from studies of handicapped children's coping (see Williamson, Zeitlin, & Szczepanski, 1989) they seemed to significantly contribute to better parenting among parents of infants and preschool children.

The importance of Zeitlin and Williamson's work lies in the fact that it has been established based on an intensive study of infants' coping behavior. However, the limitation of Zeitlin and Williamson's (1994) approach lies in the intervention targeting parents only, especially with regard to those children who were about to enter kindergarten. Their approach represents the very common idea that parents, or children's caregivers' behavior, are the major source of influence on young children's resilience (Chambers, 1999; Cohn & Campbell, 1992; Hock & Clinger, 1981; Lewis & Ramsay, 1999; Parke & Beitel, 1988; Tronick & Gianino, 1986). Following such a notion, many would try to change the parents' behavior rather than to work directly with the preschool child.

While these ideas are based on empirical evidence, there is no reason to assume that parents are the *only* possible channel for intervention when promoting preschoolers' resilience. On the contrary, the literature gives some indication that sometimes parenting characteristics are not related to preschoolers' maladaptive behaviors (Mesman & Koot, 2001), that preschoolers' emotional and social behavior can be positively changed by a direct intervention (Shure, 2001), and that sometimes coping skills training for preschoolers will achieve better results if the mother is not involved (Faust, Olson, & Rodriguez, 1991).

Moreover, the utility of addressing most efforts to promote children's resilience toward the parents, while leaving the children aside, should be seriously questioned, especially when dealing with preschoolers who are living in low-SES families or who can be labeled as at-risk preschoolers. This is due to several problems that exist while trying to intervene among parents, such as the following:

1. **Some parents are preoccupied with daily stresses of living:** Those parents of at-risk children are frequently at risk themselves, due to their personal, familial, or environmental situations. As a result, one might discover that quite a few of the parents of at-risk children are eager to see their child develop in the "proper" way. However some of them would prefer that somebody else take responsibility for that, as they are mainly preoccupied with their own survival and daily hassles.

2. **Some parents do not focus on the child's well-being:**   Some children develop resilience in order to cope with their parents' behavior and abuse; others would love to get more attention from their parents who are often preoccupied with pursuing their own well-being. These phenomena are evident not only in low-SES families but also among families of the highest SES. Hence, an attempt to change these parents' behaviors might interfere with their own needs and may result in neither collaboration nor implementation of new knowledge about their parenting. This leads to the problem of who attends parents' meetings, as is illustrated by examples 3-8.

3. **Those who cooperate with intervention programs are not always those whose children run the highest risk for maladaptive behavior:** To attend a parent's workshop in the midst of a hard day's night, when the only thing that really matters to the parent is to have some time for himself or herself, can be a lot to ask. Not surprisingly, those parents who attend such meetings are the ones whose children are very important to them. The children of other parents—those parents who love their kids not *more* than themselves but rather *as much as* themselves (not to mention those who love their kids *less* than themselves)— will be left behind, with nobody to support their positive and resiliency related development.

4. **Parents are sometimes distrustful of the educational system:** This is a well-known phenomenon all over the world (Christenson & Carroll, 1999; Israelashvili, 1995), that parents and schools have to overcome major bouts of distrust. One would speculate that this problem is critical especially for parents of at-risk children, as a significant number of the parents might have been unable to succeed during their own school years (and this, in turn, might have contributed to their current poor economic situation). That means that even if parents attend a workshop on how to promote children's resilience, some of them will not be ready to accept

the educational recommendations and suggestions (e.g., "THEY don't really know what the meaning of living the way WE live is").

5. **Some parents are troubled by other family members' problems:** The amount of familial and personal problems is not equal for all families (Israelashvili, 2003). Many times those parents who are in need of parental guidance and instruction on how to promote their child's resilience are, at the very same time, troubled with their other child(ren)'s problems. Their ability to cooperate with a workshop recommendation might also be affected by their ability to successfully manage the problems they confront with their other child(ren).

6. **Parents are not always aware of the need to avoid the transfer of knowledge and experiences from one developmental stage to another:** Needless to say, the school's recommendations and suggestions are developmentally oriented. This means that counseling a 4-year-old child is not identical to counseling a 7-year-old child, and so forth. For example, intervention by parents of infants would necessarily be different from an intervention by parents of preschoolers. One of the reasons for the limited utility of interventions that focus on changing parental behavior is the fact that, once the child has moved to a new stage in his or her life, many parents would be in need of further guidance on how to behave under these new circumstances. One popular example would be the number of parents who have been "good-enough" parents throughout the years, but eager to get some guidance on how to behave once their child has entered the stage of adolescence. Practically speaking, some core principles, such as empathic listening, problem-solving, and so forth, can be utilized across many situations, if handled age appropriately. However, during a child's development some parents may repeatedly be in need of more guidance on additional age-related principals, as well as on new ways to implement those core principals. Hence, sometimes there might be a need for a prolonged intervention, rather than a one-time workshop, in order to gain a significant and positive change in parental behavior. This includes the case of intervention that aims to promote a child's resilience.

7. **Some parents do not trust themselves:** This is the case for many parents with low self-efficacy, who tend to be overwhelmed by their parental responsibilities (Coleman & Karraker, 2003). Some of them will even feel that they are unable to manage their current parental duties and, hence, will tend to escape any additional duty that will be directed toward them. As a result, these parents are likely to implement experts' suggestions somewhat inadequately.

8. **Some parents are not reliable:** Generally speaking, parents' assessment of their young children's socio-emotional behavior is reliable

and predictive (Mendez & Fogle, 2002). Yet, sometimes mothers' reports tend to be related to mothers' own dysphoric functioning rather than to their children's actual position (Clark-Stewart, Allhusen, McDowell, Thelen, & Call, 2003). As a result, working with parents might not always be helpful.

All together, these limitations neither intend to minimize parental influence nor underestimate the importance of efforts to promote positive parenting as a way to foster children's resilience. Rather, they suggest that intervention among parents would lead to limited success, unless some efforts are devoted, at the same time, to directly promoting resilience in these parents' children. Similar recommendations have already been suggested by Ramey and Ramey (1998). After reviewing the literature on early interventions, Ramey and Ramey came to the conclusion that interventions providing direct educational experiences for young children would have more positive and enduring effects than those which rely only on intermediary routes to change children's competencies.

FACE-TO-FACE INTERVENTION TO PROMOTE PRESCHOOLERS' RESILIENCE

One qualification that parents usually have, which turn them into powerful agents of change in their children's lives, is their care for their children and their intimate and intensive relationship with them. With regard to the above mentioned list of obstacles to parental change as a source for at-risk children's change, the need arises to try to approach young children in such a way so that some of the qualities of the parent-child relationship will be supplied by someone other than the parents themselves. One possibility is to include their kindergarten teachers in the efforts to change young children's resilience. The only limitation to this possibility is the number of tasks the kindergarten teacher is supposed to accomplish along with the amount of time he/she can devote to working with each child (individually or in small groups). Another possibility is to use mentors.

In her discussion of the "ordinary magic" that leads to resilience, Masten (2001) mentions that resilience can be achieved by a person's exposure to opportunities and choices at crucial junctures in the life course. One of her examples is finding a mentor (p. 233). Accordingly, Horning and Rouse (2002) recommend "efforts to provide other relationships for the child if extended family members are not available" (p. 158). The mentor is not a replacement for the parents, but rather an adult who is aware of that specific child's needs and knows how to guide young children in managing stressful encounters.

Actually, the idea of using a mentor in order to affect a change in children's and youth's lives is not a new one. Several prevention programs—such as Cowen et al. (1996) "Primary Mental Health Prevention," Olds, Kitzman, Cole, and Robinson's (1997) "Unmarried young inner-city pregnant females" intervention, and Parra, DuBois, Neville, Pugh-Lilly and Pavinelli's (2002) "Big Brothers/Big Sisters" program—have long ago supplied evidence of the significant impact that such programs can have. As a result, it is generally agreed that mentoring relationships, whether they arise naturally or are formed through programs (Rhodes, Bogat, Roffman, Edelman, & Galasso, 2002) offer benefits to youth. Some researchers even argue that youth from disadvantaged backgrounds are the ones to benefit most from participation in mentoring programs (DuBois, Holloway, Valentine, & Cooper, 2002).

However, applying the idea of mentoring to promote preschoolers' resilience deserves more attention, due to 4-years old kindergartners' characteristics, such as: Concrete cognitive functioning; large variance in linguistic ability; preference for playing; limited ability to concentrate (15–20 minutes at most); the possibility of conflicting feelings (e.g., between loyalty to their families and eagerness to cooperate and benefit from their mentors); and, finally, limited knowledge of "the outside world" beyond the walls of their family and kindergarten.

Hence, in order to gain the benefits of mentoring while adapting it to preschoolers' characteristics, as mentioned above, we have suggested the use of animals as a moderating "vehicle." This means that the monitor will transfer knowledge and skills to these kindergarten children by engaging the children in play, painting, and stories which are related to animals' stress and coping. There are several reasons to believe that preschoolers would benefit from exposure to animals: infants know animals and "confront" them everyday; animals are concrete; children love animals; animals confront stress and use various coping behaviors; and it is easy for kids to identify with animals. The idea is not to supply "pet therapy," but rather to take advantage of animals as a tool for communication, for acquiring children's confidence in their mentors, and for enabling children to transfer knowledge from animals' lives to their own.

The A.R.Y.A. Project—A.R.Y.A.—Advancement of Resilience at a Young Age (the acronym translates to "lion" in Hebrew)—has been established at Tel Aviv University School of Education, in collaboration with TAU Price-Broday Initiation. The basic target of the project is to promote preschoolers' resilience; the first point in which positive effects are supposed to be evident is on entrance to first grade. The project addresses at-risk 4-year-old kindergarten children, Jewish and Arab, who are living in a suburb of the city of Tel-Aviv.

Below are the major characteristics of the intervention program. A detailed description of the intervention can be found in Israelashvili and Wegman-Rosi (2003).

The A.R.Y.A. Project

- *Selection and training of mentors.*   Mentors in the project are Tel Aviv University graduate students who receive remuneration for their work. Throughout the implementation of the project the mentors participate in individual and group meetings, during which they receive instruction and training.

- *Screening all children for behavioral problems.*   All children in the nominated kindergartens are screened for behavioral and emotional problems. Children with special developmental problems are encouraged to seek individual help, though they are not prevented from participating in the project.

Individual Sessions

- *Designing the setting.*   The mentor and the preschool teacher jointly design the schedule and setting in which the mentor will individually work with the kindergarten children. Each meeting with the mentor lasts for about 20 minutes during the school day. The mentor has no control over the order in which children will come into the meeting.

- *Establishing the relationship.*   In the first session, the mentor introduces her or himself, introduces the project, tells a short story about friendship between animals, and gives "reinforcement" for collaboration with her/him.

- *Choosing an animal.*   The mentor introduces the child to a variety of animals through storytelling, joint looking at animal pictures and card play, and encourages the child to choose an animal "about which we will learn together." Children are not limited to animals living in Israel, nor would they be asked to change their preference, unless such an animal does not, or has never, existed. Some of the most popular animals that children pick are: horses, butterflies, lions, turtles, dinosaurs, and monkeys. Once the child chooses an animal, most, but not all, stories, plays, and paintings featured in the meetings will refer to this animal. Selecting an animal usually takes one to two sessions.

- *Learning together.* Through games, stories, looking at pictures, and working with puppets—the mentor dialectically exposes the child to the "chosen" animal's stress and methods of coping. In the course of each individual session, the mentor guides the child to discuss what the animal might (a) "think," (b) "feel," and (c) "do" - when confronted with a stressful event.

- *Enlarging the scope of coping methods.* In each meeting a different way of coping is introduced to the child, namely, seeking social support, planning, seeking actual support, escape, active coping, disguise, demonstrating positive aspects of oneself, and self-talk/self-sing. All these ways of coping are presented to each child, but the order of their presentation is determined individually be each mentor, according to each child's actual life and personal characteristics.

- *Delivering the "message" of resilience.* Following each story/play/experience the mentor will ask: Have you ever used such a way of coping? (awareness); in what other circumstances can you use this way of coping? (implementation); what would happen if you used this way but it did not help? (encouragement); what other ways of coping could be used in the event you have just mentioned, if this way of coping didn't help?

- *Never give-up.* A major feature of the A.R.Y.A. program is that it is not an attempt to promote what may be considered "the positive methods of coping," simply because any method of coping would be positive as long as it fits the specific circumstances (Lazarus & Folkman, 1984). Alternatively, the program attempts to foster in the children a feeling of "never give-up." This goal derives from our understanding that resilience has nothing to do with the results (success) of a person's attempts to cope with stressful events but rather with the very fact that the person persistently pursues a way to change unpleasant events.

Group Activities

The mentors conduct a group activity in which three to five children are asked to solve a problem under two conditions—the first situation involves an imaginary child in a story, and the second an actual child in the group.

Upon conclusion of the project a file, including all of the child's paintings and other work, is given to the child to keep and show to her or his family and friends.

In addition to the individual and group sessions with the children, several other activities have been conducted in order to intensify the power of the intervention. These activities include:

- *Home visits.* The mentor conducts a home visit after the child has become acquainted with the mentor. During these visits the mentor introduces her/himself and the project to the child's parent(s), asks for information about the family's and child's special problems and needs, and gains an impression of the child's home environment. Later on, the mentor will try to incorporate acquired knowledge on the child's human and physical environment in his/her discussion with the child about the implementation of various methods of coping with everyday stressors.

- *A play for the children.* A play was written especially for the project, describing a boy who has to adapt to a new kindergarten due to home relocation (along with his dog). In the course of the play, the boy employs several methods of coping, all of which the children have previously discussed with their mentors. The performance of this play is followed by a group discussion of the boy's problems and coping behaviors.

- *A special guided tour to a zoo.* A special tour of Tel Aviv University's Zoological Garden is conducted. The focus of the tour, which is conducted in cooperation with the staff of the zoo, is to demonstrate the various methods of coping which animals use in their environment.

Evaluation

Short-term evaluations of participating children's behavior in preschool are collected throughout the project implementation, to evaluate their responses to the project and any observed changes in their behavior. These evaluations serve also as a baseline for the longitudinal follow-up study of project contribution to children's school adjustment.

The A.R.Y.A. project has operated for 2 years (2002-2003) in the Jaffa area, which is a mixed residential area with Jewish and Arab, most of whom are Moslems, and a few Christians, all living side by side. Accordingly, about one third of the participating children were Jews and the rest were Arabs. All children were from low-income families composed of two to nine members ($M = 4.9$). According to parents' reports, about 20% of the children were the products of high-risk pregnancies; for about 20% there had been problems during delivery; about 40% of the children had major health problem during their first two years of life; and in about 50% of the families there had been significant family problems during the previous 3 years.

These data demonstrate that the children who participated in the project were vulnerable to various developmental problems. Currently upon the entrance of its first group into elementary school, the project faces the challenge of proper evaluation, and hopefully, a demonstration that the program contributed significantly to these preschoolers' resilience. However, from the procedural point of view, the project gained a lot of support from parents, teachers, and the children themselves who expressed their enjoyment of the project throughout the year(s). However, this project is just one example of what can be done when finding new ways to promote preschoolers' resilience.

CHALLENGES FACING STUDIES OF PRESCHOOLERS' RESILIENCE

Several problems inhibit the development of extensive knowledge on preschoolers' resilience, some of them theoretical and others practical. To name a few of the problems:

1. **Understanding preschoolers' narratives about stress and coping**: Major individual differences in preschoolers' vocabulary and reasoning are evident. However, another issue that deserves more attention is the quality of the narratives preschoolers tell about stressful encounters and coping behaviors. The structure and content of such stories, while taking into account the level of the child's vocabulary, seems to be an essential step in promoting resilience. Currently there are studies on preschoolers' narratives of various emotions they have been experiencing (see Sy, DeMeis, & Scheinfield, 2003), but there is no study about the way they describe a stress episode. It seems that a detailed analysis of such stories would be a major step in comprehending what is the meaning of stress for these preschoolers in constructing proper interventions in order to promote resilience and in establishing reliable measurements of preschoolers' resilience.

2. **Establishing reliable measurements of preschoolers' resilience:** Currently, measurement of preschoolers' resilience relies on adults' reports (e.g., Karraker & Lake, 1991; Karraker, Lake, & Perry, 1994). Though such measurements yield reliable data (Israelashvili, 2003), they represent only the adults' point of view, and thus have limited utility. For

example, in the case of intervention to promote resilience, evaluation studies need to utilize reliable pre- and postmeasures of the participating children. Both parents' and teachers' evaluations seem to be too general and imprecise and thus not able to detect changes in children's resilience within the period of several months. Hence, scales that directly measure the level of preschoolers' resilience with regard to stress episodes would contribute significantly to the development of research activity in this field. Existing tests such as the Children's' Apperception Test (Bellak & Abrams, 1997) can serve as a starting point for the development of such scales.

3. **Exploring cultural differences**: Coping and resilience are dependent on the context and culture in which the child (and adult) is living. Evidence of significant cultural differences in understanding and expressing coping (see Frydenberg et al., 2003; Grotberg, 2000), even with regard to preschoolers' resilience (Israelashvili, 2003), call for further explorations of cultural differences in socialization to coping behavior, already present at such an early age.

4. **Establishing environmental intervention that promotes resilience**: The recommendation to try to promote preschoolers' resilience as has been suggested above, is only part of a more comprehensive effort that should be made to better prepare preschoolers for the transition to elementary school and for encountering stressful episodes in a more resilient way. Other additional interventions need to be directed at kindergarten teachers and communities in which the children live. In both cases the target should be an environmental change that will focus on resilience as a major motive in that kindergarten/community life.

Thinking about young children who are facing big problems in their everyday lives and their transition to school should lead to an intensive exploration of ways to increase the odds that these young children will grow to be resilient youth and happy adults.

REFERENCES

Arnold, D. H., & Doctoroff, G. L. (2003). The early education of socioeconomically disadvantaged children. *Annual Review of Psychology, 54,* 517-545.

Barton, M. L., & Zeanah, C. H. (1990). Stress in the preschool years. In E. L. Arnold (Ed.), *Childhood stress* (pp. 194-221). New York: John Wiley & Sons.

Becker, B. E., & Luthar, S. S. (2002). Social-emotional factors affecting achievement outcomes among disadvantaged students: Closing the achievement gap. *Educational Psychologist, 37,* 197-214.

Bellak, L., & Abrams, D. M. (1997). *The thematic apperception test and the children's apperception test in clinical use* (6th ed.). Boston: Allyn & Bacon.

Belsky, J., & Braungart, J. M. (1991). Are insecure avoidant infants with extensive day-care experience less stressed by and more independent in the Strange Situation? *Child Development, 62,* 567-571.

Blair, C. (2002). School readiness: Integrating cognition and emotion in a neurobiological conceptualization of children's functioning at school entry. *American Psychologist, 57,* 111-127.

Chambers, S. M. (1999). The effect of family talks on young children's development and coping. In E. Frydenberg (Ed.), *Learning to cope: Developing as a person in complex societies* (pp. 130-149). Oxford, England: Oxford University Press.

Christenson, S. L., & Carroll, E. B. (1999). Strengthening the family-school partnership through "check and connect." In E. Frydenberg (Ed.), *Learning to cope: Developing as a person in complex societies* (pp. 248-276). Oxford, England: Oxford University Press.

Clark-Stewart, K. A., Allhusen, V. D., McDowell, D. J., Thelen, L., & Call, J. D. (2003). Identifying psychological problems in young children: How do mothers compare with child psychiatrists? *Applied Developmental Psychology, 23,* 589-624.

Cohn, J. F., & Campbell, S. B. (1992). Influence of maternal depression on infant affect regulation. In D. Cicchetti & S. L. Toth (Eds.), *Developmental perspectives on depression: Vol 4. Rochester symposium on developmental psychopathology* (pp. 103-130). Rochester, NY: University of Rochester Press.

Coleman, P. K., & Karraker, K. H. (1998). Self-efficacy and parenting quality: Findings and future applications. *Developmental Review, 65,* 622-637.

Coleman, P. K., & Karraker, K. H. (2003). Maternal self-efficacy beliefs, competence in parenting, and toddlers' behavior and developmental status. *Infant Mental Health Journal, 24,* 126-148.

Connell, C. M., & Prinz, R. J. (2002). The impact of childcare and parent-child interactions on school readiness and social skills development for low-income African American children. *Journal of School Psychology, 40,* 177-193.

Cowen, E. L., Hightower, A. D., Pedro-Carroll, J. L., Work, W. C., Wyman, P. A., & Haffey, W. G. (1996). *School-based prevention for children at risk: The Primary Mental Health Project.* Washington, DC: American Psychological Association.

Cowen, E. L., Work, W. C., & Wyman, P. A. (1997). The Rochester Child Resilience Project (RCRP): Facts found, lessons learned, future directions divined. In S. S. Luthar, J. A. Burack, D. Cicetti, & J. R. Weisz. (Eds.), *Developmental psychopathology: Perspectives on adjustment, risk, and disorder* (pp. 527-547). New York: Cambridge University Press.

Cowen, E. L., Wyman, P. A., Work, W. C., & Iker, M. R. (1995). A preventive intervention for enhancing resilience among highly stressed urban children. *Journal of Primary Prevention, 15,* 247-260.

Del Gaudio Weiss, A., & Fantuzzo, J. W. (2001). Multivariate impact of health and caretaking risk factors on the school adjustment of first graders. *Journal of Community Psychology, 29,* 141-160.

Dickey, J. P., & Henderson, P. (1989). What young children say about stress and coping in school. *Health Education, 20*, 14-17.

Dockett, S., & Perry, B. (1999). Starting school: What do the children say? *Early Child Development and Care, 159*, 107-119.

DuBois, D. L., Holloway, B. E., Valentine, J. C., & Cooper, H. (2002). Effectiveness of mentoring programs for youth: A meta-analytic review. *American Journal of Community Psychology, 30*, 157-197.

Early, D. M., Pianta, R. C., Taylor, L. C., & Cox, M. (2001). Transition practices: Findings from a national survey of kindergarten teachers. *Early Childhood Education Journal, 28*, 199-206.

Faust, J., Olson, R., & Rodriguez, H. (1991). Same-day surgery preparation: Reduction of pediatric patient arousal and distress through participant modeling. *Journal of Consulting and Clinical Psychology, 59*, 475-478.

Field, T. M., McCabe, P. M., & Schneiderman, N. (Eds.). (1992). *Stress and coping in infancy and childhood.* Hillsdale, NJ: Lawrence Erlbaum Associates.

Fox, L., Dunlop, G., & Cushing, L. (2002). Early intervention, positive behavior support, and transition to school. *Journal of Emotional & Behavioral Disorders, 10*, 149-157.

Frydenberg, E. (Ed.). (1999). Constructing a research agenda. In *Learning to cope: Developing as a person in complex societies* (pp. 341-352). Oxford, England: Oxford University Press.

Frydenberg, E., & Lewis, R. (2000). Teaching coping to adolescents: When and to whom. *American Educational Research Journal, 37*, 727-745.

Frydenberg, E., Lewis, R., Kennedy, G., Ardila, R., Frindte, W., & Hannoun, R. (2003). Coping with concerns: An exploratory comparison of Australian, Colombian, German, and Palestinian adolescents. *Journal of Youth and Adolescence, 32*, 59-66.

Garmezy, N. (1993). Children in poverty: Resilience despite risk. *Psychiatry, 56*, 127-136.

Garmezy, N., Masten, A. S., & Tellegen, A. (1984). The study of stress and competence in children: A building block for developmental psychopathology. *Child Development, 55*, 97-111.

Grotberg, E. H. (2000). The International Resilience Research Project. In A. L. Comunian & U. P. Gielen (Eds.), *International perspectives on human development* (pp. 379-399). Lengerich, Germany: Pabst Science.

Gullo, D. F., & Burton, C. B. (1992). Age of entry, preschool experience, and sex as antecedents of academic readiness in kindergarten. *Early Childhood Research Quarterly, 7*, 175-186.

Gunner, M. R., & Brodersen, L. (1992). Infant stress reactions to brief maternal separations in human and nonhuman primates. In T. M. Field, P. M. McCabe, M. Philip, & N. Schneiderman (Eds.), *Stress and coping in infancy and childhood* (pp. 1-18). Hillsdale, NJ: Lawrence Erlbaum Associates.

Hock, E., & Clinger, J. B. (1981). Infant coping behaviors: Their assessment and their relationship to maternal attributes. *Journal of Genetic Psychology, 138*, 231-243.

Horning, L. E., & Rouse, K. A. G. (2002). Resilience in preschoolers and toddlers from low-income families. *Early Childhood Education Journal, 29*, 155-159.

Israelashvili, M. (1995). *Parents-school collaboration*. Monograph submitted to Israel Ministry of Education. Tel Aviv, Israel: Tel Aviv University, School of Education.

Israelashvili, M. (2001) Developmental perspective on children's exposure to stressful life events. *International Journal for Mental Health Promotion, 3*, 5-10.

Israelashvili, M. (2003). *Cultural bias in cross-informant evaluations of preschoolers.* Manuscript submitted for publication.

Israelashvili, M., & Wegman-Rozi, O. (2003). Advancement of preschoolers' resilience: The A. R. Y. A. project. *Early Childhood Education Journal, 31*, 101-105.

Jones, S. M., & Zigler, E. (2002). The Mozart effect: Not learning from history. *Journal of Applied developmental Psychology, 23*, 355-372.

Kapor-Stanulovic, N. (1999). Encounter with suffering. *American Psychologist, 54*, 1020-1027.

Karraker, K. H., & Lake, M. A. (1991). Normative stress and coping processes in infancy. In E. M. Cummings & A. L. Greene (Eds.), *Life-span developmental psychology: Perspectives on stress and coping* (pp. 85-108). Hillsdale, NJ: Lawrence Erlbaum Associates.

Karraker, K. H., Lake, M., & Perry, T. B. (1994). Infant coping with everyday stressful events. *Merrill-Palmer Quarterly, 40*, 171-189.

Kellam, S. G., Ling, X., Merisca, R., Brown, C. H., & Ialongo, N. (1998). The effect of the level of aggression in the first grade classroom on the course and malleability of aggressive behavior into middle school. *Development and Psychopathology, 10*, 165-185.

Lazarus, R. S., & Folkman, S. (1984). *Stress, appraisal and coping*. New York: Springer.

Lewis, M., & Ramsay, D. S. (1995). Developmental change in infants' responses to stress. *Child Development, 66*, 657-670.

Lewis, M., & Ramsay, D. S. (1999). Effect of maternal soothing on infant stress response. *Child Development, 70*, 11-20.

Lewit, E. M., & Baker, L. S. (1995) School readiness. *The Future of Children, 5*, 128-139.

Luthar, S. S., Doernberger, C. H., & Zigler, E. (1993). Resilience is not a unidimensional construct: Insights from a prospective study of inner-city adolescents. *Development and Psychopathology, 5*, 703-717.

Masten, A. S. (2001). Ordinary magic: Resilience processes in development. *American Psychologist, 56*, 227-238.

Masten, A. S., & Coatsworth, J. D. (1998). The development of competence in favorable and unfavorable environments: Lessons from research on successful children. *American Psychologist, 53*, 205-220.

Mendez, J. L., & Fogle, L. M. (2002). Parental reports of preschool children's social behavior: Relations among peer play, language competence, and problem behavior. *Journal of Psychoeducational Behavior, 20*, 370-385.

Mesman, J., & Koot, H. M. (2001). Early preschool predictors of preadolescent internalizing and externalizing *DSM-IV* diagnoses. *Journal of the American Academy of Child and Adolescent Psychiatry, 40*, 1029-1036.

Miliotis, D., Sesma, A., Jr., & Masten, A. S. (1999). Parenting as a protective process for school success in children from homeless families. *Early Education and Development, 10*, 111-133.

Miller, P. A., Ryan, P., & Morrison, W. (1999). Practical strategies for helping children of divorce in today's classroom. *Childhood Education, 75*, 285-289.

National Institutes of Health. (2003, January 27). *NIH Guide: Effectiveness of early childhood programs, curricula, and interventions in promoting school readiness* [Online]. Avaialable: http://www.nih.gov/rfa-hd-03-003

Olds, D., Kitzman, H., Cole, R., & Robinson, J. (1997). Theoretical foundations of a program of home visitation for pregnant women and parents of young children. *Journal of Community Psychology, 25*, 9-25.

Parke, R. D., & Beitel, A. (1988). Disappointment: When things go wrong in the transition to parenthood. *Marriage and Family Review, 12*, 221-265.

Parra, G. R., DuBois, D. L., Neville, H. A., Pugh-Lilly, A. O., & Pavinelli, N. (2002). Mentoring relationships for youth: Investigation of a process-oriented model. *Journal of Community Psychology, 30*, 367-388.

Prior, M. (1998). Resilience and coping: The role of individual temperament. In E. Frydenberg (Ed.), *Learning to cope: Developing as a person in complex societies* (pp. 33-52). Oxford, England: Oxford University Press.

Rak, C. F., & Patterson, L. E. (1996). Promoting resilience in at-risk children. *Journal of Counseling and Development, 74*, 368-373.

Ramey, C. T., & Ramey, S. L. (1998). Early intervention and early experience. *American Psychologist, 53*, 109-120.

Ramey, S. L., Lanzi, R. G., Phillips, M. M., & Ramey, C. T. (1998). Perspectives of former Head Start children and their parents on school and the transition to school. *The Elementary School Journal, 98*, 311-328.

Rhodes, J. E., Bogat, G. A., Roffman, J., Edelman, P., & Galasso, L. (2002). Youth mentoring in perspective: Introduction to the special issue. *American Journal of Community Psychology, 30*, 149-155.

Rimm-Kaufman, S., Pianta, R. C., & Cox, M. (2000). Teachers' judgment of problems in the transition to school. *Early Childhood Research Quarterly, 15*, 147-166.

Rollin, S. A., Anderson, C. W., & Buchner, R. M. (1999). Coping in children and adolescents: A prevention model for helping kids avoid or reduce at-risk behavior. In E. Frydenberg (Ed.), *Learning to cope: Developing as a person in complex societies* (pp. 299-321). Oxford, England: Oxford University Press.

Shure, M. B. (2001). I can problem solve (ICPS): An interpersonal cognitive problem solving program for children. *Residential Treatment for Children and Youth, 18*, 3-14.

Skinner, E. A., & Wellborn, J. G. (1997). Children's coping in the academic domain. In P. Wolchik & I. Sandler (Eds.), *Handbook of children's coping: Linking theory to intervention* (pp. 387-421). New York: Plenum.

Stanford, B. H., & Yamamoto, K. (Eds.). (2001). *Children and stress: Understanding and helping.* Olney, MD: Association for Childhood Education International.

Stouthamer-Loeber, M., Loeber, R., Wei, E., Farrington, D. P., & Wikstrom, P. H. (2002). Risk and protective effects in the explanation of persistent serious delinquency in boys. *Journal of Consulting and Clinical Psychology, 70*, 111-123.

Sy, S. R., DeMeis, D. K., & Scheinfield, R. E. (2003). Pre-school children's under-standing of the emotional consequences for failures to act prosaically. *British Journal of Developmental Psychology, 21*, 259-272.

Tronick, E. Z., & Gianino, A. (1986). Interactive mismatch and repair: Challenges to the coping infant. *Zero to Three, 6*, 1-6.

Tschann, J. M., Kaiser, P., Chesney, M. A., Alkon, A., & Boyce, W. T. (1996). Resilience and vulnerability among preschool children: Family functioning, temperament, and behavior problem. *American Academy of Child and Adolescent Psychiatry, 35*, 184-192.

van den Oord, E. J. C. G., & Van Rossem, R. (2002). Differences in first graders' school adjustment: The role of classroom characteristics and social structure of the group. *Journal of School Psychology, 40*, 371-394.

Wang, M. C., Haertel, G. D., & Walberg, H. J. (1997). Fostering educational resil-ience in inner-city schools. In H. J. Walberg & O. Reyes (Eds.), *Children and youth: Interdisciplinary perspectives, Vol. 7. Issues in children's and families' lives* (pp. 119-140). Thousand Oaks, CA: Sage.

Weir, R. C., & Gjerde, P. F. (2002). Preschool personality prototypes: Internal coherence, cross-study reliability, and developmental outcomes in adoles-cence. *Personality and Social Psychology Bulletin, 28*, 1229-1241.

Williamson, G. G., Zeitlin, S., & Szczepanski, M. (1989). Coping behavior: Impli-cations for disabled infants and toddlers. *Infant Mental Health Journal, 10*, 3-13.

Wyman, P. A., Cowen, E. L., Work, W. C., Hoyt-Meyers, L., Magnus, K. B., & Fagen, D. B. (1999). Caregiving and developmental factors differentiating young at-risk urban children showing resilient versus stress-affected out-comes: A replication and extension. *Child Development, 70*, 645-659.

Wyman, P. A., Cowen, E. L., Work, W. C., & Kerley, J. H. (1993). Life stress: A prospective study of urban at-risk children. *Development and Psychopathology, 5*, 649-661.

Zeitlin, S., & Williamson, G. C. (1994). *Coping in young children: Early intervention practices to enhance adaptive behavior and resilience*. Baltimore: Paul H. Brookes.

Zelikovsky, N., Rodriguez, J. R., Gidycz, C. A., & Davis, M. A. (2000). Cognitive behavioral and behavioral interventions help young children cope during a voiding cystourethrogram. *Journal of Pediatric Psychology, 25*, 535-543.

Zigler, E., Styfco, S. J., & Gilman, E. (1993). The national Head Start program for disadvantaged preschoolers. In E. Zigler, S. J. Styfco, & J. Sally (Eds.), *Head Start and beyond: A national plan for extended childhood intervention* (pp. 1-41). New Haven, CT: Yale University Press.

CHAPTER 8

TEACHING YOUNG PEOPLE
TO COPE

Erica Frydenberg
University of Melbourne, Australia

ABSTRACT

Improving children and adolescent adaptation to stress has been identified as a promising approach to preventing the development of problems and illness in young people. This chapter will cover the theoretical and conceptual framework that underlies coping and will address the relevance of this conceptualization for children, adolescents, and adults. It will consider the implications for educational practice in a general sense and more particularly focuses on the development of coping skills in school settings. The development of a coping skills program, The Best of Coping (BOC), was developed at Melbourne University as a skills-based cognitive behavioral program designed to facilitate the learning of positive thinking skills and productive coping strategies in adolescents. The outcomes of seven evaluations in a number of settings are presented. Collectively, they highlight the fact that young people can be provided with skills that enhance their ability to cope effectively with their life circumstances.

Thriving, Surviving, or Going Under: Coping with Everyday Lives, 189–206

INTRODUCTION

Schools are increasingly expected to take on more than a purely academic role in the psychosocial development of young people. There is increased pressure from parents and the community for schools to not only educate young people in literacy and numeracy, but to also provide support and guidance in relation to general well-being and mental health. State governments provide general guidelines on how schools should provide such support, with emphasis placed on primary prevention and early intervention through the delivery of coordinated and comprehensive services for young people (Department of Education Victoria, 1998). However, it is left up to each school to identify specific issues of concern in relation to their students and how they will deliver such services. Although specific issues may vary depending on the demographics of the school, some issues are universally accepted as being pertinent to young people's well-being. One such area, which has been identified as influencing adolescents' mental health, is the coping process.

The coping process is particularly important in adolescence because it has been acknowledged that there is a link between psychosocial stress and illness in adults, as well as in children and adolescents (Boyce & Jemerin, 1990). Adolescence is a time when many young people are confronted with many life stressors for the first time. They have not yet fully developed a repertoire of coping responses from which to draw, and consequently the way they deal with the stress may impact on them adversely (Patterson & McCubbin, 1987).

Researchers have examined factors that may moderate the relationship between stressors and adjustment, and characterize "resilient" children and adolescents who cope well despite developmentally adverse conditions (Ebata & Moos, 1991; Garmezy, 1983; Rutter, 1987). One of these factors is gender, as it is well acknowledged that boys and girls in general experience different mental health issues, and as such may require different preventative approaches. Indeed they do cope differently.

One way of addressing the increasing importance of identifying ways of encouraging the development of resilience to stress in adolescents as a way of combating psychological problems is to improve adaptation to stress through preventative programs (Sandler, Wolchik, MacKinnon, Ayers, & Roosa, 1997).

A primary goal of prevention is to provide adjustment enhancing skills and conditions (Raphael, 1993). Programs offer this opportunity of providing all adolescents, rather than focusing on those who may already be considered at risk of mental health problems. They provide an opportunity to develop strategies in a supportive environment, that may buffer adolescents against adverse conditions. In this way it is hoped that the severity of issues arising and the number of young people affected may be reduced.

In response to these issues, there is a clear need for schools to have access to programs that have been empirically evaluated and take factors such as gender differences into consideration, in order to provide adolescents with an opportunity to build their skills in these areas.

DEFINING COPING

There are two major theoretical approaches to stress and coping, both of which have been explored more extensively with adult groups rather than with young people. The first of these theories is the cognitive behavioral approach exemplified in the work of Lazarus (1966, 1991). The second is the Conservation of Resources (COR) theory developed by Hobfoll (1988, 1998, Hobfoll & Lilly, 1993). These theoretical approaches share some common conceptual underpinnings, but diverge in the manner in which they focus on either the cognitive processes within the individual, as in the appraisal approach of Lazarus, or the sociological context, as in the COR theory of Hobfoll. In recent years Hobfoll has extended his resource theory to emphasize communal, rather than individualistic aspects of coping (Hobfoll, 2002) and others have extended the transactional stress model to consider proactive aspects of coping (Schwarzer & Taubert, 2002; Greenglass, 2002). These researchers emphasize extensions of the coping construct to include positive strivings, which were hitherto in the domain of motivation. Proactive coping is a relatively new concept. As Greenglass points out reactive coping is about risk management and proactive coping is about goal management.

While the appraisal approach of Lazarus, which emphasizes how an individual appraises the situation and the resources which they have to deal with the situation underpins much of the research on coping reported here, the work of Hobfoll in emphasizing the social context in which the individual finds themselves, as resource rich or resource poor, also determines how they cope and has provided insights on young people's coping (McKenzie, 2001; McKenzie, Frydenberg, & Poole, 2003; see also Chapter 4, this volume).

Coping may be seen as the behavioral and cognitive efforts used by individuals to deal with the person-environment relationship (Frydenberg & Lewis, 2000). The coping resources, styles and strategies to which an individual has access and uses, all influence the way in which an individual responds to stressful situations. Coping resources include those aspects of the self, such as problem-solving skills and self-esteem, as well as the social environment (the availability of a supportive social network) that facilitate adaptation to life stress (Frydenberg & Lewis, 1993a).

Coping strategies refer to the cognitive or behavioral actions taken in the course of a particular stressful episode. These may vary across time and context depending on the stressor (Compas, 1987). There are limitless numbers of coping strategies that individuals use to manage their concerns. However, in order to study coping it is necessary to reduce the number of strategies to a manageable few, by grouping together similar ways of coping based on similarly of ideas or actions. This is achieved through various empirical procedures and the factors extracted make up the different coping strategies (Frydenberg, 1997). For the present study, the different coping actions that individuals use will be grouped according to 18 strategies identified by the Adolescent Coping Scale (Frydenberg & Lewis, 1993b). This is a scale that has been developed through a rigorous empirical procedure utilizing data obtained from Australian adolescents and as such, is seen as an appropriate measurement of coping.

These coping strategies have been grouped according to a reduced number of dimensions, which have been referred to as coping styles. Coping styles are methods of coping that characterize individuals' reactions to stress either over time or across different situations. They may partially reflect the ways of coping preferred by individuals because they are consistent with personal goals, values, and beliefs.

The most widely used model of coping, the transactional model, proposes that coping can be defined in terms of two global coping strategies: problem-focused (or behavioral) coping and emotion-focused (or cognitive) coping (Folkman, 1982; Lazarus & Folkman, 1984). Other researchers have found that the strategies can best be grouped to characterize three coping styles that represent two functional and one dysfunctional aspect of coping (Frydenberg & Lewis, 1991; Seiffge-Krenke & Shulman, 1990). The functional styles represent direct attempts to deal with the problem, with or without reference to others, while the dysfunctional styles relate to the use of nonproductive strategies. It is important to note however, that the use of the terms functional and dysfunctional styles do not refer to "good" or "bad" types of coping as coping strategies and styles are context dependent.

THE INSTRUMENT

The main evaluative tool used in the studies reported here was the Adolescent Coping Scale (ACS) (Frydenberg & Lewis, 1993b) both as part of the program and as pre- and postprogram measures.

The scale consists of 80 questions, 79 of which elicit ratings of an individual's use of 18 coping strategies, plus a final open-ended question. Scores on the scales can be expressed as percentages so that the respondents' preferred coping styles can be readily compared (for clinical and counseling purposes) to populations reported in the manual and the literature. The items on the ACS comprise 18 different scales, each containing between three and five items, and each reflecting a different coping response.

Each item in the scale, with the exception of the last one, describes a specific coping response, be it a behavior or a mind set (for example, "Talk to others to see what they would do if they had the problem"). The last item, Item 80, asks students to write down anything they do to cope, other than those things described in the preceding 79 items. To record their responses, students indicate if the coping behavior described was used "a great deal," "often," "sometimes," "very little," or "doesn't apply or don't use it" (no usage), by circling the numbers 5, 4, 3, 2, or 1 respectively. All scales are reliable with a median Cronbach alpha figure of .70. The stability of responses as measured by test retest reliability coefficients range from .44 to .81 and are in general moderate, but nevertheless satisfactory given the dynamic nature of coping.

The 18 scales of the ACS have labels that reflect the construct inherent in the items. They are recorded in Table 8.1 along with an exemplar that represents the most generic of the items on each respective scale.

In addition to providing an assessment of 18 coping strategies the ACS allows for combining scales to produce measures of three empirically defensible coping styles based on factor analysis (Frydenberg & Lewis, 1996). These three coping styles or domains referred to in this study are:

1. *Solving the Problem*, which comprises eight coping strategies (seeking social support, focus on solving the problem, physical recreation, seek relaxing diversions, investing in close friends, seek to belong, work hard and achieve, and focus on the positive) and represents a style of coping characterized by working at a problem while remaining optimistic, fit, relaxed, and socially connected.

2. *Reference to Others*, which contains four strategies (seek social support seek, spiritual support, seek professional help, and social action) and can be characterized by turning to others for support whether they are peers, professionals, or deities.

3. *Nonproductive Coping*, which comprises eight strategies (worry, seek to belong, wishful thinking, not cope, ignore the problem, tension reduction, keep to self, and self-blame). These primarily reflect a combination of what may be termed nonproductive, avoidance strategies, which are empirically associated with an inability to

Table 8.1.   The Conceptual Areas of Coping

1. **SEEK SOCIAL SUPPORT** is represented by items that indicate an inclination to share the problem with others and enlist support in its management, e.g., *Talk to other people to help me sort it out.*

2. **FOCUS ON SOLVING THE PROBLEM** is a problem-focused strategy that tackles the problem systematically by learning about it and takes into account different points of view or options, e.g., *Work at solving the problem to the best of my ability.*

3. **WORK HARD AND ACHIEVE** is a strategy describing commitment, ambition, (achieve well) and industry, e.g., *Work hard.*

4. **WORRY** is characterized by items that indicate a concern about the future in general terms or more specifically concern with happiness in the future, e.g., *Worry about what is happening*

5. **INVEST IN CLOSE FRIENDS** is about engaging in a particular intimate relationship, e.g., *Spend more time with boy/girl friend.*

6. **SEEK TO BELONG** indicates a caring and concern for one's relationship with others in general and more specifically concern with what others think, e.g., *Improve my relationship with others.*

7. **WISHFUL THINKING** is characterized by items based on hope and anticipation of a positive outcome, e.g., *Hope for the best.*

8. **SOCIAL ACTION** is about letting others know what is of concern and enlisting support by writing petitions or organizing an activity such as a meeting or a rally, e.g., *Join with people who have the same concern.*

9. **TENSION REDUCTION** is characterized by items that reflect an attempt to make oneself feel better by releasing tension, e.g., *Make myself feel better by taking alcohol, cigarettes or other drugs.*

10. **NOT COPE** consists of items that reflect the individual's inability to deal with the problem and the development of psychosomatic symptoms, e.g., *I have no way of dealing with the situation.*

11. **IGNORE THE PROBLEM** is characterized by items that reflect a conscious blocking out of the problem and resignation coupled with an acceptance that there is no way of dealing with it, e.g., *Ignore the problem.*

12. **SELF-BLAME** indicates that an individual sees themselves as responsible for the concern or worry, e.g., *Accept that I am responsible for the problem.*

13. **KEEP TO SELF** is characterized by items that reflect the individual's withdrawal from others and wish to keep others from knowing about concerns, e.g., *Keep my feelings to myself.*

14. **SEEK SPIRITUAL SUPPORT** is characterized by items that reflect prayer and belief in the assistance of a spiritual leader or Lord, e.g., *Pray for help and guidance so that everything will be all right.*

15. **FOCUS ON THE POSITIVE** is represented by items that indicate a positive and cheerful outlook on the current situation. This includes seeing the "bright side" of circumstances and seeing oneself as fortunate, e.g., *Look on the bright side of things and think of all that is good.*

16. **SEEK PROFESSIONAL HELP** denotes the use of a professional adviser, such as a teacher or counselor, e.g., *Discuss the problem with qualified people.*

17. **SEEK RELAXING DIVERSIONS** is about relaxation in general rather than about sport. It is characterized by items that describe leisure activities such as reading and painting, e.g., *Find a way to relax, for example, listen to music, read a book, play a musical instrument, watch TV.*

18. **PHYSICAL RECREATION** is characterized by items that relate to playing sport and keeping fit, e.g., *Keep fit and healthy.*

cope. These second order factors, known as coping styles, all have reliabilities exceeding 0.80 (Frydenberg & Lewis, 1996).

EFFECTIVENESS OF COPING STYLES

Although it is difficult to determine what constitutes effective coping skills, general research in the field of coping has identified types of characteristics that make an adolescent effective in coping, and thus better able to deal with stress. These characteristics have been found to include temperament, optimism, perceived personal control, familial factors (such as family cohesion, shared values, loving parents, and a relationship with at least one parent figure), flexibility, and the availability of social support (Luthar & Zigler, 1991; Frydenberg & Lewis, 2002).

Coping strategies that include problem solving and positive cognitions about a stressful situation have been found to be related to less emotional, behavioral and substance use problems (Compas, Malcarne, & Fondacaro, 1988; Ebata & Moos, 1991). In contrast, there appears to be fairly consistent evidence that the use of nonproductive coping strategies that involve avoidance, such as not thinking about the problem, are related to more mental health problems in adolescents (Ebata & Moos, 1991; Lewis & Frydenberg, 2002; Sandler et al., 1997).

GENDER AND COPING

Boys and girls are socialized differently to fit into expectations of gender roles, and into acceptable and unacceptable ways of coping. They are rewarded or punished differently for coping and failing to cope. This may result in boys and girls learning to cope with situations in different ways, and have lead to consistent gender differences in the literature (Frydenberg, 1997).

There appear to be sex differences in the use of social resources, with girls more often reporting that they seek advice, help, comfort, or sympathy from others, regardless of the problem, and more as they get older. Girls discuss their problems with others more often and try to clarify their difficulties by talking them over openly (Seiffge-Krenke, 1990).

Girls report more frequent use of a broader range of coping and that they use strategies that involve interpersonal relationships with friends, siblings, parents, and other adults. It was also found that females use more solving the problem strategies than males, whereas males resort to a greater use of humour (Patterson & McCubbin, 1987). Using the same instrument, that is, Patterson and McCubbin's 54-item A-COPE (1987), with 244 subjects, Copeland and Hess (1995) found similar results. Females used coping strategies that included a proactive orientation, catharsis, positive imagery, and self-reliance more than males. Males were more likely to use avoiding problems, physical diversions, and passive diversions.

Similar differences in the coping strategies used by Australian males and females have been found in a study of 673 students from five secondary schools (Frydenberg & Lewis, 1993a). The study found differences in four strategies that were used to varying degrees by boys and girls. Girls were found to use more social support, wishful thinking, and tension reduction strategies, whereas boys used physical recreation more than girls. Additionally, however, girls were found to employ a nonproductive style of coping more than boys, putting more energy into strategies such as worry and self-blame.

Another study reported gender differences with 442 students, (314 living in intact families, 128 students living in separated families) from six high schools in metropolitan Melbourne who completed the Specific form of the Adolescent Coping Scale. Again it was found that in general, boys reported greater use of physical recreation and ignoring of problem, as well as engaging in social action and seeking professional help (Frydenberg & Lewis, 1996). In addition, it appears that girls are more likely to draw attention to the fact that they do not feel as though they are coping, whereas boys tend to keep this to themselves (Frydenberg & Lewis, 2000). These differences may in part be due to the finding that male and female adolescents differ in their appraisal of the same normative demands. Girls evaluate the same problem as more complex and more individually caused. Furthermore, when a stressful event is over, they continue to ruminate or think about it (Seiffge-Krenke, 1990).

These gender differences may predispose boys and girls to different difficulties during adolescence. For instance, the greater use of social support has in some instances been found to be associated with better academic achievement, particularly with boys who seem to profit from using this strategy by doing better in their school work (Parsons, Frydenberg, & Poole, 1996). This is of interest given the present concern regarding boys' achievement academically in relation to girls (Teese, 1989).

AGE AND COPING

Just as there have been clear and consistent gender differences in coping, age has been found to be a consistent mediating factor (see Chapter 2 by Lewis and Frydenberg, this volume). In general, functional coping decreases with age: as they get older, boys and girls use more tension reducing strategies (Compas et al., 1988; Frydenberg & Lewis, 1993a, 1999, 2000). There seems be a slump in coping between the ages of 14-16 (Frydenberg & Lewis, 2000). It is for that reason that it is generally recommended that coping skills be taught before young people reach the senior years of their school life.

DEVELOPING COPING SKILLS

Adolescents seem to acquire coping behaviors and styles from a number of sources. These include: previous personal experience in handling similar situations; vicarious experience associated with observing the success or failure of others, especially family members; perceptions of their own physiology and inferences they make about their vulnerability; as well as social persuasion, particularly by parents, peers, and significant others (Patterson & McCubbin, 1987). During this period, adolescents may acquire coping skills through trial and error. However, going through the trial and error process may render some adolescents vulnerable to stress-related problems (Schinke, Schilling, & Snow, 1987). Coping skills programs offer adolescents the opportunity to experience a range of coping skills without the stress of a real situation (Raphael, 1993).

Introducing programs into the school setting is a way of allowing students to explore and develop an understanding of their own and alternative coping behaviours in a safe and supportive environment. However there are few tested and systematic studies of ways to promote mental health of young people (Raphael, 1993). Thus, there is a real need to develop preventative programs, particularly ones that address general coping skills and that are easily offered within a school setting.

There is considerable literature supporting the effectiveness of problem solving and affective awareness skills as a way of reducing a wide range of child mental health problems (Sandler et al., 1997). There are various approaches to developing the desired skills. Self-help publications such as *Coping for Capable Kids* (Cohen & Frydenberg, 1995), publications that bring together a body of knowledge that help clinicians and educators design programs of instruction such as *Coping Skills Intervention for Children and Adolescents* (Forman, 1992), or *Learning to Cope: Developing as a Person in Complex Societies* (Frydenberg, 1999b), or detailed programs which have been developed with the aim of building adolescents' problem-solving, decision-making, and goal-setting abilities.

One such program, The Best of Coping (Frydenberg & Brandon, 2002) has been developed for adolescents and evaluated in a number of school settings in and outside Australia. The principle that underscores the BOC is that we can all do what we do better. If we do not like how we cope in certain contexts we can learn new strategies. It is possible to enhance and develop one's coping if we have a framework within which to do that. The Adolescent Coping Scale, with its 18 conceptual areas of coping, provides a framework and language with which individuals and groups can obtain their coping profile and make changes in their coping practices. It provides the underpinning of this coping skills program. Comprising of 10 sessions, the program begins with a discussion of the meaning of coping and the different styles and strategies used to cope. Students are encouraged to think of strategies that are not helpful and find alternative strategies. Other topics that are addressed include thinking optimistically, effective communication skills, steps to take so as to achieve effective problem solving, decision making, goal setting, and time management. The program also includes a session for the practical building of those coping skills that have been learned throughout previous sessions.

More specifically, Session 1 provides an introduction to the theoretical framework and language of coping that is first introduced by the Adolescent Coping Scale and which is utilized in many of the subsequent sessions. Session 2 on Good Thinking helps young people become aware of the ways in which they can change the way they think and subsequently how they appraise events (positively or negatively), and how they cope. Session 3 has an emphasis on what not to do. We now have evidence that when it comes to coping it is important to teach young people what not to do as much as what to do. It is the use of the nonproductive coping strategies such as worry, self-blame, and tension reduction that are most readily associated with depression (Cunningham & Walker, 1999). Session 4 emphasizes communication skills, which play an important part in effective interactions. Asking for help depends on the capacity to communicate effectively. The next six sessions, Problem Solving, Making Decisions, Goal Setting, Aiming High, and Time Management provide an essential set of skills for high school students. Each of the sessions can be focused on a particular topic such as dealing with conflict, both internal and external.

EVALUATION OF THE BEST OF COPING

Seven evaluations of the Best of Coping Program, in three settings in Australia and one in Italy have been reported. See Table 8.2 for a summary of the results.

In the first setting (Study 1; Bugalski & Frydenberg, 2000) the program was conducted at a high school in Metropolitan Melbourne, Australia as part of the Year 10 (16-17 years) curriculum. The sample consisted of 113 students who were divided into the "at risk: (22), "resilient" (23) and

Table 8.2.   Best of Coping Studies

	Study	Year Level	Experimental Group	Control Group
1	Bugalski & Frydenberg (2000) Melbourne	Yr 10 (16-17 yrs)	N = 22 "at risk" ↓ nonproductive ↑ productive N = 23 "resilient" ↑ nonproductive ↓ productive N = 68 "main" ↑ nonproductive ↑ productive	N/A
2	Luscombe-Smith, Frydenberg, & Poole (2003) Melbourne	Yr 10 (16-17 yrs)	N = 83 (M = 39, F = 44) ↑ reference to others (males more than females)	N/A
3	Cotta, Frydenberg, & Poole (2000) Melbourne	Yr 7 (11-13 yrs)	N = 43 ↑ productive (trend) ↓ nonproductive (worry, wishful thinking, not cope, self-blame)	N = 45 ↑ nonproductive ↑ self-blame ↓ work hard ↓ social action
4	McCarthy (in press)	Yr 7 (11-13 yrs)	N = 179 (M = 100, F = 79) ↓ nonproductive (trend)	N = 56 (M = 33, F = 23) ↑ nonproductive (trend)
5	Tollit (2002) Melbourne	Yr 7 (11-13 yrs)	N = 57 (Female) ↑ productive (scenarios) ↓ reference to others (also at follow-up)	N = 58 (Female) ↓ productive
6	Huxley (2003) Melbourne	Year 9 (16-17 yrs)	N = 24 (N = 15 Female) ↓ tension reduction (N = 11 Male) ↑ seeking social support ↑ social action	NA
7	Ferrari, Nota, Soresi, & Frydenberg (2003) Northern Italy	15-16 yrs	N = 13 (M = 2, F = 11) ↑ focus on positive ↑ work hard ↑ solve problem ↓ wishful thinking ↓ tension reduction	N = 13 (M = 2, F = 11) ↓ solve problem ↑ wishful thinking ↑ tension reduction

↑ increase; ↓ decrease; M = male; F = female

"main group" (68) based on scores on the Children's Attributional Style Questionnaire (CASQ) (Seligman, 1995) and the Perceived Control of Internal States (PCIS) (Pallant, 2000)

Results in that study showed a significant decrease in nonproductive coping and an increase in productive coping for the at risk group, while the opposite was true for the resilient and main groups.

In the same setting the second study (Luscombe-Smith, Frydenberg, & Poole, in press) was conducted with 83 students (39 males and 44 females) in Year 10. Results for these showed a significant increase in reference to others coping postprogram.

In the second setting, a total of 323 adolescents, in Year 7 (11-13 years) were recruited from a Melbourne high school and divided into treatment and control groups, with the treatment group receiving the program through collaboration between school staff and either a school psychologist or school counselor. In Study 3 (Cotta, Frydenberg, & Poole, 2000), with a sample of 88 students, results showed significant decreases in nonproductive coping for the treatment group postprogram (as well as a trend indicating increases in productive coping). In particular, a decrease was noted in adolescents' use of worry, wishful thinking, not cope, keep to self, and, probably most importantly, self-blame. In contrast, the control group showed a significant increase in self-blame, though there were decreases on work hard and also for social action. In summary, the program appeared to be successful in reducing reliance on strategies generally labeled elsewhere as maladaptive and prevents a decrease in at least one strategy considered helpful.

In contrast, the results of Study 4 (McCarthy, 2001), conducted in the same school 2 years later, with a sample of 235 students, show a trend toward the reduction of nonproductive coping for the experimental group and an increase for the control group. Although the results failed to reach statistical significance, when examined class by class, there were clearly some classes who benefited and others who did not, indicating the importance of implementation. That is, both the training of instructors and the choice of instructors are likely to impact the outcome.

A fifth study (Tollit, 2002) with 115 Year 7 female participants who were recruited from a single-sex Catholic secondary college located in the inner city of Melbourne, Australia and whose ages ranged from 11 years to 13 years of age, with a mean age of 12 years was conducted using the ACS and three scenarios which described an academic problem, a family relationship problem, and a bullying problem. The instrument and scenarios were responded to before the program and after the treatment group completed the program. The treatment group also completed these measures at 2 months following the program implementation. Results indicated that the treatment group significantly reduced their use of reference to others coping from pretreatment to follow-up and from posttreatment to follow-up. The scenario responses indicated that there was a significant difference at postprogram between the proportion of students in the two groups who reported their likelihood of using productive coping strategies to deal with academic problems and bullying situations, with a greater portion of the treatment group including productive strategies in their response to the scenarios. Hence the program appeared to be effective in reducing reference to others coping and in promoting the use of productive coping when confronted with academic stressors and bullying predicaments.

A sixth Australian study was conducted in a Catholic co-educational school in an outer suburb of Melbourne (Huxley, 2003) ($N = 24$). A member of the school staff, a teacher-librarian, who was not the students' regular teacher, ran the study. The first eight sessions of the program were taught over 12 school class periods. The instructor kept detailed self-reflective notes relating to both the process and her own development and there was a 6-month follow-up. Changes in the students' attitudes were reflected in the coping skills questionnaire and the responses to the scenarios. Females reduced their reliance on tension reduction and increased their seeking of social support and social action. Moreover, the teacher reported changes in her own management of teacher stress and life-circumstance stress. The students singled out the teacher on many occasions to comment on their own coping and to request further sessions. Thus it would seem that the students and the instructor had developed a common language of coping. However, the responses on six-month follow-up indicated that since students had lost some of the gains made postprogram there is a need for ongoing reinforcement of coping language and skills in order for the benefits to be maintained.

Finally in a northern Italian study (Ferrari, Nota, Soresi, & Frydenberg, 2003) using an Italian translation of the BOC program, 26 participants selected from a group of 183 students in a largely rural community, who exhibited low levels of self-efficacy and problem solving abilities, participated in a 12-session implementation of the program. The student participants improved their coping and problem-solving abilities as well as demonstrating an increase in their focus on the positive and showed a reduction in wishful thinking and tension reduction.

SUMMARY AND CONCLUSION

Overall, the BOC has been found to be effective with adolescents at risk in the 16-year-old age group and with 11-13 year-olds when well-trained instructors or school counselors implemented the program. The results of Study 4 appear to indicate a potential problem relating to the implementation of the program. In Study 3, where the psychologist/counselor was actively involved in the teaching of the program together with the classroom teachers, and in which all teachers conducting the program were trained by the psychologist/counselor, the program appears to have had maximum impact. In contrast, in Study 4 only 3 of the 13 pastoral care teachers conducting the program were trained by the psychologist. They in turn trained the remaining 10 pastoral care teachers. A further difference can be noted between the training offered to teachers in Studies 3 and 4. In the former all teachers received 2 days training, in the latter three teachers received 1 day in-service and the remaining 10 received approximately a half day.

Evaluation of the program also highlights the fact that the participants' self-efficacy increased significantly when compared to nonparticipants (Bugalski & Frydenberg, 2000; Cotta, Frydenberg, & Poole, 2000). This finding suggests that the program is useful in developing a sense of psychological control for participants. A belief in one's sense of psychological control will determine whether one will attempt to cope with a situation or not. Once individuals have a sense of their own capabilities, it is more likely that they will approach their problems with the aim of solving them, rather than avoiding them. In addition, self-efficacy has also been associated with a reduction in depressive symptoms and improvements in academic performance and health (Burger, 1985). As a result, program participants with higher levels of self-efficacy would be expected to utilize more productive coping strategies and use less avoidant strategies. When the program was introduced in a girls' school (Tollit, 2002), the students reduced their resorting to the assistance of others and this was maintained over a follow-up period. When students were asked to indicate how they would cope with hypothetical situations relating to academic problems and to bullying, there was an increased usage of productive strategies postprogram. Moreover, there is emerging evidence that when teachers implement the program they benefit personally and they both adopt and promote the language of coping in their educational communities.

In the Italian study there was a most interesting finding in relation to problem solving skills in that if conflicts are construed as problems to be solved the increase in problem solving skills is useful for managing conflict, and thus a highly desirable outcome.

In general, the findings show promise for the value of the Best of Coping program for students in general and more so those "at risk." That group of young people are often the ones who manage conflict least satisfactorily. The studies clearly indicate that where teachers together with psychologists/counselors are involved in the delivery of the program to students the program was more successful, as it was where the instructors received more substantial training. Every teacher can play an important role in prevention and early intervention programs and activities that strengthen the resilience of students as they learn and develop. However, it would seem that there is a need for good training of instructors and ongoing support if the benefits are to be maximized.

Overall the studies highlight the value of teaching adolescents cognitive-based skills in coping in order to facilitate the use of interpersonal resources. However, factors that contribute to resilience over and above coping skills need to be acknowledged. For example, some exposure to stress and conflict, rather than the avoidance of these, is likely to promote healthy development. Family, peer, and school support also play an important part. Additionally, the building of resources that are perceived to be of value to young people in the management of their everyday lives, and which include coping skills, is beneficial.

Furthermore, as indicated by Lewis and Frydenberg in Chapter 1 of this volume, it is important not only to emphasize the extent of the increase or decrease of usage of a strategy but also to take into account the perceived efficacy. That is, the strategy needs to be assessed for its effectiveness as well as the extent of usage.

Nevertheless, overall, in order to foster healthy social and emotional development and equip young people with life skills we need to change the language of despair to a language of optimism and ability. Talking about coping is a step in the right direction. How people think to a large extent determines how they feel. A greater capacity to reflect on a situation and assess or develop the appropriate responses to particular circumstances that are stressful is most important. The development of coping language along with coping skills holds promise for young people's social-emotional development.

REFERENCES

Boyce, W. T., & Jemerin, J. M. (1990). Psychobiological differences in childhood stress responses: I. Patterns of illness and susceptibility. *Journal of Developmental Behavior and Pediatrics, 11*, 86-94.

Bugalski, K., & Frydenberg, E. (2000). Promoting effective coping in adolescents "at-risk" for depression. *Australian Journal of Guidance & Counseling, 10*, 111-132.

Burger, J. M. (1985). Desire for control and achievement-related behaviours. *Journal of Personality and Social Psychology, 48*, 1520-1533.

Cohen, L., & Frydenberg, E. (1995). *Coping for capable kids*. Waco, TX: Prufrock Press.

Compas, B. E. (1987). Coping with stress during childhood and adolescence. *Psychological Bulletin, 101*, 393-403.

Compas, B. E., Malcarne, V. L., & Fondacaro, K. M. (1988). Coping with stressful events in older children and young adolescents. *Journal of Consulting and Clinical Psychology, 56*, 405-411.

Copeland, E. P., & Hess, R. S. (1995). Differences in young adolescents' coping strategies based on gender and ethnicity. *Journal of Early Adolescence, 15*, 203-219.

Cotta, A., Frydenberg, E., & Poole, C. (2000). Coping skills training for adolescents at school. *The Australian Educational and Developmental Psychologist, 17,* 103-116.

Cunningham, E. G., & Walker, G. (1999). Screening for at-risk youth: Predicting adolescent depression from coping styles. *Australian Journal of Guidance and Counseling, 9,* 15-24.

Department of Education Victoria. (1998). *Framework for student support services in Victorian government schools.* Melbourne, Australia: Community Information Service.

Ebata, A. T., & Moos, R. H. (1991). Coping and adjustment in distressed and healthy adolescents. *Journal of Applied Developmental Psychology, 12,* 33-54.

Ferrari, L., Nota. L., Soresi, S., & Frydenberg, E. (2003). *"The Best of Coping": A training to improve coping strategies.* Unpublished manuscript.

Folkman, S. (1982). An approach to the measurement of coping. *Journal of Occupational Behavior, 3,* 95-107.

Forman, S. G. (1992). *Coping skills interventions for children and adolescents.* San Francisco: Jossey-Bass.

Frydenberg, E. (1997). *Adolescent coping: Research and theoretical perspectives.* London: Routledge.

Frydenberg, E. (1999a). Health, well-being & coping? What's that got to do with education? *Australian Journal of Guidance & Counseling, 9,* 1-18.

Frydenberg, E. (Ed.). (1999b). *Learning to cope: Developing as a person in complex societies.* New York: Oxford University Press.

Frydenberg, E., & Brandon, C. M. (2002). *The best of coping.* Melbourne, Australia: Oz Child.

Frydenberg, E., & Lewis, R. (1991). Adolescent coping: The different ways in which boys and girls cope. *Journal of Adolescence, 14,* 119-133.

Frydenberg, E., & Lewis, R. (1993a). Boys play sport and girls turn to others: Age gender and ethnicity as determinants of coping. *Journal of Adolescence, 16,* 252-266.

Frydenberg. E., & Lewis, R. (1993b). *Manual: The Adolescent Coping Scale.* Melbourne: Australian Council for Educational Research.

Frydenberg. E., & Lewis, R. (1996). The coping strategies used by adolescents in intact and separated families. *Australian Journal of Guidance and Counseling, 6,* 87-99.

Frydenberg, E., & Lewis, R. (1999). Things don't get better just because you're older: A case for facilitating reflection. *British Journal of Educational Psychology, 69,* 81-94.

Frydenberg. E., & Lewis, R. (2000). Teaching coping to adolescents: When and to whom? *American Educational Research Journal, 37,* 727-745.

Frydenberg, E., & Lewis, R. (2002). Adolescent wellbeing: Building young people's resources. In E. Frydenberg (Ed.), *Beyond coping: Meeting goals, vision and challenges* (pp. 175-194). New York: Oxford University Press.

Garmezy, N. (1983). Stressors of childhood. In N. Garmezy & M. Rutter (Eds.), *Stress, coping and development in children* (pp. 43-84). New York: McGraw-Hill.

Greenglass, E. R. (2002). Proactive coping and quality of life management. In E. Frydenberg (Ed.), *Beyond coping: Meeting goals, vision and challenges* (pp. 37-62). New York: Oxford University Press.

Hobfoll, S. E. (1988). *The ecology of stress*. New York: Hemisphere.

Hobfoll, S. E. (1998). *Stress, culture, and community*. New York: Plenum Press.

Hobfoll, S. E. (2002). Social and psychological resources and adaptation. *Review of General Psychology*, *6*, 307-324.

Hobfoll S. E., & Lilly, S. (1993). Resource conservation as a strategy for community psychology. *Journal of Community Psychology*, *21*, 128-148.

Huxley, L. (2003). *Teacher and student coping*. Unpublished raw data, University of Melbourne, Australia.

Lazarus, R. S. (1966). *Psychological stress and the coping process*. New York: McGraw-Hill.

Lazarus, R. S. (1991). *Emotion and adaptation*. New York: Oxford University Press.

Lazarus, R. S., & Folkman, S. (1984). *Stress, appraisal and coping*. New York: Springer.

Lewis. R., & Frydenberg, E. (2002). Concomitants of failure to cope: What we should teach adolescents about coping. *British Journal of Educational Psychology*, *72*, 419-431.

Luscombe-Smith, N., Frydenberg, E., & Poole, C. (in press). Broadening social networks: Outcomes of a coping skills program [Special issue]. *Australian Journal of Guidance and Counselling*.

Luthar, S. S., & Zigler, E. (1991). Vulnerability and competence: A review of research on resilience in childhood. *American Journal of Orthopsychiatry*, *61*, 6-22.

McCarthy, K. (2001). Assessing the effectiveness of Bright Lives–Best of Coping program in adolescents across three secondary schools in Melbourne. Unpublished master's thesis, University of Melbourne.

McKenzie, V. (2001). *Young people and their resources*. Unpublished doctoral dissertation, University of Melbourne, Australia.

McKenzie, V., Frydenberg, E., & Poole, C. (2003). *What matters to young people: The relationship between resources and coping style*. Unpublished manuscript, University of Melbourne, Australia.

Muldoon, O. T. (1996). *Stress, appraisal and coping: A psychosocial approach*. Unpublished doctoral thesis, The Queens University, Belfast.

Pallant, J. F. (2000). Development and validation of a scale to measure perceived control of internal states. *Journal of Personality Assessment*, *75*, 308-337.

Parsons, A., Frydenberg, E., & Poole, C. (1996). Overachievement and coping strategies in adolescent males. *British Journal of Educational Psychology*, *66*, 109-114.

Patterson, J. M., & McCubbin, H. I. (1987). Adolescent coping style and behaviours: Conceptualization and measurement. *Journal of Adolescence*, *10*, 163-186.

Raphael, B. (1993). Adolescent resilience: The potential impact of personal development in schools. *Journal of Paediatric Child Health*, *29*, 31-36.

Rutter, M. (1987). Psychosocial resilience and protective mechanisms. *American Journal of Orthopsychiatry*, *57*, 316-331.

Sandler, I. N., Wolchik, S. A., MacKinnon, D., Ayers, T. S., & Roosa, M. W. (1997). *Handbook of children's coping: Linking theory and intervention.* New York: Plenum Press.

Schinke, S. P., Schilling, R. F., & Snow, W. H. (1987). Stress management with adolescents at the junior high transition: An outcome evaluation of coping skills intervention. *Journal of Human Stress, 13,* 16-22.

Schwarzer, R., & Taubert, S. (2002). Tenacious goal pursuits and striving toward personal growth: Proactive coping. In E. Frydenberg (Ed.), *Beyond coping: Meeting goals, visions, and challenges* (pp. 19-36). New York: Oxford University Press.

Seiffge-Krenke, I. (1990). Developmental processes in self-concept and coping behavior. In H. Bosman & S. Jackson (Eds.), *Coping and self-concept in adolescence.* New York: Springer-Verlag.

Seiffge-Krenke, I., & Shulman, S. (1990). Coping style in adolescence: A cross-cultural study. *Journal of Cross-Cultural Psychology, 21,* 351-377.

Seligman, M. E. (1995). The optimistic child. NSW, AU: Random House Australia.

Teese, R. (1989). Gender and class in the transformation of the public high school in Melbourne, 1946-85. *History of Education Quarterly, 29,* 237-259.

Tollit, M. (2002). *Assessing the effectiveness of The Best of Coping program with female adolescent students.* Unpublished doctoral dissertation, University of Melbourne, Australia.

CHAPTER 9

SAVING STUDENTS FROM MUSIC PERFORMANCE ANXIETY

Narelle Lemon, Erica Frydenberg, and Charles Poole
University of Melbourne

ABSTRACT

When working with adolescent music students the topic of "nerves" or "stage fright" is one that often comes up, especially before a performance. "I just can't do this, can I do it another time?", "What if I make a mistake?", or "My legs won't stop shaking" indicate students who may be in danger of dropping out of music making because they are suffering from music performance anxiety. A program, Coping with Music Performance, aimed at helping senior students cope with the anxiety associated with performing music is presented, together with the results of a study of its outcomes. Students' responses to the program showed benefits in coping with the stress of performing.

Thriving, Surviving, or Going Under: Coping with Everyday Lives, 207–225

"DROWNING": THE THREAT OF FEAR OF PERFORMING

The Coping with Music Performance program was written after an extraordinarily talented senior music student came to to tell his teacher (the first named author) of his intention to quit performing music. Through several conversations with Sebastian,[1] and with his mother, it became apparent that his decision to stop playing the drums, and his guitar, was due to the pressure he felt from peers while performing. Sebastian had so many questions.

> Why do I feel this way? Where can I get help? Why don't I like performing anymore? Why do I feel so alone? I'm different; I like other styles of music! I was told that I make a better drummer than guitarist, is that true? Will I feel better? Why do I feel like I can't pick my guitar up and play like I used too? Why do I feel like such a failure?

Sebastian reminded the teacher of her own personal experiences as a tertiary music student. Memories she had put in the very back of her mind. Feelings of confusion, unanswered questions, fear from sources unknown, wanting to run away, butterflies in the stomach, feeling alone, withdrawn, and being anxious, were all too familiar. She identified with Sebastian. This was a typical case of music performance anxiety (MPA). Being without access to assistance, not knowing how to cope, accompanied by embarrassment can make performing in the music environment difficult and unpleasant. Music performance anxiety can easily give the music student an excuse to stop making music altogether. As MPA affects everyone, from beginner to the most seasoned professional (Leisner, 1995), the phenomenon needs to be understood, so that strategies for counteracting its effects can be devised.

An individual in a performance situation often experiences MPA. The anxiety is only too clearly felt by the performer, but may also be evident in aspects of the performance, and can sometimes be seen by members of the audience. Common behavioral symptoms can include:

- Shaking or trembling
- Idiosyncratic mannerisms or movements
- Change of physical appearance
- Patterns of movement with parts of or entire body
- Grimacing after a mistake
- Mechanical aspects of playing
- Desire to frequently go to the toilet
- Adrenalin rush

- "Butterflies" in the stomach
- Blurry vision of the music
- Muscle tension
- Increased heart rate
- Sweating
- Hot or cold flushes
- Nausea
- Dry mouth
- Diarrhea
- Vomiting
- Loss of appetite

Common cognitive symptoms for musicians experiencing elements of MPA include:

- Negative thoughts
- Self-doubt
- Distraction
- A feeling of impending doom
- Fear of judgment
- Worry of what peers will think
- Fear of "stuffing up"
- Memory blanks
- A feeling of panic (Dunkel, 1989; Roland, 1997)

All artists, whether they are musicians, actors, or dancers, experience some anxiety in relation to performance. Artists who experience anxiety to a severe extent call this "stage fright". For some students they may know it as "nervous anticipation," "butterflies in the stomach," "nerves," or "performance jitters." Whatever the word used to describe this problem, some self-doubt about one's ability to perform is experienced. There are numerous alternative names, but MPA has well-known symptoms that commonly occur together. Figure 9.1 shows the interrelationships between the factors involved in MPA.

Many performers tend to describe their performing experiences as frightening, overwhelming, and at times terrifying (Salmon & Meyer, 1992), with some musicians going as far as to claim that performance anxiety is an extreme fear of failure. Music performance anxiety can stem from failure, poor technical preparation and practice methods, poor control over body, unrealistic goals, insufficient performance stimulation, and

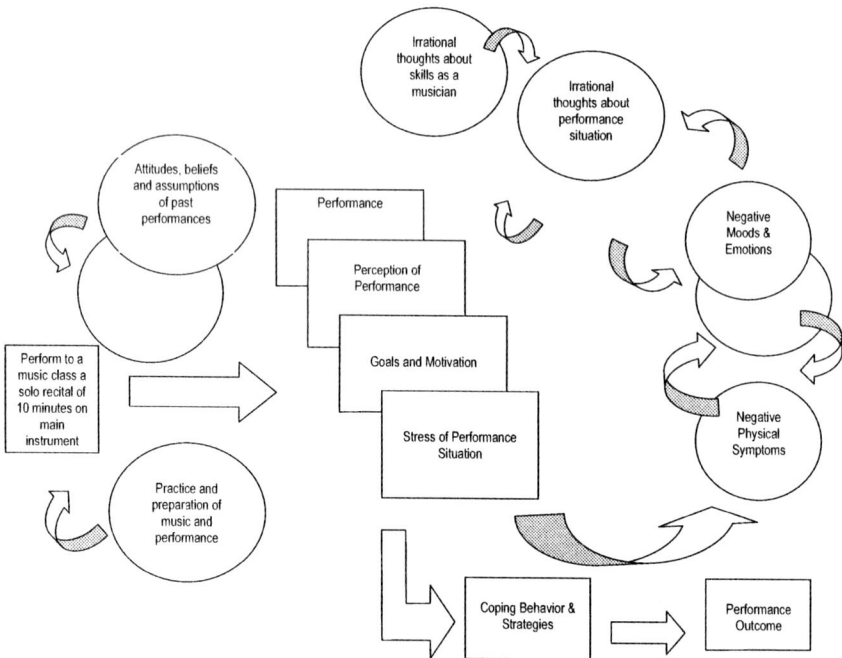

Figure 9.1.   Adolescent and the Performance Situation

lack of positive self-talk (Shaw, 1995). Music performance anxiety can be a serious problem for many musicians. Less experienced students of music can find MPA overwhelming. How can they be saved from drowning in a turbulent sea of self-doubt?

"Surviving": Using the Coping with Music Performance Program

The problem was approached by devising a set of experiences that could be undertaken by music students under the guidance of their teachers. Anxiety was taken to be the problem underlying MPA (Roland, 1997), the "fight or flight" phenomenon, which triggers symptoms such as profuse sweating, clammy hands, and rapid breathing. Although these experiences are uncomfortable, they serve a useful purpose in motivating the individual to take action. There are numerous suggestions for ways to bring this anxiety under control ranging from the very ancient techniques of yoga (Wood, 1994) through relaxation (Benson & Stuart, 1992; Roland, 1997) and aromatherapy (Bachman, 1996) to more modern suggestions such as goal setting and time management (Heller, 1999), Rational Emotive Therapy (Ellis, 1971; Reubart, 1985), and the teaching of coping strategies (Frydenberg, 1997).

Coping with Music Performance is a seven-week program designed to be accessible to the classroom music teacher. Workshops 1 to 6 run for 45 minutes each, with Workshop 7 designated for a time frame of 45-60 minutes. Activities involve diverse approaches to learning (practical, written, verbal, reflection, and role-plays) designed for use with individuals, pairs, small groups, and for the entire class as appropriate.

The program initially focuses on identifying individual coping styles and the importance of taking the initiative to choose the most effective coping strategies for the music performance situation. Students then choose individual personal goals on which to work. In the context of these goals, students learn strategies to take control of internal feelings and external reactions to difficult situations. These strategies include use of positive self-talk, problem solving and goal setting, and relaxation techniques. Strategies are practiced within the classroom and in the music performance environment. Coping with Music Performance was specifically written for the classroom music teacher to implement within the relevant upper secondary school music class or classes. Unlike some other programs that are designed for the school's welfare officer or educational psychologist to implement, this program has been designed to draw on the close relationship between a music teacher and his or her music student.

BACKGROUND TO COPING WITH MUSIC PERFORMANCE

> *I don't want to perform. I hate performing. All I want to do is*
> *drill a hole in the stage floor and jump straight down it.*
>
> —Allison (18-year-old Trumpet student)

Music Performance Anxiety (MPA) for the musician is not a new concept—particularly for those who are tertiary music students, semiprofessional, professional, or amateur musicians. For many of these performers the concept of "nerves" or "stage fright" is normal for performance situations, not necessarily a positive nor negative experience but more of one that is always present. For the adolescent music student at secondary school anxiety associated with performing is not always a good feeling. Although there are occasions on which the stress of performing elevates the performance to new heights, embarrassment is often present, together with low confidence and self-esteem, and is associated with the fear of judgment from peers. Nevertheless MPA differs from individual to individual (Hipple, 1997) with diverse origins and varying range of severity.

For the adolescent musician, performing opportunities commonly occur in the school environment, sometimes to the public, but mainly during school concerts in front of peers, teachers, and the school community.

Most adolescent music students associate "nervousness" with performance, either before, during, or after the performance. Yet their knowledge of what their body is experiencing, what they are thinking, and what they can do is extremely low. For many the concept of MPA is unknown or unclear. The school setting is an ideal setting to introduce education enhancement and intervention to the adolescent musician since it is the location in which they are mainly performing. Ideally, these skills can be maintained and utilized in situations outside school performances.

It is through experiencing the satisfaction of success, mastery, and power, that the child develops a sense of personal effectiveness and the ability to fend for him or herself physically, emotionally, socially, and educationally (Donnchadha, 2000). Personal effectiveness is not so much genetically transmitted but more environmentally learned, that is, learned from parents, teachers, friends, and other significant individuals in their lives, or through experience. In developing the Coping with Music Performance program it was expected that the seven-workshop program would have a beneficial impact on participants' music performance, in addition to their self-esteem, confidence, and overall sense of satisfaction, areas that influence an individual's general task performance.

The program aims to allow students to acquire knowledge, learn to use productive coping strategies in the music performance environment, and to address any anxiety that is present which affects the overall performance. In learning and practically applying skills throughout the workshops, it is expected that the adolescent would become more proficient in the use of productive strategies for use in the music performance environment. The focus is also on the adolescent developing skills that can be generalized to other areas of their lives. It is by having opportunities to learn, use, and practice skills that a child becomes informed in the use of social, emotional, and physical skills, which are the building blocks of effective coping (Donnchadha, 2000).

One of the fundamental focuses of the program is to allow for the music students to gain and develop effective skills to negotiate; accept others' points of view; express feelings; have sympathy; be aware of his/her body and its capabilities; share personal space without the feeling of being threatened; assert his/her position without feeling threatened; be aware of what he/she is or is not capable of doing; that it is all right to take risks, to take credit for success, to set goals, and to feel comfortable with one's self. It involves the confidence to fail and the willingness to try (Donnchadha, 2000). These skills can be practiced with peers, family, teachers, and others and are applicable to any situation, not just to music performance.

CREATING THE PROGRAM

Much of the literature refers to the professional musician or tertiary student. There is a dearth of research specific to the area of adolescent music students. Similarly there is a lack of specific strategies to assist with the anticipated symptoms. Nevertheless it is evident from the available literature that MPA is prevalent among music performers (Davis, 1994; Dunsby, 1995; Harris, 1993; Ristad, 1982; Salmon & Meyer, 1992), yet it is not clear how secondary school music students cope with this phenomenon.

IMPLICATIONS FOR THE CREATION OF THE PROGRAM

Your performance is the time when you can finally share with your listeners
what you have worked so hard in the practice room to achieve.

—Leisner (1995)

Information available on MPA includes theory, common symptoms, and expected behavior. However there is a paucity of information available explaining coping strategies. Roland (1997) is one of the few authors who suggest mental rehearsal as a strategy accompanied with some suggestions in relaxation. Like Haid (1999), Roland also emphasizes coping strategies in the area of preparation, referring to thoughts affecting health, using performance anxiety in the music setting as a working example of how cognitive restructuring or avoiding the negative stress cycle can affect anxiety. Positive self-talk and Rational Emotive Therapy strategies are discussed in depth. However, it is clear from the limited strategies presented in the literature, which are not easily accessible to the music student, that coping possibilities have not been fully investigated.

Davis, Eshelman, and McKay (1988) discuss many strategies for stress management, focusing particularly on strategies aimed at anxiety in specific situations (tests, deadlines, interviews, etc). These include progressive relaxation, breathing, meditation, imagination, self-hypnosis, thought stopping, refuting irrational ideas, coping skills training, and time management. Coping strategies in the areas of relaxation, breathing, and rational thoughts are developed more extensively by Benson and Stuart (1992) with specific examples and exercises provided. Rickard (1992) suggests relaxation and breathing primarily for dealing with anxiety in general. Dacey and Fiore (2000) also support Rational Emotive Therapy, positive thoughts, therapeutic methods, and imagination.

Generally from the literature it is evident that intervention requires comprehensive understanding of the underlying problem. Yet despite the suggestions of strategies there is a failure to provide information and to make the techniques accessible to the performer.

Rational Emotive Therapy (positive self-talk), time management and goal setting strategies (including musical preparation), breathing techniques, relaxation techniques (including yoga and aromatherapy), and constructive self-esteem techniques were used for the MPA program which has been developed for the upper secondary school music student.

FOCUS ON THE MUSIC ITSELF

Why me? Do I have to perform now? Can't somebody else go now? I really don't want to perform, those poor people who have to sit there and listen to me.

—Melissa (16-year-old vocal student)

Authors can often present MPA as an anxiety deriving from the act of one exhibiting oneself in public (Aaron, 1986). One approach to improving and overcoming MPA is to focus on the music itself to enhance the performing experience. Many writers have suggested focusing on the music itself rather than concentrating on the reaction of the audience and the subsequent anticipation of who will or might be in the audience. Often, MPA can occur through lack of readiness rather than performance anxiety itself. Focus and preparation of the music itself is of great assistance in overcoming performance anxiety (Davis, 1994; Haid, 1999).

Prior to a musical performance, the backstage chatter often revolves around the audience. Discussions like these are quite natural; however the way the performers reflect on these concerns can affect the quality of the performance. In an effort to "hype" oneself up before a performance, many musicians put more emphasis on performance anxiety than is required. This results in the musician becoming a victim of performance anxiety. Often the hype surrounding a performance backstage influences the performers anxiety levels. Unnecessary focus on the audience, the anticipation of reactions, or the size of the audience only attracts negative energy. Davis (1994) comments, that the very exhilaration that attracts musicians to live performance can also supply the emotional energy to block memory, causing the individual to freeze or to do things out of the usual during a performance.

It has been suggested that questions with unknown answers often dominate the performer's thoughts before the performance, therefore encouraging negative thought patterns. Negative thoughts need to be minimized and prevented from invading the stage (Haid, 1999). The performer must put the music ahead of all other considerations during practice sessions, rehearsals, lessons, and performances. Through focus on musical progression and passages, musicality and physical activities appropriate to the music (such as breathing), the outcome is likely to be an optimum performance. With the performer developing a heightened understanding of the music the ultimate result should be an enhanced performance experience. Many performers, especially students, are anxious because they are not adequately prepared by the time of the performance (Hipple, 1997).

THE PERFORMER IN OURSELF

Each time we experience even modest success,
we build a little more faith into our bodies.

—Ristad (1982)

Performers tend to be too self-critical during performance. Self-judgment during a performance can have both a positive and negative effect. Self-judgment may destroy the flow of an individual's thought and physical actions both in the present and into the future (Leisner, 1995). It has been suggested that the inner self (self-talk) can have a negative impact on performance situations (Green & Gallwey, 1986). Alternatively it can have a positive impact. Performers need to look at the internal process of centering, or concentrating, and collecting energies so that their body is ready for work (Tourelle & McNamara, 1998).

A silent factor most frequently experienced with MPA is the fear of failure. Even with thorough musical preparation the fear of the performance situation and the uncontrollable feeling of emotions can seem to make managing the anxiety impossible. Believing that it is acceptable to pause in the music, and knowing you have a rational method for managing errors, the likelihood of a lapse falls dramatically. With a performers mind free from worry there is room for more focus on the musical details. Therefore, the performer's body is liberated from strain and able to work to its full potential while delivering the music to an audience (Schneiderman, 1991). It is important not to confuse fear with the feeling of excitement (Dunkel, 1989).

It is all right to make a mistake. This is an important part of performing and minimizing the fear of failure. What is most important is what an individual did as a performer, not what was wrong. Vulnerability is a natural human emotion, however it is possible to control the feeling and challenge the situation. It is sometimes the fear of failing that makes one fail (Schneiderman, 1991).

"THRIVING": AN EVALUATIVE TRIAL OF THE MPA PROGRAM

Method

In a study involving the trial and evaluation of the MPA program (Lemon, 2003), 36 senior music students from Year 10 (15-16 years), 11 (16-17 years), and 12 (17-18 years) were recruited. The following procedures were followed:

1. *Reflective journal entries.*   All of the students were asked to complete reflective journal entries before a performance situation. Themes were sought and the prevalence of MPA in these students was estimated from their written response. Students were then divided into two groups. The 14 Year 10 students were regarded as a comparison group, while the 22 Year 11 and Year 12 students were involved in the seven workshops.

2. *Workshop ratings.*   At the conclusion of each of the first six workshops each of the Year 11 and Year 12 students completed a rating scale. Students rated their perceptions of the workshop to a series of positively toned statements on a five-point Likert-style scale ranging from "Strongly disagree" to "Strongly agree." Four items were common to each evaluation: I feel more positive about performing solo to an audience, I feel my performing experiences will improve, I learnt at least one productive coping strategy today that I can use in my next performance, and I developed my knowledge about MPA. The scores on these items were averaged for the 13 subjects who had participated in all workshops. The ratings were then subjected to a one-way repeated measures analysis of variance with tests of polynomial trends.

3. *Adolescent Coping Scale (ACS).*   All students involved in the program completed the Adolescent Coping Scale (Frydenberg & Lewis, 1993) at the beginning, during, and at end of the workshop series. By examining the patterns of the means and correlating the final rankings for both the experimental and comparison groups it

was possible to assess changes in the extent to which the various coping strategies were used. (See Chapter 9, this issue).

4. *The "Scenario" task.*   Scenarios were used to obtain a qualitative evaluation of student progress. The first scenario recounted a 17-year-old student musician's difficulties as a result of MPA. Two further scenarios with similar content were presented in later sessions. All scenarios were set in the secondary school environment and were familiar descriptions of performance situations for the adolescent music student. Students were asked in the first of the programmed sessions to write what they would do if they were in this position. This "Scenario" task was repeated at the end of the series. Informal comparison of the differences in responding was used to suggest gains made as a result of participation in the program.

Results

Reflective Journal Entries

Several themes emerged on examination of the diary entries, which clearly displayed adolescents' views of the performance environment. It was apparent that the need for practice and levels of being underprepared were common concerns. Concern about lack of preparation and practice in the music performance setting may have been due to an adolescent's inexperience in the area of performance preparation. Inconsistency of practice strategies, techniques, and time was evident in performances, not only through observation but also in students' general comments and preperformance conversations with peers. A reliance on trial and error of how much practice was required before a performance was a common strategy. If a performance had been successful in the past with little preparation, often the adolescent musician would expect this to be the pattern for subsequent performances. However, if the subsequent performance was not successful, little acknowledgment was made of the need for additional preparation and the need to improve practice strategies, particularly where the trial and error process fails to benefit the performer. The adolescent musician tends not to adjust the process when a less successful performance takes place.

Before the adolescent musicians participated in the MPA program it was evident in the journal reflections that students experienced a variety of MPA symptoms. Worry about self-image, lack of practice, an overall focus on making mistakes during the performance, and the subsequent judgment that the audience may make, and what others would think, were MPA symptoms that were rated highly.

I'm a bit scared.... I am a bit nervous that I will forget the words of a song. I'm shaking a bit at the moment but I think I'll be okay. The other thing is I'm going to go red up on stage. I'm concentrating on getting my performance right. (Alex)

After participating in the MPA program the reflections of the adolescent music students demonstrated themes consistent with preprogram reflections, particularly in the areas of worry about making mistakes and of what others think. The theme of MPA symptoms was also present, however to varying degrees and at a reduced level. Lack of preparation for the performance was also a strongly emerging theme. Overall, while the themes remained, the frequency and intensity of the concerns decreased.

I keep thinking people won't like my performance and that I am going to make a really stupid mistake. I'm scared of getting up in front of my classmates and performing. I would like to have had this over and done with so I didn't have to worry about it. (Oliver)

Many of the students referred to using various relaxation techniques as coping strategies before and during the performance. This was interpreted as a positive outcome of Workshop 5 of the MPA program, where students were taught relaxation exercises such as stretching, yoga, aromatherapy, and breathing.

I'm feeling OK leading up to the performance. Not really nervous at the moment but a bit I guess. I used relaxation techniques last night and I think they have helped a lot. (Janelle)

In the 1-month postprogram follow-up journal reflections and performance observations, the senior music students indicated a remarkable improvement in the type and severity of MPA symptoms displayed; while some remained consistent, others decreased as a result of skills acquired from the MPA program. In particular, the adolescent music students reported that some symptoms of MPA were present immediately before or at the beginning of the performance, rather than over a longer period of time.

I'm fine. Not nervous. Will be later when it comes closer to my performance. (Matthew)

Students indicated that worry about making mistakes while performing in front of others, and that being under prepared was a consistent fear and apprehension. Again, references to use of relaxation techniques were also frequently noted.

I don't feel too nervous today. I know the pieces reasonably well so I don't feel that scared. I am a bit hot and I have a bit of a headache but I should be ok. (Travis)

Workshop Ratings

There was a strong linear trend $(F(1, 12) = 40.06, p < .001)$. The means rose from Workshop 1 to Workshop 6 as follows: 3.02, 3.33, 3.71, 3.94, 3.69, 4.50. From considerable doubt at first, support rose to a very strong level after Workshop 6. The one deviation from linearity, a slight drop for Workshop 5, was also significant $(F(1, 12) = 11.47, p = .006)$. This may be evidence of less enthusiasm on the part of some students to participate in the practical exercises associated with the alternative therapies involving breathing, stretching, and yoga.

Adolescent Coping Scale (ACS)

The responses to the scales showed little change from preprogram to 1-month follow-up. This is not entirely unexpected where small group numbers are involved. The workshop group showed an unexpected increase in seeking spiritual support, as did the comparison group. Focus on the positive showed the opposite trend, decreasing in both workshop and comparison groups. It may be that we are learning more about fatigue in doing the same scale several times than we are about differences made by workshop participation. This suggestion was supported by the highly significant Spearman's rank order correlation coefficient between group rankings of .873. The major discrepancies in ordering were on tension reduction and self-blame where the workshop group ranked higher on both. This suggests that the few differences found might have more to do with the age of the students. Frydenberg and Lewis (1993) report similar trends among older secondary students.

The "Scenario" Task

Student participants responded to three scenarios during the study. The responses were then analyzed in correspondence with the coping strategies specified with the ACS, however some additional miscellaneous items (Can't relate to scenario, noncoherent response, not worry, positive self-talk, reflect, build confidence, relaxation, and medication) were also indicated. Students responded to the scenarios with suggestions of coping strategies they would use for the specific situation.

When the responses to the scenarios were categorized according to the 18 conceptual areas of coping the results indicated that the music students used the strategies of focus of solving the problem, invest in close friends, and focus on the positive when confronted with similar situations of MPA in the performance environment. The programs participants

Table 9.1.   ACS Descriptive Statistics for Workshop and Comparison Groups over Time

	Time 1		Time 2		Time 3	
	Mean	SD	Mean	SD	Mean	SD
SEEK TO BELONG						
Experimental	12.77	3.86	13.00	4.05	11.94	3.42
Control	12.35	4.30	13.44	3.97	9.83	3.88
SEEK SOCIAL SUPPORT						
Experimental	12.63	5.87	12.86	4.27	11.31	4.83
Control	14.57	5.21	13.66	3.50	12.16	4.87
SOLVE THE PROBLEM						
Experimental	15.59	5.20	15.60	4.79	14.94	4.64
Control	15.07	3.58	17.77	3.52	15.41	4.96
WORK HARD & ACHIEVE						
Experimental	18.18	3.71	17.60	3.15	17.21	3.55
Control	17.28	4.39	19.00	3.00	15.41	5.45
WORRY						
Experimental	14.50	5.07	14.20	4.24	12.78	4.61
Control	12.76	4.38	11.66	3.46	9.16	3.45
INVEST IN FRIENDS						
Experimental	13.40	5.09	14.53	4.40	11.36	3.96
Control	11.38	3.94	10.88	2.97	8.08	3.02
WISHFUL THINKING						
Experimental	15.95	4.57	14.13	3.71	14.36	2.94
Control	14.35	5.56	14.11	4.70	12.33	5.29
NOT COPE						
Experimental	10.59	4.58	10.60	3.62	10.05	3.42
Control	9.85	4.22	9.66	2.95	7.58	2.81
TENSION REDUCTION						
Experimental	11.59	3.97	12.20	4.09	11.00	4.64
Control	9.07	3.87	9.00	2.34	7.41	2.53
IGNORE THE PROBLEM						
Experimental	9.81	3.63	9.26	3.15	9.27	3.17
Control	8.35	3.31	10.22	3.23	8.00	3.41
SELF BLAME						
Experimental	10.54	4.05	11.13	3.04	10.84	4.29
Control	8.35	3.15	8.88	3.17	7.33	2.96
KEEP TO SELF						
Experimental	11.18	4.81	11.73	3.73	10.73	3.69
Control	9.23	3.51	11.11	3.68	9.50	3.52
SEEK SPIRITUAL SUPPORT						
Experimental	7.09	5.26	8.93	5.21	11.00	2.70
Control	5.50	3.43	4.66	2.00	9.91	3.39
FOCUS ON POSITIVE						
Experimental	12.18	3.91	11.86	2.82	7.94	5.99
Control	12.57	3.32	12.33	1.50	4.16	.57

(continued)

Table 9.1. **Continued**

	Time 1		Time 2		Time 3	
	Mean	*SD*	*Mean*	*SD*	*Mean*	*SD*
SEEK PROFESSIONAL HELP						
Experimental	6.77	3.25	8.20	3.72	6.47	3.23
Control	7.28	4.08	8.55	3.94	5.75	2.30
RELAXATION						
Experimental	11.31	2.69	11.06	1.70	10.52	2.67
Control	10.57	3.03	10.66	2.59	8.00	3.16
SOCIAL ACTION						
Experimental	6.04	2.51	7.00	3.79	5.94	2.48
Control	6.78	3.37	5.33	1.50	4.41	.79
PHYSICAL RECREATION						
Experimental	7.13	2.74	8.40	2.87	7.73	3.26
Control	7.92	3.30	9.88	3.10	7.33	2.80

indicated high preference for use of relaxation techniques and positive self-talk; concepts they learned during the completion of the MPA program.

The 18 coping categories were combined according to the three coping styles (namely, solving the problem, reference to others, nonproductive) coping. In doing this the results suggest that the workshop group increased their use of the coping style, solving the problem (namely, seek relaxing diversions, focus on solving the problem, work hard and achieve, seek to belong, invest in close friends, focus on the positive, and physical recreation), while reference to others (namely, seek social support, seek spiritual support, seek professional help, and social action) and nonproductive coping (namely, keep to self, not coping, worry, ignore the problem, self-blame, wishful thinking, and tension reduction) styles reduced (see Table 9.2).

It is interesting to note that students' reference to Miscellaneous Items, including items such as not worry, positive self-talk, and relaxation (yoga, aromatherapy, breathing exercises) increased remarkably over time. The students who did not participate in the program had altered responses over time also. This may be suggest that the students interest and knowledge was changing due to skills that were self-taught and from motivation to learn more about their own coping strategies and styles. This can be seen in the increased use of solving the problem as a coping strategy.

Of particular interest was the students' positive change over time in relating to the scenarios. Reference to others was mentioned predominantly as a means of coping for music students. This took the form of practicing performance techniques and pieces in front of family or

**Table 9.2.   Scenario Responses Based on Frequency of
Coping Style and Miscellaneous Items**

	Time 1		Time 3	
Coping Style	Workshop Group	Comparison Group	Workshop Group	Comparison Group
Solving the problem	56	38	79	49
Reference to others	16	16	10	8
Nonproductive coping	17	9	7	1
Miscellaneous items	28	20	46	12

friends. The students also mentioned the use of relaxation techniques taught in Workshop 5. In the scenario responses, students frequently mentioned yoga, breathing, and stretching exercises, with an increase over time. Females referred to this strategy more than males. There were indications that not worrying had also become a MPA coping strategy that was applied by the students in performance situations, with males tending to refer more to this strategy. The response of can't relate to this scenario reduced considerably over the time span of the program, indicating students were better able to relate to scenarios after gaining knowledge of MPA.

Conclusion

Participating adolescent musicians in the trial implementation of the MPA program indicated that they understood the aims of the program and agreed that each workshop achieved the stated aims. Over time students felt more comfortable about discussing MPA and the signs they experienced in the music performance environment. Further development occurred with improved relationships among the students and between the students and the music teacher, both within the classroom and outside. Students often discussed MPA in performances outside of the classroom and in performance situations involving different music students. The participants of the program developed the language to be able to describe what they were experiencing and were able to identify signs of MPA. This is an indication of the success of the program. The importance of preparation for the performance situation, and especially for those who do experience symptoms of MPA is vital (Greene, 2001; Kenny, 2002; Tarrant, 2002). In particular, Kenny reports that musicians need to spend more time on preparation before a performance. This was found to be the case in this study. After participating in the program, students were able to acknowledge the need for preparation. They also recognized that the lack of preparation is very evident to the audience and fellow performers. During Workshop 6 students were introduced to issues associated with time management and goal setting. Discussions occurred about senior music students having differing goals for music performance. Yet regardless of these goals, time management skills in preparation and rehearsal are vital in all situations. Prior to the program, students often announced to the audience that they were not prepared but still maintained they would be able to "carry off" their performance. It became evident to the students at the conclusion of the program and during the follow-up program performance that preparation was required. It was evident to the audience when practice and preparation were lacking. During, and leading into, the follow-up program performance, students began to practice specifically for the performance with acknowledgment of this occurring through their reflective journal entries and postperformance comments.

It became evident through observations and reflective journals that once students were taught skills in the area of relaxation, these techniques were utilized to cope with MPA before, during, and after a musical performance. Students often referred to use of breathing and yoga exercises in preparing for their performances through their journal reflections. The increase in range of coping strategies of the adolescent musicians participating in the program over time displayed the ability of the students to gain knowledge in coping strategies for MPA. Through the development of coping strategies, the overall aims of the program were met with considerable success. Students gained knowledge in MPA signs and symptoms, strategies (productive and nonproductive), and were able to practice strategies and skills in the music performance environment. Most importantly the students were able to acknowledge that individuals have different symptoms and experiences related to performing.

NOTES

1. All names mentioned throughout this chapter have been changed to preserve confidentiality.

REFERENCES

Aaron, S. (1986). *Stage fright: Its role in acting*. Chicago: The University of Chicago Press.
Bachmann, M. (1996). *Introducing aromatherapy*. New South Wales, Australia: Philip Mathews Book.

Benson, H., & Stuart, E. (1992). *The wellness book: The comprehensive guide to maintaining health and treating stress-related illness.* New York: Birch Lane Press.

Betts, K., Hayward, D., & Garnham, N. (2001). *Quantitative analysis in the social sciences: An introduction.* Melbourne, Australia: Tertiary Press.

Dacey, J., & Fiore, L. (2000). *Your anxious child: How parents and teachers can relieve anxiety in children.* San Francisco: Jossey-Bass.

Davis, M., Eshelman, R., & McKay, M. (1988). *The relaxation and stress reduction workbook.* Oakland, CA: New Harbinger Publications.

Davis, R. (1994). Performance anxiety. *The American Music Teacher, 44,* 24-28.

Donnchadha, R. (2000). *The confident child: A guide to fostering personal effectiveness in children.* Dublin: Newleaf.

Dunkel, S. E. (1989). *The audition process: Anxiety management and coping strategies.* New York: Pendragon Press.

Dunsby, J. (1995). *Performing music: Shared concerns.* Oxford, England: Clarendon Press.

Ellis, A. (1971). *Growth through reason: Verbatim cases in rational emotive therapy.* Palo Alto, CA: Science and Behavior Books.

Frydenberg, E. (1997). *Adolescent coping: Theoretical and research perspectives.* London: Routledge.

Frydenberg, E., & Lewis, R. (1993). *Adolescent Coping Scale: Administrator's manual.* Melbourne: Australian Council for Educational Research.

Green, B., & Gallwey, T. (1986). *The inner game of music.* London: Pan Books.

Greene, D. (2001). *Audition success: An Olympic psychologist teaches performing artists how to win.* New York: Broadway Books.

Haid, K. (1999). *Coping with performance anxiety.* Presentation at Music Educators National Conference, Melbourne, Australia.

Harris, C. J. (1993). *Research into the effects of a strategy designed to decrease music performance anxiety and enhance the self-esteem of adolescents.* Unpublished master's thesis, University of Melbourne, Melbourne, Australia.

Heller, S. (1999). *Conquering fear and anxiety.* New York: Alpha Books.

Hipple, J. (1997, May). *Music performance anxiety: An overview of technological advances in therapy, psychopharmacology & bio-feedback.* Paper presented at the International Conference on Counseling, Beijing, China.

Kenny, D. (2002, July). *Theory and therapy in music performance anxiety: Harmony or counterpoint.* Paper presented at the Stress and Anxiety Research Conference, Melbourne, Australia.

Leisner, D. (1995). Six golden rules for conquering performance anxiety. *American SpringTeacher, 45*(2). Available: http://www.davidleisner.com/guitarcomposer/noname.html

Lemon, N. (2003). *Coping with music performance: A program for upper secondary school music students.* Unpublished master thesis, University of Melbourne, Melbourne, Australia.

Reubart, D. (1985). *Anxiety and musical performance: On playing the piano from memory.* New York: Da Capo Press.

Rickard, J. (1992). *Relaxation for children.* Melbourne, Australia: Collins Dove.

Ristad, E. (1982). *A soprano on her head: Right-side-up reflections on life and other performances.* Moab, UT: Real People Press.

Roland, D. (1997). *The confident performer*. Sydney, Australia: Currency Press.

Salmon, P., & Meyer, R. (1992). *Notes from the green room: Coping with stress and anxiety in musical performance*. New York: Lexington Book.

Schneiderman, B. (1991). *The confident performer: The art of preparing*. St Louis, MO: MMB Music.

Shaw, M. (1995). *Your anxious child: Raising a healthy child in a frightening world*. New York: Birch Lane.

Tarrant, R. (2002, July). *Who gets butterflies? An investigation of incidence and cause of performance anxiety in a group of student musicians*. Paper presented at the Stress and Anxiety Research Conference, Melbourne, Australia.

Tourelle, L., & McNamara, M. (1998). *Performance—A practical approach to drama*. Melbourne, Australia: Heinemann.

Wood, L. (1994). *Yoga for you*. New York: Dolphin Press.

CHAPTER 10

A MODEL COUNSELING INTERVENTION PROGRAM TO PREPARE ADOLESCENTS FOR COPING WITH WORK-FAMILY CONFLICT

Rachel Gali Cinamon
Tel Aviv University, Israel

Yisrael Rich
Bar Ilan University, Israel

ABSTRACT

Men and women in Western society now commonly pursue careers while concomitantly functioning as spouses and parents. This combination of roles frequently leads to significant stress, often termed by researchers as work-family conflict. This stress results from the natural desire to succeed in both domains alongside limitations of one's time and energy. Much research over the last 20 years has demonstrated the negative ramifications of this stress in the family domain as well as in the work domain (e.g., poor family relations; low job commitment and satisfaction). These negative outcomes highlight the need for educational and counseling interventions that pro-

Thriving, Surviving, or Going Under: Coping with Everyday Lives, 227–254
Copyright © 2004 by Information Age Publishing
All rights of reproduction in any form reserved.

vide adolescents with appropriate coping skills for more satisfactory blending of critical life roles. Based on theory and research on work-family
conflict and adolescent development, this chapter presents an intervention
model that includes elements of enhanced self-awareness about future life
roles as well as planning and coping skills that ameliorate the conflict.

INTRODUCTION

Important changes in the nature of families and the workforce, such as
growing numbers of dual career couples and working mothers with young
children, have increased the likelihood that male and female employees
today have both substantial household obligations and major work
responsibilities (Allen, Herst, Bruck, & Sutton, 2000; Bond, Galinsky, &
Swanberg, 1998). Active participation in two demanding spheres may
benefit the individual but also might accrue high costs and stress. The
combination of work and family roles could comprise a source of stress
because of ongoing and, frequently, relentless demands on the individual's time and energy. Occupational health researchers commonly cite a
widespread effect of this stress: the work-family conflict (Frone, 2003).
Work-family conflict comprises a form of inter-role conflict in which pressures from work and family roles are incompatible (Greenhaus & Beutell,
1985).

Researchers have associated work-family conflict with a number of dysfunctional outcomes in the work and in the family domains. Numerous
studies have shown that work-family conflict predicts work dissatisfaction
or distress (Carlson & Kacmar, 2000; Frone, Barnes, & Farrell, 1994;
Frone, Yardley, & Markel, 1997) as well as negative behavioral work outcomes such as burnout (Bacharach, Bamberger, & Conley, 1991) and
absenteeism, tardiness, and poor role performance at work (Frone, Yardley, & Markel, 1997; Howson & O'Driscoll, 1996). Regarding the family
domain, studies found that work-family conflict predicts family dissatisfaction or distress (Carlson & Kacmar, 2000; Frone, Barnes, & Farrell,
1994; Frone, Yardley, & Markel, 1997), low levels of family well-being
(Kinnunen & Mauno, 1998), and poor family-related role performance
(Frone, Yardley, & Markel, 1997; Howson & O'Driscoll, 1996). Research
also revealed this conflict's negative correlation with employees' mental
health, physical health, and health-related behaviors whereas it correlated
positively with psychological distress (Kirchmeyer & Cohen, 1999; Marks,
1998), self-reported poor physical health (Grzywacz, & Marks, 2000), and
life dissatisfaction (Netemeyer, Boles, & McMurrian, 1996). These findings underscore the need for organizations to help their employees cope
with this sort of stress and reduce levels of work-family conflict, in order to

increase employee's occupational performance as well as their life satisfaction and well-being.

Indeed, the literature describes organizational work-family initiatives
and family-friendly organizational policies that aim to help employees
balance work and family life and ease the conflict (e.g., Frankel, 1998;
Galinsky & Bond, 1998). These initiatives include flexible work arrangements, family leave, dependent-care assistance, and general resource services (Frone, 2003). However, organization officials are free to decide if
and how to implement such policies, are more likely to operate family-
friendly services if managers believe that such policies will yield financial
benefits to the organization, and carry no legal responsibility for promoting their employees' ability to cope with the conflict (Heaney, 2003).
Despite the promotion of such family-friendly policies, no consistent
research evidence exists to clearly substantiate the contribution of these
policies to the reduction of work-family conflict. Along with methodologi-
cal explanations for the inconclusive research findings such as inconsistent measures of the conflict (Frone & Yardley, 1996), Frone (2003)
emphasized the fact that many employees do not use the services and
benefits offered to them by employers. Employees may feel uncomfortable utilizing available perks because of a perceived gap between formal
organizational policies and management level criticism about "exploiting" the organization or mixing home and work needs.

Since many male and female employees today suffer from the stress of
work-family conflict and insufficient solutions are provided by employers,
it is important to seek additional strategies to promote mental and physical health and reduce this conflict. Many scholars have called for primary
prevention to help young adults prepare for the complex task of balancing work and family lives (Granrose, 1985; Weitzman, 1994). Support for
this direction of intervention emerges from research on adolescents'
future plans. The fundamental changes in the world of work and in families have also manifested themselves in the career plans of many adolescents in western societies, who report an intention to blend these two
important life roles (Kerpelman & Schvaneveldt, 1999; Kulik, 1998;
Novack & Novack, 1996; Peake & Harris, 2002; Rich & Golan, 1992).
Female adolescents attribute high importance to the family role as well as
to the work role (Archer, 1989). They expect to become very involved in
both (Betz, 1993; Farber, 1996; Greene & Wheatley, 1992; Phillips &
Imhoff, 1997) and they plan to work most of their lives without significant
career interruption to care for their families (Blau & Ferber, 1992; Reskin
& Padavic, 2001). Similar patterns have also been found among male adolescents who place high importance on their marital and parental roles,
along with their career (Gerson, 1989; Willinger, 1993).

PREVENTIVE COPING WITH WORK-FAMILY CONFLICT

Adolescents' plans to participate actively in both work and family roles indicate that, like the adult employees of today, they will feel the stress of combining work and family roles and will likely experience its harsh effects unless they are afforded effective and timely intervention. Therefore, it is crucial to enhance their ability to manage multiple roles and, specifically, to learn how to blend their work and family roles effectively. They need to acquire skills that will help them handle the conflict successfully and, under ideal conditions, to prevent its occurrence.

Unfortunately, many organizations do not accept the responsibility to promote employees' health in a proactive manner and simply ignore workers' stress as long as it does not impair their job functioning. Instead, the educational system becomes a primary social institution that can provide guidance to teens to deliberate and decide about the importance of various life roles, to acquire the astuteness required to manage multiple roles, and to deal with the ensuing stress. Clearly, one aspect of preparing our secondary students to enter the adult world is to assist them in the transition from school to work (Solberg, Howard, Blustein, & Close, 2002) and one facet of this preparation is to provide them with the cognitive and emotional skills that will enable them to cope effectively with the stress of multiple adult roles.

The strategy of preventive intervention that targets adolescents before they embark into the world of work in order to strengthen their ability to manage multiple roles and their sense of efficacy regarding coping with stressful situations, coincides with wellness and positive psychology perspectives within counseling and educational psychology. Seligman and Csikzentmihalyi (2000), for example, highlighted the importance of sustained commitment to developing positive individual traits and institutions with favorable practices for improving quality of life and preventing pathology. This approach also appears in recent stress and coping literature where the concept of preventive coping has become a prominent conceptual addition to the positive psychology perspective. Preventive coping (Aspinwall & Taylor 1997; Greenglass, 2000; Greenglass, Schwarzer, & Taubert, 1999; Schwarzer, 2000) deals with goal-oriented, long-term behaviors of individuals *before* significant stress occurs. It may be defined as an effort to build up resources that lessen the likelihood of the onset of stressful events and reduce the severity of the consequences of stress, should it occur. While earlier coping was seen as primarily reactive, strategies used only after stress had been experienced, preventive coping is seen as something one can do before stress occurs. Individuals are not only reactive, but capable of initiating constructive paths of action and creating opportunities for growth that minimize harmful stress. Coping becomes especially concerned with determination of goals and ways of accomplishing them by means of resources the individual has rendered available for utilization.

Application of the concept of preventive coping to the case of preparing adolescents for the task of blending work and family roles means that educators are enjoined to assist students to build personal resources that will enable them to reduce the probability of experiencing significant work-family conflict in the future. It is inappropriate to wait until young people assume roles of full-time employees and parents and experience the stress of work-family conflict and only then take action to reduce the stress. According to the preventive coping approach, adolescents can be prepared, even before entering adulthood, to avoid the conflict or to handle it successfully if it appears in the future. Interventions could focus on enhancement of adolescents' general resources and resilience in order to boost their personal fulfillment in work and family roles. Although our primary concern is with the potential self-actualization gains accruing to individuals, there is good reason to believe that this strategy will also provide economic benefits for the workplace.

We suggest that development of such a counseling intervention for high school students can yield positive outcomes if it is grounded in adolescents' exploration processes and identity formation, in theory and research explaining work-family conflict, in models of self-efficacy, and in research on career interventions methods. Each of these elements and their implications for preparing adolescents to blend work and family roles is described below. A more detailed description of an intervention program will follow.

EXPLORATION PROCESSES AND IDENTITY FORMATION

At the transition to adulthood, adolescents become increasingly focused on their anticipated identities in career, marriage, and parenthood. Erikson (1980) described adolescence as a time of identity formation that he called "psychosocial moratorium." Identity formation involves exploring or "trying on" different identity possibilities (Marcia, 1994). Cote and Levine (1988) argued that in late adolescence, youngsters experience social pressure to explore their emerging identities. Markus and Nurius (1986) called such anticipated identities "possible selves"—developing but not yet true identities. Like true identities, they consist of organized self-views and perceived expectations from others (Stryker & Serpe, 1994). During the process of identity exploration, possible selves comprise aspects of the self that are most fragile and vulnerable to change following feedback from the environment (Markus & Nurius, 1986). Possible selves may be perceived as only "virtual reality" yet they hold important meanings for the adolescents' future. When a teenager works part-time in a fast-food restaurant while striving to keep up her grades in school and a meaningful relationship with her boyfriend, comments from significant others on her role management provide her with information on her ability to handle multiple roles in the future. She may reflect on the importance of the various life roles she presently experiences and how she might blend comparable roles in the future.

The postmodern age in Western society has complicated this process of exploration even further. Dramatic changes in the nature of the world of work and the nature of families hamper young people's ability to anticipate these possible selves. A multitude of alternatives are now available to young people and the exploration process has become much more complex. The advent of modern business practices, economic globalization, and the proliferation of information technology have all contributed to the creation of a 24-hour society that places great demands on employees' time and energy. Companies and organizations often seek totally devoted employees who can work in shifts to keep up with demands for rapid, immediate products and services (Smith, Folkard, & Fuller, 2003). The sweeping process of globalization, in particular, has increased international competition, stress for companies and individuals, and job insecurity (Tetrick & Quick, 2003). Most people can no longer expect to spend their working lives in the same job or even in the same organization. The rapid technological changes and modifications in organizational and occupational structures are reshaping the world of work, increasing the number of self-employed (Aronsson, 1999) and the number of workers who opt for other forms of flexible employment such as home-based, temporary, or contract work (Benach, Fernando, Platt, Diez-Roux, & Muntaner, 2000). Globalization may result in increased employee relocation or displacement (Frumkin, 1998). Unemployment, fear of unemployment, and migration can render stress and negative effects on the health of workers as well as their families (Tetrick & Quick, 2003). In sum, the postmodern pattern of extremely dynamic work environments frequently requires people to restructure their identities more than one time during their careers. For adolescents focusing on anticipated career roles, the future appears very unclear and even threatening.

Technological, economical, and cultural changes in industrial society have also lead to dramatic changes in the definition and nature of the family (Bourdieu, 1996; Stacey, 1990). The institution of "nuclear family" with a father and mother no longer comprises the only available structure for raising children and has undergone a steady process of individualization and democratization (Beck & Beck-Gernsheim, 1995; Beck-Gernsheim, 1998). For many, the individual has become the center of the family, with his or her wishes, dreams, and needs at the focus of concern rather than those of the family as a collective (see Gergen, 1991). Authoritarian and even authoritative parenting patterns have given way to democratic or laissez faire styles. Diverse sorts of previously nontraditional families have become legitimized and legalized (e.g., dual career couples, dual earner families, single parent families, homosexual/lesbian families). Along with the potential that the redefined family structure offers, it also constitutes a source of conflict, instability, and fragility because the family's very existence depends on the motivation of each member to continue to be part of the family (Cheal, 1993; Stacey, 1990, 1992).

Thus, adult roles in the postmodern world, with their dynamic and diverse nature, have complicated adolescents' capacity to explore possible "worker" selves and possible "family member" selves, let alone contemplate role combinations. Indeed, the desire to explore possible selves may have diminished considerably because teenagers' perceptions of the worlds of work and family as bombarded by constant change may lead them to conclude that exploration at this stage is premature. This complexity raises the need to provide appropriate knowledge to adolescents and to offer guidance and purposeful mediation throughout an adolescent's exploration process. Increased familiarity with the postmodern world's work pressures and characterizations of family may strengthen adolescents' sense of self-efficacy regarding their ability to successfully negotiate conflicting demands. It is worth noting that those individuals who are likely candidates to provide knowledge and mediation, such as, parents, educators, and counselors, may also require extensive self-exploration because they, too, are in a process of ongoing change in their perceptions of life roles and their management.

Despite the centrality of the exploration process in adolescents and the virtual certainty that they will experience multiple roles, most of the literature on this topic focuses only on occupational exploration, and considerably less has been written about family and other role exploration. Occupational exploration comprises one of the central elements in most career choice and developmental theories, and in career intervention practice (Blustein, 1997; Gottfredson, 1996; Niles, Anderson, & Goodnough, 1998). A key assumption of career theories maintains that engaging in vocational exploration fosters awareness of one's internal attributes and dreams and knowledge about one's educational and vocational options, thereby facilitating the establishment of a meaningful work life (Blustein, 1997; Gottfredson, 1996; Holland, 1997). We assert a similar assumption regarding the beneficial effects of engaging in an integrative endeavor of *occupational* exploration alongside *family*-role exploration, thereby facilitating the establishment of a meaningful blend of work and family domains with fewer conflicts. Indeed, the aforementioned current trend in career interventions—the focus on occupational exploration while virtually ignoring its mutual relationship role with family roles—is incongruent with the most broadly supported theory in the field of career development, that of Donald Super (1990), which emphasizes the need to relate to *all* life roles in order to understand vocational behavior and development.

Recently, Flum and Blustein (2000) suggested a shift in vocational exploration to include a more ongoing and integrative exploration of work, family, and other life roles. Rather than view exploration merely as an early stage in the career development process, Flum and Blustein (p. 345) described exploration as a "critical means by which individuals can construct themselves and re-explore and reconstruct themselves through the life span and across life roles." This new approach to exploration suggests that when individuals construct their identity as a result of exploration, the process of self-construction engenders further exploration. Exploration of the identity of the worker role, for example, can lead to exploration of family roles, and vice versa. In brief, exploration is viewed as an ongoing recursive process.

Adolescents who explore a possible worker self may actually try to combine that role with a possible set of intimate relations, receiving practical experience as well as feedback from the environment, which will serve as a source for further exploration. Berzonsky (1995) showed that adolescents are open to identity-relevant feedback and that adolescents in psychosocial moratorium are more likely to internalize negative self-appraisals than are individuals at other life stages. Therefore, feedback from the social environment regarding the adolescent's ability to blend life roles needs to be offered with great sensitivity because it can play a crucial role in shaping future plans. If an adolescent girl expresses her plan to pursue a nontraditional occupation such as engineering alongside conventional family roles, but receives negative feedback that emphasizes the difficulties of blending motherhood and engineering, she may rethink her occupational plans. She may thus lose a satisfying vocation, society may lose an excellent engineer and she may become a frustrated mother and spouse because she interpreted the feedback as blocking her aspirations for self-realization. Most certainly we are not suggesting that adolescents should be spared knowledge of real difficulties and dilemmas that they may encounter in realizing their wishes to combine family and work roles. However, their awareness should be cultivated in ways that facilitate adolescents' ability to make their own tentative decisions after serious reflection about the potential rewards and sacrifices of different role combinations.

The crucial effect of this "trying out" process during adolescence suggests that this is a critical period for implementing primary intervention programs to mediate these exploration processes and help adolescents become familiar with future internal and external resources and barriers. Such an intervention, spanning a dual perspective of work and family roles and their combinations, should help adolescents gain insight into their attitudes, aptitudes, and interests in both roles and should also provide knowledge about different sorts of role blending that is embedded in an understanding of the continuing dynamic changes in the world of work and the nature of the family. It is vital that adolescent exploration goes beyond stereotypical and superficial inquiry and that it delves thoughtfully into the personal meanings they attribute to life roles. During this journey into oneself, the individual is invited to follow paths that may prove difficult and even painful, as personal meanings, values and goals are examined. What does it mean to me to be a parent? Do I want to be like my parents? What is important to me as a spouse? What do I want from work? What am I willing to do and to forgo to thrive in these roles? Attempts to answer these important questions, even it they are only partial and tentative, should help adolescents to plan their future more coherently in ways that maximize the likelihood of realizing the life story each would like to fulfill.

This process of exploring possible selves while examining issues of quality of performance in each role and how to combine work and family roles holds great promise to help adolescents establish the cycle of "constructing, re-exploring, and re-constructing" themselves as advocated by Flum and Blustein (2000). Interventions that encourage adolescents to examine their own future and to shape it according to their own versions of the "good life" should enhance their sense of autonomy alongside feelings of personal responsibility for the outcomes of their decisions. Thus, it is reasonable to believe that programs designed to prepare young people to cope proactively with work-family conflict may have far-reaching effects on identity clarification throughout the life span.

WORK-FAMILY CONFLICT

Social roles play an important function in the lives of all individuals (Clark, 2000). They help us define who we are, they influence what we do, and we attribute different meanings and levels of importance to them. Greenhaus and Beutell (1985), who established the theoretical framework for work-family research, proposed that work-family conflict intensifies when either work or family roles are salient and central to the person's self-concept. They theorized that the more important a role is to an individual, the more time and energy that person will invest in it, which will allow less time and energy for other roles. A recent study (Cinamon &

Rich, 2002a) demonstrated the importance of examining the relative salience of both work *and* family roles. People who attributed high importance to both roles revealed the highest levels of work-family conflict, compared to persons who ascribed high importance to one role and low importance to the other role. In addition to role salience, personal role meanings should be examined (e.g., Cinamon & Rich, 2002b; Cook, 1994). Two individuals, for example, may assign a similar level of importance to the family role but may ascribe different personal meanings to this role that will affect levels of work-family conflict and how it is expressed in everyday life. One person may view the family role as establishing close relationships with family members, whereas the other person may interpret the family role as being a good breadwinner. The influence of role salience and role meanings on individuals' thinking and behavior at work and at home indicates the need to weave these variables into any prevention program aimed at reducing future conflict.

After adolescents determine their role salience and role meanings, personal role redefinition can significantly contribute to coping. Hall (1972) proposed the concept of personal role redefinition as one of three coping behaviors to address the work-family conflict. Personal role redefinition refers to altering one's internal conception of role demands including changing one's attitude toward roles. This coping strategy may help adolescents adopt an internal locus of control over decisions about their own role hierarchy and about increasing or decreasing role salience. Redefinition may help youngsters develop a sense of coherence (personal confidence that the world is manageable and purposeful) that is crucial to helping them to create and achieve their goals (Antonovsky, 1987, 1993). It can also build a confidence that they know themselves and have the ability to monitor their own feelings and thoughts. Ryff and Singer (1998) noted that sense of coherence is a core feature of positive human health.

Another important aspect of work-family conflict research involves the influence of stress and support variables. Recent research highlighted the influence of stress and support variables from the work domain and the family domain on work-family conflict (Burke & Greenglass, 1999). Regarding the work domain, conflict increased, for example, when the individual spent many hours at work away from home (Frone et al., 1997; Parasurman, Yasmin, Purohit, Veronica, & Beutell, 1996). In contrast, research indicated that conflict decreased when the person experienced flexible work hours and managerial support (Lee, 1983; Staines & Pleck, 1983; Thomas & Ganster, 1995). With regard to family-related stress and support variables, research has linked high levels of work-family conflict to the presence of small children in the home (Lewis & Cooper, 1998) and to many hours invested in housework (Voydanoff, 1988). On the other hand, spousal support emerged as a factor moderating the conflict (Matsui, Ohsawa, & Onglatco, 1995). Several studies have shown that only some adolescents, mostly girls, are aware of the family domain's impact on their ability to fulfill their career and family plans. Baber and Monaghan (1988), for instance, found that adolescent girls who plan nontraditional, demanding careers expect to have fewer children compared to adolescent girls who plan traditional careers. Likewise, Hallet and Gilbert (1997) reported that career-oriented adolescent girls expect their future spouse to hold feminist attitudes and share household obligations. We were unable to find research examining adolescent awareness about work domain variables that may influence family plans, like flexible working hours or managerial support.

These findings suggest the potential benefits of intervention to promote adolescents' awareness of the interdependence of stress and support variables from both domains. Adolescents must realize that their vocational success and fulfillment are most likely related to their family development. For example, to bring a child into a family that already has young children, and at the same time to take on a new job or position, may be extremely stressful. In addition to assisting young people in the process of exploration, interventions should teach adolescents to seek occupations and organizations with policies conducive to fulfilling their family plan, like on-site daycare, flexible working hours, or manager support. In a parallel manner, interventions should help teenagers think insightfully about their family goals and how to accomplish them in light of their work aspirations. Of critical importance is the enhancement of adolescents' awareness and exploration while avoiding pressure on them to arrive at firm plans. Counseling programs should also provide information and guidance on how to establish social support, how to arrive at satisfactory arrangements regarding sharing housework, and so on. These are crucial skills that most young people need to learn and do not have structured opportunities to develop. Thus, they should be an important component of any prevention program that focuses on the work-family conflict.

SELF-EFFICACY AND WORK-FAMILY CONFLICT

Compared to the larger body of research on role characteristics as potential causes of work-family conflict, only a few studies have examined the contribution of personality variables to the conflict (Frone, 2003). These studies demonstrated that high levels of hardiness, extraversion, and self-esteem were associated with lower levels of work-family conflict (Bernas & Major, 2000; Grzywacz & Marks, 2000). Social cognitive theory is a prominent scholarly resource that can advance understanding of the relations between personal variables and work-family conflict. Social cognitive career theory (SCCT; Lent, Brown, & Hackett, 1994) applies Bandura's (1986) social cognitive theory to career development processes. Assuming that people are active agents in their environments, SCCT emphasizes the interactive roles of personal, contextual, and behavioral variables influencing career goals, actions, and achievements. The major construct in this theory, self-efficacy, comprises the belief in one's ability to perform specific tasks. Self-efficacy beliefs help determine individuals' willingness to initiate specific behaviors, their persistence in the face of barriers and conflicts, and their level of competence in executing behaviors (Bandura, 1986). Self-efficacy theory proposes that the probability of engaging in an activity and executing it successfully is determined in part by the degree to which individuals believe they can effectively perform the behavior (Bandura, 1986). Schwarzer and Renner (2000) related self-efficacy to proactive coping, counting "coping self-efficacy" as one of the personal resource factors that boost resilience and moderate stress. They defined it as an optimistic self-belief of being able to cope successfully with the particular situation at hand. Accordingly, adolescents' plans to actively participate in work and family roles may be affected by their sense of self-efficacy in handling the conflicts arising from their role combination. These beliefs emerge from a complex process of self-perceptions that involves four components: performance mastery experiences, verbal persuasion, and support from others; and physical states and reactions in the context of task performance (Bandura, 1986).

Self-efficacy beliefs are an important aspect of career development. Research indicates that academic self-efficacy strongly predicts academic achievement and persistence (Hackett, Betz, Casas, & Rocha-Singh, 1992). Many researchers who investigated career self-efficacy reported a positive correlation between adolescents' high self-efficacy in a specific occupation and their willingness to choose this occupation (Tang, Foad, & Smith, 1999). High self-efficacy in a specific occupation also correlated positively with high career aspirations for that occupation (Nauta, Epperson & Kahn, 1998). Perceptions of low self-efficacy in certain occupations may contribute to individuals' premature elimination of those possible career options (Betz & Hackett, 1981). Similar patterns emerged in research dealing with self-efficacy in family roles. First, parental self-efficacy, referring to persons' beliefs about their ability to succeed in the parental role/tasks, correlated positively with good adaptation to the parental role (Ardelt & Eccles, 2001). Second, marital self-efficacy emerged as a predictor of marital satisfaction (Finchman, Harold, & Gano-Phillips, 2000). These studies demonstrated the vital relevance of self-efficacy on behavior in both the work and family domains. Therefore, perceived low self-efficacy in managing the work-family conflict may lead to the premature elimination of some career or family options that require a challenging blend of work and family roles. Recent research demonstrated that self-efficacy concerning work-family conflict management correlated negatively with expectations of work-family conflict, and correlated positively with career plans that intensively combined work and family roles (Cinamon, 2003). On the basis of the above research, we need to be especially sensitive to adolescents who report low self-efficacy for managing the work-family conflict because they may try to avoid stress by shunning specific occupations that they consider very demanding and stressful, or by curtailing their family plans in order to achieve their occupational goals.

Many authors have recommended efficacy-enhancing interventions due the strong impact of self-efficacy on development (Brown & Lent, 1996; Hackett & Byars, 1996; Swanson & Woitke, 1997). These recommendations would appear relevant, too, for career intervention programs aimed at increasing self-efficacy concerning coping with work-family conflict. The interventions should be based on exploiting several sources of self-efficacy: personal achievement, performance, and exposure to role models (Bandura, 1986). People take on multiple social roles from birth, immediately becoming a son or daughter, grandchild, sibling, patient in a doctor's care, etc. Young children already combine family roles as a brother or niece along with a preschool student role and a role in the community. Their own successful experience with current personal role combinations may provide a good frame of reference for establishing high efficacy to combine work and family roles in the future. Allowing adolescents to explore and appreciate their current ability to combine life roles (like student, family member, friend, etc.) may foster efficacy beliefs in their capability for blending future work and family roles despite conflicting demands for time, energy and emotional allegiance. Additionally, personal exposure to men and women who succeed in blending work and family roles with low levels of work-family conflict may also contribute to the establishment of high self-efficacy concerning work-family conflict management. Interventions can provide such exposure by introducing adolescents to gender- and culture-matched role models who successfully combine life roles. The adolescent should feel that the person they encounter is from a similar background, and if that person accomplished a satisfactory blending of roles, then "so can I." Special attention during this meeting should be devoted to determining the resources that help blend roles and analyzing the barriers that impede role combination.

CAREER INTERVENTIONS AND IMPLEMENTATION

Career intervention programs are widespread and empirical evidence supports their contribution to participants' career development (Brown & Ryan Krane, 2000; Lapan & Kosciulek, 2001; Savickas, 1999; Whiston & Sexton, 1998). The career intervention literature, as well as the literature of other intervention programs, has directed a fair amount of attention to the issue of targets of change, but relatively little to issues of strategy (Heaney, 2003). Accordingly, the current chapter will describe the intervention program and will discuss questions of strategy in some detail. Certain career development methods and techniques have emerged as effective for most clients. Ryan (1999) conducted a series of meta-analytic studies that investigated whether the presence of various intervention components (e.g., written exercises, computer activities) is linked with outcome measures associated with satisfying career choices like vocational identity and career maturity. Findings showed that outcome measures were more strongly influenced by intervention methods than by participant characteristics. The effectiveness of group interventions also emerged. Brown and Ryan Krane (2000) concluded that career interventions are significantly more effective if the interventions (a) allow participants to clarify their goals in writing, (b) provide participants with individualized interpretations and feedback, (c) give current career information, (d) include role models, and (e) help participants develop support networks that will facilitate their pursuit of career aspirations.

The intervention program described below was designed to implement these five effective components in the area of both work and family roles. Written goal clarification exercises encourage participants to recode reflections, thoughts, and feelings regarding their work and family plans. Written exercises also can help participants establish work and family goals and plan for their implementation with special consideration to the conflicts these goals may evoke. Individual interpretation and feedback comprises another important aspect of this process, mediating each participant's difficulties that may arise due to the planned combination of roles, as well as highlighting the support variables that may be of assistance and the stress variables that may pose obstructions. Most career intervention programs provide occupational information about the world of work. In line with an approach aiming to prepare adolescents for work-family conflict, interventions should also include information about the family domain, such as different sorts of families (dual career families, single-parent families, traditional families), the developmental cycle of the family, the family's different support systems, factors that can cause stress to the family, as well as resources that help families. Information may be obtained through the counselor-facilitator, other group members, computers, or outside sources. Guest speakers may act as role models. They should include male and female guests who play an active role in both domains and who can achieve a level of self-disclosure and intimacy that facilitates participants' exploration. Inclusion of models from the same culture and socioeconomic class as the participants may also be a critical determinant. Finally, in line with work-family conflict research that demonstrated the impact of social support in reducing the conflict, interventions should assist participants to recognize people who may help assist them physically and morally to combine work and family roles and to nurture supportive relationships.

An important aspect of any intervention program is the issue of implementation. Implementation of career health promotion programs within organizations in general and school organizations in particular is very complicated because it is intricately related to organizational and individual level variables (e.g. Heaney, 2003; Lytle, Ward, Nader, Pedersen, & Williston, 2003). One of the primary barriers within the school organization is the time pressures and constraints of schools that render low priority for health promotion activities (Lytle et al., 2003). It is a great challenge to convince school leaders to invest school time and energy to promote the necessary knowledge, skills, attitudes, and self-efficacy for coping with work-family conflict. Other organizational pitfalls of school program implementation include lack of ongoing systematic staff development and the lack of sufficient funds for "nonessential" materials and equipment (Lytle et al., 2003; Sheppard, 2002). Although school counselors or other mental health workers may be the professionals responsible for the contents and forms of implementation of programs for work-family conflict prevention, the active support and cooperation of the principal and other administrative staff are crucial. These school officials usually have a broad system-wide perspective on the school; they have some control over material and human resources at the organizational level; and they have means to contribute to creating a climate that values the intervention. Thus, the success of the intervention program is considerably more likely when school professionals from both of these domains work together to develop the program.

GENDER DIFFERENCES IN
WORK-FAMILY CONFLICT AND COPING

One of the interesting topics regarding planning and implementing intervention programs on work and family roles is related to gender. Are there gender differences that render it desirable to design distinctive programs for male and female adolescents? If there are gender differences, can we exploit them in order to achieve our goals?

Gender differences in work and family experiences have been a consistently important theme in work-family research (Cinamon & Rich, 2002b; Lewis & Cooper, 1999). Based on Greenhaus and Beutell's (1985) argument about the importance of role salience to the work-family conflict, many scholars have speculated that women experience more work-family conflict than men due to their typically greater home responsibilities and their allocation of more importance to family roles. However, most recent research has discovered that men and women do *not* differ on their level of work-family conflict (Blanchard-Fields, Chen, & Hebert, 1997; Duxbury & Higgins, 1991; Grzywacz & Marks, 2000; Wallace, 1997). These unanticipated results regarding the lack of gender differences on level of work-family conflict raise the possibility that researchers' emphasis on between-gender differences may cover important within-gender variation in work-family conflict. Gender identity can not be separated from other identity issues. Rather, it is part of a complex psychological and social process whereby men and women adopt varying degrees of traditionally masculine and feminine roles and responsibilities (Anderson & Leslie, 1991). A host of social and cultural factors, as well as individual abilities and personality characteristics, mediate the relationship between gender and work-family conflict (Farmer, 1985). Thus, individual variation within gender can be a valuable source of information in order to explain differences among persons regarding work-family conflict. Indeed, a study by Cinamon and Rich (2002b) showed within and between gender differences. Comparisons between men and women showed that overall females had higher levels of work-family conflict. However, when men and women attributed similar levels of importance and value to work and family roles, they also shared similar levels of work-family conflict. This and other research emphasize the need to attend to the variation in men's and women's beliefs about the importance of work and family roles, rather than to generalize to all men and to all women based on gender alone (Cinamon & Rich, 2002b; Kerpelman & Schvaneveldt, 1999).

This body of research does not allow us to make unequivocal recommendations regarding the offering of intervention programs to prevent or minimize work-family conflict in homogeneous or heterogeneous gender groups of adolescents. Several supporting arguments can be offered for each position. For example, some adolescents might feel greater emotional and social security in homogeneous gender groups. As a result, they are more likely to explore their identities insightfully, to express themselves freely and they may sense greater empathy for the opinions and concerns of their group members. Also, they may be more willing to take riskier positions because there are fewer concerns about negative repercussions within the group.

Heterogeneous gender groups have important advantages as well. More varied career goals and aspirations may be discussed and legitimized in heterogeneous groups. In general, males and females are provided the opportunity to broaden their horizons and to learn from other gender persons with whom they probably have shared fewer intimate conversations on personal meanings related to work and family. Heterogeneous groups of adolescents can also stimulate thoughtful discussions about gender and work roles. In particular, young men and women can hear about the desires, dreams and demands of other gender persons regarding blending family and work roles. They may begin to experience confrontations and negotiations regarding priorities, sharing of duties and maximizing self-realization for both family members. They may also begin to learn how other gender persons utilize strategies to resolve problems. For example, considerable research has demonstrated that women are more likely than men to seek advice, information, practical assistance and/or emotional support from others in their social networks when they have a problem (Greenglass, 2000). These are issues that commonly arise between dual career spouses when seeking to define their work and family roles or when dealing with work-family conflict.

As noted above, sifting through this literature to evaluate its implications for establishing homogenous or heterogeneous gender groups does not yield an unambiguous answer. Nevertheless, the promise inherent in heterogeneous groupings leads us to favor this arrangement in most cases. However, we also encourage forming homogeneous settings for those activities where participants might benefit from a greater sense of security and intimacy. Of special importance is that in making the decision about homogeneous or heterogeneous groups, school leaders should pay special attention to local considerations, such as the relations between the boys and girls that will comprise the group, their vocational maturity, how stereotyped is their thinking about gender roles and other issues that will affect the quality of group interaction.

DESCRIPTION OF AN INTERVENTION PROGRAM

The program consists of 8 to 10 weekly 90-minute workshop meetings held in high school, with 7 to 12 male and female participants aged 16 to 18 years. Its objectives may entail a variety of topics including: increasing personal awareness about work and family role identity; clarifying relevant attitudes, values, interests; increasing self-efficacy concerning role management; and providing information about work-family conflict and ways to reduce it. The program consists of three units:

1. *Exploration* of personal identity.
2. *Information* about work, family, and work-family conflict.
3. Transferring *skills* of role management.

The *exploration* unit aims to foster participants' exploration of the social roles that comprise their identity as family member, student, worker, friend, and so forth, and the hierarchical importance of these social roles. This unit focuses on future work roles (entry level, executive; colleague, boss) as well as family roles (spouse, parent). To explore the future hierarchical importance of life roles, adolescents are urged to ask themselves about their current role salience as a student, peer, family member, and worker: *Which are the most important roles for me? Why are they important? How do I know they are so important? Which role is the least important? Was it always like that?* Participants can individually create their own current structure of identity based on engagement in present social roles, ranking them in descending order from the most important role to the least important. As a stimulus, the facilitator can write the names of different life roles onto cards. Participants choose those cards with the roles they feel comprise their current or future identity, and arrange them in order. Another stimulus can be a diagram of six circles, with five circles surrounding one central circle. Participants are invited to write their names in the center circle and to insert in the surrounding circles those social roles that comprise their identity. Then they are asked to mark the most important role and the least important one. Group discussion focuses on the relative importance of different roles, on the legitimacy of each individual maintaining a unique hierarchy, on different personal meanings of importance, as well as on changes in role meanings and importance over time.

In this unit it is important to clarify with participants their current role conflicts, using guiding questions such as: *Which roles seem to clash with one another? If all roles are important, how do I set priorities? How do I manage demands on my time and energy?* Facilitators devote special attention to participants' present ability to combine roles: *What helps me combine roles? What makes it more difficult? How do I solve problems when they arise?* Facilitators also clarify gender variations, cultural variations, and individual variations. Participants are expected to gain the understanding that the determination of role hierarchies, modes of combining roles, perceived role conflict and ways of ameliorating it are related to the individuals' belief system and are subject to his or her influence. Moreover, it is very helpful to inform participants of the temporary and dynamic nature of role importance hierarchies. Participants receive feedback from the facilitator as well as from the other participants.

In the identity component of this exploration unit, participants also explore role meanings by asking questions such as: *What does it mean for me to be a student? A family member? A friend? What kind of parent will I be? What kind of worker? What kind of parent/worker do I want to be? What is a good parent/worker?*

In line with Brown and Ryan Krane's (2000) recommendations, among other tasks in this unit, participants write their personal goals for work roles and family roles. The facilitators give personal feedback regarding these goals, and other group members provide feedback within group discussions. The mutual relationship between work and family roles is emphasized in this unit.

Role-playing is also a very useful technique during this unit. Participants are invited to act out different anticipated roles such as "yourself 10 years from now at work." The role play is guided by questions such as: *Where is the scene happening? What is my job there? Who are my colleagues? How do I feel at work?* A group discussion helps the "actor" explore the work role, with special attention to the role's salience and personal meanings that emerged through the role play. Participants are offered multiple opportunities to experience different possible worker selves and are invited to play the same role with different salience levels and meanings. The role play session is a wonderful opportunity that enables several participants to explore diverse roles in different situations and to expose themselves to the reactions of a number of individuals who are undergoing similar exploration processes. A comparable procedure is implemented for the family roles. The group discusses gender and cultural differences as these emerge. Personal and group discussion and feedback from participants and the facilitator help the adolescents explore their feelings and attitudes toward the different possible selves they played in each role. Although the discussion may focus on the events and feelings expressed in the role play, it is important to adopt a future orientation so that participants will internalize the idea that personal and social change is likely to occur and the exploration will continue.

Special attention is given to exploring possible combinations of work and family roles. Several diagrams presenting different relations between work and family can provide interesting stimuli such as: (a) Two separate circles depicting no relations between work and family reflecting the myth of separate worlds. (b) Ying and yang within the same circle describing relatively harmonic relations. (c) Overlapping circles of family and work, with the family circle encroaching, in varying degrees, on the work circle (representing conflict where family intrudes into work). (d) Overlapping circles of family and work, with the work circle encroaching, in varying amounts, on the family circle (representing conflict where work intrudes into family). Participants can be invited to select the "ideal" diagram or the "worst" diagram and explain why. The meeting should include discussion and role play of different role combinations, with a focus on the conflicts that these combinations elicit and possible solutions.

The *information* unit includes knowledge regarding the world of work, the variation within different family structures, and about the work-family conflict. Regarding the world of work, participants actively learn about the different occupations that exist in their environment. It is especially important to expose young people from economically depressed areas to occupations not commonly found in their immediate environment. The facilitator also helps participants become familiar with different computer resources for career decision making (e.g., see Gati, 1996). Most information about different occupations describes the job's characteristics, the abilities and educational credentials needed. The current intervention sees as particularly valuable information on the flexibility of different occupations with regard to blending life roles and the aspects of each occupation that influence and are influenced by family. Participants are encouraged to learn how to use computers to search statistical websites and to read newspaper articles on the labor market and to consider analyses of the implications of these trends on family roles. Opportunities to practice getting this information are an integral part of the unit.

Alongside exposure to different occupations, adolescents need to become familiar with different configurations of families (e.g., traditional, dual career families, dual earner families, one-parent family, etc.). Group discussion can focus on the barriers and resources within each type of family regarding work and family role combinations. This unit can also include an active search by participants for statistical data regarding men's and women's work within different family arrangements.

Another important issue in this unit is knowledge about work-family conflict. Participants become familiar with the phenomenon, its characteristics, and its detrimental results. Special attention is given to teaching adolescents about the contribution of stress and support variables from the work domain and from the family domain. To insure that learning does not remain on an abstract level, participants practice how to communicate in appropriate ways with their supervisors, colleagues and spouse. They learn to recognize signs of stress in themselves or in their work colleagues and family members so they can restructure their schedules and priorities when necessary in order to prevent undue pressures. These management skills are crucial for participants' future ability to blend life roles effectively and to minimize work-family stress.

In line with Brown and Ryan Krane's (2000) recommendation, in this unit adolescents meet men and women from their social and cultural background who have combined a successful career and active participation in their family. Following the understanding deriving from self-efficacy theory (Bandura, 1986), it is important that the role models as well as the facilitator encourage participants to blend work and family roles, affirming their belief that the adolescents can achieve this blend effectively. Counselors-facilitators prepare invited role models before the presentation to assure that they will support the core messages of the intervention. Role models need to be familiar with the purpose of the intervention and its main components and they are guided to tell their story so as to encourage students to believe in themselves. They also describe the kinds of problems they have encountered, how they overcame them, and resources they used that proved helpful.

The *transferring skills* unit comprises mainly role-playing activities and personal and group feedback. Participants receive short stories describing conflicts of both types: work events interfering in family life (e.g., missing your child's party due to a demanding period at work) and family events interfering in work life (e.g., missing work due to your child's illness). These can also be presented in a computerized manner for tryout and feedback before role-playing. Participants also role-play their reactions to these stories on the basis of their tentative identity emphases (as expressed in the exploration unit) and on the knowledge they gained in the information unit. The group discusses these role-played reactions in terms of whether the reaction reduces or increases the conflict. Using knowledge gained in the information unit, participants can role-play various responses that might help them reduce the conflict (reschedule their day, ask for help, seek support, etc.). The facilitator invites adolescents to role-play actual conflicts between current life roles, for example, conflicts in friendship roles. Participants can act out their actual attempts to solve and handle these actual or anticipated conflicts. The facilitator reinforces effective solutions after the group discussion. Participants receive encouragement about their current ability to handle role conflict and their capacity to use that ability and knowledge in the future. Throughout this unit activities focus on how to relate to and manage conflict based on the participant's chosen identities. However, as the unit unfolds, the experiential learning stimulates some participants to question the wisdom of the relative importance of their chosen life roles. Counselors are aware that it may be necessary, even at this phase, to provide opportunities for participants to reconsider this fundamental issue.

FINAL COMMENTS

This chapter provides the rationale for and describes a counseling intervention aimed to increase adolescents' ability to blend work and family roles effectively and to prevent or moderate the negative effects of work-family conflict. The intervention is grounded in the literature on work-family conflict, which portrays this conflict as a major stress variable in male and female employees in Western societies. It is founded on the assumption that educational authorities should take responsibility for proactively increasing students' resilience and ability to cope with future stress. The program suggests a three component structure that includes exercises drawing from the literature on effective career intervention programs: exploration, information, and skill training.

Due to the limited scope of this chapter, we did not elaborate on the cultural aspects of work-family conflict or on the implications of culture for developing and implementing the intervention program. Yet, we believe that this is a very important issue. As Heppner and Heppner (2003) suggested, cultural decontextualization has limited both the extent and the applicability of our understanding of career interventions. To understand career intervention fully, we must examine not only what we do therapeutically, but also the reactions that such interventions incur from the socio-cultural and physical environments in which our clients must implement their choices. The entire topic that we have discussed in this chapter is imbued with cultural and moral values. Work, family, life role salience, personal meanings and appropriate or effective role blending are all deeply affected by the social and cultural environment of participants. Facilitators are therefore urged to examine their own beliefs and values about work and family roles for both genders and to carefully avoid imposing their own values regarding appropriate role combinations onto their group participants. Furthermore, intervention programs will most likely fail if they clash with the adolescent's family and social milieu. Hence, career intervention programs that aim to prepare adolescents to cope effectively with work-family conflict would do well to collaborate with families and to respect the values and traditions of the participants.

REFERENCES

Anderson, E. A., & Leslie, L. A. (1991). Coping with employment and family stress: Employment arrangement and gender differences. *Sex Roles, 24*, 223-231.

Aronsson, G. (1999). Influence of worklife on public health. *Scandinavian Journal of Work Enviroment Health, 25*, 597-604.

Allen, T. D., Herst, D. E., Burck, C. S., & Sutton, M. (2000). Consequences associated with work to family conflict: A review and agenda for future research. *Journal of Occupational Health Psychology, 5,* 278-308.

Antonovsky, A. (1987). *Unraveling the mysteries of health.* San Francisco: Jossey-Bass.

Antonovsky, A. (1993). The structure and properties of the sense of coherence scale. *Social Science and Medicine, 36,* 725-734.

Archer, S. L. (1989). Gender differences in identity development: Issues of process, domain, and timing. *Journal of Adolescence, 12,* 117-138.

Aspinwall, L. G., & Taylor, S. E. (1997). A stitch in time: Self-regulation and proactive coping. *Psychological Bulletin, 121,* 417-436.

Ardelt, M., & Eccles, J. S. (2001). Effects of mothers' parental efficacy beliefs and promotive parenting strategies on inner-city youth. *Journal of Family Issues, 22,* 944-972.

Baber, K. M., & Monaghan, P. (1988). College women's career and motherhood expectations: New options, old dilemmas. *Sex Roles, 19,* 189-203.

Bacharach, S. B., Bamberger, P., & Conley, S. (1991). *Journal of Organizational Behavior, 12,* 39-53.

Bandura, A. (1986). *Social foundations of thought and action: A social cognitive theory.* Englewood Cliffs, NJ: Prentice-Hall.

Beck, U., & Beck-Gernsheim, E. (1995). *The normal chaos of love.* Cambridge, England: Polity Press.

Beck-Gernsheim, E. (1998). On the way to a post-familial family: From a community of a need to elective affinities. *Theory, Culture and Society, 15,* 53-70.

Benach, J., Fernando, G. B., Platt, S., Diez-Roux, A., & Muntaner, C. (2000). The health-damaging potential of new types of flexibile employment: A challenge for public health researchers. *American Journal of Public Health, 90,* 1316-1317.

Bernas, K. H., & Major, A. D. (2000). Contributors to stress resistance: Testing a model of women's work-family conflict. *Psychology of Women Quarterly, 24,* 170-178.

Berzonsky, M. D. (1995). Public self-presentations and self-conceptions: The moderating role identity status. *The Journal of Social Psychology, 135,* 737-745.

Betz, N. C. (1993). Women's career development. In F. L. Denmark & M. A. Paludi (Eds.), *Psychology of women: A handbook of issues and theories* (pp. 627-684). Westport, CT: Greenwood Press.

Betz, N. E., & Hackett, G. (1981). The relationship of career-related self-efficacy expectations to perceived career options in college women and men. *Journal of Counseling Psychology, 28,* 399-410.

Blanchard-Field, F., Chen, Y., & Herbert, C. E. (1997). Interrole conflict as a function of life stage, gender, and gender-related personality attributes. *Sex Roles, 37,* 155-174.

Blau, F. D., & Ferber M. A. (1991). Career plans and expectations of young women and men: The earnings gap and labor force participation. *Journal of Human Resources, 26,* 581-607.

Blustein, D. L. (1997). A context-rich perspective of career exploration across the life roles. *Career Development Quarterly, 45,* 260-274.

Bond, J. T., Galinsky, E., & Swanberg, J. E. (1998). *The 1997 national study of the chancing workforce.* New York: Families and Work Institute.

Bourdieu, P. (1996). The family as a realized category. *Theory, Culture and Society, 13,* 19-26.

Brown, S. D., & Lent, R. W. (1996). A social cognitive framework for career choice counseling. *Career Development Quarterly, 44,* 354-366.

Brown, S. D., & Ryan Krane, N. E. (2000). Four (or five) sessions and a cloud of dust: Old assumptions and new observations about career counseling. In S. D. Brown & R. W. Lent (Eds.), *Handbook of counseling psychology* (3rd ed., pp. 740-766). New York: Wiley.

Burke, R. J., & Greenglass, E. R. (1999). Work-family conflict, spouse support, and nursing staff well being during organizational restructuring. *Journal of Occupational Health Psychology, 4,* 327-336.

Carlson, D. S., & Kacmar, K. M. (2000). Work-family conflict in the organization: Do live role values make a differences? *Journal of Management, 26,* 1031-1054.

Cheal, D. (1993). Unity and difference in postmodern families. *Journal of Family Issues, 14,* 5-19.

Cinamon, R. G. (2003). *Work-family conflict management self-efficacy and career plan among Israeli students.* Manuscript submitted for publication.

Cinamon, R. G., & Rich, Y. (2002a). Profiles of attribution of importance to life roles and their implications for the work-family conflict. *Journal of Counseling Psychology, 49,* 212-220.

Cinamon, R. G., & Rich, Y. (2002b). Gender differences in attribution of importance to life roles. *Sex Roles, 47,* 531-541.

Clark, S. C. (2000). Work/family border theory: A new theory of work/family balance. *Human Relations, 53,* 747-770.

Cook, E. P. (1994). Role salience and multiple roles: A gender perspective. *Career Development Quarterly, 43,* 85-95.

Cote, J. E., & Levine, C. (1998). A critical examination of the ego identity status paradigm. *Developmental Review, 8,* 147-184.

Duxbury, L. E., & Higgins, C. A. (1991). Gender differences in work-family conflict. *Journal of Applied Psychology, 76,* 60-73.

Erikson, E. H. (1980). *Identity and life cycle.* New York: Norton.

Farber, R. S. (1996). An integrated perspective on women's career development within a family. *American Journal of Family Therapy, 24,* 329-342.

Farmer, H. (1985). Model of career and achievement motivation for women and men. *Journal of Counseling Psychology, 32,* 360-390.

Finchman, F. D., Harold, G. T., & Gano-Phillips, S. (2000). The longitudinal association between attributions and marital satisfaction: Direction of effects and role of efficacy expectations. *Journal of Family Psychology, 14,* 267-285.

Flum, H., & Blustein, D. L. (2000). Reinvigorating the study of vocational exploration: A framework for research. *Journal of Vocational Behavior, 56,* 380-404.

Frankel, M. (1998). Creating the family friendly workplace: Barriers and solutions. In S. Klarreich (Ed.), *Handbook of organizational health psychology: Programs to make the workplace healthier* (pp. 79-100). Madison, CT: Psychosocial Press.

Frone, M. R. (2003). Work-family balance. In J. C. Quick & L. E. Tetrick (Eds.), *Handbook of occupational health psychology* (pp. 143-162). Washington, DC: APA.

Frone, M. R. Barnes, G. M., & Farrell, M. P. (1994). Relationship of work-family conflict to substance use among employed mothers: The role of negative affect. *Journal of Marriage and the Family, 56,* 1019-1030.

Frone, M. R., & Yardley, J. K. (1996). Work-place family-supportive programs: Predictors of employed parents' importance ratings. *Journal of Occupational and Organizational Psychology, 69,* 351-366.

Frone, M. R., Yardley, J. K., & Markel, K. S. (1997). Developing and testing an integrative model of the work family interface. *Journal of Vocational Behavior, 50,* 145-167.

Frumkin, H. (1998). Free-trade agreements. In J. M. Stellman (Ed.), *Encyclopedia of occupational health and safety* (Vol. 1, pp. 2013-2017). Geneva, Switzerland: Imternational Labour Office.

Galinsky, E., & Bond, J. T. (1998). *The 1998 business work-life study: A sourcebook.* New York: Families and Work Institute.

Gati, I. (1998). Using career-related aspects to elicit preferences and characterize occupations for a better person-environment fit. *Journal of Vocational Behavior, 52,* 343-356.

Gergen, K. J. (1991). *The saturated self: Dilemmas of identity in contemporary life.* New York: Basic Books.

Gerson, M. J. (1989). Tomorrow's fathers: The anticipation of fatherhood. In S. H. Cath, A. Gerwitt, & L. Gunsberg (Eds.), *Fathers and their families* (pp. 127-144). Hillsdale, NJ: The Analytic Press.

Gottfredson, G. D. (1996). Some direct measures of career status: Putting multiple theories into practice. In M. L. Savickas & W. B. Walsh (Eds.), *Handbook of career counseling theory and practice* (pp. 213-236). Palo Alto, CA: Davies-Black.

Granrose, C. S. (1985). Plans for careers among college women who expect to have families. *Vocational Guidance Quarterly, 33,* 284-295.

Greene, A. L. & Wheatley, S. M. (1992). "I've got a lot to do and I don't think I'll have the time": Gender differences in late adolescents; narratives of the future. *Journal of Youth and Adolescence, 21,* 667-686.

Greenglass, E. R. (2000, July). *Work rage and its psychological implications.* Paper presented at the 21st International STAR Conference, Bratislava, Slovakia.

Greenglass, E. R., Schwarzer, R., & Taubert, S. (1999). *The Proactive Coping Inventory (PCI): A multidimensional research instrument* [On-line]. Available: http://www.psych.yorku.ca/greenglass/

Greenhaus, J. H., & Beutell, N. J. (1985). Source of conflict between work and family roles. *Academy Management Review, 10,* 77-88.

Grzywacz, J. G., & Marks, N. F. (2000). Reconceptualizing the work family interface: An ecological perspective on the correlates of positive and negative spillover between work and family. *Journal of Occupational Health Psychology, 5,* 111-126.

Hackett, G., & Byars, A. M. (1996). Social cognitive theory and the career development of African American women. *Career Development Quarterly, 44,* 322-340.

Hackett, G., Betz, N. E., Casas, J. M., & Rocha-Singh, I. A. (1992). Gender, ethnicity, and social cognitive factors predicting the academic achievment of students in engineering. *Journal of Counseling Psychology, 39,* 527-538.

Hall, D. T. (1972). A model of coping with role conflict: The role behavior of college educated women. *Administrative Science Quarterly, 17*, 471-486.

Hallett, M. B., & Gilbert, L. A. (1997). Variables differentiating university women considering role-sharing and conventional dual-career marriage. *Journal of Vocational Behavior, 50*, 308-322.

Heaney, C. A. (2003). Worksite health intervention: Targets for change and strategies for attaining them. In J. C. Quick & L. E. Tetrick (Eds.), *Handbook of occupational health psychology* (pp. 305-323). Washington, DC: APA.

Heppner, M. J., & Heppner, P. P. (2003). Identifying process variables in career counseling: A research agenda. *Journal of Vocational Behavior, 62*, 429-452.

Holland, J. L. (1997). *Making vocational choices: A theory of vocational personalities and work environments* (3rd ed.). Odessa, FL: Psychological Assessment Resources.

Howson, M., & O'Driscoll, M. P. (1996). *Satisfaction with children and job-family conflict: Implication for absenteeism, lateness, and turnover.* Unpublished manuscript, University of Waikato, Hamilton, New Zealand.

Kerpelman, J. L., & Schvaneveldt, P. L. (1999). Young adults' anticipated identity importance of career, marital, and parental roles: Comparisons of men and women with different role balance orientations. *Sex Roles, 41*, 189-217.

Kinnunen, U., & Mauno, S. (1998). Antecedents and outcomes of work-family conflict among employed women and men in Finland. *Human Relations, 51*, 157-177.

Kirchmeyer, C., & Cohen, A. (1999). Different strategies for managing the work/non work interface: A test for unique pathways to outcomes. *Work and Stress, 13*, 59-73.

Kulik, L. (1998). Inter-and intra-gender differences in life orientations and work attitudes in Israel: A comparative analysis. *International Journal for the Advancement of Counseling, 20*, 95-111.

Lapan, R. T., & Kosciulek, J. F. (2001). Toward a community career system program evaluation framework. *Journal of counseling and development, 79*, 3-15.

Lee, R. A. (1983). Flextime and conjugal roles. *Journal of Occupational Behavior, 4*, 297-315.

Lent, R. W., Brown, S. D., &Hackett, G. (1994). Toward a unifying social cognitive theory of career and academic interest, choice, and performance. *Journal of Vocational Behavior, 45*, 79-122.

Lewis, S. N., & Cooper, C. L. (1998). Stress in dual earner families. In B. A. Gutek, A. Stomberg, & L. Larwood (Eds.), *Women and work* (Vol. 3, pp. 139-168). Newbury Park, CA: Sage.

Lytle, L. A., Ward, A., Nader, P. R., Pederson, S., & Williston, B. J. (2003). Maintenance of a health promotion program in elementary schools: Results from the CATCH-ON study-key information interviews. *Health Education and Behavior, 30*, 503-518.

Marcia, J. E. (1994). The empirical study of ego identity. In H. A. Bosma, T. L. Graafsma, H. D. Grotevant, & D. J. de Levita (Eds.), *Identity and development: An interdisciplinary approach* (pp. 97-80). Thousand Oaks, CA: Sage Publications.

Marks, N. F. (1998). Does it hurt to care? Caregiving, work-family conflict, and midlife well-being. *Journal of Marriage and the Family, 60*, 951-966.

Markus, H., & Nurius, P. (1986). Possible selves. *American Psychologist, 41*, 954-969.

Matsui, T., Ohsawa, T., & Onglatco, M. (1995). Work-family conflict: The stress-buffering effects of husband support and coping behavior among Japanese married working women. *Journal of Vocational Behavior, 47*, 178-192.

Nauta, M. M., Epperson, D. L., & Kahn, J. H. (1998). A multiple-groups analysis of predictors of higher level career aspirations among women in mathematics, science, and engineering majors. *Journal of Counseling Psychology, 45*, 483-496.

Netemeyer, R. G., Boles, J. S., & McMurrian, R. (1996). Development and validation of work-family conflict and family-work conflict scales. *Journal of Applied Psychology, 81*, 400-410.

Niles, S. P., Goodnough, G., & Anderson, W. P., Jr. (1998). Exploration to foster career development. *Career Development Quarterly, 46*, 262-275.

Novack, L. L., & Novack, D. R. (1996). Being female in the eighties and nineties: Conflicts between new opportunities and traditional expectation among white, middle class, heterosexual college women. *Sex Roles, 35*, 57-77.

Parasurman, S., Yasmin, S. P., Purohit, Y., Veronica, M., & Beutell, N. (1996). Work and family variables, entrepreneurial career success and psychological well-being. *Journal of Vocational Behavior, 48*, 275-300.

Peake, A., & Harris, K. L. (2002). Young adults' attitudes toward multiple role planning: The influence of gender, career traditionality and marriage plans. *Journal of Vocational Behavior, 60*, 405-421.

Phillips, S. D., & Imhoff, A. R. (1997). Women and career development: A decade of research. *Annual Review of Psychology, 48*, 31-59.

Reskin, B. F., & Padavic I. (2001). The doctrine of separate spheres. In R. Satow (Ed.), *Gender and social life* (pp. 57-62). Needham Heights, MA: Allyn & Bacon.

Rich, Y., & Golan, R. (1992). Career plans for male-dominated occupations among female senior in religious and secular high schools. *Adolescence, 27*, 73-86.

Ryan, N. E. (1999). *Career counseling and career choice goal attainment: A meta-analytically derived model for career counseling practice.* Unpublished doctoral dissertation, Loyola University, Chicago.

Ryff, C. D., & Singer, B. (1998). The contours of positive human health. *Psychologocal Inquiry, 9*, 1-28.

Savickas, M. L., (1999) The transition from school to work: A developmental perspective. *Career Development Quarterly, 47*, 326-36.

Schwarzer, R. (2000). Manage stress at work through preventive and proactive coping. In E. A. Locke (Ed.), *The Blackwell handbook of principles of organizational behavior* (pp. 342-355). Oxford, England: Blackwell.

Schwarzer, R., & Renner, B. (2000). Social-cognitive predictors of health behavior: Action self-efficacy and coping self-efficacy. *Health Psychology, 19*, 487-495.

Seligman, M., & Csikszentmihalyi, M. (2000). Positive psychology: An introduction. *American Psychologist, 55*, 5-14.

Sheppard, R. R. (2002). The utility of a school-initiated character education program. *Dissertation abstracts international section A: Humanities and social sciences, 63*, 2149.

Solberg, V. S., Howard, K. A., Blustein, D. L., & Close, W. (2002). Career development in the schools: Connecting school-to-work-to-life. *Counseling Psychology, 30*, 705-725.

Smith, C. S., Folkard, S., & Fuller, A. (2003). Shiftwork and working hours. In J. C. Quick & L. E. Tetrick (Eds.), *Handbook of occupational health psychology* (pp. 163-184). Washington, DC: APA.

Stacey, J. (1990). *Brave new families*. New-York: Basic Book.

Stacey, J. (1992). Backward toward the postmodern family. In B. Thorne & M. Yalom (Eds.), *Rethinking the family, some feminist questions* (pp. 91-118). Boston: Northeastern University Press.

Staines, G. L., & Pleck, J. H. (1983). *The impact of work schedules on the family*. Ann Arbor, MI: Institute for Social Research.

Stryker, S., & Serpe, R. T. (1994). Identity salience and psychological centrality: equivalent, overlapping, or complementary concepts? *Social Psychology Quarterly, 57*, 16-35.

Super, D. E. (1990). A life-span, life-space approach to career development. In D. Brown & L. Brooks (Eds.), *Career choice and development: Applying contemporary theories to practice* (2nd ed., pp. 197-261). San Francisco: Jossey-Bass.

Swanson, J. L., & Woitke, M. B. (1997). Theory into practice in career assessment for women: Assessment and Interventions regarding perceived career barriers. *Journal of Career Assessment, 5*, 443-462.

Tang, M., Foad, N. A., & Smith, P. L. (1999). Asian Americans career choices: A path model to examine factors influencing their career choices. *Journal of Vocational Behavior, 54*, 142-157.

Tetrick, L. E., & Quick, J. C. (2003). Prevention at work: Public health in occupational settings. In J. C. Quick & L. E. Tetrick (Eds.) *Handbook of occupational health psychology* (pp. 3-17). Washington, DC: APA.

Thomas, L. T., & Ganster, D. C. (1995). Impact of family supportive work variables on work family conflict and strain: A control perspective. *Journal of Applied Psychology, 80*, 6-15.

Voydanoff, P. (1988). Work role characteristics, family structure demands, and work/family conflict. *Journal of Marriage and the Family, 50*, 749-761.

Wallace, J. E. (1997). It's about time: A study of hours worked and work spillover among law firm lawyers. *Journal of Vocational Behavior, 50*, 227-248.

Weitzman, L. M. (1994). Multiple-role realism: A theoretical framework for the process of planning to combine career and family roles. *Applied and Preventive Psychology, 3*, 15-25.

Whiston, S. C., & Sexton, T. L. (1998). A review of school counseling outcome research: Implications for practice. *Journal of Counseling and Development, 76*, 412-426.

Willinger, B. (1993). Resistance and change: College men's attitudes toward family and work in the 1980's. In J. C. Hood (Ed.), *Men, work, and family: Research on men and masculinities series* (Vol. 4, pp. 108-130). Newbury Park, CA: Sage.

CHAPTER 11

THREE KEYS TO THRIVING

David W. Johnson and Roger T. Johnson
University of Minnesota

ABSTRACT

There are three key elements to thriving. First, a person needs to build cooperative relationships with others in which they work together to achieve common goals. Being part of a cooperative enterprise creates a shared sense of accomplishment, positive relationships, social support systems, high self-esteem, psychological health, and social competencies, all of which are necessary to thrive and survive. Second, the quality of any relationship depends on resolving conflicts constructively. The more central the relationship to a person's survival, the more important it is to resolve conflicts constructively. Keys to doing so are engaging in problem-solving negotiations and peer mediation. Finally, the relationships in which a person thrives are based on a set of civic values in which the well-being of others and the common good are as valued as self-interests.

Sooner or later, everyone encounters adversity in his or her life. Pain, suffering, and hardship are part of the human experience and make their way into everyone's life. Often at unforeseen, surprising times, individuals are faced with misfortune or a calamity, such as rejection by valued others, death of a loved one, or serious illness. Thus, a person is faced with a

Thriving, Surviving, or Going Under: Coping with Everyday Lives, 255–273
Copyright © 2004 by Information Age Publishing

255

traumatic set of circumstances that causes a high degree of psychological discomfort and a major invalidation of the person's important assumptions about oneself and the nature of the world in which one lives. The person experiences both distress and a striving for growth. Inherent in facing such *adversity* (i.e., misfortune that taxes or exceeds the person's resources) is a demand for change. For some, the changes are for the worse, resulting in psychological distress or illness, a loss of valued resources (such as relationships or employment), or physical injury or illness. For others, the changes are for the better, resulting in increased self-understanding, better relationships, increased competencies, success, and personal strength, courage, resolve, grace, and humor. Such positive changes are known as thriving. Thriving may be reflected in three general domains (Calhoun & Tedeschi, 1998; Tedeschi & Calhoun, 1995):

1. Changes in perception of self: View of self as vulnerable to difficulties in life but self-reliant and capable of coping with difficult challenges.
2. Changes in relationships with others: Improved relationships characterized by increased emotional closeness, increased freedom to express emotions, and increased sympathy and understanding for the suffering of others.
3. Changes in philosophy of life: A deeper appreciation for life along with new life directions and priorities, changes in life priorities, increased experience of existential wisdom, and greater interest in and openness to spiritual and religious matters.

The approaches in identifying the factors that determine whether a person deteriorates or thrives as the result of adversity may be classified as either focusing on the independent person or the interdependent person. The *independent-self approach* to thriving views the person as an independent, isolated individual separate and apart from all other individuals and who, therefore, deals with a set of circumstances on his or her own with only his or her own resources (Johnson, 2003; Johnson & F. Johnson, 2003). This approach emphasizes teaching each person a set of cognitive strategies (such as positive appraisal, optimism, focusing on the problem, noting positive events, appraisal of situational meaning, and others) that the person uses to cope with a traumatic set of circumstances. The danger in viewing thriving as an individual activity is that social isolation tends to magnify the impact of adversity. The *interdependent-self approach* to thriving views the person as being imbedded in networks of interdependent relationships such as family, friendships, church, community, country, and who, therefore, deals with circumstances as a member of relational networks that provide resources above and beyond the individual's own

(Johnson, 2003). Thriving is viewed as resulting from joint problem solving, social support, social comparison, joint identity, intimate conversations, physical contact, and so forth. From this approach, thriving in the midst of a traumatic set of circumstances requires the ability to build and maintain interdependent relationships. Doing so involves managing conflicts constructively and establishing values and norms concerning mutual support and assistance.

Of the two approaches, the interdependent-self approach seems most promising for both prevention and treatment programs. While there are no easy recipes for dealing with adversity, thriving requires being involved with other people. Isolated and detached individuals generally do not have the resources to thrive (Johnson & Johnson, 1989). Supportive, caring, cooperative, and committed relationships tend to lessen the impact of adverse events, provide opportunities for intimate and personal conversations and problem solving, create opportunities for seeing adverse events from a variety of perspectives, provide reality checks on perceptions and analyses, give reassurance that one has the strength to persevere, and provide many other positive benefits. Even within caring relationships, and frequently during crises when individuals are upset and stressed, conflicts occur that must be managed in constructive ways. Knowing how to resolve conflicts skillfully, therefore, is an essential aspect of facing and dealing with a traumatic set of circumstances. Finally, it is especially during crises that a person's values and attitudes are revealed. People, who are quite civil when they are calm and situations are supportive, may treat others in rude and unconcerned ways when they are under stress. When crises occur, an individual needs values that help him or her maintain caring and committed relationships and manage conflicts constructively.

Interdependent-self prevention programs involve giving individuals the competencies and values they need to build and maintain extended support networks within which conflicts are managed constructively. When a traumatic set of circumstances occurs, the requirements for thriving are then in place. Treatment programs involve increasing the person's network of supportive and caring relationships, ensuring that the conflicts that occur are managed constructively, and helping the person internalize the values underlying caring and committed relationships and constructive conflict resolution. Prevention almost always is more effective than treatment. Children, adolescents, and young adults may be prepared to thrive in adversity through their experiences in schools. In this chapter, a prevention program (although it also may be used for treatment) is described that is aimed at preparing students to thrive during a traumatic set of circumstances. This program, which is being implemented in schools throughout many different parts of the world, is known as the

Three Cs. It is aimed at establishing and teaching students how to establish cooperative community, constructive conflict, and civic values. This program entails the three steps of learning how to thrive in the face of adversity.

THREE Cs PROGRAM: THE THREE STEPS OF THRIVING

Working cooperatively with peers, resolving conflicts constructively, and internalizing prosocial values are experiences that all children, adolescents, and young adults need if they are to thrive while dealing with adversity constructively. The Three Cs program is an example of the interrelationships among theory, research, and practice. It is directly based on social interdependence and conflict theories, and the theories have been validated by a great deal of research on cooperation (Johnson & Johnson, 1989), constructive controversy (Johnson & Johnson, 1995b), and the peacemaker program (Johnson & Johnson, 1995a, 1996a, 2002). While the Three Cs program may be implemented in any social system, it is primarily within educational organizations that it has been field tested and validated. The program has been implemented in a wide variety of schools throughout North, Central, and South America, Europe, Africa, the Middle East, and Asia, with inner-city, lower-class students and with upper-class private school students and with everyone in between, and in schools in third world as well as industrialized countries. The widespread implementation of the Three Cs program gives it a generalizability not found in most educational programs.

COOPERATIVE COMMUNITY

There are so many reasons why a person facing a traumatic set of circumstances needs to be a member of a caring, committed, and cooperative community that only a few may be listed here. An important aspect of thriving is having personal, intimate conversations with caring and committed individuals about the nature of the adversity and its effects on the person. If nothing else, these conversations take place with a psychotherapist. In these conversations, preferably with friends and family, the person struggles to rebuild or repair fundamental assumptions that order his or her experience. Meaning is obtained primarily through interpersonal processes in which consensual validation is achieved, not through isolated rumination. Thriving requires accurate perceptions of the traumatic events and constructing meaning from those perceptions.

There is considerable danger in not checking the accuracy of one's perceptions by comparing them with the perceptions of others. Voltaire said, "What is madness? To have erroneous perceptions and to reason correctly from them." Many people who act in ways that are seen as pathological are reasoning with insufficient data or rigidly defending the wrong assumptions about the nature of their life and the world they live in. In order to thrive while facing traumatic events often requires demolishing old cognitive structures that provided a map for life and building new ones.

There are paradoxes in dealing with adversity (Calhoun & Tedeschi, 1998). A person facing adversity must be active while letting time take its course, must accept help while recognizing that ultimately no one else can manage the trauma, and must leave the trauma in the past while weaving it into the future. These paradoxes are typically discovered and accepted in conversations with caring and accepting others, not in isolation.

Thriving often requires changing one's view of oneself and modifying one's personal identity. A person's identity tends to be social, developed by comparing oneself with others and defining oneself by the groups one is a member of. The stronger the positive interdependence linking oneself with others, the stronger one's identification with the group, the more one's identity is derived from group membership, the more one's self-esteem and self-worth are derived from group membership, the more qualities of the group that become incorporated into one's self-definition, the more the group influences one's perspective, the more empathy one feels for other members, and the more help and support one receives from other group members (Johnson & Johnson, 2003). When faced with adversity, group memberships are anchors that help clarify one's identity and self-worth.

One of the last phases of thriving is being able to describe the traumatic events to oneself and others. A personal narrative is created to organize information about oneself and the events in one's life. This personal narrative is created in conversations with caring and committed others and needs to be told to caring and committed others.

Finally, Bandura (1997) suggests that overcoming many of the significant problems that affect people's lives, such as poverty, prejudice, and political oppression, requires action at the collective level. It takes more than oneself to solve most of life's problems. Other people are needed, and individuals facing challenges need to mobilize joint action to solve their problems. Thus, learning how to thrive in the midst of a traumatic set of circumstances requires knowing how to organize and maintain cooperative efforts.

STEP ONE: COOPERATIVE EFFORTS AND COMMUNITY

- Step One: Learn how to build and maintain cooperative efforts in which positive relationships are characterized by caring, commitment, and support.

By its very definition, the demands of adversity tend to exceed the person's resources. That is what makes it adversity. It is through one's relationships with people who share common goals and who usually live in the same locality (and are therefore available to provide help and support) that a person is able to thrive while dealing with traumatic events. In other words, it takes a community. Communities are built on *positive interdependence* (cooperation), which exists when individuals work together to achieve mutual goals. Cooperation may be contrasted with *negative interdependence* or competition (i.e., when individuals work against each other to achieve a goal that only one or a few may attain) and *social independence* or individualistic efforts (i.e., when the outcomes of each person are unaffected by others' actions).

In school, students can learn how to build and maintain the interdependent relationships within which they will receive the help and assistance they need to deal effectively with a traumatic set of circumstances. Some of the relationships established in schools may last for the rest of their lives. Students learn about cooperation through experiencing it. When teachers structure learning situations cooperatively, students are placed in a situation in which they promote each other's success, give each other support and help, experience joint success, and work to benefit others as well as themselves. When teachers structure learning situations competitively, students are placed in a situation in which they oppose each other's success, obstruct each other's efforts, and work toward depriving others of success. When teachers structure learning situations individualistically, students are placed in a situation where each person works alone for self-benefit only. There has been a great deal of research comparing the relative efficacy of cooperative, competitive, and individualistic efforts. The many outcomes studies may be subsumed within the three broad and interrelated outcomes (see Figure 11.1 and Table 11.1) (Johnson & Johnson, 1989). Compared to competitive and individualistic efforts, cooperation tends to promote:

1.   Greater effort exerted to achieve (higher achievement and greater productivity, more frequent use of higher-level reasoning, more frequent generation of new ideas and solutions, greater intrinsic and achievement motivation, greater long-term retention, more

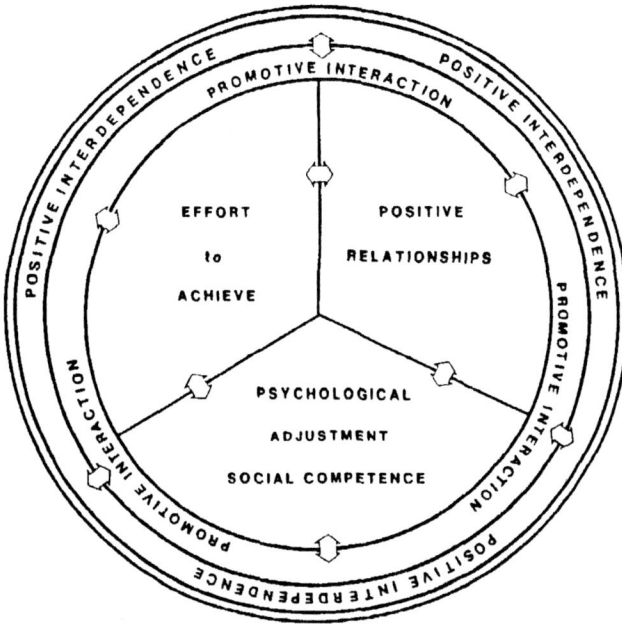

Reprinted with permission from Johnson and Johnson (1989).

Figure 11.1.   Outcome of Cooperative Learning

Table 11.1.   Mean Effect Sizes for Impact of Social Interdependence on Dependent Variables

	Cooperative vs. Competitive	Cooperative vs. Individualistic	Competitive vs. Individualistic
Achievement	0.67	0.64	0.30
Interpersonal Attraction	0.67	0.60	0.08
Social Support	0.62	0.70	−0.13
Self-Esteem	0.58	0.44	−0.23

Reprinted with permission from Johnson and Johnson (1989).

on-task behavior, and greater transfer of what is learned within one situation to another).

2.   Higher quality of relationships among participants (greater interpersonal attraction, liking, cohesion and esprit de corps, valuing of heterogeneity, and task-oriented and personal support). It is difficult to overemphasize the importance of these research results as friends give a person a developmental advantage and not having

friends places a person at risk for a wide variety of negative experiences and action patterns.

3. Greater psychological adjustment (greater psychological health, greater social competencies, higher self-esteem, a shared identity, and greater ability to cope with stress and adversity).

These outcomes result only when cooperation is structured effectively. Effective cooperation requires that five basic elements be carefully structured into the situation (Johnson & Johnson, 1989; Johnson, Johnson, & Holubec, 1998a) (see Table 11.1). First, there must be a strong sense of **positive interdependence**, so individuals believe they are linked with others so they cannot succeed unless the others do (and vice versa). Individuals must believe that they sink or swim together. Positive interdependence may be structured through mutual goals, joint rewards, divided resources, complementary roles, and a shared identity. Second, each collaborator must be **individually accountable** to do his or her fair share of the work. Third, collaborators must have the opportunity to **promote each other's success** by helping, assisting, supporting, encouraging, and praising each other's efforts to achieve. Fourth, working together cooperatively requires **interpersonal and small group skills**, such as leadership, decision-making, trust-building, communication, and conflict-management skills. Finally, cooperative groups must engage in **group processing**, which exists when group members discuss how well they are achieving their goals and maintaining effective working relationships.

Levels of Interdependence

Positive interdependence may be structured at all levels of school life. The heart of a cooperative school community is the predominant use of cooperative learning. **Cooperative learning** is the instructional use of small groups so that students work together to maximize their own and each other's learning (Johnson, Johnson, & Holubec, 1998a). Any assignment in any curriculum, in any subject area, for any age student can be done cooperatively. There are three types of cooperative learning (Johnson, Johnson, & Holubec, 1998a, 1998b): Formal cooperative learning, informal cooperative learning, and cooperative base groups.

Formal cooperative learning consists of students working together, for one class period to several weeks, to achieve shared learning goals and complete jointly specific tasks and assignments (such as decision making or problem solving, completing a curriculum unit, writing a report, conducting a survey or experiment, or reading a chapter or reference book, learning vocabulary, or answering questions at the end of the chapter). Any course requirement or assignment may be structured to include formal cooperative learning.

Informal cooperative learning consists of having students work together to achieve a joint learning goal in temporary, ad-hoc groups that last from a few minutes to one class period. During a lecture, demonstration, or film, informal cooperative learning can be used to focus student attention on the material to be learned, set a mood conducive to learning, help set expectations as to what will be covered in a class session, ensure that students cognitively process and rehearse the material being taught, summarize what was learned and precue the next session, and provide closure to an instructional session. Informal cooperative learning groups are often organized so that students engage in 3- to 5-minute focused discussions before and after a lecture and 2- to 3-minute turn-to-your-partner discussions interspersed throughout a lecture.

Cooperative base groups are long-term, heterogeneous cooperative learning groups with stable membership. Base groups give the support, help, encouragement, and assistance each member needs to make academic progress (attend class, complete all assignments, learn) and develop cognitively and socially in healthy ways. Base groups are permanent (lasting from one to several years) and provide the long-term, caring peer relationships necessary to influence members consistently to work hard in school.

In addition to cooperative learning, positive interdependence can be extended through all levels of the school (Johnson & Johnson, 1994). **Classroom interdependence** may be created through such procedures as class goals, rewards or celebrations, class roles (such as establishing a classroom government), or dividing resources among all class members (having the class publish a newsletter in which each cooperative group contributes one article). **Interclass interdependence** may be created through organizing several classes into a "neighborhood" and having them engage in joint projects. **School interdependence** may be structured through displaying the school's goals, organizing faculty into collegial teaching teams and study groups, using cooperative groups during faculty meetings, and conducting all-school projects. Projects with parents, such as creating a "strategic plan" or raising money, create **school-parent interdependence**. Finally, **school-neighborhood interdependence** may be created by mutual projects; such as having neighborhood members play in the school band or having students and neighborhood members jointly clean up a park.

STEP TWO: CONSTRUCTIVE CONFLICT RESOLUTION

- Step Two: Resolve conflicts within cooperative relationships constructively.

Adversity often springs from conflict with others, and even when it does not, while facing a set of traumatic circumstances, it becomes even more important than usual to manage the conflicts that occur constructively. Many of these conflicts may be with the people who are providing help and support. Conflicts, however, do not need to be avoided. When conflicts are managed constructively, they can increase (a) individuals' energy, curiosity, and motivation, (b) achievement, retention, insight, creativity, problem-solving, and synthesis, (c) healthy cognitive and social development, (d) clarification of own and others' identity, commitments, and values, (e) quality of relationships, and (f) many other positive outcomes (Johnson & Johnson, 1995a, 1995b, 1996a). Managing conflicts constructively depends on (a) clear procedures for managing conflicts, (b) individuals being skilled in the use of the procedures and value using them, and (c) community and organizational norms and values encouraging and supporting the use of the procedures. Faculty and staff need to teach students (and learn themselves) three procedures for managing conflicts: academic controversy, problem-solving negotiation, and peer mediation procedures (see Table 11.2).

Table 11.2.   Types of Conflict

Academic Controversy	Conflicts of Interest
One person's ideas, information, theories, conclusions, and opinions are incompatible with those of another and the two seek to reach an agreement.	The actions of one person attempting to maximize benefits prevents, blocks, or interferes with another person maximizing their benefits.
Controversy Procedure	**Integrative (Problem-Solving) Negotiations**
Research & prepare positions	Describe wants
Present & advocate positions	Describe feelings
Refute opposing position & refute attacks on own position	Describe reasons for wants & feelings
Reverse perspectives	Take other's perspective
Synthesize & integrate best evidence & reasoning from all sides	Invent three optional agreements that maximize joint outcomes
	Choose one and formalize agreement

Reprinted with permission from Johnson and Johnson (1989).

Academic Controversies

Thriving does not mean agreeing with other people's advice, analyses of the situation, or recommendations for action. To thrive, a person must be able to resolve conflicts among ideas constructively. Conflicts among ideas are known as controversies. A **controversy** exists when one person's ideas, opinions, information, theories, or conclusions are incompatible with those of another and the two seek to reach an agreement (Johnson & Johnson, 1979, 1995b). Controversies are resolved by engaging in what Aristotle called **deliberate discourse** (i.e., the discussion of the advantages and disadvantages of proposed actions) aimed at synthesizing novel solutions (i.e., **creative problem solving**). By engaging in academic controversies as part of the instructional program, students learn how to engage in effective interpersonal decision making and resolve conflicts between one's own and other people's ideas. Teachers may structure an academic controversy by randomly assigning students to heterogeneous cooperative learning groups of four members (Johnson & Johnson, 1995b). The groups are given an issue on which to write a report and pass a test. Each cooperative group is divided into two pairs. One pair is given the "con" position on the issue and the other pair is given the "pro" position. Each pair is given the instructional materials needed to define their position and point them toward supporting information. The cooperative goal of reaching a consensus on the issue (by synthesizing the best reasoning from both sides) and writing a quality group report is highlighted. Students then:

1. **Research and Prepare a Position:**   Each pair develops the position assigned, learns the relevant information, and plans how to present the best case possible to the other pair. Near the end of the period pairs are encouraged to compare notes with pairs from other groups who represent the same position.
2. **Present and Advocate their Position:**   Each pair makes their presentation to the opposing pair. Each member of the pair has to participate in the presentation. Students are to be as persuasive and convincing as possible. Members of the opposing pair are encouraged to take notes, listen carefully to learn the information being presented, and clarify anything they do not understand.
3. **3. Refute Opposing Position And Rebut Attacks on their Own:** Students argue forcefully and persuasively for their position, presenting as many facts as they can to support their point of view. Students analyze and critically evaluate the information, rationale, and inductive and deductive reasoning of the opposing pair, asking them for the facts that support their point of view. They refute

the arguments of the opposing pair and rebut attacks on their position. They discuss the issue, following a set of rules to help them criticize ideas without criticizing people, differentiate the two positions, and assess the degree of evidence and logic supporting each position. They keep in mind that the issue is complex and they need to know both sides to write a good report.

4. **Reverse Perspectives:**   The pairs reverse perspectives and present each other's positions. In arguing for the opposing position, students are forceful and persuasive. They add any new information that the opposing pair did not think to present. They strive to see the issue from both perspectives simultaneously.

5. **Synthesize and Integrate the Best Evidence and Reasoning into a Joint Position:**   The four group members drop all advocacy and synthesize and integrate what they know into a joint position to which all sides can agree. They (a) finalize the report (the teacher evaluates reports on the quality of the writing, the logical presentation of evidence, and the oral presentation of the report to the class), (b) present their conclusions to the class (all four members of the group are required to participate orally in the presentation), (c) individually take the test covering both sides of the issue (if every member of the group achieves up to criterion, they all receive bonus points), and (d) process how well they worked together and how they could be even more effective next time.

Benefits of Controversy

As Thomas Jefferson noted, *"Difference of opinion leads to inquiry, and inquiry to truth."* Over the past 30 years we have conducted over 25 research studies on the impact of academic controversy and numerous other researchers have conducted studies directly on controversy and in related areas (Johnson & Johnson, 1989, 1995b). The considerable research available indicates that intellectual "disputed passages" create higher achievement (characterized by higher achievement, longer retention, more frequent use of higher-level reasoning and metacognitive thought, more critical thinking, greater creativity, and continuing motivation to learn), more positive interpersonal relationships, and greater psychological health when they (a) occur within cooperative learning groups and (b) are carefully structured to ensure that students manage them constructively (Johnson & Johnson, 1989, 1995b) (see Table 11.3). Engaging in a controversy can also be fun, enjoyable, and exciting. Two of the most important aspects for learning how to thrive, however, are (a) the emphasis on viewing the issue from both perspectives and (b) learning that con-

Table 11.3.   Meta-Analysis of Controversy Studies: Mean Effect Size

Dependent Variable	Controversy/ Concurrence Seeking	Controversy/ Debate	Controversy/ Individualistic Efforts
Achievement	0.68	0.40	0.87
Cognitive Reasoning	0.62	1.35	0.90
Perspective Taking	0.91	0.22	0.86
Motivation	0.75	0.45	0.71
Attitudes Toward Task	0.58	0.81	0.64
Interpersonal Attraction	0.24	0.72	0.81
Social Support	0.32	0.92	1.52
Self-Esteem	0.39	0.51	0.85

Reprinted with permission from Johnson and Johnson (1989).

flicts can have positive outcomes when people listen to each other and work cooperatively to reach solutions.

Conflict Resolution Training

If students are to resolve conflicts constructively, they must learn how to resolve conflicts of interests. *Conflict of interests* exist when the actions of one person attempting to maximize his or her wants and benefits prevents, blocks, or interferes with another person maximizing his or her wants and benefits. Conflict resolution and peer mediation programs have their roots in four sources (Johnson & Johnson, 1995a): Researchers in the field of conflict resolution, advocates of nonviolence, antinuclear war activists, and members of the legal profession. The research-based peer mediation programs began in the 1960s with the *Teaching Students to be Peacemakers Program* (Johnson, 1970; Johnson & Johnson, 1995a, 1995b). It was derived from social interdependence theory (Deutsch, 1949; Johnson & Johnson, 1989) and focused on teaching all students in a school the nature of conflict, how to use an integrative (problem-solving) negotiation procedure, and how to mediate peer conflicts. All students then take turns in being a class and school mediator.

Problem-Solving Negotiations

To resolve conflicts of interests, individuals may negotiate using a **distributive** or "win-lose" procedure (where one person benefits only if the opponent agrees to make a concession) or an **integrative** or problem solving procedure (where disputants work together to create an agreement that benefits everyone involved). In ongoing relationships, only the integrative or problem solving procedure should be used, as distributive negotiations tend to result in destructive outcomes and integrative negotiations tend to result in constructive outcomes. The steps in using problem solving negotiations are (Johnson & Johnson, 1995a) (a) describing what you want, (b) describing how you feel, (c) describing the reasons for your wants and feelings, (d) taking the other's perspective and summarizing your understanding of what the other person wants, how the other person feels, and the reasons underlying both, (e) inventing three optional plans to resolve the conflict that maximize joint benefits, and (f) choosing one and formalizing the agreement with a hand shake.

Peer Mediation

Once the problem-solving negotiation procedure is learned, all members of the school community need to learn how to mediate conflicts of interests (Johnson & Johnson, 1995a). A **mediator** is a neutral person who helps two or more people resolve their conflict, usually by negotiating an integrative agreement. Mediation is not arbitration. **Arbitration** is the submission of a dispute to a disinterested third party (such as a teacher or principal) who makes a final and binding judgment as to how the conflict will be resolved. Mediation consists of the four steps of (a) ending hostilities, (b) ensuring disputants are committed to the mediation process, (c) helping disputants successfully engage in problem-solving negotiations, and (d) formalizing the agreement (Johnson & Johnson, 1995a).

Once students understand how to negotiate and mediate, the peacemaker program is implemented. Each day the teacher selects two class members to serve as official mediators. Any conflicts students cannot resolve themselves are referred to the mediators. The mediators wear official T-shirts, patrol the playground and lunchroom, and are available to mediate any conflicts that occur in the classroom or school. An example is as follows.

During lunch on the playground, a ball rolls out of bounds during a lively game of soccer. A cluster of students walking by laugh as one of them kicks the ball away from the player trying to retrieve it. An argument ensues. A pair of peer mediators with clipboards in hand quickly approach the two disputants. "Would you like some help resolving your conflict?" So begins the mediation process through which the disputants arrive at a mutually agreeable solution that makes both happy. They shake hands as friends and return to their activities while the peer mediators make a note of the resolution, then continue to be available for other schoolmates who may need help resolving conflicts.

The role of mediator is rotated so that all students in the class or school serve as mediators an equal amount of time. Initially, students mediate in pairs. This ensures that shy or nonverbal students get the same amount of experience as more extroverted and verbally fluent students. Mediating classmates' conflicts is perhaps the most effective way of teaching students the need for the skillful use of each step of the negotiation procedure. If peer mediation fails, the teacher mediates the conflict. If teacher mediation fails, the teacher arbitrates by deciding who is right and who is wrong. If that fails, the principal mediates the conflict. If that fails, the principal arbitrates.

Additional lessons are needed to refine and upgrade students' skills in using the negotiation and mediation procedures. Gaining real expertise in resolving conflicts constructively takes years of training and practice. Negotiation and mediation training may become part of the fabric of school life by integrating them into academic lessons. Literature, history, and science units typically involve conflict and most lessons in these subject areas can be modified to include role playing situations in which the negotiation and/or mediation procedures are practiced. The *Teaching Students to be Peacemakers Program* may be retaught each year in an increasingly sophisticated and complex way, thus becoming a 12-year spiral program. Twelve years of training and practice will result in a person with considerable expertise in resolving conflicts constructively.

Benefits of Conflict Resolution and Peer Mediation Programs

We have conducted seventeen studies on implementing the Peacemaker Program in schools involving students from kindergarten through the ninth-grade and several other researchers have conducted relevant studies (Johnson & Johnson, 2002). The studies were conducted in rural, suburban, and urban settings. From Table 11.4 it may be seen that students tended to learn the negotiation and mediation procedures, retain their knowledge throughout the school year and into the following year, apply the procedures to their and other people's conflicts, transfer the procedures to nonclassroom settings such as the playground and lunchroom, transfer the procedures to nonschool settings such as the home, use the procedures similarly in family and school settings, and (when given the option) engage in problem-solving rather than win-lose negotiations. In addition, students' attitudes toward conflict tended to became more

Table 11.4.   Mean Effect Sizes Peacemaker Studies

Dependent Variable	Mean	Standard Deviation	Number of Effects
Learned Procedure	2.25	1.98	13
Learned Procedure – Retention	3.34	4.16	9
Applied Procedure	2.16	1.31	4
Application – Retention	0.46	0.16	3
Strategy Constructiveness	1.60	1.70	12
Constructiveness – Retention	1.10	0.53	10
Strategy Two-Concerns	1.10	0.46	5
Two-Concerns – Retention	0.45	0.20	2
Integrative Negotiation	0.98	0.36	5
Quality of Solutions	0.73	0	1
Positive Attitude	1.07	0.25	5
Negative Attitude	–0.61	0.37	2
Academic Achievement	0.88	0.09	5
Academic Retention	0.70	0.31	4

Reprinted with permission from: Johnson, D. W., & Johnson, R. (1989).

positive. Students learned to view conflicts as potentially positive and faculty and parents viewed the conflict training as constructive and helpful. Finally, when integrated into academic units, the conflict resolution training tended to increase academic achievement and long-term retention of the academic material. Academic units, especially in subject areas such as literature and history, provide a setting to understand conflicts, practice how to resolve them, and use them to gain insight into the material being studied.

The result was that students tended to resolve their conflicts without the involvement of faculty and administrators. Classroom management problems, in other words, tended to be significantly reduced. The number of discipline problems teachers had to deal with decreased by about 60% and referrals to administrators dropped about 90%.

STEP THREE: CIVIC VALUES

- Step Three: Internalize the values underlying cooperation and constructive resolution of controversies and conflicts of interests.

Students are sitting in a circle on the carpet. A class meeting is in progress. Today the issue is respect. One of the students risked telling her classmates that she felt hurt during recess the day before because she was trying to tell kids the rules to a new game, but nobody would listen. So began a discussion on what it means to be respectful, why that is important, and the sharing of everyone's personal experiences of times they felt respected versus not respected.

Positive development of students requires that all members of the school community adopt a set of civic values (Johnson & Johnson, 1996b, 1999). To create the common culture that defines a community, there must be common goals and shared values that help define appropriate behavior and increasing the quality of life within the community. These common values provide internal resources to thrive while facing adversity. A learning community cannot exist in schools dominated by (a) competition where students are taught to value striving for their personal success at the expense of others or (b) individualistic efforts where students value only their own self-interests. Rather, students need to internalize values underlying cooperation and integrative negotiations, such as commitment to the common good and to the well being of other members, a sense of responsibility to contribute one's fair share of the work, respect for the efforts of others and for them as people, behaving with integrity, caring for other members, compassion when other members are in need, and appreciation of diversity. Such civic values both underlie and are promoted by the cooperation and constructive conflict resolution that take place in the school.

While there are a wide variety of programs to teach students values, in order to make value development a hidden curriculum beneath the surface of school life students should spend most of their school time working in cooperative learning groups and should be taught how to manage both controversies and conflicts of interests constructively. It is through the ebb-and-flow of daily life in the school that values are most effectively taught, and these values should (a) assume a positive view of human nature, (b) be aimed at developing individuals who are active advocates for democracy and social justice, and (c) focus students beyond selfishness toward improving the quality of life for all students and the common good.

CONCLUSIONS AND SUMMARY

When faced with adversity and challenges, individuals may deteriorate or grow. When faced with a severe threat, a person may go beyond surviving or recovering to thriving. In contrast to vulnerability / deficit models of health, a focus on thriving emphasizes that facing adversity and challenges can result in growth and enhanced well-being beyond where one was prior to the challenge. The aftermath of facing a crisis can be post-traumatic growth. In a sense, thriving involves triumph in the face of trauma. There are two approaches to thriving. The interdependent-self approach emphasizes building and maintaining networks of supportive and caring relationships within which individuals are committed to each other's well-being as well as their own. The independent-self approach emphasizes cognitive strategies to manage adverse events. While the latter approach has considerable value, the former approach is the most powerful and has the most data validating its effectiveness.

There are three steps in learning how to thrive while facing a set of traumatic circumstances. First, a person needs to build cooperative relationships with others in which they work together to achieve common goals. Being part of a cooperative enterprise creates a shared sense of accomplishment, positive relationships, social support systems, high self-esteem, psychological health, and social competencies, all of which are necessary to thrive and survive. Second, a person needs to be able to resolve the conflicts that occur as part of the adversity or as part of the thriving constructively. The more central the relationship to a person's survival, the more important it is to resolve conflicts constructively. Keys to doing so are engaging in problem-solving negotiations and peer mediation. Finally, a person needs to internalize the civic values underlying cooperation and constructive conflict resolution. Being involved in supportive and caring relationships is enhanced by valuing the well-being of others and the common good.

REFERENCES

Bandura, A. (1997). Self-efficacy: *The exercise of control*. New York: W. H. Freeman.

Calhoun, L., & Tedeschi, R. (1998). Beyond recovery from trauma: Implications for clinical practice and research. *Journal of Social Issues, 54*, 357-371.

Deutsch, M. (1949). A theory of cooperation and competition. *Human Relations, 2*, 129-152.

Johnson, D. W. (1970). *Social psychology of education*. New York: Holt, Rinehart, & Winston.

Johnson, D. W. (2003). *Reaching out: Interpersonal effectiveness and self-actualization* (8th ed.). Boston: Allyn & Bacon.

Johnson D. W., & Johnson, F. (2003). *Joining together: Group theory and group skills* (8th ed.). Boston: Allyn & Bacon.

Johnson, D. W., & Johnson, R. (1979). Conflict in the classroom: Controversy and learning. *Review of Educational Research, 49*, 51-61.

Johnson, D. W., & Johnson, R. (1989). *Cooperation and competition: Theory and research*. Edina, MN: Interaction Book Company.

Johnson, D. W., & Johnson, R. (1994). *Leading the cooperative school* (2nd ed.). Edina, MN: Interaction Book Company.

Johnson, D. W., & Johnson, R. (1995a). *Teaching students to be peacemakers* (3rd ed.). Edina, MN: Interaction Book Company.

Johnson, D. W., & Johnson, R. (1995b). *Creative controversy: Intellectual challenge in the classroom* (3rd ed.). Edina, MN: Interaction Book Company.

Johnson, D. W., & Johnson, R. (1996a). Conflict resolution and peer mediation programs in elementary and secondary schools: A review of the research. *Review of Educational Research, 66,* 459-506.

Johnson, D. W., & Johnson, R. (1996b). Cooperative learning and traditional American values. *NASSP Bulletin, 80*(579), 11-18.

Johnson, D. W., & Johnson, R. (1999). Cooperative learning, values, and culturally plural classrooms. In M. Leicester, C. Modgill , & S. Modgil (Eds.), *Values, the classroom, and cultural diversity.* London: Cassell PLC.

Johnson, R., & Johnson, D. W. (2002). Teaching Students to be Peacemakers: A meta-analysis. *Journal of Research in Education, 12,* 25-39.

Johnson, D. W., & Johnson, R. (2003). *New developments in social interdependence theory.* Report, Cooperative Learning Center, University of Minnesota. Submitted for publication.

Johnson, D. W., Johnson, R., & Holubec, E. (1998a). *Cooperation in the classroom* (6th ed.). Edina, MN: Interaction Book Company.

Johnson, D. W., Johnson, R., & Holubec, E. (1998b). *Advanced cooperative learning* (3rd ed.). Edina, MN: Interaction Book Company.

Tedeschi, R., & Calhoun, L. (1995). *Trauma and transformation: Growing in the aftermath of suffering.* Thousand Oaks, CA: Sage Publications.

PART IV

TEACHER AND PARENT COPING

The final chapters in this volume address more specifically issues of adult coping. If young people are to cope effectively we need to consider how adults around them cope. The first chapter in this section introduces a model for developing the coping skills of parents of "at- risk" children and adolescents. The final chapter identifies teachers as exemplars of a professional group who need to avoid burnout and the ways in which that can be done.

CHAPTER 12

COPING STRATEGIES FOR PARENTS

Stephen A. Rollin, Tam Dao, and Jennifer L. Holland
Florida State University

ABSTRACT

This chapter is designed to review the literature on coping for adults, with particular emphasis placed on coping strategies for parents of at-risk children and adolescents. The chapter has four main purposes. First, the framework is discussed utilizing coping and development research and theories. Second, to increase awareness for parents and professionals coping strategies are considered. Third, models, examples, and strategies are provided to assist parents and professionals to identify risk and protective factors. Lastly, examples of situation-specific coping strategies are identified and discussed.

> *In today's world parents find themselves at the mercy of a society which imposes pressures and priorities that allow neither time nor place for meaningful activities and relations between children and adults, which downgrade the role of parents and the functions of parenthood, and which prevent the parent from doing things he wants to do as a guide, friend, and companion to his children.*
>
> —Urie Bronfenbrenner (1979, p. 662)

Thriving, Surviving, or Going Under: Coping with Everyday Lives, 277–303
Copyright © 2004 by Information Age Publishing

INTRODUCTION

Developmental psychologist Urie Bronfenbrenner reveals the challenge facing parents, who must learn to successfully cope with the stressful demands of society, to effectively nurture the development of their children. Lisa Kudrow, a movie actress, exemplifies the challenge when she describes her role conflict; "Three weeks after I had Julian I filmed a small part in *Analyze This* with Robert De Niro. I felt guilty taking my son on a plane to New York, *so mommy can do a movie*"(Motherhood, 2003).

It is not unreasonable to expect that parents will face a host of taxing events and situations during the years of their children's development. These challenging situations and events can present themselves in many forms, ranging from a child having difficulties with school to a child who is involved with substance use. As Urie Bronfenbrenner implied, it is also not uncommon for parents to overlook the fact that in its simplest form, coping can be one technique that parents can learn to employ successfully to deal with these types of demands.

In this chapter the literature on coping for adults, with particular emphasis placed on coping strategies for parents of at-risk children and adolescents is considered. First, coping and developmental research and theories from mainstream psychology are summarized to provide a framework for suggested coping strategies. Second, the chapter is intended to have practical applications for parents and mental health professionals, by increasing awareness about coping strategies for parents and highlighting coping strategies as a central factor affecting the development of children. Third, the chapter includes a self-evaluation checklist to assist parents and professionals in identifying general risk and protective factors among the family and children, and to serve as a catalyst for opening the communication process between parents, professionals, and children. And finally, using the framework proposed by other researchers in the area of stress and coping, situation-specific coping strategies for parents of at-risk children and adolescent will be identified and discussed.

"TRICKLE-DOWN EFFECT"

It is without a question, the significance of family influence on adolescent development has been well established in the field of psychology. Since Bell's 1968 article, "Reinterpretation of direction of effects in studies of socialization," in which he suggested models of socialization to account for child influence in studies of parent-child interactions, new waves of research explicating the role of family members on adolescent development have emerged (Cremeens, Lindsey, & Caldera, 2002). According to Cremeens, Lindsey, and Caldera (2002), one of several archetypes emerging from the literature for understanding family dynamics is Bronfenbrenner's (1979) ecological-developmental theory, which examined the child's development within the context of the system of relationships that forms the child's environment. Another prominent paradigm addressing parent-child interaction is that of Sameroff's Transactional Theory. According to Sameroff (1975), the development of the child occurs as a transactional process between the parent and the child. To be more specific, children's actions elicit parental responses and parental responses in turn, bring about children's actions. As a result of this interaction over time, the child and the parents develop consistent patterns of behaviors. The works of Ainsworth and Bowlby (1954), Lollis and Kuczynski (1997), and Almeida, Wethington, and Chandler (1999) on attachment patterns of children accentuated yet another theoretical perspective on the influence of family members on child and adolescent development. According to these authors, the interaction between the parent and the child plays a pivotal role in the development of the child. To clarify, the dyadic parent-child relationship is established on the reaction of parents to a child's styles of responding, which in turn has consequences on the child's impetus and capability to explore the environment. These influential studies in the areas of ecological-developmental theories, transactional processes between the family and the child, and attachment patterns of children with their caregivers have shed light on the impact of family dynamics on children 's development. As a result of the overwhelming evidence suggesting the importance of parent-child interactions and as shown in Figure 12.1, it is the authors' belief that effective coping strategies for parents are

SYSTEM

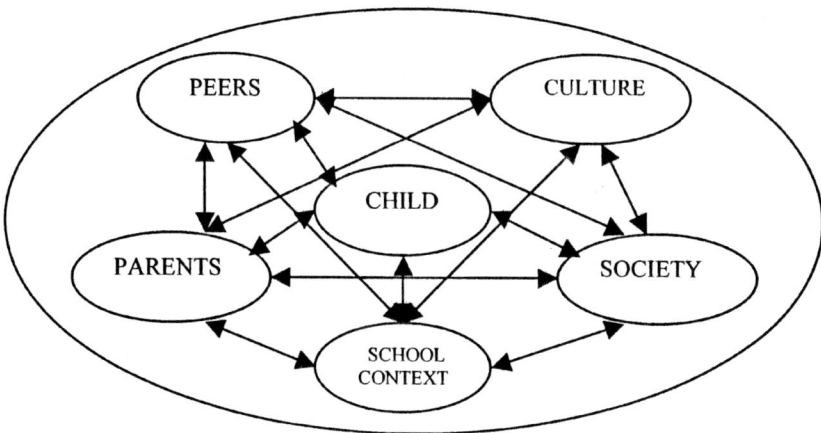

Figure 12.1.   Child Focused System Model

just one of a host of crucial elements in the equation for healthy child and adolescent development. Figure 12.1 illustrates how the child is at the center of the system, and reveals other factors that influence the child.

From Figure 12.1 it can be seen that the child is in the center of the diagram. The child's behavior, attitude, and feelings all impinge and are affected by forces in the system such as peers, culture, parents, society, and school context. As a part of the diagnostic process, it is important for the parent to note the interactive dimensions of this closed system. Noting that any changes in any one of the components will have an impact on the child and how the child relates to the system. From a diagnostic perspective this model allows the parents to identify those forces that affect the child.

COPING RESEARCH AND
THEORY FORM GENERAL PSYCHOLOGY

Stress and coping have been a topic of considerable interest over the years and is a widely studied phenomenon in the general psychology literature today (Hobfoll, Schwarzer, & Chon 1998). Hobfoll and colleagues indicated that stress takes place when resources are lost, threatened with loss, or unsuccessfully devoted. Over the years, psychologists have defined coping in a number of different ways. One of the numerous models of stress and coping examines coping as a degree or amount of stressor that an organism can tolerate, while placing little emphasis on an individual's cognition and coping process (Houston, 1987). Some typical studies that adopt this perspective are commonly found in laboratory settings in which researchers want to ascertain whether certain laboratory animals, such as mice are able to cope with the varying amounts of volts of electric shock. However, due to lack of emphasis on cognition and the coping process, this paradigm of stress and coping is seldom utilized today (Hardy, Jones, & Gould, 1996).

The psychoanalytic perspective characterizes coping in a different way. According to Folkman (1992), coping provides the individual with an unconscious defense mechanism that allows the individual to manage instinct, affect, and stress. To be more specific, the employment of altruism, sublimation, and humor are considered advanced forms of coping that allow the individual to manage stressful situations and events. The paradigm of stress and coping from the psychoanalytic perspective, however, has not gone unchallenged by critics who argue that the emphasis lies solely within the individual, with scarce weight given to the importance of the situation. Additional criticisms suggest that little attention was paid to the problem solving functions of coping, and the inherent difficulties of measuring unconscious processes (Folkman, 1992).

The dominant model flourishing in the stress and coping research was a model proposed by Lazarus and Folkman (1984) in a volume entitled *Stress, Appraisal, and Coping.* According to the stress and coping model posited by Lazarus and Folkman, the stress-coping process utilizes the transactional-theory perspective, which was highlighted earlier. Based on this view, coping is defined as "a process of constantly changing cognitive and behavioral efforts to manage specific external and/or internal demands or conflicts appraised as taxing or exceeding one's resources" (Lazarus & Folkman, 1984, p. 141). According to Lazarus and Folkman, the coping process begins with an individual's appraisal of the demands placed on the individual by the environment. In the Lazarus and Folkman model, stress is comprised of events and responses to it, the process initiated by the evaluation of the situation (primary appraisal) to determine if the demands are likely to be stressful and a judgment of resources (secondary appraisal) available for influencing and controlling the perceived stressors. Collectively, primary appraisal and secondary appraisal determine the attribute and quantity of stress an individual ultimately perceives, which in turn, influence how the individual copes.

The two most widely accepted coping categories are problem-focused and emotion-focused coping (Folkman & Lazarus, 1980). According to Folkman and Lazarus, problem-focused coping consists of efforts to manipulate or organize the problem that is causing the stress for individual. Emotion-focused coping, on the other hand, entails moderating the emotional responses, which result from the problem that causes stress for the individual. Table 12.1 is an adapted model of the process of active problem-focused and emotion-focused coping as utilized with substance abuse problems.

Folkman and Lazarus (1980), theorized that problem-focused coping is employed more often when situations are perceived as amenable to change and resources are available to deal with stressors, while emotion-focused coping is employed most often in situations that are perceived as inflexible and resources are perceived as inadequate or unavailable to deal with stressors. An example is presented to illustrate the difference between the two coping categories.

Mary is single parent who is raising two boys on her own, ages 7 and 16 in a rural neighborhood. Mary's closest relative lives in a nearby city approximately 50 miles away. She often works 50-60 hours a week on minimum wage earnings to support her children. She recently received a call from the school counselor in the school where one of her two boys

Table 12.1.   Problem-Focused and
Emotion-Focused Coping with Substance Use

Active Problem-Focused	*Active Emotion-Focused*
1. Parents can set up a time to sit down, listen, and understand what are some concerns, fears, acceptance, and/or denial an individual may have regarding substance use. Parents can help reshape ideas that their children may have obtained from the media or peers.	1. Parents can learn and engage in meditation techniques to reduce the level of stress.
2. Parents can help their child feel good about themselves. When parents praise efforts and accomplishments and when parents correct the child's actions by disapproving their actions instead of criticizing the child, parents are able to improve self-esteem.	2. Parents can acquire knowledge and practice relaxation methods.
3. Parents can proactively meet teachers, school counselors, other school administrator to understand problem within the context.	3. Parents can apply cognitive strategies to change the meaning of the situation. This can be done with the guidance of a mental health professional.
4. Parents can help their child develop strong values to make rational decisions based on facts about alcohol, tobacco, and other drugs (also see p. 297) to buffer against peer pressures. Parents can accomplished this through informal and/or formal discussions with John.	4. Parents can engage in physiological exercise to reduce stress and tension.
5. Parents can encourage their child to participate in healthy productive extra-curricular activities. Parents can encourage their children to participate in after school activities to decrease the opportunity for experimenting with ATODs.	5. Parents can participate in local social support groups.
6. Parents can actively seek support and understanding from other parents who are dealing with similar problems.	
7. Parents can seek family counseling with a mental health professional specializing in substance use.	

attend school. The school counselor reported that the 7-year-old child has been tested for learning disabilities and was diagnosed as having dyslexia. The school counselor also suggested that it was essential that Mary come to school on a regular basis to meet, discuss, and stay current with her child's situation. According to the Lazarus and Folkman model, Mary, at the outset, would appraise the school counselor's diagnosis and warning. In this primary appraisal, Mary would assess the plausibility of the school counselor's diagnosis and warning, rather than seeing it as a threat. If Mary believes in the veracity of the diagnosis and warning, secondary appraisal would occur. If Mary feels capable of handling her child's condition, she is more likely to employ problem-focused coping (e.g., work less hours). However, if Mary believes in the counselor's genuineness, but secondary appraisal were less helpful with regard to her child's condition, that is, she did not feel that she had the resources to cope, she is likely to become anxious or worry or just ignore the problem (all negative coping strategies).

At the risk of oversimplifying the subject, research studies on general coping often emphasize one of two routes, active or avoidant strategies (Snyder & Pulvers, 2001). For an individual, active coping strategies can be either behavioral or psychological responses designed to change the nature of the stressor to the individual or the actual reconstruction of meaning of the stressor to the individual. Avoidant coping strategies, on the other hand, are behaviors and/or mental states that steer individuals from directly addressing and dealing with stressful events (Holahan & Moos, 1987). A review of the relevant research literature on which coping path to take has offered inconsistent findings and suggestions. According to Snyder and Pulvers (2001), adopting an avoidant strategy is not adaptive, often making matters worse for the individual trying to deal with the problem. Moos (1986), argues specific coping strategies are not inherently adaptive or maladaptive. Instead, they are very much situation specific. Therefore, the ultimate goal in successful coping rests on the ability to access a broad range of responses to deal effectively with situations, as opposed to any one response to manage the ever-changing environment. Taking Moos' argument into consideration, one of the main goals of this chapter is to identify coping strategies for parents of at-risk children and adolescents that are situation specific. These situation-specific coping strategies are intended for parents and mental health professionals, who are less adept with the research literature regarding stress and coping. Therefore, it is not the purpose of this chapter to provide a universal model of adaptive coping strategies for parents of at-risk children and adolescents. Instead, the purpose is to aid the healthy development of at-risk children and adolescents by teaching parents how to utilize situation-specific coping strategies. Before we proceed to discuss strategies for parents, a brief discussion of general risk and protective factors for children and adolescents is essential.

GENERAL RISK AND PROTECTIVE FACTORS

Decades of research have established the association between specific risk and protective factors and the likelihood that children and adolescents will be exposed to at-risk behaviors. According to the Study Group on Very Young Offenders, a group of 39 experts on child delinquency and child psychopathology organized by the Office of Juvenile Justice and Delinquency Prevention (OJJDP), certain risk factors have been identified in longitudinal studies as predictors of adolescent health and behavior problems (Office of Juvenile Justice & Delinquency Prevention, 1999). These longitudinal studies have often recognized that risk and protective factors operate in several domains: the individual child, the child's peer groups, the child's family, the child's school, and the child's neighborhood and community.

According to the study group, risk factors that are associated with child delinquency were defined as an individual's genetic, emotional, cognitive, physical, and social characteristics. These individual risk factors included early antisocial behavior, emotional factors (i.e., high behavioral activation and low behavioral inhibition), poor cognitive development, low intelligence, and hyperactivity. These aforementioned risk factors have been identified as good predictors of later delinquency, prosocial behaviors (i.e., helping, sharing, and cooperation), being female, and having good cognitive performance appear to serve as protective factors.

Peer relationships and family milieu have also been identified as relating to later child delinquency. Family risk factors include inadequate parenting practices (i.e., high level of parent-child conflict, poor monitoring, and low level of positive involvement), family violence (i.e., children witnessing physical and verbal spouse abuse), parental divorce, parental psychopathology, teenage parenthood, family structure, and family size. Peer risk factors include association with deviant peers and peer rejection. On the other hand, peer and family protective factors that reduce risk of delinquency include positive social orientation, strong family attachment, and healthy family beliefs, values, and standards for appropriate behaviors.

The child's socialization process within the school context and the child's surrounding environment has also been identified as predicting child and adolescent delinquency. School factors such as poor academic performance, low academic aspiration, lack of attachment to school environment, and low commitment to school were identified as predictors of later delinquency. Neighborhood and community factors such as family poverty, disorganized neighborhoods, availability of drugs and firearms, and low neighborhood attachment have also been identified as possibly contributing to later delinquency. Protective factors for the school, neighborhood, and community include opportunities for school involvement, reward, recognition and opportunity for prosocial activities, good academic performance, and healthy community beliefs and standards for appropriate behavior.

No single risk factor will lead a child or adolescent to delinquency, it is the increase in risk factors with the decrease in protective factors that increases the likelihood of juvenile delinquency (Office of Juvenile Justice & Delinquency Prevention, 1999). As a result, it is imperative that mental health professionals and parents become aware of these factors and understand how these influences can provide important guidance and direction to prevention and early intervention for juvenile delinquents.

AT-RISK AREAS FOR CHILDREN AND ADOLESCENTS

The following domains have been selected to discuss the positive coping model and possible situation-specific coping strategies for parents. The decision to narrow the infinite number of possible domains to discuss was arduous, drawing primarily from the knowledge and experiences of the authors in the area of school psychology, statistics from both the Office of Juvenile Justice and Delinquency Prevention (OJJDP), National Institute of Mental Health (NIMH), and the Department of Education. The remainder of the chapter will concentrate on situation-specific coping strategies within the positive coping model for parents in the areas of poor academic achievement and substance use. However, the positive coping model and the coping strategies provided are simple and straightforward enough to be applied to other high-risk areas.

POSITIVE COPING MODEL

The positive coping model will serve as a guide to help individuals gain a better understanding of the perceived stress, to appraise the significance of the perceived stress, and to provide individuals with situation-specific coping strategies to effectively deal with the perceived stress. The positive coping model proposed is heavily influenced by the literature in the area of decision making. In particular, the decision-making model (CASVE cycle) proposed by Reardon, Lenz, Sampson, and Peterson (2000) was adapted to incorporate situation-specific coping strategies for parents.

Data Gathering

The first stage we recommend for an individual attempting to alleviate the amount of stress they perceive is *data gathering*. During this stage attempts are made to gather as much information as possible that relates to the stimulus and environment. By engaging in this process, an individual can position himself/herself to better understand what is causing the stress and how the stress can be alleviated. In order to effectively gather information relating to the stress, an individual must create an environment in which the lines of communication are opened (i.e., talking with members who experienced similar situations). Effective communication allows for the exchange of information between the individual experiencing the stress and his/her environment. When an individual is increasingly aware of the stress and contextual circumstances relating to the stress, the individual can begin to identify the source(s) of stress, evaluate the source(s) of stress, and explore its cause(s).

One of the ways parents can open lines of communication with their children is to collaboratively work on the self-evaluation checklist provided in the chapter. By responding to the questions on the self-evaluation tool, both parents and children become more informed about general risk and protective factors among children. Furthermore, by working together to evaluate individual, family, and social characteristics, parents and children can better understand the source of the stress, the context in which it operates, and more importantly, they can strengthen the communication process between parents and children.

Evaluation

The word evaluation best describes the second stage of the model recommended for individuals who want to reduce the level of perceived stress. In this particular stage, an individual examines, and evaluates the situation, to fully understand their perceived stress and their ability to respond effectively to the stressor. An individual in this stage asks questions like "What is causing me to feel this way and why am I feeling like this in this situation?" "What do I need to know about myself and my situation to alleviate my stress?" "Do I have what it takes to help me, or do I need to ask for help?" "Who has gone through similar situations and what have they done to respond to those situations?" The evaluation stage is important because it allows an individual to resist the temptation to act impulsively to remove the stressor.

The evaluation stage incorporates components similar to the stress and coping model proposed by Folkman and Lazarus (1980). As stated earlier, the coping process begins with an individual's appraisal of the demands placed on the individual by the environment. Based on this primary and secondary appraisal of stress, the attribute and severity of the stress an individual ultimately perceives will eventually influence how the individual copes.

Synthesis

The term synthesis is used to describe the third stage in our stress-reducing model. Individuals in this stage are asking and addressing the basic question of "What can I do to alleviate my stress?" In the synthesis stage, individuals brainstorm the possible options for removing the stressor. We recommend that individuals adopt situation-specific coping strategies. The situation-specific coping strategies recommended are based on the generally accepted coping categories proposed by Folkman and Lazarus (1980), Frydenberg and Lewis (1993), and the extensive research conducted on active and avoidance coping strategies. As stated earlier, Folkman and Lazarus categorized coping into problem-focused and emotion-focused coping. Additional researchers, such as Snyder and Pulvers (2001) and Holahan and Moos (1987) recognized active and avoidance coping strategies. The situation-specific model proposed is based on the combination of problem-focused, emotion-focused, and active coping. Due to extensive research suggesting that avoidant strategies are not adaptive, often making matters worse for the individual trying to deal with the problem, we will not present strategies that we consider to demonstrate avoidant-like behaviors. However, as stated earlier, we do adopt Moos' argument, in that specific coping strategies are not inherently adaptive or maladaptive. The possible combination of strategies we propose, neither active problem-focused, active emotion-focused, nor the combination of the two is inherently superior. Instead, they are equally adaptive for parents, depending largely on the individual and the context.

Planning

Once individuals identify the coping strategy or strategies they feel comfortable adopting to alleviate their perceived stress, individuals are prepared for the planning stage. In the planning stage, individuals can effectively implement a particular coping strategy or a combination of coping strategies by engaging in goal-directed behaviors such as preparation and experimenting. Preparation involves generating a plan for reducing stress and experimenting entails using a trial-and-error approach to gain knowledge of what is most effective in regards to reducing stress for the individual.

Implementation

The final stage in our stress-reducing model is called implementation. Individuals in this stage choose a particular coping strategy or a combination of coping strategies to alleviate their perceived stress. Implementation involves converting ideas and thoughts into actions and developing a sequence of rational steps to achieve the primary goal of stress reduction. An important component within the implementation stage for individuals is the ability to have the continuous option to return to the data generation stage if the chosen option was ineffective in reducing the perceived stress. The option to return to the data generation stage provides what we call a recursive feedback loop. This gives parents an opportunity to revisit any of the above stages before deciding on their action plan.

The implementation stage includes more than simply choosing a particular coping strategy or a combination of coping strategies. In the implementation stage, it is important that individuals evaluate the coping strategy or strategies in terms of how it affects both the individual and others. One of the questions individuals should ask and address in this stage is "If I decide to use this coping strategy, then how would it affect myself, my friends, my spouse, my children, and others who are significant to me?" We recommend that individuals evaluate their selected coping strategy or strategies by examining both costs and benefits to themseleves and others. In addition to examining both costs and benefits to self and others, individuals should examine the stressor within its context. It is recommended that individuals ask two questions when examining the stressor within its context: "How quickly can I resolve this problem?" and "Is this stressor habitual or ephemeral?" These two questions if asked and addressed will allow individuals to simultaneously take into consideration the self, the environment, and the stressor when deciding the most optimal coping strategy or strategies. Figure 12.2 provides a model for positive coping that integrates all of the aforementioned steps. This figure is provided as a visual representation of the sequential and recursive steps when integrating coping strategies.

In addition, a checklist is provided for parents and children to use to gather data (See Tables 12.2, 12.3, & 12.4).

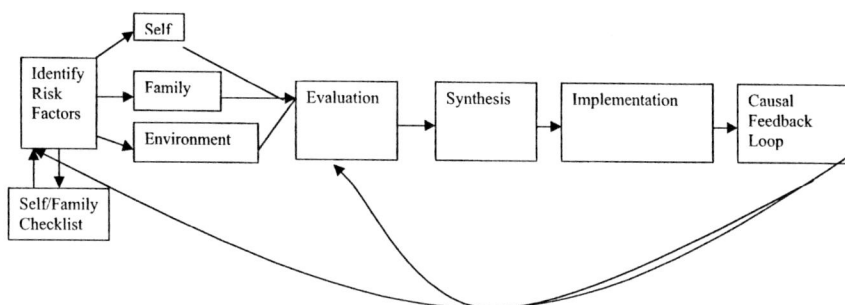

Steps to be Completed During Each Phase of Figure 12.2

I.   Identify Risk and Protective Factors
   a.   Checklist
II. Self, Family, and Environment
   a.   Interview child and/or adult
   b.   Open discussion about risk and protective factors
   c.   Talk with peers, school, and family members
III. Evaluation
   a.   Is there a problem?
   b.   Is there a common theme?
   c.   Is there a specific domain (i.e., family, self, environment)?
   d.   What is the duration of the problem?
   e.   Type of problem?
   f.   Impact of problem?
IV. Synthesis
   a.   Take all information and reduce to specific problem area(s)
   b.   Identify negative self-talk
   c.   Identify positive self-talk
   d.   What tools do you have available for help?
   e.   What do you need?
   f.   Identify problem or emotion focused
   g.   What is the accessibility to change?
V.   Implementation
   a.   Feasibility, skills, or outside resources
   b.   Costs
      i.   Social
      ii. Financial
   c.   Time
   d.   Consequences
   e.   Unintended consequences
   f.   Sustaining power or long-term effects
   g.   Increase protective factors
   h.   Decrease risk factors
VI. Causal Feedback Loop
   a.   Internal feedback
   b.   External feedback (friends and family)
   c.   Retrospection

Figure 12.2.   Model for Positive Coping

Table 12.2.   Family Risk and Protective Factors: Checklist for Kids

Rish Factors

Indicate answer by circling the appropriate response

Question	N (No) or Y (Yes)	
1. I frequently argue with my parents.	N	Y
2. My parents would not be that upset if I used alcohol or other substances.	N	Y
3. My parents and I don't communicate.	N	Y
4. My parents are too (strict/lenient).	N	Y
5. I can't discuss alcohol or drugs with my parents.	N	Y
6. My family often lets me down.	N	Y
7. I am embarrassed by my family.	N	Y
8. I often get into trouble with the law.	N	Y
9. I have problems dealing with stress.	N	Y
10. I don't expect much from my parents.	N	Y
11. My parents have unclear rules, guidelines, and expectations.	N	Y
12. My parents and/or siblings use drugs and/or alcohol.	N	Y
13. I do not feel close to my family.	N	Y
14. I have been physically or sexually abused by a family member.	N	Y
15. My parents do not care if I get into trouble with the law.	N	Y
16. My parents do not care about my schoolwork or grades.	N	Y
17. My family moves frequently.	N	Y
18. My parents don't know who my friends are.	N	Y
19. My parents are frequently unemployed.	N	Y
20. I do not enjoy spending time with my family.	N	Y

Protective Factors

Question	N (No) or Y (Yes)	
1. Our family can openly discuss feelings.	N	Y
2. I enjoy spending time with my family.	N	Y
3. I enjoy talking to my family.	N	Y
4. My family is supportive.	N	Y
5. I am not ashamed of my family.	N	Y
6. My family does not frequently (3 times per week) use alcohol.	N	Y
7. My family does not frequently (3 times per week) use substances.	N	Y
8. My parents and I communicate well.	N	Y
9. My family is always there for me.	N	Y
10. I feel close to my family.	N	Y
11. My parents provide adequate supervision.	N	Y
12. My parents are consistent with discipline.	N	Y
13. The expectations from my parents are stated clearly.	N	Y
14. My parents expectations do not change on a daily/weekly basis.	N	Y
15. My parents give me frequent praise.	N	Y
16. My parents do not have very high and unrealistic expectations.	N	Y
17. My parents and I spend quality time together.	N	Y
18. Our family deals well with stressful situations.	N	Y
19. My parents are employed most of the time.	N	Y
20. I feel like my family has enough money.	N	Y

*It is recommended that you use this checklist as a guide to identify risk and protective factors, and areas of concern, so that as a family you can sit down and discuss items endorsed.

Table 12.3. Family Risk and Protective Factors: Checklist for Parents

Risk Factors

Indicate answer by circling the appropriate response

Question	N (No) or Y (Yes)	
1. I frequently argue with my kids.	N	Y
2. I frequently use drugs or alcohol.	N	Y
3. My kids and I don't communicate.	N	Y
4. I am too (strict/lenient).	N	Y
5. I can't discuss alcohol or drugs with my kids.	N	Y
6. My kids often let me down.	N	Y
7. I am embarrassed by my kids.	N	Y
8. My kids often get into trouble with the law.	N	Y
9. I have problems dealing with stress.	N	Y
10. I don't expect much from my kids.	N	Y
11. I have unclear rules, guidelines, and expectations for my kids.	N	Y
12. My kids use drugs and/or alcohol.	N	Y
13. I do not feel close to my kids.	N	Y
14. I have been physically or sexually abused by a family member.	N	Y
15. I do not care if my kids get into trouble with the law.	N	Y
16. I do not care about my kids' schoolwork or grades.	N	Y
17. We move frequently.	N	Y
18. I don't know who my kid's friends are.	N	Y
19. I am frequently unemployed.	N	Y
20. I do not enjoy spending time with my kids.	N	Y

Protective Factors

Question	N (No) or Y (Yes)	
1. Our family can openly discuss feelings.	N	Y
2. I enjoy spending time with my kids.	N	Y
3. I enjoy talking to my kids.	N	Y
4. Our family is supportive.	N	Y
5. I am not ashamed of my kids.	N	Y
6. I do not frequently (3 times per week) use alcohol.	N	Y
7. I do not frequently (3 times per week) use substances.	N	Y
8. My kids and I communicate well.	N	Y
9. I am always there for my kids.	N	Y
10. I feel close to my kids.	N	Y
11. I provide adequate supervision.	N	Y
12. I am consistent with discipline.	N	Y
13. My expectations are stated clearly.	N	Y
14. My expectations do not change on a daily/weekly basis.	N	Y
15. I provide frequent praise for my kids.	N	Y
16. I do not have very high and unrealistic expectations.	N	Y
17. I spend quality time with my kids.	N	Y
18. Our family deals well with stressful situations.	N	Y
19. I am employed most of the time.	N	Y
20. I feel like we make enough money to live comfortably.	N	Y

* It is recommended that you use this checklist as a guide to identify risk and protective factors, and areas of concern, so that as a family you can sit down and discuss items endorsed.

Table 12.4.   Individual Risk and Protective Factors: Checklist for Kids/Parents

Risk Factors

Indicate answer by circling the appropriate response

Question	N (No) or Y (Yes)
1. I don't have many friends.	N Y
2. It is difficult to make new friends.	N Y
3. I often feel lonely.	N Y
4. I don't like the way I act.	N Y
5. I don't like the way I look.	N Y
6. My life is all mixed up.	N Y
7. I can't do most things I try.	N Y
8. I often get into physical fights.	N Y
9. I break things on purpose.	N Y
10. I get mad easily.	N Y
11. Bad things usually happen to me.	N Y
12. I don't think I will ever be successful.	N Y
13. I don't like to help others.	N Y
14. I never do my part.	N Y
15. I don't enjoy being part of a team.	N Y
16. Marijuana makes me happy.	N Y
17. I use alcohol frequently (3 times per week).	N Y
18. I can't wait to be old enough to drink.	N Y
19. I am curious about alcohol and other drugs.	N Y
20. I have been in trouble with the law.	N Y

Protective Factors

Question	N (No) or Y (Yes)
1. I have a lot of friends.	N Y
2. It is easy to make new friends.	N Y
3. I like myself.	N Y
4. I like the way I act.	N Y
5. I like the way I look.	N Y
6. I like to be with other people.	N Y
7. I can do most things I try.	N Y
8. I do not get into physical fights.	N Y
9. I always help others out.	N Y
10. I am able to cope well with stress.	N Y
11. I know that I will be successful.	N Y
12. I can do anything I set my mind to.	N Y
13. I generally follow rules.	N Y
14. I make good grades in school.	N Y
15. I have control over what happens to me.	N Y
16. I don't have many friends who use alcohol or other drugs.	N Y
17. I do not use alcohol frequently (3 times per week).	N Y
18. I do not use drugs.	N Y
19. I am not curious about alcohol and other drugs.	N Y
20. I have not been in trouble with the law.	N Y

*It is recommended that you use this checklist as a guide to identify risk and protective factors, and areas of concern, so that as a family you can sit down and discuss items endorsed.

THE SCHOOL CONTEXT

It has been well documented that youth who do not complete high school are often faced with many more problems in later life than do youth who graduate from high school. Among the problems for school dropouts is the widening gap between dropouts and graduates in future earnings and opportunities. According to the National Center for Education Statistics, male and female college graduates earned 60% to 95% more, respectively, than those who only completed high school. Furthermore, males and females who dropped out of high school earned 27% to 30% less, respectively, than peers who have earned a high school diploma. The knowledge of the consequences of failing to complete high school is even more vexing if the prevalence rates of academic failure are mentioned. The National Center for Education Statistics provided national data indicating between 347,000 and 544,000 10th through 12th grade students left school each year without successfully completing a high school degree. In addition, 5 out of every 100 young adults enrolled in high school in October 1999 left school before October 2000 without successfully completing a high school degree. Many studies conducted by the Federal government and private organizations have produced new information regarding school dropouts and academic outcomes. To acquire updated statistics on school dropouts and academic outcomes, we found that the National Center for Education Statistics and the Department of Education were most valuable.

Who is at Risk of Dropping Out?

The following information has been identified by Coley (1995) to indicate that, in general, certain groups of youth have more difficulties with school, thus more likely to leave school before graduating, although not every youth in these categories end up dropping out of school before they graduate. However, these categories are important to note, in order to prevent some youth from leaving school prematurely. According to Schwartz (1995), students in large cities are twice more likely to leave school before graduating than nonurban youth. And of those who drop out, more than half leave by the 10 grade, 20% leave by the eighth grade, and 3% stop by the fourth grade. In terms of ethnic differences, youth who identify themselves as Hispanics are twice as likely as those of African American descent to drop out, while Caucasian and Asian American students are least likely to drop out. Furthermore, youth of Hispanic descent have a one-to-four ratio in dropping out and nearly half leave by the eighth grade.

Reasons for Dropping Out

According to Coley (1995) students drop out for many reasons. In interviews conducted with high school dropouts, they reported both school problems and personal factors as reasons for dropping out. Some of the school factors reported include a "dislike for the school in general, receiving failing grades or unable to keep up with school work, did not get along with teachers, didn't fit in, had disciplinary problems such as suspension and expulsion, and didn't feel safe at school." Personal factors mentioned were, "had to support the family, problems with substance abuse, trouble managing both school and work, became a parent, wanted to become a parent, wanted to travel, and had friends who dropped out." Some adolescents, however, are able to get through a difficult period with minimal assistance from teachers, parents and/or significant others. However, when the impediments become profuse and last longer than one grading period or when the child exhibits chronic academic failures, the role of parents and significant others takes a more crucial function in alleviating the academic problems of the child.

Based on the alarming data provided by the National Center for Education Statistics (2003), it is not unreasonable to surmise that countless teens will experience a time in which maintaining adequate school performance becomes challenging and difficult. As a result, parents need to have access to a broad range of strategies to deal effectively with both their behaviors and emotions, consequently affecting their children's behaviors and emotions.

The remainder of the chapter presents case vignettes along with an illustration of the positive coping stages so as to highlight the application of coping strategies for parents of at-risk children and adolescent.

Case Vignette 1

John is currently a freshman at Spring Woods High School. John's parents have been concerned about his recent low quiz grades in physical science, English, and algebra I. On John's first report card, he received one A, three Bs, and three Cs. After this report card, John's parents, aware that he has been a relatively good student throughout elementary and middle school and never in any real danger of failing a subject, told him that he needs to reduce his social activities until his grades improve. His parents, over the next few months, monitored his social activities. However, on John's subsequent report card, he received two Bs, two Cs, and three Fs. John's parents came home from work and discovered their son's grades with a note from the school counselor suggesting that John may have to retake physical science, English, and algebra I in summer school in order to pass the ninth grade. After briefly talking to John, he stated that "school is not for everyone" and that he is seriously considering dropping out of school.

Data Gathering

One method of gathering information for the parents regarding John's academic difficulties is to set up a time to discuss John's schoolwork with his teachers, school counselor, principal, and other pertinent school administrators. Only after having an in-depth discussion with these individuals can John's parents really understand the problem within the context. Another method of gathering information for parents is to proactively set up a time to sit down and listen to John so as to understand his fears and concerns. One way parents can start a meaningful discussion with John is by collaboratively working with John on the self-evaluation checklist. In doing so, John's parents can utilize the self-evaluation checklist to identify general risk and protective factors. In addition to being able to identify risk and protective factors, John's parents can use the self-evaluation checklist as a vehicle to open the lines of communication with John. As a result of efficiently gathering data through communication, the stress of witnessing your child facing school difficulties can no longer be ignored and the process to analyze the sources of the problem and explore its causes has begun.

Evaluation

In this particular stage, the parents should take a moment to examine, consider, and evaluate the situation to fully understand their perceived stress and their ability to respond effectively to the stressor. One approach is to improve self-knowledge in the areas of coping skills, as well as to expand knowledge regarding possible coping strategies. To be more specific, John's parents could examine what coping strategies they have utilized in the past, on what circumstances, and how effective were they in alleviating the stress. By examining past coping strategies, John's parents are able to create a mental model of the stressor in relation to past coping strategies. This, in turn, will allow John's parents to accurately appraise both the stressor and the resources available for influencing and controlling the perceived stressors.

Synthesis

In the synthesis stage, the dominant question for parents is "What can I do to alleviate my stress?" As stated earlier, of the possible combination of strategies we proposed, neither active problem-focused, active emotion-focused, nor the combination of the two is inherently superior. Instead, they are equally adaptive to parents, depending largely on the individual and the context. Without effective coping strategies for parents, John's academic difficulties could easily escalate to become something more serious, such as dropping out of school (Dryfoos, 1990). Because problems often vary from situation to situation, effective coping strategies need to be flexible in order that individuals adapt appropriately.

Implementation

In the implementation stage, John's parents choose a particular coping strategy or a combination of coping strategies to alleviate the stress of witnessing his difficulties in school. To reiterate our point, it is not the purpose of this chapter to provide a universal model of adaptive coping strategies for parents of at-risk children and adolescents. Instead, our focus is on the positive coping model and to aid the healthy development of at-risk children and adolescents by increasing parents' awareness in situation-specific coping strategies. In the implementation stage, John's parents will decide on what coping strategies to utilize. The important point here is not what strategy or strategies they have chosen but that they have the ability to continue to monitor the effectiveness of these strategies through internal and/or external feedback. (See Chapter 2 by Lewis and Frydenberg, this volume, where it is pointed out that it is the self-appraised value or quality of a strategy that matters not just its use). In this particular case, internal feedback for John's parents could be the persistent feelings of stress. On the other hand, external feedback could come from reactions and comments made by significant others, such as "You look tired and stressed out all the time."

In addition to monitoring internal and external feedback, it is recommended that John's parents evaluate their coping strategy or combination of strategies by including an assessment of the costs and benefits to self and others with an emphasis on John. To fully weigh the costs and benefits of a particular coping strategy or combination of strategies, John's parents should determine whether this situation has a realistic potential for quick resolution and whether this situation is of a chronic or fleeting nature. For example, if John's parents were to adopt an active problem-focused strategy, such as creating time to spend with John to try to listen and understand John's fears and concerns, questions like "How do I adjust my work time to be more available to John?" and "How will John respond when approached about this situation?" needs to be asked and addressed.

ALCOHOL, TOBACCO, AND OTHER DRUGS (ATODS)

Over the last few decades, the literature regarding substance use among children and adolescent has been growing substantially, especially in the development of adolescent substance abuse (McGillicuddy, Rychtarik, Duquette, & Morsheimer, 2001). This statement should be of no surprise given the findings reported by federal agencies, such as the Office of Juvenile Justice and Delinquency Prevention (1999). According to OJJDP, in 1998, the Monitoring the Future Study asked a nationally representative sample of nearly 50,000 secondary school students in public and private schools to describe their drug use patterns through self-administered questionnaires. The following were reported (Office of Juvenile Justice & Delinquency Prevention, 1999):

1. In 1998, 54% of all high school seniors said they had at least tried illicit drugs. While almost half of high school seniors used marijuana at least once, 37% said they had used it in the past year, 23% said they used it in the previous month, and 6% said they had used marijuana on 20 or more occasions in the previous 30 days.

2. In 1998, 4 in 5 high school seniors said they had tried alcohol at least once; half said they had used it in the previous month. Even among eighth graders, the use of alcohol was high; one half had tried alcohol, almost one quarter had used it in the month prior to the survey. In regards to heavy drinking (defined as five or more drinks in a row), 31% of seniors, 24% sophomores, and 14% of eighth graders reported this behavior.

3. In 1998, 65% of seniors and 46% of eighth graders had tried cigarettes. In regards to smoking cigarettes on a regular basis, 22% of seniors, 16% of sophomores, and 9% of eighth graders reported this behavior.

Who is At-risk of Substance Use?

According to OJJDP, teenagers in general are at risk for developing serious alcohol and drug problems when the following components are included: (1) a family history of substance abuse, (2) when diagnosed with a mental disorder such as depression, AD/HD, conduct disorder, and so forth, (3) when children have low self-esteems, and (4) when children feel alienated from the mainstream. In terms of socio-demographics, males are more likely than females to consume an alcoholic beverage or to consume alcohol heavily. In regards to ethnicity, African Americans have lower drug, alcohol, and tobacco use rates than Whites.

Due to the striking statistics provided by OJJDP, it is imperative that parents have access to a broad range of strategies to deal effectively with the substance abuse of children and adolescent. Empirical studies demonstrate that the causal direction of the parent behavior-adolescent substance abuse is more bidirectional and reciprocal than unidirectional. Drawing from this perspective, it is hypothesized that effective parental coping in response to children and adolescent substance use will improve the overall psychological functioning of the parents and in turn, diminish children and adolescent substance use. Alternatively, ineffective coping strategies will lead to maintained or increased child and adolescent substance use.

Case Vignette 2

Over the last few years, David's overall grades have been slowly dropping from primarily As to Cs and Ds. David has been a relatively good student throughout his middle school years, without demonstrating any particular behaviors to be of tremendous concern to his parents. His father and mother stated that ever since David entered high school, his grades have been dropping and he seems to care less about school. His parents also stated that they are not particularly pleased about David's choice of friends. David's parents have been concerned about David's substance use primarily for two reasons. A few weeks ago, David's parents, suspicious of their child's behaviors over the last few months, decided to look through some of David's personal belongings. They discovered a small bag of marijuana hidden away under some sweaters in the back of his clothes drawer. Last week, David's parents were called to the school because David and some other teens were suspected of smoking marijuana during lunch break. When the teens were confronted they denied the accusations. However, when David's parents arrived at school, they had no doubt that David had smoked marijuana during lunch break because not only were his pupils dilated but he also smelled of pot.

Data Gathering

In this scenario, David's parents would benefit tremendously if they first gather information from David's school administrators, school counselor, teachers, and peers about his academic, social, and behavioral functioning. By opening up the communication lines with other individuals, David's parents are better able to understand what exactly is going on before and after school. A one-on-one conversation with the school counselor, David's teachers, and/or his peers will provide valuable information to be analyzed later. These sources of information are based on first-hand accounts from individuals who interact with David on a regular basis in various environmental contexts. After gathering information from other individuals it would be also be beneficial to set up a time to sit down, listen, and understand what are the concerns, fears, acceptance, and/or denial David may have regarding substance use. As stated earlier, David's parents can utilize the self-evaluation checklist provided as a vehicle to discussing David's behaviors. By having a positive conversation with David, it will be more likely that he will open up and communicate with his parents.

Evaluation

In the evaluation stage, David's parents should take a moment to assess the plausibility of David using marijuana or other illicit drugs. Based on his past behaviors (marijuana found in his drawer, the school incident involving marijuana, and information gathered through the others), this primary appraisal appears accurate and secondary appraisal is needed. To fully understand the situation and their ability to respond effectively to the stressor, David's parents need to analyze the information they have obtained in the data gathering stage, the coping strategies they have used in the past for similar incidents, and the effectiveness of these coping strategies in alleviating the stress. For example, David's parents may want to look closely at how they handled similar situations in the past when David has been in trouble. Questions such as, "do I usually ignore these things and wait until he comes and talks to me?", "do I confront and accuse him of his actions?", "do I exaggerate or minimize the situation?", and "are these strategies effective in dealing with the situation?" need to be answered honestly before proceeding to the implementation stage. Only after asking these questions and answering them honestly are parents able to determine what it is that they can do to alleviate the problem.

Synthesis

When David's parents are in the synthesis stage, they will ultimately have to answer the question "What can I do to solve this problem?" If David's parents take the time to gather information from others and evaluate the problem within its contexts, answering the question of what resources are available becomes significantly easier. As stated earlier, of the possible combination of strategies we proposed, neither active problem-focused, active emotion-focused, nor the combination of the two is inherently superior. Instead, they are equally adaptive to parents, depending largely on the individual and the context. In Table 12.1, we proposed the following strategies, based on dominant research in the areas of problem-focused, emotion-focused, active, and avoidant categories and strategies, for parents who are faced with the challenge of coping with children who are engaged in substance use.

Implementation

After accurately appraising both the stressor and the resources available for influencing and controlling the perceived stressors, David's parents should choose a particular coping strategy or a combination of coping strategies to alleviate the stress of having a child involved in substance use. In the implementation stage, David's parents will decide on what coping strategy or strategies to utilize. Again, the important point is not what strategy or strategies David's parents chose, but that they have the ability to continue to monitor the effectiveness of the strategy or strategies through internal and/or external feedback. In this particular case, internal feedback for David's parents could be the persistent feelings of worrying, lack of sleep, loss of motivation, and chronic fatigue. On the other hand, external feedback could come from reactions and comments made by significant others, such as "We need you to come to school to pick up your child. We currently have him in the office because he was caught having drugs on school grounds."

In addition to monitoring internal and external feedback, it is recommended that David's parents evaluate their coping strategy or combination of strategies by including an assessment of both costs and benefits to self and others with an emphasis on David. To fully weigh up the costs and benefits of a particular coping strategy or combination of strategies, David's parents should determine whether this situation has a realistic potential for quick resolution and whether this situation is of a chronic or fleeting nature.

CONCLUSION

In today's society, parents are being challenged with numerous situations and circumstances that have the capacity to produce stress and anxiety. It is not unreasonable to expect that parents will face a host of taxing events and situations during the years of their children and adolescent's development. As illustrated in the chapter, these challenging situations and events can present themselves in many forms, ranging from a child having difficulties with school to a child who is involved with substance use.

There is a broad body of literature examining family influence on children and adolescent development. Two broad generalizations can be made about these studies. First, the studies in the area of ecological-developmental theories, transactional processes between family and the child, and attachment patterns of children with their caregivers have shed light on the impact of family dynamics on children's development. Second, these studies demonstrate the importance of parent-child interactions as one of a host of crucial components in the equation of healthy child and adolescent development.

Drawing from research studies in the areas of parent-child interaction and stress and coping, we have provided a positive coping model including situation-specific coping strategies for parents with an emphasis on the positive coping model as a central factor affecting the development of children. We strongly believe that the positive coping model and the coping strategies provided are simple and straightforward enough that it can and should be applied to other high-risk areas. In addition to providing a model for coping, we have also included a self-evaluation tool to assist parents and professionals in identifying general risk and protective factors among children. The self-evaluation tool can also serve both as tool to identify general risk and protective factors among children and/or act as a catalyst in opening the communication lines between parents, children, and professionals.

REFERENCES

Almeida, D. M., Wethington, E., & Chandler, A. L. (1999). Daily transmission of tensions between marital dyads and parent-child dyads. *Journal of Marriage and the Family, 61*, 49-61.

Ainsworth, M. D., & Bowlby, J. (1954). Research strategy in the study of mother-child separation. *Courrier, 4*, 105-131.

Bell, R. Q. (1968). Reinterpretation of direction of effects in studies of socialization. *Psychological Review, 71*, 81-95.

Bronfenbrenner, U. (1979). *The ecology of human development.* Cambridge, MA: Harvard University Press.

Coley, R. J. (1995). *Dreams deferred: High school dropouts in the United States.* Princeton, NJ: Educational Testing Service, Policy Information Center.

Cremeens, P. R., Lindsey, E. W., & Caldera, Y. M. (2002). Bidirectionality in socialization relationships: Child effects on father perceptions of the marital relationships. *National Social Science Association Journal, 19*, 1-9. Available: http://www.nssa.us/nssajrnl/19-1/htm/3/3.htm

Dryfoos, J. (1990). *Adolescents at risk: Prevalence and prevention*. New York: Oxford University Press.

Folkman, S. (1992). Making the case for coping. In B. N. Carpenter (Ed.), *Personal coping: Theory, research and application* (pp. 31-46). Westport, CT: Praeger/Greenwood Group.

Folkman, S., & Lazarus, R. S. (1980). An analysis of coping in a middle-aged community sample. *Journal of Health and Social Behavior, 21*, 219-239.

Frydenberg, E., & Lewis, R. (1993). *Manual: The Adolescent Coping scale*. Melbourne: Australian Council for Educational Research.

Hardy, L., Jones, G., & Gould, D. (1996). *Understanding psychological preparation for sport*. New York: John Wiley & Sons.

Hobfoll, S. E., Schwarzer, S., & Chon, K. (1998). Disentangling the stress labyrinth: Interpreting the meaning of stress as it is studied. *Anxiety Stress and Coping, 11*, 181-212.

Holahan, C. J., & Moos, R. H. (1987). Risk, resistance, and psychological distress: A longitudinal analysis with adults and children. *Journal of Abnormal Psychology, 96*, 3-13.

Houston, K. B. (1987). Stress and coping. In C. R. Snyder & C. E. Ford (Eds.), *Coping with negative life events: Clinical and social psychological perspectives* (pp. 373-399). New York: Plenum Press.

Lazarus, R. S., & Folkman, S. (1984). *Stress, appraisal, and coping*. New York: Springer.

Lollis, S., & Kuczynski, L. (1997). Beyond one hand clapping: Seeing bidirectionality in parent-child relations. *Journal of Social and Personal Relationships, 14*, 441-461.

McGillicuddy, N. B., Rychtarik, R. G., Duquette, J. A., & Morsheimer, E. T. (2001). Development of a skill training program for parents of substance-abusing adolescents. *Journal of Substance Abuse Treatment, 20*, 59-68.

Motherhood. (2003, June 2). *Parents @ work: Celebrity mummies!* [On-line]. Available: http://www.motherhood.com

Moos, R. H. (1986). *Coping with life crises: An integrated approach*. New York: Plenum.

National Center for Education Statistics. (n.d.). *The condition of education* [On-line]. Available: http://nces.ed.gov//programs/coe

Office of Juvenile Justice & Delinquency Prevention. (1999). *Juvenile offenders and victims: The 1999 national report* [On-line]. Available: http://www.ncjrs.org/html/ojjdp/nationalreport99/toc.html

Reardon, R. C., Lenz, J. G., Sampson, J. P., & Peterson, G. W. (2000). *Career development and planning: A comprehensive approach*. Stamford, CT: Thomson Learning.

Sameroff, A. (1975). Transactional models in early social relations. *Human Development, 18*, 65-79.

Schwartz, W. (1995). *School dropouts: New information about an old problem*. New York: Office of Educational Research and Improvement, U.S. Department of Education. (Eric Document Reproduction Service No. EDOUD965).

Snyder, C. R., & Pulvers, K. M. (2001). Dr. Seuss, the coping machine, and "Oh the places you'll go." In C. R. Snyder (Ed.), *Coping with stress: Effective people and processes* (pp. 3-29). New York: Oxford University Press.

CHAPTER 13

DIRECTIONS IN TEACHER TRAINING FOR LOW-BURNOUT TEACHING

Lessons from the Research

Isaac A Friedman
The Henrietta Szold Institute
The National Institute for Research in the Behavioral Sciences

ABSTRACT

Burnout is a psychological syndrome comprising senses of exhaustion, unaccomplishment, and depersonalization that manifests itself in professionals working with people in need of help, of treatment, or of instruction. Different sources of stress leading to burnout have been identified in the literature. This chapter uses Friedman's Shattered Dreams model of teacher stress and burnout to establish directions in training teachers for a more successful, low-burnout teaching career. These directions involve the acquisition of four basic professional abilities: (a) leadership skills (classic and postmodern), (b) self-regulation skills, (c) organizational efficacy skills, and (d) skills for evading the burnout trap. The chapter argues that these skills can be learned and applied by trainee teachers, and be used effectively.

Thriving, Surviving, or Going Under: Coping with Everyday Lives, 305–326

Burnout is a psychological syndrome that manifests itself in professionals working with people in need of help, of instruction, or of treatment. Many definitions have been suggested for the phenomenon of burnout in professionals in all kinds of human service fields, including teaching and administration in educational settings. The current conceptualization of professional burnout in human service professions now views burnout as involving three elements: exhaustion, nonaccomplishment and depersonalization (Maslach & Jackson, 1981).

Various professionals have been found to suffer from exhaustion and nonaccomplishment, whereas depersonalization, meaning an alienated, negative, or even a hostile attitude toward others, was found to exist mainly among those involved in assisting, instructing, or treating other people. Feelings of ineffectiveness in fulfilling role-related tasks, and a sense of professional nonaccomplishment accompanied by feelings of professional incompetence are now considered the primary psychological factor in professional burnout for all service professions. Feelings of exhaustion are a response to the stress generated by role demands and the sense of being unable to perform role-related tasks that are required or expected. People who are in a state of burnout tend to reduce their involvement in work and even renounce their ambitions of dedicating themselves to the job and the clients.

Teachers are conscious of the burnout feeling produced by teaching and of its causes and consequences. Participants in workshops designed to treat teacher burnout, conducted by the author, have described burnout in the following ways (Friedman & Lotan, 1993):

- Burnout is when teachers feel "wiped out." A burned out teacher is someone who is completely exhausted, physically and mentally. Regarding myself, I don't feel I am the same person I was 10 years ago. Today, I react completely differently to what happens in class and at school (homeroom teacher for 17 years).

- A burned out teacher means a tired teacher. Personally, I want to do more, but I lack the emotional strength and feel I need help (homeroom teacher for 20 years).

- Burned out teachers are teachers who are away from work a lot as a result of illness. They show symptoms of fatigue, depression. and a reluctance to work (teacher for specific subjects, 10 years experience).

- As a burned out teacher, I feel that my work doesn't contribute much, and the fact is I don't really care about it anymore. I feel like a mechanical engineer whose work is with machinery, not people (homeroom teacher of 25 years).

Recent literature has shown that burnout occurs and develops along two distinct tracks (Friedman, 1996):

1. *A cognitive track.* There is a conscious sense of a lack of success and professional nonfulfillment.
2. *An emotional track.* This begins with a sense of emotional overload that intensifies and develops into feelings of emotional exhaustion.

As time passes, burnout progresses along these tracks attacking the professional in a pincer movement. There are naturally differences along both tracks, owing to the professional's personality, experience, and training and also to the amount of social and organizational support he or she receives. For example, someone who is more of a "thinking" than a "feeling" type will tend to "move" along the cognitive track of burnout, while someone who is a "feeling" type will tend to progress along the emotional track.

The main theme underlying this chapter is that a perceived discrepancy may exist between a teacher's professional competence and actual achievements, successes, or failures, and that such discrepancy can be a significant source of stress. By understanding the stages through which the teacher passes in discovering this discrepancy we might improve our understanding of the burnout phenomenon and develop more effective treatment. One very important contributor to burnout has been identified as the shattering of professional dreams (Friedman, 2000).

SOURCES AND CAUSES OF BURNOUT

Consensus exists among researchers that the burnout process begins with exposure to work stressors. Stress is normally the result of a lack of fit between the individual and one's environment. Theories maintain that stress stems from an imbalance between professional demands and the professional's personal competence, and from a lack of fit between the support and assistance rendered to the professional by his or her milieu (colleagues, superiors, resources), and ambient demands posed on him or her, such as, achievements, success, and effective use of resources (French, Caplan, & Van Harrison, 1982). According to another, somewhat different theory, our general experience of work is two dimensional in terms of challenges and skills. If the challenges are numerous and fairly difficult, and the skills inadequate to meet them, professionals experience anxiety and stress. Conversely, if an individual has superfluous skills in addition to those needed to meet the challenges, he or she will become stressed, bored, and unhappy (Csikszentmihalyi, 1990). All theories of stress have one thing in common: an emphasis on the gap existing between the expected and the actual in terms of performance capability, skills, resources, and success.

Research into the origins of teacher burnout in different cultures and at different points in time reveals that factors associated with teacher-student relations represent the main cause of burnout (Friedman & Lotan, 1985). Teacher-perceived discrepancies between expectations and classroom reality were found to be related to controlling disciplinary problems, motivating and encouraging students to do well at school and maintaining positive social relations in the classroom (Milstein & Golaszewski, 1985). An Israeli study of elementary school teachers (Friedman, 1995), involving some 350 teachers and 1,150 pupils, uncovered the areas in which teachers experience a gap between their expectations and their actual experiences with pupils. Those areas were: respect toward the teacher, sociability, and attentiveness. In each of these three areas it was found that when teachers are treated disrespectfully, or are not shown warmth and friendliness, or if students are not attentive and committed to learning, feelings of unaccomplishment and disappointment arise, representing a major cause of burnout. It is worth noting that in this study (Friedman, 1995) the first two areas (respectfulness and friendliness toward the teacher) concern the interpersonal relations aspect of teachers and pupils, whereas the third area (attentiveness) concerns the task element of the teacher's work (teaching and educating, class management, etc.). Moreover, the respectfulness element of the interpersonal relations between teachers and pupils was found to have the greatest impact on burnout. A gap existing in the expectations regarding the task aspect of the teacher's work made an additional contribution to burnout, albeit to a lesser degree than the interpersonal relations. The study also found that pupils realize that disrespectful behavior toward teachers inflicts on teachers enormous stress, whereas reluctance to learn, inattentiveness and low achievements are less stressful to the teachers. The findings of that study support the hypothesis that a discrepancy between teacher expectations, hopes for warmth and respect and for helping pupils to learn and succeed, and harsh reality are a major cause of burnout.

For teachers, like any professionals, professional self-image is an important factor, and according to recognized stress theories, differences between the teacher's self-image and perceived reality can produce stress. In a study carried out by Friedman and Farber (1992), gaps were found in the professional image the teacher ascribes to himself, and the image the teacher believes is ascribed to him or her by pupils, parents, school colleagues and the principal. The gap between teacher's self-perception and pupils' perceptions of their teacher's professional competence was found to be a major source of stress. Gaps between the teacher's self-perception and the parents' and principal's perception of the teacher were found less of a stressor.

UNDERSTANDING BURNOUT IN TERMS OF A DISCREPANCY BETWEEN BELIEFS AND REALITY IN PROFESSIONAL SELF-EFFICACY

The studies cited above and other recent studies (see Maslach & Leiter, 1997; Schaufeli, Maslach, & Marek, 1993; Travers & Cooper, 1996), demonstrate clearly that the gap between the professional's perception of his or her own professional competence and professional expectations, and the reality in which that professional competence is reflected, is a major stressor conducive to burnout. Cherniss (1995) has explored the crisis that professionals undergo in the transition from studying and training to hands-on work in their first few months on the job, among teachers, nurses, psychologists, and lawyers. He found that recently qualified professionals were excited about helping and saving others, but that the real world they confronted was not what they expected. Rather, it was brimming with unpredicted frustrations and a failure by their work environment to render them support. Almost all professionals believed that their studies and training had failed to prepare them for the challenges ahead. They expected matters to improve, and often this was the case. However, for many, the stress proved unbearable. They sobered up from their desire to help and contribute and lost their enthusiasm and vigor: they became burned out. Cherniss concluded that professionals set out with unrealistic expectations and that these expectations by and large served as a major cause of their downfall. They fall prey to the "professional mystique"—a romantic belief that professional work is full of feelings of vocation and satisfaction.

Gavish (1997) carried out a study to explore the phenomenon of "reality shock" among teachers in mainstream and special education in Israel. Teachers in their first year of teaching reported their professional feelings and teaching experiences. According to the study, we can classify teachers' feelings in their first year of work as a process that develops in the following three main stages:

Stage 1: Crisis

Teachers described this stage using terms like shock, nightmare, catastrophe, collapse, suffering, despair, crisis, and stress. During this stage, the teacher is at a loss regarding how to cope with the harsh, newly-discovered reality: keeping the children quiet, handling class discipline problems, dealing with problems like apathy, reluctance to learn, and social problems in the classroom.

Stage 2: Fatigue and Exhaustion

The second stage of the novice teacher's professional career is marked by fatigue and exhaustion. Teachers report that they still like the children and teaching, but that the stress and tension that teaching generates is so distressing they are considering leaving teaching. The teachers described their disappointment with teaching in the following four areas:

1. *Pupil-related problems.*   Most problems were associated with pupils with special needs and behavioral problems. Such problems provided the greatest source of frustration and disenchantment. The overall feeling was one of helplessness and an inability to function effectively.
2. *Overload.*   Teachers reported that their first steps in teaching were overly demanding, requiring them to work large numbers of hours inside and outside the classroom.
3. *Criticism.*   Demands on teachers are accompanied by criticism, either perceived or real, from pupils, parents, colleagues, and the principal.
4. *Nonrecognition and lack of reward.*   The teacher's great effort goes unrecognized—even if the pay is adequate. Teachers feel a lack of reward and praise for their work.

Stage 3: Adaptation and Reconciliation

In stage three, teachers accept and adapt to reality. In this manner they solve the existential problem. Adjustment entails learning new teaching methods, and above all, looking for a compromise between the teaching standard they first dreamed of and a standard that reality dictates.

Naturally, each teacher will respond differently at being exposed to a disappointing and tough reality. However, there seems to be a lot of similarity in the reactions to this reality shock. A common response is to lower expectations of teaching and focus on goals perceived as offering more immediate and unambivalent satisfaction. In these cases teachers may think: "Since my efforts have been fruitless, I will choose an easier, more certain path in teaching from now on. It will suffice if I just teach at the level of the pupils' ability— without insisting on any particular way which seems highly appropriate". Another common response is to blame the pupils, even after lowering expectations of them and setting achievable goals. This marks a change from their previous attitude when they first took up teaching. They do not blame themselves any more for what happens in class and school. Another common response is to tone down the warmth and affection shown to pupils. From this point on, the path leading to depersonalization may not be long.

The problems teachers encounter and experience most intensely, particularly in their first year of teaching, relate to the interpersonal relations between themselves and their environment in both the classroom and the school contexts. These problems consist of difficulties with their pupils; criticism of their work from pupils, parents, colleagues, and principals; and no recognition or reward. In addition, teachers experience problems with their role-related tasks (overload). No significant discrepancy between expectations and the reality of routine teaching tasks was found in any of the studies reported in recent years.

Five main stressors in a teacher's professional work can be identified, the chief of which is the professional skills crisis (Friedman, 2000). Professionals are usually expected to possess skills that will allow them to reach every pupil, even the most problematic. Teachers who cannot do this are seen as uncaring, lacking flair, or both. The expertise that the professional is equipped with following training is intended to make the teacher feel "on top of things" under all circumstances and at any time. Professionals, however, are not always sure of what to do in certain practical situations: teachers, on their first day of teaching, find themselves standing before a class full of children, not knowing what to do first. Young professionals tend to blame themselves for a lack of success. Such self-indictment produces feelings of despair and failure and a sense of being unfit to fulfill their role and vocation.

The second source of stress relates to the confrontation with staff in the organizational system employing the professional. The anticipated professional autonomy is soon discovered to be an unrealistic dream, since the professionals are not permitted to take autonomous decisions and work as they see fit, independently of those around (or above) them. The professionals not only feel that the system places all kinds of strange demands on them, but that even in matters of agreement, the environment fails to provide them with proper support or permit their work to run smoothly (Friedman, 1999).

The third cause of stress in professional work concerns difficulties and problems with service recipients, which prevent the professional from functioning with the right amount of effectiveness. The "service recipients" in teaching are the pupils and their parents. The most common difficulties are unresponsiveness, lack of discipline, reluctance to learn and obey the teacher's instructions (pupils), and noncooperation, interference, and even harassment (by parents). Professionals who do not surmount these impediments indict themselves as lacking the necessary professional skills. Another difficulty pertaining to service recipients concerns their lack of expressed appreciation for the professionals' work. This lack of appreciation might be accepted with better understanding if the professionals had more confidence and felt no need for approval and recognition of their professional competence—especially from service recipients.

The fourth source of stress identified is boredom and monotony. Employment in public service should be interesting and meaningful. However, teachers report that after working with pupils for two months, the teaching routine turns destructive.

The fifth source of stress seems to be the absence of support from colleagues and lack of collegiality. Professionals go to work expecting to find enthusiastic, supportive, and empathic friends. Instead, they meet apathetic reactions, lack of interest, and on occasion, hostility. Furthermore, public support for the professional's work, which is supposed to help those requiring support, is perceived as inadequate or missing.

FRIEDMAN'S "SHATTERED DREAMS" MODEL OF TEACHER BURNOUT

The gap between a teacher's subjective perception of efficacy and that teacher's experience of classroom practice is central in understanding burnout, and may also point to several key factors in its prevention. The typical behaviors indicative of teacher efficacy are the ability to stimulate and motivate pupils and instill values, the ability to improvise in unforeseen classroom situations, ability to control disciplinary infractions without undue effort, ability to influence colleagues, assertiveness when dealing with the school administration, familiarity and resourcefulness regarding the organization, and in exercising influence in the school (Friedman & Kass, 2000, 2002). A gap is sensed in perceptions of teacher efficacy when a teacher, who embarked on a teaching career with a sense of vocation and social and educational idealism, is exposed to the reality of the job routine: the teacher's dreams of a satisfying and rewarding professional career may then be shattered. Examining the process whereby professional dreams are smashed, especially among novice teachers, will most likely further our understanding and our ability to treat and minimize the occurrence of burnout.

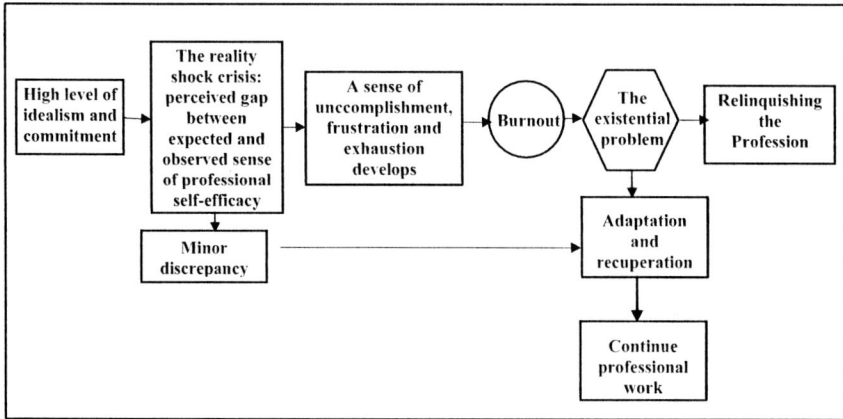

Figure 13.1.   The "Shattered Dreams" Model: An Illustration of the Professional Efficacy Discrepancy approach to Understanding Burnout

Friedman (2000) devised a burnout process model based on the professional efficacy discrepancy approach for studying burnout named the "shattered dreams" model. The underlying assumption of this model is that burnout occurs as the result of a gap between reality and how the individual subjectively perceives their professional efficacy, or by a gap between the person's expectation in prospect and the same person's experience in practice.

The following stages can be tracked in the model (see Figure 1):

1. Teachers start out with idealistic feelings and a great sense of commitment to teaching and to education.

2. Once they begin teaching and are exposed to school reality, teachers undergo a "reality shock." Facing this reality shock means, in practical terms that what was learned during the training period, and what was expected, is not what seems to be the reality of work-life at school. Psychologically, novice teachers are exposed to certain suppressor factors which inhibit those intrinsic and extrinsic success expectations. The reality shock may be regarded as their response to the perceived discrepancy between their sense of professional self-efficacy and their actual efficacy. Teachers may experience difficulties in four areas of efficacy: pupil-related tasks, school-related tasks, relationships with pupils, and relations with colleagues and school administration.

3. Teachers perceive the greatest gap in the relations' arena, especially those interrelations with pupils, colleagues, and the adminis-

tration. They also perceive a considerable gap in their school related functions, in particular in their ability to acquire school resources to aid them in fulfilling their professional duties.

4. Teachers develop a sense of professional failure, which grows into a feeling of personal failure, frustration, and physical and mental exhaustion. This feeling is accompanied by a negative emotional reaction to pupils. In the teaching profession, especially in Israel, teachers did not report "pure" depersonalization, but noted other harsh feelings toward the pupils (e.g., blaming them for not doing well in their studies, questioning their desire to learn and to invest time and effort in learning). These combined feelings produce the sense of burnout, which the teacher clearly experiences at this stage.

5. The teacher faces an existential problem that is personal and social in nature. The teacher is at a crossroad and must decide which way to go. At this point, some decide to leave teaching. Others, however, opt to continue.

6. The teachers who decide to remain in teaching now enter the stage of accepting reality, adapting psychologically and professionally, and trying to overcome obstacles. At this point, some lower their expectations and, through a process of rationalization, construct a professional perspective that is compatible with their lowered expectations and with their work circumstances.

It is worth noting that at the various stages of the process, especially the first ("reality shock") and fifth stages (deciding to stay in teaching), teachers strongly stress their dissatisfaction with the professional training they received, their initial reception at their job, and the lack of personal and professional support from their school.

DEVELOPING NECESSARY PROFESSIONAL SKILLS FOR LOW-BURNOUT TEACHING

The need to develop skills for low-burnout teaching is based on the assumption that burnout is a perceived sense of professional failure. Therefore, skills for low-burnout teaching include skills for successful teaching. In addition there is an underlying psychological assumption here that success in fulfilling a professional assignment depends also on the professional's ability to cope with those suppressor factors that inhibit the sense of intrinsic and extrinsic success. Many of these defensive abilities can be developed through appropriate training.

Teaching is a demanding professional career marked by considerable tension stemming from different sources. It is generally a "high-burnout" job. Since we cannot prevent teacher burnout completely, certain professional skills can be used to alleviate the stresses of teaching and help to make this important profession a "low burnout" as opposed to a "high-burnout" profession.

The following describes four important skills that can help in achieving low-burnout teaching:

1. Leadership skills (classic and postmodern).
2. Organizational efficacy skills.
3. Self-regulation skills.
4. Skills for evading the burnout trap.

These skills can all be learned and applied by trainee teachers following theoretical studies and practice.

Classical Leadership Skills

A classroom teacher is a leader in every sense. He or she is heading a group of pupils, is involved in planning class work, organizing and supervising pupils' work, and directing their learning. The teacher also coordinates learning topics, motivates pupils, and focuses on the following eight typical activities:

1. Defining learning goals and planning activities to attaining these goals.
2. Providing resources needed to achieve these goals.
3. Planning and establishing the setting for the pupils' activities.
4. Supporting and assisting group work and interpupil relations.
5. Fostering group cohesion among students.
6. Nurturing a sense of satisfaction and fulfillment among pupils (and their parents).
7. Encouraging pupils, as a group, to organize activities that will help them achieve their goals.
8. Nurturing the pupil as an individual and as having a role of a "learner."

The eight activities listed above relate to the teacher's work and are familiar to anyone who is teaching or has taught, are distinct leadership activities applicable to the leader of any group, and of course to teachers. A leader requires several basic skills, the main of which are these (Stogdill, 1974):

1. Ability to persuade a group to undertake agreed upon activities.
2. Ability to cope with ambivalent situations.
3. Ability to plan work and achievement.
4. Ability to evaluate situations and draw conclusions.
5. Ability to influence senior colleagues (principal, administration).
6. Directing the group toward activities aimed at achieving goals.
7. Ability to structure the work of the group.
8. Nurturing the individual: the ability to show empathy and consideration for group members.

Postmodern Leadership Skills

Leadership studies of the 1990s treated leadership as a human activity that combines classical leadership and management—two activities, which for years were considered separate and distinct activities. In the age of empowerment, it is also thought that the leader must be able to delegate authority effectively by giving up some portions of authority domains and ensure that group members can optimally receive the powers delegated to them. Now, the ability to dissever from portions of power and authority of the leadership role is considered one of the most important skills of the modern leader. This skill gained particular emphasis when the human side of the leader's behavior was singled out and was reflected in two alternative patterns of leadership: transactional leadership and transformational leadership.

Transactional leadership is the style of leadership where leaders can offer followers suitable remuneration for their labor or support. In this way, followers obtain appreciation and reward.

Transformational leadership occurs in visionary leaders having an ability to stimulate group members to follow them in realizing their vision. In postmodern leadership theory, the ability to formulate and realize a vision is a critical factor. Such ability can be expressed through three key areas of leader behavior: pointing to the direction of action, guiding others, and arousing drive and inspiration. These three processes, which are presently considered the heart of postmodern leadership theory, can typically be found in teachers and educational staff.

My main proposition here is that since teachers are leaders in every way, they must be trained for their role, just as leaders are trained for theirs. And just as the training for leaders is neither short nor simple, training for teachers should neither be short or simple. For low burnout these skills need to be taught in a practical and applied form aimed at assisting teachers in classroom management.

There are several practical methods of training novice teachers in using leadership skills, the most important of these being psychodrama and role-playing. These techniques require participants to act out leadership roles in which they address typical problems with varying conditions of audience cooperation. In role-playing, one person plays the leader, while the rest of the group are the "followers." Modeling desired behaviors and reinforcing their use in role-playing could also help in translating theory into practice.

Regarding teachers, I wish to emphasize the need to encourage greater awareness and sensitivity toward followers (pupils) and to some extent toward colleagues and principals. In order to deepen awareness and sensitivity, the teacher—as leader—must acquire five basic skills:

1. Greater sensitivity toward followers' needs and aspirations.

2. Greater openness and sharing of information with followers.

3. Share responsibility for decision making with followers.

4. Bring about closer reciprocal relations, cultivate friendlier, more egalitarian relations with followers.

5. Establish and run less structured patterns of activity; encourage followers to be more personally involved.

Organizational Efficacy Skills

Friedman and Kass (2000, 2002) have found that organizational efficacy is an important component of teachers' sense of professional efficacy. Organizational efficacy is teacher's sense of being able to influence school goals and the way they are realized. It involves teachers' interrelations with colleagues and the school principal. Teachers who had mastered organizational skills experience low levels of burnout (Friedman, 2003).

Teacher burnout research in Israel and elsewhere in the world has identified the main organizational skills that can help in reducing teacher burnout (Friedman, 1999):

1. Ability to avoid interpersonal and intraorganizational conflicts and to resolve them should they arise. Such conflicts may most likely involve allocation of resources, work arrangements, division of responsibility among staff and interpersonal issues.

2. Ability to prompt and obtain organizational support and use it as needed.

3. Ability to overcome organizational impediments, mostly those regarding communication and the use of scarce resources.

4. Ability to view organizational change as a positive endeavor (not as a loss), to identify and emphasize the benefits of change as opposed to its shortcomings.

5. Ability to utilize personal and organizational development programs; ability to extend intellectual curiosity and love of learning and improvement.

Administrators can be of great assistance in helping teachers to avoid interrole and intrarole conflicts. It is important that these should be avoided to reduce burnout.

Self-regulation Skills

Self-regulation relates to the psychological system through which the professional monitors his or her own actions, evaluates their consequences and adopts measures to alter his or her behavior. This system applies to self-determined goals and rules of conduct that shape the person's behavior. These rules of conduct concern the behavior that is expected from the individual under certain circumstances, standards of performance that a behavior is intended to achieve, and the outcomes (positive or negative) of success or failure in the intended performance levels (Mischele, Shoda, & Rodriguez, 1989). Studies have examined the outcomes of some self-regulation techniques aimed at significantly improving performance in achieving operative goals (Latham & Frayne, 1989). Examples of such techniques are self-evaluation based on accepted performance standards, self-learning, attentiveness, and openness to change (see Sarason, 1979). Some of the ways of changing situations that can produce success using self-regulatory techniques are described in studies published over the past two decades (see, for example, Rodriquez, Mischele, & Shoda, 1989).

The development of self-regulatory skills requires certain cognitive tools and a belief that it is possible to apply these tools effectively (Bandura, 1991). Such tools include self-observation of activities undertaken by the individual, applying personal standards for judging and directing personal performance, enlisting personal competencies to influence and direct personal efforts and harnessing appropriate strategies to achieve success (Zimmerman & Martinez-Pons, 1990). Self-regulation skills require the following capabilities:

1. *Goal setting.* Belief in one's own ability influences the choice of one's goals and determines the commitment to achieving these goals. When one sees oneself as talented and highly able, one chooses tough and highly challenging goals (Bandura, 1986). There is a potential danger in this, as the novice teacher needs realistic rather than tough and challenging goals.

2. *Self-esteem.* Self-esteem is a function of the satisfaction that people derive from achievement and the results of attaining personal goals. Achieving positive self-esteem requires clear criteria for success or failure, setting of priorities among those criteria, and an ability to assign each criterion to its appropriate level of predetermined priority (Zimmerman & Bandura, 1994). To help in building self-esteem, appropriate and realistic personal goals need to be set.

3. *Self-observation.* Self-observation does not only refer to the technical observation of a person's conduct by themselves, but to a process that distinguishes between actions requiring special attention, those actions of a lesser importance, which require limited attention (Bandura, 1986).

4. *Planning and time management.* Vital to the success of self-regulation is an ability to schedule planned activities well and to efficiently manage time required for each stage of implementation (Zimmerman, Greenberg, & Weinstein, 1994).

All these skills need to be practiced thoroughly by trainee teachers under protected conditions during their training. It is important to note that it is not enough simply to acquire self-regulation skills. Rather, one should be taught to apply these skills determinedly in the face of any problems, stressors, or temptations that can potentially distract one from implementing actions designed to realize predetermined goals.

Skills For Evading the Burnout Trap

As in any other profession, teaching requires "life skills" which will allow the professional to function within limiting organizational frameworks, and in the long run, preserve teachers' professional sparkle. Three specific life skills are worth mentioning here:

1. *Well-balanced career drive.*   Drive is a basic human impulse and no one is suggesting that one should try to repress professional drive. The fact, however, is that professionals who fall into the burnout trap are those who set themselves particularly high, unrealistic, goals. The way to evade the burnout trap is therefore to set achievable goals and design a plan of action to achieve them in stages.

2. *Seek meaning in achievable objectives.*   "Reality shock" research demonstrates that at the outset of their careers, professionals look forward to enjoying "meaningful work." They join the public service in a desire to "give to others," and also perhaps to "improve the world" and "educate the future generation." These goals affect their choice of profession and lend great meaning to their lives. The reality they encounter is that their goals are not easily achievable, which makes this the main contributor to the reality shock of professionals in their novice year of work.

   A life skill that can help professionals escape the burnout trap is the ability to moderate expectations regarding the meaningfulness of the work, without trivializing it. One way to achieve this is to look for alternative meanings at work that are sufficiently important, although different from the original meaning, which is apparently too hard for the professional to realize.

3. *Balancing work, family, and leisure.*   This balance is vital to any job, and is especially important in the teaching profession, which by its very nature "invades" the person's private domain, often interfering with the practitioner's domestic life.

BUILDING UP AND CONSERVING SENSE OF PROFESSIONAL SELF-EFFICACY

The important difference between new teachers who are treading the road to burnout and teachers who are on the highway to professional accomplishment is their sense of professional self-efficacy, or in short "teacher efficacy." According to self-efficacy theory, a belief in one's personal competence affects one's performance due to four mediating processes: (1) motivating; (2) cognitive; (3) affective, and (4) choice processes.

Motivating processes involve establishing goals and expectations regarding the outcomes of the goals. Cognitive processes involve expectations regarding success or failure scenarios and expectations with regard to options of enlisting the support of one's environment. Affective processes involve one's feelings regarding future scenarios. Choice processes are those that orient the individual toward preferring one goal to another (Bandura, 1986).

Teachers with a strong sense of efficacy are able to withstand the reality shock test, persevere with their careers, and enjoy satisfaction from it. Teachers whose sense of efficacy has been significantly undermined following their brush with reality fall into the burnout trap. The question is what can produce a strong sense of efficacy in teachers, and how does one sustain it in the long run?

The mass of research on the professional self-efficacy in different fields provides a fair amount of information on the sources of self-efficacy and how to create and nourish it. Bandura (1997) suggests four factors that can help in the building and maintenance of self-efficacy:

1.   Previous success experiences serving as inspiration and a model for imitation.
2.   Experiences within a supporting group of professionals.
3.   Social support.
4.   Physiological stimuli as performance quality indicators.

I will now describe the factors put forward by Bandura and discuss the practical implications of each with regard to preparing teachers for a low-burnout career.

PREVIOUS SUCCESS EXPERIENCES SERVING AS INSPIRATION AND A MODEL FOR IMITATION

Prior success in the professional's life can offer a source of inspiration and a model for future accomplishment. Earlier experiences of success are an important base for creating and maintaining teacher efficacy, as they provide powerful testimony that the professional is capable of doing whatever is necessary to succeed. For someone to have a strong, stable sense of efficacy, prior experiences of overcoming obstacles through sustained effort should occur. Difficult events or situations in the past in which the professional has prevailed can confirm that success is achievable with rigorous and sustained effort. When individuals face new challenges they draw on encouraging evidence from their past with regard to their successes and how these were achieved. This helps the individual to convince him or herself that he/she is capable of succeeding now and in the future. Documenting past successes in one's memory should include keeping records of how these successes were achieved. Thus, if one is not successful in the present, one can explore the relationship between resources invested and results. When people can ascribe a failed performance to unsuitable strategies more than to a lack of ability, the failure will paradoxically enhance the feeling of efficacy since they believe that improved strategies will yield success in the future. In contrast, when work under optimal conditions is accompanied by failure, the professional is signaled that he lacks the appropriate ability to perform the work required. Under these circumstances, failure in tasks recognized as relatively easy can exert a destructive impact on perceived self-efficacy.

The practical implications of the above in terms of teacher training are that while training, teachers should receive an opportunity to experience situations that are generally considered problematic in a supervised and controlled manner. Such experience can be via simulations of staged and filmed incidents or through field practice. Field experience during teacher training already forms part of teacher training programs offered by colleges, but does not consistently receive the emphasis it deserves. Particularly, questions of teacher-student relations, disciplinary problems, student motivation, relations with parents, and so forth, are conspicuous by their absence.

EXPERIENCES WITHIN A
SUPPORTING GROUP OF PROFESSIONALS

Support given by a group of professionals for problem solving and addressing pertinent issues can be very effective. If professionals within the group are all involved in the same type of activities, it is possible to learn from colleagues' mistakes and successes, not just from one's own. Discussing examples of activities with colleagues is an effective way of enhancing the professional's sense of self-efficacy. People can assess their own abilities relative to those of others, social comparison being a very important factor in evaluating personal competence.

The practical implications of the above, in terms of teacher training, concern the methodology of utilizing the experiential component of gearing up for work. Teaching situations (e.g., teaching new material), handling discipline problems, bolstering social cohesion, and resolving classroom management issues, should be carried out in a group context with each group member addressing the identical problem, in turn. The others in the group can then evaluate their peers, offer comments, and suggest remedies or improvements.

TRAINING WITHIN A SOCIAL SUPPORT CONTEXT

Social support can reinforce the professional's confidence in his or her ability to realize his or her goals. It is easier to sustain a feeling of self-efficacy and to empower it when confronted with a challenging situation if others whom the individual deems important express confidence in his or her ability and do not convey skepticism. Although verbal support alone may have a limited effect in reinforcing perceived efficacy, it can encourage someone to work on him or herself—if the positive evaluation is within realistic limits. People who are given constructive verbal encouragement from significant others have a tendency to draw upon greater personal resources in order to carry out their mission successfully.

Trainees themselves, while preparing for a professional career, should try to refine their sensibilities and be conscious of environmental assessment, particularly with regard to suggestions for changing a mode of conduct in cases of low levels of success or failure. The following processes are vital to achieving greater levels of awareness:

1. *Attentiveness.*   Awareness determines what the person discerns, what he hears, and what he does not want to hear. Items of information on different subjects receive differing degrees of importance.

2. *Data recall and processing.*   These determine which aspects of the data gathered will be recalled and the meaning of each piece of information.

3. *Implementation.*   Knowing what to do with each item of data, that is, developing ways of improving work related activities on the basis of evaluation and criticism from the environment.

4. *Motivation.*   Showing consistency in implementing the changes decided on using the processes described above.

USE OF PHYSIOLOGICAL STIMULI AS PERFORMANCE QUALITY INDICATORS

Physiological states such as tension, "heaviness," and so forth, offer the professional important indicators regarding success and failure. People say, "When I carried out a certain type of activity, I had butterflies in my stomach." For many, such sensations are an indication that they are not competent enough to undertake such an action.

It is extremely useful for trainee teachers to familiarize themselves with stress management methods and techniques. These techniques can help the person bolster their sense of self-efficacy, as well as significantly alleviate work-related stressors and the burnout that usually ensues. The following are the four most popular, commonly suggested methods of stress reduction:

1. *Physical activities.*   It is possible to achieve significant relaxation with 5-30 minutes of rhythmic exercise or brisk physical activity.

2. *Relaxation.*   Numerous relaxation techniques exist that can be practiced at home or at work: breathing exercises, releasing muscle tension, and techniques to help one unwind mentally.

3. *Biofeedback.*   This involves gaining voluntary control of physiological mechanisms: brain waves, heart rate, muscle tension, stomach acidity, and blood pressure. The positive benefits of biofeedback are reduced tension, fewer headaches, and lower stress-related (emotional) blood pressure levels.

4. *Cognitive-behavioral techniques.*   The purpose of cognitive-behavioral techniques is to encourage people to reevaluate or gain fresh insight into stressful situations, and by doing so reduce their stressful effect. These techniques involve reassessing personal expectations and standards by thrusting aside thoughts that confer exaggerated importance to stress or anxiety inducing activities.

SUMMARY

Newly qualified teachers set off with high expectations, a deep faith in the power of education, distant, grand goals founded on this belief, confidence in their own personal and professional ability to achieve these, and other, no less lofty goals. Early in the teacher's career he or she discovers a gap between the harsh realities of teaching and these initial beliefs and certainties. The wider the gap, the more intensely this gap is perceived, the greater the teacher's emotional stress will be, and the higher the chances of burnout. From the studies outlined above, we find that the key to understanding and preventing burnout is the relationship between the teacher's perceived professional competencies and skills, and the work-related demands and overload that are exerted on these abilities and skills. The less favorable this relationship is to the abilities and skills, the greater the burnout will be.

The practical suggestions offered here aim to boost the teacher's professional capabilities, particularly in areas that receive less emphasis during teacher training: leadership skills, skills for fruitful interpersonal relations, and finally, organizational skills. Regarding leadership skills, the skills used in transactional and transformational leadership are stressed and so are issues such as involvement of pupils and colleagues in the delegation of authority processes. Regarding interpersonal skills, the subjects highlighted are self-regulation skills and skills that can help the professional avoid the trap of burnout. On the subject of organizational skills, we emphasize the skills needed in dealing with conflict, gaining others' support, communication, coping with change, and pursuing a program of personal and organizational development.

REFERENCES

Bandura, A. (1986). *Social foundations of thought and action: A social cognitive theory.* Englewood Cliffs, NJ: Prentice-Hall.

Bandura, A. (1991). Social cognitive theory of self-regulation. *Organizational Behavior and Human Performance, 50,* 248-287.

Bandura, A. (1997). *Self efficacy: The exercise of control.* New York: Freeman.

Cherniss, C. (1995). *Beyond burnout.* New York: Routledge.

Csikszentmihalyi, M. (1990). *Flow, the psychology of optimal experience.* New York: Harper Perennial.

French, J. R. P., Caplan, R. D., & Van Harrison, R. (1982). *The mechanisms of job stress and strain.* Chichester, England: Wiley & Sons.

Friedman, I. A. (1995). Student behavior patterns contributing to teacher burnout. *Journal of Educational Research, 88,* 281-289.

Friedman, I. A. (1996). Multiple pathways to burnout: Cognitive and emotional scenarios in teacher burnout. *Anxiety, Stress, and Coping, 9,* 245-259.

Friedman, I. A. (1999). *Teacher burnout. The concept and its measurement.* Jerusalem: The Henrietta Szold Institute.

Friedman, I. A. (2000). Burnout in teachers: Shattered dreams of impeccable professional performance. *Journal of Clinical Psychology, 56,* 595-606.

Friedman, I. A. (2003). Self-efficacy and burnout in teaching: The importance of interpersonal-relations efficacy. *Social Psychology of Education, 6,* 191-215.

Friedman, I. A., & Farber, B. A. (1992). Professional self-concept as a predictor of teacher burnout. *Journal of Educational Research, 86,* 28-57.

Friedman, I. A., & Kass, E. (2000). *Teacher efficacy: The concept and its measurement.* Jerusalem: The Henrietta Szold Institute.

Friedman, I. A., & Kass, E. (2002). Teacher self-efficacy: A classroom-organization conceptualization. *Teaching and Teacher education, 18,* 675-686.

Friedman, I. A., & Lotan, I. (1985). *Burnout in elementary teachers in Israel.* Jerusalem: The Henrietta Szold Institute.

Friedman, I. A., & Lotan, I. (1993). *Stress and burnout in teaching—causes and prevention measures.* Jerusalem: The Henrietta Szold Institute.

Gavish, B. (1997). *The reality shock: Teacher experiences in their first year in teaching.* Unpublished research report, The Hebrew University, Jerusalem.

Latham, G. P., & Frayne, C. A. (1989). Self management training for increasing job attendance: A follow up and replication. *Journal of Applied Psychology, 74,* 411-416.

Maslach, C., & Jackson, S. (1981). The measurement of experienced burnout. *Journal of Occupational Behavior, 2,* 99-113.

Maslach, C., & Leiter, M. (1997). *The truth about burnout.* San Francisco: Jossey-Bass.

Milstein, M., & Golaszewski, T. (1985). Effects of organizationally based and individually based stress management efforts in elementary school settings. *Urban Education, 49*, 389-409.

Mischele, W., Shoda, Y., & Rodriguez, M. L. (1989). Delay of gratification in children. *Science, 244*, 933-938.

Rodriguez, M. L., Mischele, W., & Shoda, Y. (1989). Cognitive person variables in the delay of gratification of older children at risk. *Journal of Personality and Social Psychology, 57*, 358-367.

Sarason, I. G. (1979). Three lacunae of cognitive therapy. *Cognitive Therapy and Research, 3*, 223-235.

Schaufeli, W. B., Maslach, C., & Marek, T. (1993). *Professional burnout.* Washington, DC: Taylor & Francis.

Stogdill, R. M. (1974). *Handbook of leadership.* New York: The Free Press.

Travers, C. J., & Cooper, C. L. (1996). *Teachers under pressure.* London: Routledge.

Zimmerman, B. J., & Bandura, A. (1994). Impact of self-regulatory influences on writing course attainment. *American Educational Research Journal, 31*, 845-862.

Zimmerman, B. J., Greenberg, D., & Weinstein, C. E. (1994). Self-regulating academic study time: A strategy approach. In D. H. Schunk & B. J. Zimmerman (Eds.), *Self-regulation of learning and performance: Issues and educational application* (pp. 181-199). Hillsdale, NJ: Erlbaum.

Zimmerman, B. J., & Martinez-Pons, M. (1990). Student differences in self-regulated learning. *Journal of Educational Psychology, 82,* 51-59.

Printed in the United States
21457LVS00004BA/45-162